D1255697

This book sets out to interpret Euripides' *The Trojan Women* in the light of a view of tragedy which sees its function, as it was understood in classical Athens, as being didactic. This function, the author argues, was carried out by an examination of the ideology to which the audience subscribed. *The Trojan Women*, powerfully exploiting the dramatic context of the aftermath of the Trojan War, is a remarkable example of tragic teaching. The play questions a series of mutually reinforcing polarities (man/god; man/woman; Greek/barbarian; free/slave) through which an Athenian citizen defined himself, and also examines the dangers of rhetoric and the value of victory in war. By making the didactic function of tragedy the basis of interpretation, the author is able to offer a coherent view of a number of long-standing problems in Euripidean and tragic criticism, namely the relation of Euripides to the sophists, the pervasive self-reference and anachronism in Euripides, the problem of contemporary reference, and the construction and importance of the tragic scene.

The book, which makes use of recent scholarship both in Classics and in critical theory, should be read by all those interested in Greek tragedy and in the culture of late fifth-century Athens.

CAMBRIDGE CLASSICAL STUDIES

General editors
M. F. BURNYEAT, M. K. HOPKINS, M. D. REEVE,
A. M. SNODGRASS

EURIPIDEAN POLEMIC

EURIPIDEAN POLEMIC

The Trojan Women and the function of tragedy

N. T. CROALLY
Dulwich College, London

CAMBRIDGE
UNIVERSITY PRESS

Published by the Press Syndicate of the University of Cambridge
The Pitt Building, Trumpington Street, Cambridge CB2 1RP
40 West 20th Street, New York, NY 10011-4211, USA
10 Stamford Road, Oakleigh, Melbourne 3166, Australia

© Faculty of Classics, University of Cambridge 1994

First published 1994

Printed in Great Britain at the University Press, Cambridge

A catalogue record for this book is available from the British Library

Library of Congress cataloguing in publication data
Croally, N. T.
Euripidean polemic: The Trojan women and the function of tragedy / N. T. Croally.
p.   cm. – (Cambridge classical studies)
Includes bibliographical references.
ISBN 0 521 46490 0 (hardback)
1. Euripides. Trojan women. 2. Euripides – Political and social views.
3. Didactic drama, Greek – History and criticism. 4. Hecuba (Legendary character)
in literature. 5. Women and literature – Greece. 6. Trojan War in literature.
7. Polemics. 8. Tragedy. I. Title. II. Series.
PA3973.T83C76   1994
882'.01—dc20   93-44672 CIP

ISBN 0 521 46490 0 hardback

DISCARDED
WIDENER UNIVERSITY

WIDENER UNIVERSITY
WOLFGRAM
LIBRARY
CHESTER, PA.

AO

CONTENTS

CONTENTS

ACKNOWLEDGEMENTS

I owe much to many. For constructive responses I would like to thank John Henderson, Geoffrey Lloyd, Costas Valakas, Barbara Goff, Paul Cartledge, Oliver Taplin, Dan Burnstone and various audiences at the Graduate Literary Seminar of the Cambridge University Classics Faculty. In America, Bob Mielke has been a friend and a constant source of intellectual stimulation. Richard Hunter and Richard Buxton, the examiners of the doctoral thesis on which this book is based, were most helpful in indicating errors and areas which needed further consideration. Pauline Hire, the anonymous Press reader and, especially, Professor Michael Reeve have offered helpful advice, allowing me to attempt to turn a thesis into a book. Pat Easterling, who was my first thesis supervisor, both urged scholarly caution and encouraged me to experiment in interpretive techniques. For many years now, Simon Goldhill has criticized my work aggressively and constructively. We do not always agree, but, as Blake said, without contraries, no progression. I wish to thank two close friends. Nick de Somogyi has discussed many general points with me. That our interests have converged in the provocative relations between war and tragedy (the Renaissance in his case), after we began our respective research on such different paths, has been a source of both enlightenment and delight. Linda Mack has always been willing to argue any and every point, all the more helpfully because from a less engaged and more philosophical position. Lastly, I wish to thank my parents for their support.

ABBREVIATIONS

AC	*L'Antiquité Classique*
AJP	*American Journal of Philology*
BICS	*Bulletin of the Institute of Classical Studies*
CA	*Classical Antiquity*
CB	*The Classical Bulletin*
CJ	*Classical Journal*
C&M	*Classica et Mediaevalia*
CP	*Classical Philology*
CQ	*Classical Quarterly*
CR	*Classical Review*
CW	*Classical World*
DK	Diels, H. and Kranz, W. eds. *Die Fragmente der Vorsokratiker*. 3 vols. Berlin, 1952.
FGH	*Fragmente der griechischen Historiker*
G&R	*Greece & Rome*
GRBS	*Greek, Roman and Byzantine Studies*
HSCP	*Harvard Studies in Classical Philology*
HTR	*Harvard Theological Review*
ICS	*Illinois Classical Studies*
IG	*Inscriptiones Graecae*
JHS	*Journal of Hellenic Studies*
LEC	*Les Etudes Classiques*
NLH	*New Literary History*
PCA	*Proceedings of the Classical Association*
PCPS	*Proceedings of the Cambridge Philological Society*
QFC	*Quaderni di Filologia Classica*
QS	*Quaderni di Storia*
REG	*Revue des Etudes Grecques*
RhM	*Rheinisches Museum für Philologie*
RPh	*Revue de Philologie*

SicGym	*Siculorum Gymnasium*
TAPA	*Transactions of the American Philological Association*
YCS	*Yale Classical Studies*
WHB	*Wiener humanistische Blätter*
WJ	*Würzburger Jahrbücher für die Altertumswissenschaft*
WS	*Wiener Studien*
WZ Halle	*Wissenschaftliche Zeitschrift der Martin-Luther-Universität, Halle-Wittenberg*
ZPE	*Zeitschrift für Papyrologie und Epigraphik*

INTRODUCTION

My subject is Euripidean tragedy and how, in the cultural and dramatic context of war, it performs its didactic function. For the most part, and for reasons which will become clear, I have concentrated on *The Trojan Women* (*Troades*). Behind this enterprise lies a view of the nature of fifth-century Athenian tragedy, which it seems proper to enunciate in this introduction.[1]

Greek tragedy is a discourse of the fifth-century Athenian *polis*; it is a product of a culture distant in time and, in many ways, different in character.[2] Unlike any literary event we know in the modern western world, the tragedies were performed on an occasion of great political importance. The Athenian *polis* was involved in the production of tragedy both directly and indirectly. The invention of tragedy, of theatre, is dependent itself on the invention of politics. While politics was a panhellenic phenomenon, the development of democracy at Athens allowed in a more thoroughgoing way what

---

[1] References to classical texts follow by and large the system of abbreviation used in the *Oxford Classical Dictionary*. I have, however, referred to some plays of Aristophanes and some dialogues of Plato by their English titles or by abbreviations of those titles (e.g. *Clouds*, *Laws*, *Rep.* for *Republic*, *Prot.* for *Protagoras*). The tragedies of Euripides are referred to by title alone. With other texts the author is given except when the context makes authorship clear.

[2] We should emphasize the difference between the classical Greek *polis* and the modern state, which is neatly summarized by R. Osborne (1985), 8–9: 'One indication of the degree of difference between *polis* and state lies in the fact that we cannot, and feel no pressure to, identify "state" and citizens in the way that the *polis* was felt to be co-extensive with the citizen body... Modern conceptions of the state may extend beyond the citizen body, as in those which stress the state as a hierarchical socio-political organization, which will, of course, embrace disenfranchised as well as citizens; or it may be divorced from the citizen body, as in "the distinctively modern idea of the State as a form of public power separate from both the ruler and the ruled".' The quotation is taken from Skinner, *The Foundations of Modern Political Thought*. Cambridge, 1978, p. 254. Also see Arist. *Pol.* 1252b27ff., 1276b1–2ff. For other work on the *polis*, see e.g. Ehrenberg (1960); M. Finley (1983). Kolb (1979), 530 is blunt: 'Das Theater war "die Polis".'

Geoffrey Lloyd has called the potential for radical innovation, access to debate, the habit of scrutiny and the expectation of rational justification for positions held.[3] In the democracy, the widening of the franchise was more extreme, the right to speak openly more acceptable, and the politicization of discourse more complete. Tragedy was such a discourse. For it was not merely an art form. The Greeks had no obvious equivalent for our concept of art, and the cluster of words which together approximate to what we might consider to be art have different, often political origins, meanings and applications (e.g. *sophia* – wisdom or skill, *technē* – art or skill, *poiēsis* – creation or production). Tragedy was, in fact, an institution, 'a new type of spectacle in the system of the city-state's public festivals'.[4]

Although tragedies were performed at many festivals throughout Attica, the most important was the Great Dionysia.[5] While the very appearance of tragedy at a festival marks its public nature, the city was also directly involved in selecting and funding the plays. It was the Council (*Boulē*) which, along with one of the chief magistrates (the *archōn epōnumos*), selected those who would judge the contests of both poets and protagonists.[6] It was that same *archōn* who chose both which poets were to be allowed the honour of having their plays performed,[7] and the plays' sponsors (*chorēgoi*), who would train and support the chorus.[8] But tragedy is not only to be seen as a discourse whose production was a matter of public

---

[3] On the relations between the developments of Greek thought and politics, and the role played by such factors as slavery and literacy, see G. Lloyd (1979), 226–64, esp. p. 258; (1988). On the Greek invention of politics, see M. Finley (1983).

[4] Vernant and Vidal-Naquet (1988), 23. At Athens there were probably twice as many festivals in the fifth century as in any other city; see Ps. Xen. *Ath. Pol.* 3.2; Thuc. 2.38.1.

[5] Taplin (1977), 17 reminds us of the passage in Plato (*Rep.* 475d) where Glaucon talks of theatre-lovers going to both City and Rural Dionysia to see as many plays as possible.

[6] Pickard-Cambridge (1968²), 96–7. Gregory (1991), 5–6 has carefully discussed the democratic aspects of the Great Dionysia. My treatment of the issue is therefore brief. Connor (1990) argues that the Great Dionysia was instituted after the Peisistratid regime and was closely bound to the democracy.

[7] Pickard-Cambridge (1968²), 84.

[8] On this and the various duties of a *chorēgos*, as well as on the probable selection of the choruses themselves, see Pickard-Cambridge (1968²), 71–99.

concern; it must also be viewed as reflecting the aims and methods of the democracy. First, tragedy was funded either directly by the *polis*, which paid the honorarium to competing poets, or through the system called the liturgy (the funding of state projects by private individuals, a sort of indirect taxation; in the case of tragedy, it was called the *chorēgia*).[9] The *chorēgia* almost matched the trierarchy in expense and would thus seem to be valued almost as highly as the defence of fatherland or the extension of empire.[10] Indeed, it might be said that the enforcement of the liturgy, as a system of finance, powerfully illustrates the political power of the poorer citizens (*dēmos* in one of its senses: Ps. Xen. *Ath. Pol.* 1.13).[11] There are five other ways in which the production of tragedy manifests public and democratic features. (1) The selection of the judges was organized through the ten tribes, thus reflecting the formation of the state; and its method was sortitive, the electoral method basic to the democracy. (2) It was possibly followed by a special assembly which discussed the conduct of the officials organizing the festival, thus maintaining the democratic notion of accountability. (3) Public records were kept of the festival, noting *archōn*'s name and the various prizes awarded.[12] (4) Just as jury pay had the effect of allowing the non-propertied to participate in the legal processes of the democracy, so Pericles' establishment of subsidized theatre tickets (the *theōrika*) enabled the poor to see the plays (Plut. *Per.* 9.2–3). (5) Generally the dramatic festival shared the competitive nature of the public sphere as a whole. Tragedy was agonistic, and both dramatists and protagonists competed for prizes, just like athletes in the Olympic games (Plut. *Cim.* 8.7–9).[13]

---

[9] For the *chorēgia*, as well as for the trierarchy, an element of compulsion is attested in the existence of *antidosis*, whereby a citizen who claimed insufficient funds could indicate others better placed to pay for a chorus or a ship. See Lysias 24.9; Xen. *Oec.* 7.3; Dem. 21.156. On liturgies and taxes in the Athenian democracy, see Ober (1989), 199ff.; Christ (1990).

[10] Most expensive dithyrambic chorus 5,000 dr.; most expensive tragic chorus 3,000 dr., for which see Lysias 21.1. The trierarchy is estimated to have cost about a talent (6,000 dr.) in the fifth century; see Pickard-Cambridge (1968²), 77–8, 87.

[11] See e.g. M. Finley (1983), 36–40.   [12] Pickard-Cambridge (1968²), 71–3.

[13] Pickard-Cambridge (1968²), 93ff.

Finally, and most importantly, the plays were massively attended. Pickard-Cambridge estimated the size of the audience to be between 14,000 and 17,000; Taplin 15,000.[14] The importance of such large numbers can be gleaned from a comparison with the probable attendance figures for the Assembly in the fifth century, apparently about 6,000.[15] It would seem, then, that the audiences at the Great Dionysia represented a considerably greater proportion of the citizen population than either the Assembly or the law courts, although we must remember that foreigners and other non-citizens were present.[16] Whether women were present remains a problem. The fifth-century – mainly Aristophanic – evidence appears inconclusive, although the presence of boys (*Clouds* 537–9; *Peace* 50–3, 765–6), metics and foreigners (*Ach.* 502–8), and, for the fourth century, even prisoners is attested (Dem. 22.68; Pl. *Laws* 637b). The later evidence is doubtful too. The story of pregnant women giving birth after seeing the first appearance of the Eumenides can probably be put down to a desire to describe the theatrical effect in an extreme way (*Life of Aeschylus* 9; Pollux 4.110). The evidence of Plato – that tragedy was merely rhetoric which would appeal only to slaves, children and women (*Gorg.* 502b–d; *Laws* 817c) – could be understood as simply an insulting reference to a hypothetical audience of the least discrimination. However, a recent article by Jeffrey Henderson persuasively argues that women were not excluded from the festival. Briefly his argument is this: since other types of non-citizen are present, why should women be absent? The festival was not only a political event but a religious one as well: ritual occasions tended to be more inclusive. The general lack of acknowledgement of women's presence and the conventional addressing of the audience as male may be explained by the difference between a notional audience

---

[14] Pickard-Cambridge (1968²), 236; Taplin (1977), 10.

[15] Hansen (1976); M. Finley (1983), 73ff. Hansen (1987), 14–18 makes the point that Athenian ideology regularly claimed that all citizens attended the Assembly meetings.

[16] Gregory (1991), 5. Henderson (1991), 145 speculates that citizens may have been outnumbered by non-citizens. This seems highly unlikely in the fifth century but may possibly have been true by Menander's time; see Wiles (1991), 15.

composed only of citizens and the actual one. Once these three arguments are accepted, what evidence there is of women's presence can be viewed more positively. Still, whether women attended the plays or not, the point remains that the audience was very large and did represent a significant proportion of the citizen body.[17]

The ceremonies which preceded the plays also demonstrate the political nature of the festival.[18] The generals, the highest officers of state, sacrificed to various deities; the tribute from the allies was displayed (there were representatives of those allies in the audience); crowns were awarded to citizens who had served the city conspicuously well; finally, there was a procession of the orphans of war, educated at state expense as far as adulthood. This celebration of democratic ideology – a festal equivalent of the Funeral Oration – has been well described by Goldhill: 'It was a demonstration before the city and its many international visitors of the power of the *polis* of Athens . . . It was a public display of the success in military terms of the city. It used the state to glorify the state.'[19] The Great Dionysia, then, to its audience of Athenians and allies alike, was a central event of civic discourse. The ceremonies show that civic discourse championing itself; they show the self-image of Athens at its most potent, but also at its most complex. For the tragedies which follow represent the tensions and ambiguities of the very ideology of which tragedy is a product.

An event of great civic importance in fifth-century Athens was also inevitably of religious significance. Just as Athens honours itself at the festival, so, unsurprisingly, it honours

[17] Henderson (1991). Henderson also argues that if women were present they would have been seated in a separate area.

[18] The evidence for the pre-play ceremonies is collected in Deubner (1959), 138–42; Pickard-Cambridge (1968[2]), 57ff. The significance of the ceremonies is discussed in detail in Goldhill (1987); Meier (1988), 62–74.

[19] (1987), 61. Meier (1988), 69–70 argues well that the ceremonies express the power of the Athenian state and the sacrifices which individuals must make in its service. Phalluses were also sent by the allies, 'the surrender of their masculine force to Athens' (Reckford (1987), 22). It should also be noted that the seating in the auditorium was divided into tribes, forming 'a kind of map of the civic corporations' (Winkler (1985), 30).

Dionysus. In the orchestra of the theatre stood the *thumelē*, the stone altar at which libations were offered to the god. The priest of Dionysus had a reserved seat. Before the festival in the theatre began, ephebes enacted the advent of Dionysus by carrying his statue from near where the Academy later stood to Eleutherae (where sacrifices were performed and hymns sung) and then back to the theatre.[20] But, even in antiquity, there was some consternation about the precise relation between Dionysus and tragedy, indeed between Dionysus and the *polis* (Plut. *Quaest. Conv.* 1.1.5 [615a]). For, if 'tragedy could be said to be a manifestation of the city turning itself into theatre, presenting itself on stage before its assembled citizens',[21] then the connection between Dionysus and tragedy is one of political importance. Since the tragedies were performed in a context of ceremony which glorified Dionysus as well as the city, I think we have to assume that tragedy itself was a performance in honour of the god. But in order to understand more precisely what the relation between the god and the theatre was, it is necessary to look briefly at Dionysus and his religion.

There is no very good evidence about how Dionysus was worshipped or the nature of Greek Maenadism in fifth-century Attica. Five important features can be extracted from the scholarly discussions.[22] First, Dionysus' position among the Olympian gods is somewhat anomalous. He is often called a new god, or a late addition to the pantheon, or foreign to established Greek religion (whatever that may be), mainly because of his general absence from Homer.[23] Second,

---

[20] Pickard-Cambridge (1968²), 60–1; Vernant and Vidal-Naquet (1988), 182.

[21] Vernant and Vidal-Naquet (1988),185; see also Seaford (1984), 1ff. on the relations between Dionysus, satyr drama and tragedy. Winkler (1985), 51 believes that there was nothing Dionysiac about tragedy – see also Taplin (1978), 162 – which was performed instead 'to display the *polis'* finely tuned sense of discipline and impulse, of youth's incorporation into a competitive harmony of tribes and age classes. It so happens, *ex post facto*, that Dionysus can be seen as an appropriate patron for such a display.' This rather misses the point: whatever the origins of tragedy, what we are trying to explain is why Dionysus was an appropriate patron, *ex post facto* or otherwise.

[22] See e.g. Henrichs (1978), (1982), (1984); Daraki (1985).

[23] Farnell (1909), 85–9, 134; Vernant and Vidal-Naquet (1986), 38–9, who also make the point that Dionysus is mentioned in the Linear B tablets.

although Dionysus had his effects on men – satyrs were male, drinking at the symposium and participation in the Dionysiac Mysteries were male activities – the most spectacular and subversive Dionysiac behaviour seems to have been perpetrated by women.[24] Perhaps, then, we should not be surprised by the number of transgressive and dangerous women in tragedy. Third, Dionysus is an ambivalent god, though perhaps polyvalent would be a better word. Commonly known as a god of wine, he is also attached to the fig (Ath. 78c);[25] by his association with wine, he stands as a god both of cultivation and of ecstasy and wildness. At his most potent, Dionysus is a god whose powers transgress cultural boundaries.[26] Fourth, Dionysus is a god who oversees a number of festivals. Apart from the Great Dionysia, we know about the Anthesteria, the Lenaia, the Rustic Dionysia and the Agrionia.[27] Finally, Dionysus, as one might expect of the god of the theatre, is a god associated with the mask. There is evidence which suggests that he was not always represented anthropomorphically and was sometimes worshipped as a mask hung on a pillar.[28]

All of the features described – the strangeness, the relation with women normally excluded from the public space of the city, the doubleness and ambivalence, the transgressiveness, the association with the mask – indicate a profound and appropriate relation between Dionysus and tragedy. The god of illusion, deception, ecstasy and transgression sits very well as the patron of the theatre. The relation of the god to the mask and the fact that Dionysus was always worshipped in theatrical ways[29] also stress the appropriateness of the relation. But

[24] Winnington-Ingram (1948), 155; Kraemer (1979).

[25] Farnell (1909), 118–20; Burkert (1985), 166.

[26] As C. Segal (1982), 4 puts it: 'The Dionysiac includes the dissolution of limits, the spanning of logical contradictions, the suspension of logically imposed categories, and the exploration of the inbetweenness and reversibility in spirit that may veer abruptly from play and wonder to unrestrained savagery.'

[27] Burkert (1985), 163; Deubner (1959), 93–123.

[28] Burkert (1985), 162; Foley (1985), 253; Calame (1986); Vernant and Vidal-Naquet (1986), 38–9; Frontisi-Ducroux (1989); Adrados (1975), 256–7, 333 (Dionysus as 'the only god who retained mimetic characteristics').

[29] Goldhill (1986), 273: 'theatre is itself an essentially Dionysiac experience, where men play roles of others'; see also (1986), 78; (1987); Vernant and Vidal-Naquet (1988), 181–206.

it is not only the attributes of the god which focus our attention on tragedy as Dionysiac; it is also the effect that his worship has on his followers.

Here, we are limited in what we can say because the evidence is slim and rests, for the most part, on Euripides' *Bacchae*. Still, it can be reasonably asserted that the Dionysiac
involves an ecstatic loss of self, a transgression of mundane
perceptions: 'The whole point of Dionysism [*sic*] ... is to
become other oneself.'[30] One can see that the experience of
watching strange fictional figures on stage, of identifying with
some of those figures, of becoming involved in the drama,
could be said to be Dionysiac. As Vernant has said, the connection between tragedy and Dionysus is based on the opening up of a 'new space in Greek culture, the space of the
imaginary'.[31] Also important here is the fact that before the
Great Dionysia a statue of Dionysus was carried to and from
Eleutherae (later, certainly, by ephebes).[32] The enactment of
the advent of Dionysus is of interest, not only because it
marks one feature of the god, namely that he is always arriving from outside (unlike other gods), but also because it
marks the city's attempted appropriation of this strange and
troublesome divinity.[33] But this is always something of a
problem. The festival attempts to incorporate the irrational
elements embodied by Dionysus, and tries to present that incorporation as a successful taming of the wild god, attempts
which are undermined by tragedy's representation of extreme
transgression (e.g. Medea, Oedipus). This apparent inconsistency is especially sharp in the case of *Bacchae*, where the play
'denies what the ritual context affirms'.[34] A flux is established
between the ritual and tragic Dionysus. But, then, that is not

---

[30] Vernant and Vidal-Naquet (1988), 204. See also Simon (1978), 251–9; Detienne
(1986); Bruit Zaidman and Schmitt Pantel (1992), 198.

[31] Vernant and Vidal-Naquet (1988), 187; see also 205.

[32] Pickard-Cambridge (1968[2]), 59–61; Goldhill (1987), 59.

[33] Bérard and Bron (1986). For apparent Athenian reluctance to accept Dionysus
initially, see sch. ad Ar. *Ach.* 243; though note that at Heraia Dionysus had the
epithet *politēs*, and in Tralles, Teos and Magnesia, *dēmosios*; see Farnell (1909),
135.

[34] C. Segal (1982), 14; see also Seaford (1981).

inappropriate for the festival of Dionysus, which was a sacred and carnival time.[35] Modern study of the carnival, which began with Bakhtin, has something to offer.[36]

In the work of Bakhtin, the carnival is the scene of inversions and transgressions, the scene of the other; it 'challenges god, authority and social law'.[37] It 'plays its games in an inbetween time of temporary chaos and anarchy';[38] it is 'a populist, utopian vision of the world which provides through its inversions of hierarchy a critique of dominant culture'.[39] It is a place where prohibitions tend to disappear, and where culturally determined distinctions become problematic. But, in adopting this model of the carnivalesque festival, the language of critics has sometimes slipped into unnecessary hyperbole. Girard, for instance, claims that in a festival all distinctions are 'swept away', 'destroyed', 'effaced'.[40] If distinctions are effaced or destroyed – and it is not clear that they are – the effect is temporary. A happier description is that they are inverted, subverted or perverted. But the power of all these three processes depends on some persistence of the distinctions which are being so treated. Also, on the one hand, the carnivalesque is not uniquely Dionysian; and, on the other, not all festivals were modelled on carnivalesque reversal (e.g. the Panathenaea).[41] Indeed, Plato can even think of festivals as edifying public occasions without any hint of disorder (*Laws* 653c7ff.). When using the idea of carnival, we must be careful to be historically specific. Carrière has noted the carnivalesque origins of Dionysiac ritual but has quite rightly also insisted on its politicization in such festivals as the Great Dionysia.[42] While the Bakhtinian model sees carnival as the inversion of hierarchy, this cannot quite apply to the Great

[35] Reckford (1987), 20.
[36] There is a very good discussion of Bakhtin in White and Stallybrass (1986). See now Goldhill (1991), 176–88 on the application of Bakhtin to fifth-century Attic comedy.
[37] Kristeva (1981), 79–80.
[38] Reckford (1987), 100–1; see also Adrados (1975), 371–4.
[39] Goldhill (1991), 178.
[40] Girard (1977), 126–8; Foley (1985), 234 uses similar terminology.
[41] Adrados (1975), 245; Buxton (1987), 199.
[42] Carrière (1979), 22ff.; see also Goldhill (1991), 182–3.

Dionysia, where authority and hierarchy were explicitly celebrated and where the audience – the citizen body – represents
authority.[43] Still, the emphasis on challenge and inversion
taking place at a special time is useful for the study of tragedy.
To describe carnival at its most general, we can say that it is a
challenging and festive release from the everyday, from the
self. Tragedy, with its transport of the audience into a fictional
world of role-playing, masks and the transgressive behaviour
of figures from another time and place, offers such a release.

I believe that approaching tragedy as civic discourse is fruitful, and that stressing its significance as a specific discourse
arising out of a specific politics and religion different from our
own will yield something more interesting than the reduction
of tragedy to a literary form.[44] More was – and is – at stake
than such traditional interests of literary criticism as the unity
of the text, or the consistency of the author's use of imagery.
And the Athenian audience was probably aware of this
too. For it was blessed – some would say burdened – with a
degree of political responsibility which most of us will never
experience.[45]

Without taking on board the conclusions drawn by Marxists about the production of literature,[46] one can assert that to
ask about the production of tragedy helps to evaluate its
nature as a discourse of the *polis*. By production I mean

[43] Goldhill (1991), 176–88.
[44] Heath (1989) argues, rightly, that we must be careful not to impose anachronistic
categories of thematic unity on classical texts. He claims to find, principally in
Plato and Aristotle, that, in fact, the Greeks had a 'centrifugal' rather than 'cen-
tripetal' notion of unity. However, Plato and Aristotle are not necessarily (or even
probably) representative of a fifth-century consensus about the unity of works of
literature. Nor is it self-evident (and Heath has no fifth-century evidence) that the
'coherence' of a work of literature (Heath's initial alternative) is applicable to
tragedy. Also, the application of the term 'literature' to tragedy (which Heath
maintains) could be as anachronistic as the search for a particular idea of unity;
see Loraux (1986), 245; Longo (1990).
[45] This is the emphasis of M. Finley's work; see (1973), (1983). Goldhill (1987), 69
rightly warns that we must not be tempted to construct a uniform, homogeneous
audience response.
[46] I.e. that literature must compete in a market, that it is a form of social and
economic production and a producer of wealth for its publisher; see Williams
(1977); Macherey (1978); Macherey and Balibar (1981). There were, of course, no
publishers in fifth-century Athens; see Baldry (1971), 6ff.; Knox (1985).

the factors which enabled tragedy to be performed (what Foucault might call its 'conditions of possibility'); or, more conventionally, the context of tragedy, context, that is, as 'a necessary complicity between the interlocutor and the audience'.[47] Although, for the sake of clarity, an artificial distinction will be maintained between the context of the plays and the plays themselves (describing the former by and large as a pre-text of the latter), I hope that the impression that the reader will receive is one of the interdependence of these factors; of context not as merely an environment, or a cause absent from its effect, but as a continuous and necessary presence in the tragedies. Like many recent works of classical scholarship, then, this thesis is indebted to the work of Vernant (and those associated with him), who has championed the study of tragedy as an institution within the *polis*, as a part of civic discourse.

It is no innovation to build an interpretation of tragedy from an understanding of the relations between the *polis*, the Great Dionysia, the god Dionysus and the tragic dramas performed in his honour. Nor could any originality be claimed for asserting the need to read Euripides and his *Troades* alongside the provocative and revolutionary texts of the sophists and Thucydides' narrative of the Peloponnesian War.[48] Nor is it new to see in Euripides a certain decadence. However, the novelty of the thesis presented here consists in arguments which are germane to tragedy generally as well as to Euripides. For tragedy in general, it is argued that its didactic function, which partly constitutes its privileged position in Athenian civic discourse, should be made the basis of interpretation. The processes of tragic didacticism are considered in detail. This has afforded insights into the connection between the pleasure of watching tragedy and the teaching it conveys, as well as into the fact that tragic teaching comprises the questioning of received wisdom. It is further argued that

---

[47] Vernant (1970), 273.
[48] E.g. Decharme (1893); A. Thomson (1898); Nestle (1901); J. Finley (1938); Rohdich (1968).

such questioning can be achieved most potently when the dramatic context is that of war and its aftermath. The complex relations between tragedy, ideology and war are, I believe, relevant to all extant tragedy. In the second and third chapters, an interpretation of *Troades* is offered which demonstrates how the play performs its function. It does so by examining a series of interdependent and mutually reinforcing polarities, which the audience employed in its self-definition. Again, this is part of the practice sustained by all tragedy and so I mean my analysis, in the sense that it draws all the polarities together rather than concentrating on one, to be a model for reading other plays. For Euripides, there are more particular suggestions. First, war is not only used as a frame, or as a dramatic context for questioning, but is itself questioned. Second, the didactic project is seen to be dependent on an overriding, but slippery polarity: self/other. What I hope to show in this connection is that Euripides produces a distinctive dramatic world, where the relations of similarity and difference to the world of the audience are themselves different from those that we find in the other tragedians; and that this, along with all the other stylistic peculiarities of Euripidean drama, must be seen in relation to the didactic function.

A critical vocabulary has been adopted from a variety of sources. In brief, tragedy is placed in relation to ideology, its ideological operations and strategies viewed under the polarity self/other. Ideology. Self/other. The modern resonances are many and varied. Finley, in a forthright wish not to impose modern concepts on alien societies, denied the existence of ideology in ancient Greece.[49] However, it seems petulant not to use a word which, with some tampering and fine-tuning, becomes a very valuable way of grasping what it is exactly that tragedy questions. 'Self' and 'other' are essential to my project. First, because it is clear that the Greeks themselves thought in polarities, and used various opposed categories to define themselves. The self is used to refer to the Athenian citizen and to all the ideas and experiences with

---

[49] (1973), 50–4, 66; but compare Lanza and Vegetti (1975).

which he might identify; the other is that which he variously excludes, at the level of ideology, from the self. Second, self/other has also provided a fruitful way to comprehend the experience of going to a theatre to watch fictional, often alien, characters on a stage, characters who are, in various permutations, culturally, ethnically, socially and sexually different from the members of the audience and who inhabit dramatic worlds which are spatially and temporally different. In attempting to get to grips with the movement between the self and the other which the theatrical experience of emotional identification and involvement with fictional figures surely necessitates, we find ourselves in a world where the analysis of the spatial operations performed by tragedy becomes important (anyway, the importance of spatial distinctions to the Greeks can be easily demonstrated; see chapter four). But these are general points. We must be mindful of the fact that the Theatre of Dionysus occupied a special place at the centre of Athens, very near, in fact, to the meeting place of the Assembly. We must also remember that the theatre is divided into two obvious spaces, that of the auditorium and that of the performing area (with its spatially distinct *orchēstra* and *skēnē*). Even more important, the audience will see a dramatic world, normally set in the past and in a different place, created before them. As spectators, they were free to make the journey into the representation. Given that these were the conditions of the watching of tragedy, I believe in general that criticism of tragedy will have to become more sophisticated in its awareness of the spatial operations which tragedy enacts.

Euripides continues to provoke diverse interpretations. Kovacs argues that if we read him 'straight', 'at face value', 'naively' and 'unsuspiciously', we will find ourselves with an unironic Euripides, one who has more in common with Aeschylus and Sophocles than is normally supposed; something, in fact, of a traditionalist. Michelini argues for a Euripides who must be viewed against the Sophoclean norm: his theatre is perverse, outrageous, multiple and grotesque. McDermott sees Euripides subverting traditional assumptions but not replacing them with any new vision; at the centre of his art, she argues, there is anomaly and deformation. Gregory depicts Euripides as a poet who, like the other tragedians, tried to reconcile the traditional aristocratic values embodied in myth with the democratic order of Athens and whose plays become bearers of democratic ideology.[50] Some of these views will be analysed and some contested in the pages which follow. As has already been said, Euripides provides his audience with a distinctive dramatic world. But to understand his differences from Aeschylus and Sophocles, we must also recognize the similarities. We must also acknowledge, however, that it is difficult to talk in terms of tragic convention or of a tragic norm. The sample we have of even the three great tragedians is small; and there is, at best, only fragmentary comparative material from either the fifth or the fourth century. And, as Gregory rightly says, it is not valid to see Euripides transgressing norms or confronting conventions which he may have helped to develop.[51] It is indeed a problem with Michelini's thesis that, on the basis of the number of his victories, she too quickly identifies Sophocles as the tragic norm. Such a position underestimates the possibility (I would say the fact) that Euripides not only reacted against Sophocles; he also influenced him (and vice versa).[52] That which, for convenience, we call the tragic norm is in fact something which was always developing and never quite fixed. This can be seen from the three plays we know about which treated contemporary material – Phrynichus' *Capture of Miletus* (492 BC), *Phoenissae* (477–476 BC) and Aeschylus' *Persae* (472 BC) – and the very different audience reactions they provoked, and also from Agathon's experiment in pure fiction late in the fifth century.[53] That is to say, what constituted an acceptable dramatic world for tragedy was being worked out as the genre developed. We should also remember that tragedy de-

---

[50] Kovacs (1987); Michelini (1987); McDermott (1989); Gregory (1991).
[51] Gregory (1991), 16 n.35.
[52] *Philoctetes* would seem to be the most Euripidean of Sophocles' extant dramas; see Craik (1979); Greengard (1987).
[53] Knox (1979), 7–8.

veloped in response to contemporary events, to other literary genres and other discourses, and to its own increasing self-consciousness, its awareness of the creation of a tragic tradition. If Euripides is different, those differences are of degree, rather than kind. There is in Euripides a complication in identifying the 'other', produced by a bewildering and distinctively extreme flux between the two terms of a polarity. In Euripides, the audience also saw the comic invade the tragic space more regularly and more inappropriately, and that same space pervaded by Gorgianic rhetoric, with all its troubling consequences. They experienced a more persistent anachronism and more frequent self-reference. All of these things – present to a lesser degree in Aeschylus and Sophocles – produced a dramatic world peculiar to Euripides. It might be argued that, through the complication of otherness, Euripides questions the didactic function itself; it is certainly true to say that the creation of a distinctive dramatic world allows the poet to pose distinctive, even disturbing problems. In saying all this, I offer both a new interpretation of Euripides' provocative poetics (based on the spatial strategies of his plays and necessitating the use of various spatial terms, such as 'site') and of his relationship with the sophists. The latter has been noted often and often used too in an appreciation (and denigration) of the peculiarities of Euripidean drama. The relation is important since the appearance of sophistic elements in Euripides manifests one element of those spatial strategies. For the sophists, unlike tragedians, spoke from no place of importance such as the theatre, and their invitation to appear on Euripides' tragic stage marks the poet's determination to allow what is marginal to speak at the centre.

In my interpretation of *Troades*, then, readers will not find long discussions of dramatic structure (as it is ordinarily understood), nor of the characterization;[54] nor of Euripides as

---

[54] On the topic of characterization, see Pelling (1990), with bibliography there. The modern era of interpretation of Euripides in terms of dramatic structure and motif was initiated by Strohm (1957); see also Conacher (1967); Steidle (1968); Burnett (1971).

patriot, anti-war poet, feminist, misogynist, oligarch, sophist, anti-sophist or grocer's son.[55] Instead, they will find a reading which hopes in part to provide models for the interpretation of other tragedies and also to mark *Troades* of extant tragedies as perhaps the most extreme self-examination produced by Athens. That Euripides, as I present him, more often questions than affirms, more often makes things difficult rather than easy, is not my view alone, and I believe that enough evidence is offered here to support it.[56] However, the more or less constant demonstration of Euripides' questioning of received wisdom can lead to tedious repetitions of certain terms, such as 'problematic'. Still, too many critics believe that to identify a problem is to justify saying nothing categorical and substantial. Far from it: the process initiates discussion, and stimulates inquiry. That the problems posed by Euripides so often seem to be insoluble and so often seem to arise out of the confrontation of internally inconsistent rhetorics or irrational characters may irritate logicians; but it also allows us to recognize the sophistication with which the tragic form (and Euripides) responded to the world.

[55] The use of biography, or intellectual positions Euripides supposedly held, has always been a strong current in Euripidean criticism. See e.g. Decharme (1893); A. Thomson (1898); Nestle (1901); Grube (1941); Pohlenz (1954²); Rohdich (1968); Vellacott (1975); for trenchant criticism of such approaches, see Longo (1990). Michelini's first chapter (1987) surveys the main trends in Euripidean criticism to the present day.

[56] Buxton (1988) believes that 'bafflement' is a particular characteristic of Euripidean tragedy (he is arguing against what he sees as an excessive and deconstructionist tendency to problematize interpretation). By bafflement, he means that which the audience may feel on viewing the multiple perspectives offered on why events in the play have occurred (though he also notes the ambiguity of tragic irony and the inevitably baffling nature of the divine). Obviously, Buxton is dealing with something entirely different from the display of giddying rhetoric and unstable meaning which the interpretation of *Oresteia* by Goldhill (1984) produces. In trying to assess the relative extremity (or modernity, if you will) of the tragic art of the three great Athenian dramatists, it is not clear that asking 'why do events occur in the play' (as Buxton does) is helpful. My own attempt to understand the peculiar force of Euripidean tragedy begins neither with the demonstration of inherent and eternal difficulties of language (though it will be important) nor with a concentration on plot, but with the emphasis on the didactic function of tragedy and Euripides' relation to it.

1

TEACHING, IDEOLOGY AND WAR

The didactic production

Was tragedy supposed to teach? Many scholars have assumed that it did have some educative function and effect.[1] Arrowsmith's description – 'a democratic *paideia* in itself' – can stand as a summary of this position.[2] To talk about the didactic function of tragedy is both to indicate perhaps the most important condition of the production of tragedy and to make a historical point about both authorial and audience expectations. However, since approaching tragedy in terms of its function or its effects has recently been challenged, it is worth while laying out the evidence in support of analysing tragedy as an educative discourse.

In classical antiquity poets were figures of some authority, regarded as 'masters of truth' (to use Detienne's phrase), as experts in ethical and spiritual matters, as wise men to whom one listened for guidance. Near the beginning of *Republic* 10 Socrates confesses his affection for Homer, whom he describes as the first teacher and guide of all tragic poets (*Rep.* 595c1–2: 'πρῶτος διδάσκαλός τε καὶ ἡγεμών'). A little later, Socrates advises Glaucon that when he bumps into admirers of Homer, who claim that he has educated Greece (606e1–5: 'ὡς τὴν Ἑλλάδα πεπαίδευκεν'), he should patronize them as good but limited men. In both these instances Plato does not say anything surprising; he is in fact reporting a widespread belief in Homer the teacher. We find that same belief mentioned, though criticized, in Xenophanes (DK 21B10), in Isocrates

---

[1] Blundell (1989), 1–25; Buxton (1982), 1; Cantarella (1965), 51; Euben (1986), 23; Harriott (1969), 107; Havelock (1963), 47–9; (1982), 264ff.; Jaeger (1939), 239; Kolb (1979), 505–7; Laín Entralgo (1970), 206–15; Schlesinger (1963), 47; Walcot (1976); Walton (1984), 31; Woodbury (1986), 247–9.

[2] (1963), 33

(*Paneg.* 159) and throughout another of Plato's dialogues –
Ion – where the rhapsode after whom the dialogue is named
claims that Homer is the best teacher of everything from military strategy to carpentry.[3] Indeed, poetry was an integral
part of the education of potential citizens.[4] Discourses
deemed to have the potential to transmit wisdom were not
divided in the way in which they came to be after Plato challenged the authority of poetry.[5] The distinction was not so
much between philosophy and literature as between prose and
verse. There was a venerable tradition of wise men who wrote
in verse, including Xenophanes, Heraclitus, Parmenides, Solon and Theognis. Nussbaum reminds us of an illuminating
passage from Heraclitus (DK 22B40), where he acknowledges
that his competition was Hesiod, Pythagoras, Xenophanes
and Hecataeus: 'In our terms, he has named a didactic poet, a
seer and oral philosopher, a philosopher who wrote in verse,
and a writer of prose ethnographical treatises.'[6] There seems
so far no reason to doubt that the Athenian tragedians continue this role of poet as thinker and teacher. Euripides himself is significantly described as the philosopher of the theatre
(Ath. 158e).

The evidence concerning the symposium also suggests a didactic function for poetry. Authors as distant from each other
as Theognis and Plato agree in seeing the symposium as a
model for the city, a gathering where men may examine themselves in a playful but nevertheless important way. Here we
should note the repeated use of the word 'βάσανος' ('touch-
stone', 'test': Theog. 415–18, 447–52, 1105–6, 1164; Pl. *Laws*
649d10, 650a2, 650b4) to describe the symposium. Moreover,
at the symposium poetry plays a significant part in teaching

---

[3] Hesiod is also called a teacher in a sarcastic fragment of Heraclitus (DK 22B57).

[4] Pl. *Rep.* 367e; Pl. *Laws* 654a–b. On the education of Athenian citizens, see Marrou
(1956). On the importance of poetry and singing in Greek culture and education,
see Detienne (1967); Svenbro (1976); Calame (1977).

[5] At Pl. *Rep.* 607b5 Socrates mentions the ancient contest ('παλαιά ... διαφορά')
between poetry and philosophy. Goldhill (1991), 168 n.2 is partly right to say that
this is 'a typical strategy of both myth and rhetoric – to construct a teleological
narrative to explain a present structure', but it should be remembered that
Xenophanes and Heraclitus had long before questioned the authority of poets.

[6] Nussbaum (1986), 123.

the participants the characteristics required of them to be good men. That the symposium was a place for education and that poetry was an element in that education is made clear at Theognis 27–30:

σοὶ δ' ἐγὼ εὖ φρονέων ὑποθήσομαι, οἷάπερ αὐτὸς
   Κύρν' ἀπὸ τῶν ἀγαθῶν παῖς ἔτ' ἐὼν ἔμαθον.
πέπνυσο, μηδ' αἰσχροῖσιν ἐπ' ἔργμασι μηδ' ἀδίκοισιν
   τιμὰς μηδ' ἀρετὰς ἕλκεο μηδ' ἄφενος.

And, being well disposed towards you, I shall lay out the things which
I, Kurnus, learned from good men when I was still a child.
Be wise, and do not drag either your honour or your virtue
or your wealth towards shameful or unjust deeds.

Similar statements both of general didactic intentions and of particular advice can be found throughout Theognis (see 31ff., 61ff., 101ff., 1165–6).[7]

The fifth century saw further considerations of the function of the poet. Protagoras makes it clear that he sees poets, as well as prophets, musicians and gymnasts, as sophists, their ostensible careers merely being a mask for their real profession. Protagoras also confesses that he is a sophist and a teacher: it is to be presumed, then, that poets (and he mentions Homer, Hesiod and Simonides by name) were teachers as well (Pl. *Prot.* 317a–b). And the fact that two eminent 'sophists', Hippias and Gorgias, donned the purple robes of rhapsodes (DK 82A9) not only supports Protagoras' argument that sophists needed to disguise their true identities; it also demonstrates a sophistic attempt to appropriate rhapsodic authority, an authority which was rooted in the teachings of Homer.[8]

These examples should alert us to the fact that, although we can say that poetry was generally presumed to be educative, its didactic authority did not go unchallenged. The sophists,

---

[7] For a good collection of articles concerning the symposium, see Murray (1990), but most especially the papers by Lissarrague and Pellizer; see also Lissarrague (1990b). For Theognis and the symposium, see Levine (1985).

[8] Empedocles may also have worn the robes of the rhapsode: D.L. 8.73. On rhapsodes, see Svenbro (1976), 8off.; Herington (1985), 167–77, who collects the evidence. See Hartog (1988), 361, who characterizes Herodotus as a mixture of rhapsode and sophist.

offering a wide range of teaching for various fees, were competing to become authoritative voices within the *polis*. Plato, with his criticisms of both sophistic and poetic teaching, allows us to see that education in late fifth-century Athens was 'a source of conflict rather than social stability'.[9] Tragedy itself, in terms of poetic teaching, was a relative newcomer struggling to match the pre-eminence of Homer, which was panhellenic and rarely questioned (though see n. 5), even in Athens.[10] Tragic teaching was also institutionalized in a competition – a democratic *agōn* – where, along with comedy, it engaged in a 'contest of public voices'.[11] Yet tragedy, as a home-grown Athenian discourse sponsored by the *polis*, did acquire a particular prestige.[12] For this reason, and also because of the crisis of the final years of the war, it does not seem insignificant that Aristophanes dramatized the recall of a tragedian to come back and guide Athens in her hour of need. It is, of course, the *agōn* of the *Frogs* between 'Euripides' and 'Aeschylus' which is the main evidence for tragic didacticism. While the civic theme dominates the play, the reference to the function of tragedy is explicit. Euripides claims to have taught the audience to talk or to babble (954: 'λαλεῖν ἐδίδαξα'); Aeschylus agrees (954–5, 1069). In a longer passage Euripides also asserts that he has instructed (972: 'εἰσηγησάμην') people to think (971: 'φρονεῖν), to use reason and reflection (973: 'λογισμόν'; 974: 'σκέψιν'), so that they can think (974: 'νοεῖν') and make distinctions (975: 'διειδέναι'), to manage their households better (976–7) and, finally, to ask questions (977–9). Aeschylus' teaching is more traditional. At 1025–6 he says that his production (the word used is 'διδάξας') taught ('ἐξεδίδαξα') people to want to win. At 1029ff. he gives a list of poet-teachers who have preceded him: Orpheus taught the Mysteries and a hatred of murder; Musaeus medicine and divination; Hesiod farming; and, lastly, Homer, from

---

[9] Goldhill (1991), 169; see also G. Lloyd (1988), 84ff.
[10] Herington (1985), 135–40; Michelini (1987), 62.
[11] Goldhill (1991), 167–76.
[12] See Foley (1988) on Aristophanes' appropriation of tragedy's prestige.

whom Aeschylus claims his own inspiration (1040–2), war. In a famous couplet Aeschylus states: 'Boys have teachers, young men poets' (1054–5: 'τοῖς μὲν γὰρ παιδαρίοισιν/ἐστὶ διδάσκαλος ὅστις φράζει τοῖσιν δ' ἡβῶσι ποιηταί'). Perhaps most explicit though is when Aeschylus asks Euripides why a poet should be respected. This is Euripides' answer (1009–10):

> δεξιότητος καὶ νουθεσίας, ὅτι βελτίους τε ποιοῦμεν
> τοὺς ἀνθρώπους ἐν ταῖς πόλεσιν.

> For his mental dexterity and advice, and because we make men in cities better.

Heath has questioned the validity of a comic poet's evidence. And in principle he is right to do so, especially as there is a possibility that, in order to ridicule the amorality of 'Euripides', the statements of tragic didacticism have been exaggerated. But Heath neglects to consider that 'Euripides' and 'Aeschylus' agree on this one basic thing: tragedy *is* supposed to make citizens better. Moreover, the didactic function of tragedy is a premise for the *Frogs*, one on which a lot of the jokes depend; and, to be funny, jokes in turn depend on a 'degree of cultural consensus'.[13] Still, the point remains that the only explicit evidence that tragedy was considered to be didactic is in a comedy, where tragedy is parodied and the claims of the two competing tragedians are often undercut.[14] Also, nowhere in the *agōn* of *Frogs* does comedy make any claims to teach, something which it is fond of doing elsewhere (*Ach.* 633–5; *Frogs* 686–7). On this basis it has been argued that comedy is excluded from the *agōn* because the Athenians have excluded it from the number of didactic discourses and that the teaching which 'Euripides' and 'Aeschylus' eventually offer is typically tragic in its vagueness: specific political advice is really the function of comedy. Such a challenge

---

[13] Gregory (1991), 3–4; Heath (1987a), 45. Guépin (1968), 222 notes that the two poets agree about the didactic function, but thinks that they are wrong to do so, though he gives no reason why.

[14] Goldhill (1991), 201–22.

to tragic didacticism depends, of course, on the continuing perception of its reality; it also once again demonstrates the competitive nature of poetic teaching.[15]

Heath has not only questioned the evidence of Aristophanes; he has also challenged the very idea of analysing tragedy in terms of its function and effects.[16] His argument, briefly, is this: there are, of course, didactic *uses* made of tragedy, but that is not necessarily the concern of the tragedian. Since didactic intentions are not necessary, they are not essential, and therefore not worth considering. Furthermore, none of the ancient authors who reflect on tragedy ever mentions didactic intentions. Indeed, Heath believes that, along with the author of the *Dissoi Logoi*, the poets had no interest in teaching at all (DK 90.3.17; see also DK 90.2.28):

καὶ τοὶ ποιηταὶ οὐ [το] ποτὶ ἀλάθειαν ἀλλὰ ποτὶ τὰς ἁδονὰς
τῶν ἀνθρώπων τὰ ποιήματα ποιέοντι.

And poets write their poems not for the sake of the truth but to give men pleasure.

Of course, Heath could only hold such a position by believing that a didactic intention would have to be expressed in terms of the imparting of truth, which is by no means self-evident. Also, he has paid insufficient attention to the value of the remark from the *Dissoi Logoi*: we need not believe the author of a handbook of sophistic argumentation. And the positions adopted in the *Dissoi Logoi* seem to have the character of exercises in argument: the statement which Heath quotes comes as part of a response to the Gorgianic point that it is just for tragedians and painters to deceive (DK 90.3.10; DK 82B23). For that reason, to use one of the two arguments as historical evidence is questionable. Furthermore, the author of the *Dissoi Logoi* does not speak from a position of cultural authority, as a comic or tragic poet chosen for the Great Dionysia may be said to.

---

[15] Heiden (1991). Taplin (1983) argues that Ar. *Ach.* 500 may also be used to emphasize the case for tragic didacticism.
[16] Heath (1987a), 46–7, 88.

Heath, then, adopts a quasi-Platonic position, in which tragedy is merely a spectacle with strong emotional effects on the audience (see e.g. Pl. *Rep.* 605c10–d5).[17] However, Plato not only attacks the Athenians' enjoyment of poetry and tragedy, which he obviously believes they found unharmful; he also criticizes poetry for being negatively didactic, since it has the ability to corrupt even the most upright (*Rep.* 605c6–8). The role of poetry in transmitting values and beliefs, in educating citizens, is precisely what Plato objects to. And the depth of his criticism stands as evidence for the authority of poets.[18] Further, it is improbable that, in the absence of institutionalized education, the cultural authority of poets which I have described and to which Heath himself refers was caused simply by their being entertainers. Heath, though, makes the mistake of assuming that the pleasure of watching drama and the emotions it arouses prohibit the possibility of there being any intellectual appreciation of tragedy. While the relationship between pleasure and knowledge and Plato's and Aristotle's views of that relationship are complex, there is no reason to assume that pleasure and knowledge are mutually exclusive. But this is a difficult topic and one that requires treatment in some detail here.

Plato's criticism of tragedy has two parts: one works through the ontological status of mimesis; the other by describing the effects of tragedy.[19] *Republic* 10 states clearly that tragedy's relationship to the truth is always problematic, since it is itself an imitation of mere appearance. That is, a philosopher is obliged to take mimesis as a serious threat to the

---

[17] Heath (1987a), 80 argues that it is sufficient to say that the audience was aesthetically satisfied by an ordered sequence of events which provoked emotions. As I suggest, Heath has no evidence for this claim, and has to misinterpret Aristotle for support.

[18] Jones (1962), 52.

[19] The bibliography on Plato's criticism of poetry generally and tragedy in particular is very large. I shall not refer at every point to all the scholars from whom I have learned, but I have found these authors useful: Halliwell (1986a); Harriott (1969); Havelock (1963); Heath (1987a); Jones (1962); Kennedy (1963); Mullen (1982); Nussbaum (1986); Prendergast (1986); Redfield (1975); de Romilly (1975); Salkever (1986); C. Segal (1962).

apprehension of truth, and, in Plato's case, to propose its exclusion from the *polis*. Having argued that mimesis is dangerous, it is not surprising that Plato should describe the effects of tragedy in the way that he does. The aim of tragedy, according to Plato, is to give pleasure to its audience; and it does this by playing on its emotions, arousing fear and pity and anger and so on.[20] Because nakedly pleasurable, tragedy is morally bankrupt; worse, it corrupts. Its failure to penetrate the world of reason is accentuated by the fact that poets are not rational creatures, but ecstatic and mad.[21] The discourse they create is a form of rhetoric, and therefore, in Plato's terms, mere unknowing flattery.[22] In agreement with Gorgias, Plato points out that words have a magic that can infect the soul of the listener; in opposition to Gorgias, this is proposed as another criticism of tragedy's irrationality and immorality.[23] Most straightforwardly, though, tragedy lies.[24] Finally, and most relevant to my argument, tragedy is, in Platonic terms, unable to educate. Genuine education for Plato takes place between

[20] *Ion* 535b–e; *Gorg.* 501e–502b; *Rep.* 392a–b, 539b, 603–5d, 606b, 607a; *Laws* 655c–d, 660e, 667b, 700e, 802c–d, 817a–d.

[21] Poets as mad: *Ion* 533e; *Phdr.* 244bff., 245a. There is a criticism of this position in the *Poetics* (1455a32–3). Aeschylus is 'mad' at *Frogs* 814ff.

[22] *Gorg.* 463aff., 464c–d, 502b–d; *Rep.* 473a; *Laws* 700d–e, 817b, 909b.

[23] Rhetoric, that is, aims at 'ψυχαγωγία': *Phdr.* 261aff., 271c. It is Gorgias' *Helen* that is the key text for this view of rhetoric. I will be discussing it below.

[24] Prendergast (1986), 9–10 argues that Plato attacks mimesis not because it lies, but rather because the proliferation of images produced by mimesis undermines proper classification. This underestimates the weight of Platonic evidence in favour of the view that mimesis lies: see e.g. *Meno* 76e; *Crat.* 408c; *Rep.* 382d. That poetry lies was anyway a traditional complaint: Solon fr. 21; Hom. *Od.* 13.294, 14.387, 19.203 (and see Arist. *Poet.* 1460a17ff.); Plut. *Sol.* 29.4 (Solon telling Thespis he is a liar); Parmenides DK 28B8.52; Theog. 27; cf. Heraclitus (Kahn 12, 19, 21, 22); Pind. *Nem.* 7.21, *Ol.* 1.28; *HF* 1346. Harriott (1969), 112 points out that the word for lie ('ψεῦδος') covers a large semantic ground, and is thus difficult to translate and interpret. Similar problems over Gorgias' description of tragedy as *apatē* (DK 82B23; cf. *Helen* 9, 11). Many scholars have agonized over Gorgias' meaning, e.g. Untersteiner (1954),108ff.; Rosenmeyer (1955); C. Segal (1962); Verdenius (1981); Walsh (1984), 81ff.; Heath (1987a), 40. But the most convenient translation of the word is 'fiction', making Gorgias' statement fairly simple: one gains more benefit from theatre if one knows it is theatre and not the 'real' world (see chapter four: 'Self-reference: the audience and the play'). The only critic I can find who has also made this very straightforward suggestion is Laín Entralgo (1970), 221. Yet its problem lies in its straightforwardness. It is indeed convenient to translate *apatē* as fiction (or illusion), but to do so neglects the negative connotations of the word and Gorgias' provocativeness in using it as he does; see Bain (1987), 1.

one teacher and one pupil.[25] Tragedy cannot do this for the obvious reason of its public performance. In remarking on all this, Plato adopts an elitist tone, complaining of the mob of judges, the noise of the audience, and the fact that the only criterion used by the judges is pleasure felt by the audience.[26] As Salkever says, for Plato 'the political context of tragedy is such that it is utterly impossible for a tragedian to be both successful and at the same time a practitioner of genuinely cathartic *paideia*'.[27]

For Plato, then, as for the author of the *Dissoi Logoi*, tragedy is a discourse which, contrary to its culturally validated function, produces pleasure and nothing else. Despite what the audience may believe, it has no cognitive value whatsoever. How to respond? First, it is significant to note that Plato, the inventor of philosophy, the instigator of the battle – still continuing – between philosophy and literature for the ground of truth, the man who advocated the exclusion of poetry from the utopian state, wrote a philosophy making full use of the literary devices of image and metaphor, myth, drama and characterization.[28] Aristotle alerts us to this by his indecision over which literary genre the Socratic dialogues should best be placed in (*Poet.* 1447b11ff.). Similarly, Plato, keen to privilege the serious, quite frequently alludes to his own discourse as a game.[29]

Second, Plato's objection to tragedy is, as I said, dependent

---

[25] *Laws* 666d–667a. Salkever (1986), 282–3 describes the aim of Platonic education as the attempt to enforce a recognition of the inadequacy of the idea that happiness, the meaning of life, lies in the fulfilment of desire; see *Soph.* 230b; *Laws* 686eff. Interestingly enough, such a paideia is named 'καθαρτική' (*Soph.* 231b).

[26] *Gorg.* 502b–e; *Rep.* 604e; *Laws* 655e, 876b.

[27] (1986), 285.

[28] For the use of myth, see *Rep.* 501e; *Laws* 752a. Plato was of course a poet himself when young. And for the utopian city as the best mimesis of all, see *Laws* 817b.

[29] *Gorg.* 481b–e; *Rep.* 536c; *Parm.* 137b; *Statesman* 268d; *Tim.* 59c–d; *Laws* 803b–e; see also Derrida (1981), 157. See Huizinga (1955), 110ff. on riddle-solving and the origin of philosophy. Gorgias *Helen* 21 famously calls itself a joke ('παίγνιον'). As Huizinga (1955), 147 says, sophistic discourse questions the hierarchy of the serious over the playful; the *On Not Being* of Gorgias still baffles many, who expect it to be either a joke or serious philosophy; one of the challenges of the piece, though, is precisely to such an hierarchization; see Gomperz (1965), 35: 'Der "philosophische Nihilismus" des Gorgias ist aus der Geschichte der Philosophie zu streichen.'

on a certain, very tendentious opinion about the ontological status of mimesis. This opinion is in turn based on the theory of Forms, which is itself controversial.[30] Also, Plato's criticism of tragedy is philosophically inspired and is, explicitly in the *Republic* and the *Laws*, part of a utopian project. So, even if we were to agree with Plato's prescriptions, that would not alter the historical fact of tragedy's didactic function. Indeed it is that function, and the authority that accompanied it, which is at the core of Plato's anti-tragic complaint. Tragedy, supposedly educative, is dismissed because of its pernicious moral effects.[31] Like 'Aeschylus' in Aristophanes' *Frogs* (see 1049ff.), Plato seems to believe that people will imitate what they see on stage before them; that the representation of evil, for instance, will inevitably make people bad. That is, Plato has a limited and somewhat naive view of representation, seeing only its effects and assuming that the fact of representation is equivalent to condoning the activity represented (e.g. heroes weep; it is therefore acceptable to do so). This becomes explicit when Socrates and his co-discoursers discuss what sort of poetry, in terms of subject matter and manner of presentation, will be acceptable. Certain themes, certain musical accompaniments (the exciting ones), are rendered impermissible.[32] So, Plato does not doubt that Athenians expected tragedy to teach, and that such a function was deemed an essential feature of tragic discourse. No, his position was that it was a bad sort of teaching (because based on mimesis, and because of the context of its performance), and that it taught bad things (criticism of the gods, weakness in men and so on).

Heath also uses the evidence of Aristotle: because the *Poetics* make no overt reference to the function of tragedy,

---

[30] Ryle (1967).

[31] *Ion* 535c–e; *Rep.* 605c, 606a–b; *Soph.* 234e1–2. Blundell (1989), 15: 'Plato mistrusts the poets not merely as "teachers" of a rival brand of categorical wisdom, but as purveyors of a plurality of viewpoints with which the performer and audience are induced to sympathize.'

[32] For Plato's criticism of 'γοητεία' (sorcery), see *Soph.* 234c4–7; *Rep.* 602d, 605a; *Laws* 909b; cf. *Menex.* 235a–c. *Rep.* 377e–380c restricts poetic writing about the gods; 386ff. discusses the underworld, and proposes restrictions on the vocabulary of pity and fear, and lamentations; 398e: the Ionian and Lydian modes are to be disallowed; *Laws* 656d5–e4: dances are also to be legislated against.

that function is therefore of no importance. First, arguments from silence are not reliable, but anyway his observation rests on a debatable interpretation of the *Poetics*. Not all scholars agree that Aristotle neglects the educative role of tragedy. Second, even if it were possible to argue that he does, he may be wrong to do so. One can, in fact, respond to Plato through Aristotle. After Plato, as one critic says, tragedy needs an Aristotle.[33] Aristotle not only deals with Plato's depiction of tragedy as an emotional threat to the authority of reason and its distance from the truth;[34] he also opens up for us an area of debate concerning the relationship between the pleasure of watching a play (or reading it) and the intellectual, cognitive benefits which Aristotle claims that poetry provides.[35]

Aristotle does not exclude mimesis from the realm of knowledge. For Aristotle, mimesis is natural, it distinguishes men from animals, it is pleasurable and 'through mimesis man takes his first steps in understanding' (*Poet.* 1448b5ff.: 'τὰς μαθήσεις ποιεῖται διὰ μιμήσεως τὰς πρώτας').[36] Men learn through mimesis, then. While mimesis is rooted in human nature, the mimetic arts rationalize and exploit man's mimetic inclination. Halliwell summarizes: 'successful mimesis is of significance in Aristotle's eyes, and can be vindicated against Platonic condemnation, because it fulfils man's natural potential to understand reality by reconstituting it in some of the materials over which he has rational control'.[37] Aristotelian

[33] Nussbaum (1986), 393. Though see Halliwell (1984), 67, who says that Aristotle's rapprochement with tragedy was 'an attempt to woo it over to philosophy's side [rather] than meet it on its own terms'.

[34] Jones (1962), 21.

[35] I am not going to be able to consider all aspects of the *Poetics*. I have found these critics generally useful: des Bouvrie (1988); Else (1957); Halliwell (1986a) and (1987); Heath (1987a); Jones (1962); Laín Entralgo (1970); Lear (1988); Nussbaum (1986); Redfield (1975); Ricoeur (1984); Russell (1981); Salkever (1986); Sifakis (1986). Havelock (1982), 286ff. notes how Euripides' language in the *Frogs* has a vocabulary of cognition which, Havelock believes, is an effect of a culture increasingly using writing. On the relationship between the characteristics of Euripidean tragedy, as represented in Aristophanes' *Frogs*, and books, see Woodbury (1986). On the rates of literacy in fifth-century Athens, see Harvey (1966).

[36] On the importance of play in culture, see Huizinga (1955); Caillois (1962); Reckford (1987), 242. On mimesis as standing for a general view of art, see Arist. *Rhet.* 1371b4–8. On pleasure from mimesis compare Arist. *De Part. An.* 645a7–15.

[37] (1986a), 81.

mimesis not only anwers Plato; it does so by bringing together pleasure and knowledge. For pleasure, like mimesis, is natural (Arist. *Rhet.* 1369b33–4; Arist. *Eth. Nic.* 1177a16–17, 1177b30–1, 1154b16–17). The need to take pleasure in appropriate things was an important part of Aristotle's ethics. Given that Aristotle seems to accept that taking pleasure in mimesis was also natural, it follows that an appropriate thing in which to take pleasure would be tragedy. In some sense, then, he agrees with Plato. The audience does indeed take pleasure in watching the plays, and part of that pleasure is emotionally based. But again that is not *per se* objectionable, because emotions also have cognitive value. As valid responses to the world, emotions do not preclude thought, as Plato insists. Put another way, cognition and emotion come together in Aristotle's thought in the concept of pleasure. Even an aspect of the *Poetics* which most commentators have found inconsistent or unpleasing – the devaluation of the tragic spectacle – can be understood, as Halliwell demonstrates, as further evidence of Aristotle's keenness to assert the cognitive value of tragedy over its sensual appeal (see *Poet.* 1410b16ff., 1453b7ff.). Tragedy, in fact, has an important role to play in the direction of the emotions, whereby they 'become better attuned to the perception of reality ... and better disposed towards virtue'.[38] Or, as Jones has it, there is 'more to be gained by educating the emotions than repressing them'.[39]

'"The theatre", Grillparzer rightly stated, "is not a correctional institution for rascals, nor an elementary school for the irresponsible." But neither is it, I add, merely a place to shiver and weep pleasurably.'[40] Laín Entralgo is right. But the relationship between the pleasure of tragedy and tragic didacticism remains difficult to pin down. In the *Poetics*, the key passage is in chapter four (1448b4ff.), where pleasure and learning coincide in the experience of mimesis.[41] As Sifakis

[38] Halliwell (1986a), 197.   [39] Jones (1962), 21.
[40] Laín Entralgo (1970), 203.
[41] In the famous opening to the *Metaphysics* Aristotle makes an implicit connection between pleasure and knowledge: 'πάντες ἄνθρωποι τοῦ εἰδέναι ὀρέγονται φύσει' ('all men by nature desire to understand'). See also Arist. *Rhet.* 1410b13–15; Ath. 223b (specifically on tragedy). Note *Hipp.* 173.

28

points out, the idea that art will be indirectly instructive by being pleasurable is not especially controversial, but to claim that the experience of tragedy will be pleasurable *because* it is instructive is another matter.[42] But there is really no way to argue in any detail about this because Aristotle seems to take it as a premise: it is just a fact that learning something is pleasurable. That is, pleasure and knowledge are not deemed mutually exclusive, rather, together, and in appropriate form, they define the tragic experience. Still, it is unfortunate that Aristotle says nothing about the cognitive content of watching tragedy. Laín Entralgo speculates that the 'οἰκεία ἡδονή' (pleasure proper to tragedy) which Aristotle talks about is getting to know yourself better.[43] But, while Aristotle offers no detailed comment on this matter, he does assert that tragedy has an intellectual importance. Schlesinger is quite wrong to say that 'Aristotle was enough of a Platonist to discard the possibility of a service by drama to the intellect and to morals on the ground that drama did badly what only philosophy could do.'[44] On the contrary, Aristotle seems to have assumed that a discourse which dealt with the grave subjects of war, transgression, familial ties, social organization, the nature of goodness and reality, was a discourse that made a valid and far from negligible contribution to the philosophical project (understood in its most general sense).

Pleasure and learning also come together in the experience of grief and lamentation. The idea that represented grief would cause an audience pleasure was traditional in classical

---

[42] Sifakis (1986), 212. Barthes (1976) is an idiosyncratic meditation on the question: what if knowledge is delicious? Eagleton, 'Poetry, Pleasure and Politics' in (1986) is, as its title suggests, a consideration of pleasure's political effects and significances; see also F. Jameson, 'Pleasure: A Political Issue' in (1988). Interestingly, Brecht did not fail to see the importance of the relation between pleasure and knowledge for his theatre: 'Our theatre must encourage the thrill of comprehension and train people in the pleasure of changing reality' (quoted by Fisher (1963), 8). I am suggesting that a political form of theatre such as tragedy (political in a different sense from Brecht's of course) will similarly conflate the two terms. On the meaning of 'συλλογίζεσθαι' (normally: reckon, conclude, infer) at *Poet.* 1448b16, see Redfield (1975), 54; Sifakis (1986), 215; Lear (1988), 307 n.43.

[43] (1970), 236; see also Halliwell (1986a), 74ff.

[44] (1963), 41.

antiquity.[45] In the fifth century it is a feature of the surviving fragments of Gorgias (*Helen* 9–10), and it continues to be so in Aristotle (*Poet.* 1449b27; see also Pl. *Ion* 535c–d). If we combine this idea with another current both in tragedy and in discussion of it – 'πάθει μάθος'/'learning through suffering' – we can see a glimpse of how a play like *Troades*, with its unremitting representation of woe and misery, might provide the pleasure that accompanied learning. Indeed, in *Troades* (608–9), the chorus make the link between grief, song and pleasure explicit:[46]

> ὡς ἡδὺ δάκρυα τοῖς κακῶς πεπραγόσιν
> θρήνων τ' ὀδυρμοὶ μοῦσά θ' ἢ λύπας ἔχει.

> How sweet are tears for those in trouble
> and the songs of lamentation and the music of grief.

As Jaeger puts it: 'Suffering entails the force of knowledge.'[47]

Aristotle's response to Plato and his timely reaffirmation of the cognitive, intellectual and emotional effects of tragedy all come together in the difficult and much discussed term *catharsis*.[48] Although the term is only mentioned once in the *Poetics* (1449b24–8), it seems to be central to Aristotle's theory of tragedy. The obscurity of the concept has provoked a large and varied response. But it is not necessary here to enter into the debate, except to say that this concept, with its medical, religious and intellectual connotations, allows tragic discourse to have emotional, intellectual, therapeutic and didactic effects.[49] As a summary of this position, I quote Halliwell:

---

[45] Hom. *Il.* 23.98, 108; 24.507; Hom. *Od.* 4.113, 183; 19.249; and see e.g. Alexiou (1974).

[46] On Aeschylus and *pathei mathos*, see *Ag.* 176–8, 250–1; Lebeck (1971), 25–36. On Euripides' development of pathetic effects, see de Romilly (1986), 73–115.

[47] (1939), 273.

[48] des Bouvrie (1988); Else (1957); Halliwell (1986a) and (1987); Heath (1987a); Keesey (1979); Laín Entralgo (1970), 185ff.; Lear (1988); Nussbaum (1986), 389ff.; Pucci (1980), esp. 170–2; Reckford (1987), 47, 467; Redfield (1975), 67ff.; Russell (1981), 93ff.

[49] For summaries of positions taken over the source of *catharsis* and its best translation, see Halliwell (1986a), 351ff. Lear (1988) has some good arguments against both the purgation/purification and the clarification/education theories of *catharsis*. His own definition is that *catharsis* allows a release of emotion within a safe enviroment (one produced by mimesis) and that it consoles the audience as to the

'Tragic catharsis cannot easily be supposed to be separable from the integrated experience of tragedy – an experience which is both cognitive and emotional, and which rests on the understanding of the universals embodied in the mimetic representation.'[50]

Three final aspects of Aristotle's approach to tragedy need to be mentioned. Given that he denies the spectacle of tragedy any importance in the production of the appropriate effect of catharsis,[51] it becomes obvious that those effects will be produced almost completely by the words of tragedy. In this we can again trace traditional elements. Using tragic sources alone, we can see that the word (i.e. language) has a wide range of abilities, including pacification (Aesch. *Pers.* 837), irresistibility (Aesch. *Sept.* 715), and enchantment (*Andr.* 290).[52] Aristotle would seem to be allying himself with the opinion that words have a magical power, most emphatically expressed in Gorgias' *Helen*.[53] And the power of the *logos* is such that it can soothe and, more particularly, cure. This may sound bizarre, but there seems to have been a respectable school of opinion (before Plato at any rate) which asserted

---

existence of a rational world. On Gorgias as a precursor of Aristotle and poetics, see *Helen* 9 and 14; C. Segal (1962), 120, 132; Kennedy (1963), 169; de Romilly (1975), 5.

[50] (1986a), 200.

[51] Halliwell is quite right to accuse Aristotle of an ambivalent attitude towards spectacle. Though he downgrades it, he also describes it with the powerful Gorgianic adjective 'ψυχαγωγικόν' (1450b16: 'magically persuasive'/'seductive'); see Halliwell (1986a), 66–7, 341. Heath (1987a), 32 calls spectacle an 'ancillary pleasure'. On what Aristotle is actually referring to by spectacle, see Halliwell (1986a), 339, who plumps for just actors rather than the whole visual experience. Aristotle seems to be underestimating the importance of sight to knowledge, as Ricoeur (1984), 49 points out. This is strange because elsewhere (*Metaph.* 980a21–7) Aristotle himself asserts it. Generally, on the question of 'insight', knowledge and seeing in a tragic context, see Goldhill (1986), 199–221. Finally, Halliwell (1986a), 342 makes the important point that Aristotle may be responding to a fourth-century penchant for overstressing the visual side of tragedy.

[52] For further examples, see Laín Entralgo (1970), 67–8.

[53] De Romilly (1973), (1975); Walsh (1984). For the magic of words, see Hom. *Od.* 11.334; 13.294; 14.387; 18.282–3; Archil. fr. 106; Pind. *Nem.* 4.1–5. See Laín Entralgo (1970), 60–4 for a long list of references to appearances of the word 'θέλγω' (soothe etc.). On 'γοητεία' (sorcery) and 'κήλησις' (enchantment), see e.g. Pl. *Prot.* 315a, 328d; *Menex.* 235a2–3; *Rep.* 413c4, 601b; and n.32 above; on 'ψυχαγωγία' (magical persuasion; seductiveness), see Ar. *Birds* 1555; Pl. *Phdr.* 261a, 271c; Xen. *Mem.* 3.10.6.

this feature of the power of the word. Gorgias, of course, claims that he can cure people with his rhetoric (Pl. *Gorg.* 456b; for the Socratic response, see *Gorg.* 459aff.); and Antiphon, another sophist, is said to have established a surgery which treated ailments with the same instrument: the therapy of the word.[54] Gorgias, again, stresses the physical impact that *logoi* can have,[55] most famously when he states in the *Helen* that words act on the soul in the same way as *pharmaka* on the body (*Helen* 14).[56]

Tragedy has intellectual validity because unlike history, and more like philosophy, it deals in generalities, or universals (Arist. *Poet.* 1451b5–11; see also *Rhet.* 1356b). That fact contributes to Aristotle's ultimate disagreement with Plato, which concerns the educability of the *dēmos.* Aristotle does not quite

---

[54] Generally, see Laín Entralgo (1970). On Pythagorean and Heraclitean logotherapy, see Laín Entralgo (1970), 76ff. Note also D.L. 8.59, where it is said that Gorgias saw Empedocles healing. Tragic instances: Aesch. *PV* 377–80, 698–9; *Hipp.* 668–71; *Andr.* 93–5; see de Romilly (1973), 162 and (1975), 14.

[55] It is worth noting here Pucci (1980), writing about *Medea*, who attempts to construct an idea of a remedial discourse of pity which 'settles in a specific way the relationship between the self and the other' (p.16; and see p.55); also Pucci (1977). (Note H. Thompson (1952) on the existence of an Altar of Pity in Athens, which contained, significantly for Pucci since he concentrates on the one play, a representation of Medea.) Through a community of pain, the pain of the self receives the tragic remedy through the other. Some of what Pucci says can be accommodated in my more sociological approach to tragic exemplification: first, there is the idea that speech in the presence of another person (an other) is itself consoling (Soph. *Phil.* 692–4; and see Laín Entralgo (1970), 69); second that pleasure is, as Reckford said, 'always intensified by contrast' (1987), 6; third, it was an axiom of fifth-century medicine that you treated opposites with opposites (*On Ancient Medicine* 13; *Breaths* 1; see Arist. *Eth. Nic.* 1104b17ff., *Eth. Eud.* 1220a36ff.; G. Lloyd (1966), 21–2). Tragic therapy would then work through the self and the other, which in a more political sense is what I am arguing for. Indeed, the conflation of medicine and rhetoric is not new, but Gorgianic: see de Romilly (1973), 162; it is also fairly Platonic: *Phdr.* 259c – people become absent from themselves in the thrill of song; see Derrida (1981), 68. One problem with Pucci's theory is that he pays inadequate attention to the political context and nature of tragedy. In stressing the individual, emotional and psychological response he neglects the communal and public atmosphere in which such an experience would occur. He also fails to consider the social construction of the other (women, barbarians, slaves) and the relation between that and the tragic representation of the other.

[56] Note also Hom. *Od.* 1.337ff.; Theog. 52ff.; 98ff., 102–3; Aesch. *Ag.* 16ff.; *Hipp.* 478; *Supp.* 79; *Tro.* 472ff.; *Bacch.* 326–7. For an analysis of the *Medea* in terms of the *pharmakon*, see Pucci (1980), *passim.* For a more general idea of the physical impact of words, see DK 82A4, where Gorgias is said to have stunned the Athenians with his new rhetoric in 427 BC. This is the idea of *ekplēxis*, on which see *Helen* 6, 8, 9, 10–14; note also *Tro.* 183, Thuc. 6.36.2.

share Plato's contempt for the people; indeed, in the *Politics* he asserts that the many may be capable of better judgements than the few (*Pol.* 1283b, 1286a). The task of education in Aristotle's view is to convince people that living a disorderly life based on the fulfilment of desire and appetite will eventually prove self-destructive (*Pol.* 1266b, 1278b, 1319b). Tragedy, then, in its representation of reversal, and its stimulation of recognition of the instability of social order, provides a check on communal desire. Working in tandem with *nomoi*, i.e. with ideology, it provides a *paideia* whose significance affects both the private and the public lives of the citizens. One of the emotions that Aristotle argues that tragedy produces, namely fear, is also an emotion that elsewhere he describes as a provocation to deliberate (*Rhet.* 1385b).[57]

This last argument of Aristotle's shares with Plato the attempt to make tragedy work for one distinctive philosophical system. Although the latter believes that tragedy may teach but does so with corrupting effects, and the former implies it is educative and properly so, they both seem to accept that the cultural expectation of tragedy in fifth-century Athens was that it should teach. Aristotle qualifies Plato's zealous attempt to deny tragedy any rationality. Tragedy teaches, but it is both an emotional and an intellectual experience; it offers knowledge, about the self and the other and their constructions, and it gives pleasure in so doing. In an appropriately Dionysiac manner it offers something that is both painful and pleasurable, but which is still didactic.

But to understand why tragedy met Athens' need for a discourse which could stimulate, excite, provoke and question, we do not really need to appropriate Aristotle and Plato. Instead, we have to consider tragedy as a rhetorical discourse related to, and informed by, the profoundly important concept of *peithō*. It could be argued that discourses were not judged by the criterion of their truth content before Plato, though we should add before Thucydides, in that the historian

---

[57] See Aesch. *Eum.* 517–19, 698–9 and Soph. *Aj.* 1073–6, where a slightly different connection is made between fear and political organization.

offered an empirical alternative to Plato's absolutism.[58] That is not to say that truth as a concept was absent from fifth-century culture, but that it was constructed in the terms of *peithō*, and that discourses were judged not so much on the basis of their reflection of the truth, but on the basis of their power, their persuasiveness.[59] Athenians were in Cleon's words 'spectators of speeches' (Thuc. 3.38.4: 'θεαταὶ τῶν λόγων') and 'speaking – speaking well – was at once knowledge and power'.[60] While Walsh is correct to assert that the power of Homer, Hesiod and Pindar lies in their 'art of pleasing truth ... of truthful enchantment', the emphasis must be placed as heavily on the 'pleasing' as on the 'truth'.[61] The power of persuasion is most glamorously and shockingly advanced by Gorgias, for whom *logos* becomes a mighty tyrant with the power to enslave its audience (*Helen* 8–9; see Pl. *Gorg.* 452e; Hecuba also talks of *peithō* as a tyrant at *Hec.* 816). The ambiguous relationship of tragedy as rhetoric to truth is made manifest not only in rhetoric's natural attachment to the contingent, the malleable and the relative, but also, more provocatively, in Gorgias' notion of tragedy as *apatē* (deception). Tragedy is a fiction, an inventor of discourses; it represents conflict in opinion and ideology; it has characters trying to cope with their predicaments with the techniques of persuasion that were so ubiquitous in democratic Athens.

As rhetoric, and as *peithō*,[62] it is perfectly consistent that tragedy should be an educative discourse. Rhetoric was an integral and necessary part of any citizen's education, for the democracy depended on citizens' ability to argue and persuade, although the extent of that dependence is a matter of

---

[58] Thucydides offered, in what must be counted as an 'epistemological break', the idea of verifiability, a truth empirically tested; see Hartog (1982). Plato ignores the challenge.

[59] Note Parmenides DK 28B2.3–4: 'Πειθοῦς ἐστι κέλευθος ('Αληθείη γὰρ ὀπηδεῖ)'/ 'There is a path of Persuasion (it accompanies Truth).' Beauty is sometimes seen as a guarantee of truth; see Verdenius (1981),122; Buxton (1982), 43.

[60] Laín Entralgo (1970), 63.   [61] Walsh (1984), 107.

[62] In later times, at any rate, the priestess of *peithō* had a reserved seat for the performances of tragedy: *IG* III. 351; Buxton (1982), 35.

debate. Education also conventionally made use of poetry. Both poetry and rhetoric achieve their aims by using both intellectual and emotional factors, by giving pleasure and offering knowledge. Tragedy, then, meets the discursive requirements of Athens, because as a rhetorical discourse it follows that it will be instructive and pleasurable.[63]

Heath, however, further argues that the strength of the emotive theory of tragedy is that it can be applied to the audience, whereas the didactic theory cannot.[64] Surely this is mistaken. That we do not know precisely what the didactic effects were is not an argument for either their non-existence or their unimportance. Given that tragedy was a discourse authorized by the *polis* to be performed at a great public festival, and given that everyone seemed to agree that poetry had some educative force, it would seem reasonable to suppose that that consensus informed the production of tragedy. Tragedies were produced to be performed for audiences, who, through response and interpretation, were therefore actively involved in constructions of meaning. Their interpretations would be affected by a network of ideological forces, but one of those forces was precisely that tragedy had a didactic function. The audience presumably intended to interpret a play as a didactic discourse; that is, the function and the expectation of it are interdependent. In fact, the production and the function of tragedy are brought together in one word: *didaskein*.[65] Heath offers no evidence as to why tragedians should be blind to the cultural conditions in which they lived and worked. As regular members of the audience themselves, there seems no reason to doubt that they were aware that tragedy was expected to be paideutic. If we can talk about tragic authors' intentions – possible, though difficult, and of doubtful value – it seems probable that they were informed by the culturally and politi-

---

[63] *Peithō* may be said to have been expected to be pleasurable through its association with eroticism, seductiveness and, most specifically, Aphrodite: Paus. 1.43.6, 1.22.3; Pind. *Pyth.* 9.39; Aesch. *Supp.* 1040–1, *Cho.* 726; Soph. *Trach.* 661; *Hec.* 824ff. See also C. Segal (1962), 112, 122–8; Laín Entralgo (1970), 64–7; Verdenius (1981); Buxton (1982), 31ff.; Walsh (1984), 106.

[64] Heath (1987a), 45.   [65] Gregory (1991), 2.

cally validated function of tragedy. All our evidence about the social prestige of poets, the use of poetry in education and so on, would mean that if tragedy was primarily for entertainment, it would be, as poetry, an extraordinary exception. Heath fails to offer the extraordinary evidence which he would need to demonstrate such an exception. Nor does he explain why he prefers the evidence of the culturally unauthorized author of a handbook of sophistic argumentation to that of a comic poet, chosen by Athenians, as it were, as their representative. More importantly, Aristophanes' *Frogs* reminds us that tragedy was a discourse in part defined by its function: that is, tragedy was tragedy in so far as it attempted to teach. That is why there is no evidence about the didactic intentions of tragedians, for it is assumed that their intentions are not separable from tragedy's perceived effects.

The problems in Heath's attempted exclusion of didacticism are most manifest, however, when he says that, while our culture expects art to have something serious to say, we must accept that that may be culturally relative.[66] Indeed. But the terms in which Heath has expressed this are themselves anachronistic. Art is not a category which we can simply impose on fifth-century Athens. The evidence tells us, more precisely than Heath, that poetry was expected to teach (seriously or otherwise). I do not deny that watching tragedy was an aesthetic experience, just that aesthetic enjoyment does not preclude learning. The experience of watching tragedy could not help but involve the audience in considerations of some seriousness (whatever their actual content), for, in an obvious way, tragedy presents stories of suffering and loss, conflict and catastrophe (one could go on). Why choose these stories simply to entertain?

Perhaps the impetus for Heath's dismissal of tragic didacticism comes from a very understandable incomprehension of the context in which tragedy took place. It certainly looks alien to us to place a privileged and educative discourse in a festival with overtones of the carnivalesque. How are these carnival qualities related to tragedy's function? Because trag-

[66] (1987a), 79.

edy embodies the Dionysiac features of transgression and challenge. The point is put most neutrally by Victor Turner: 'By means of such genres as theatre ... performances are presented which probe a community's weaknesses, call its leaders to account, desacralize its most cherished values and beliefs, portray its characteristic conflicts and suggest remedies for them.'[67] In this description we can recognize some of the qualities of both tragedy and comedy. Earlier I said that tragedy offered a Dionysiac release, but release from what, into what and for what purpose? The members of the audience are released from the structures (and strictures) of their selves and their society, so that they may identify with the alien, fictional figures on the stage. The plays offer the opportunity to observe social structures from an abnormal perspective, leading the audience (potentially) to understand the artificial nature of cultural order.[68] That is, the audience have the occasion to examine themselves in the other-world of the drama. The key to the processes of tragic didacticism may lie in this idea of the fictional other-world. The claim that tragedy taught by providing simple moral lessons, and by acting as a storehouse for pithy maxims, would indeed describe a disappointing and reductive form of teaching.[69] Most scholars agree, yet they themselves, with a firm vagueness, then proceed to describe tragic didacticism with an unhelpful degree of generality.[70] Nor does it help to transform tragedy into pseudo-philosophy (in the modern, more restricted sense).[71]

---

[67] (1982), 11.   [68] C. Segal (1982), 14; Foley (1985), 234.

[69] Heath (1987a), 47.

[70] 'Seeing examples of learning is surely an important part of our learning' (Nussbaum (1986), 128). Tragedy 'can make its audience more inclined to act well', and the audience learn that serious mistakes are possible, that 'wealth does not necessarily bring happiness, and familial order is both fragile and precious' (Salkever (1986), 300). 'In sum, Tragedy was a form of public discourse that inculcated civic virtue and enhanced the citizen audience's capacity to act with foresight and judge with insight' (Euben (1986), 23). See also Schlesinger (1963), 37; Walcot (1976), 4.

[71] Nussbaum (1986), 127: 'Drama can contribute to our understanding of an ethical issue by *motivating* an argument or an enquiry. By showing us how and why characters who are not professional philosophers [*sic*] enter into argument, and by showing us what sorts of problems call forth philosophising, and what contribution philosophy makes to their work on the problems, it can show us, better than a single-voiced work, why and when we ourselves should care about ethical reflection.' I am sure Plato would have been interested to learn that tragedy was really promotional literature for philosophy.

How, then, does tragedy teach? The most convincing attempt to date to answer this question is based on a certain theory of ritual and sacrifice. Here, sacrifice becomes a frame into which a community can divert the violence which otherwise would explode between members of the community. The sacrificial victim, normally an innocent domestic animal, is conceived as a sort of 'other'.[72] In the theatre, Athens invents imaginary spaces: Argos, Thebes, Troy. Zeitlin, also making use of psychoanalytic theory,[73] has considered the second of these in detail. Thebes, she argues, is an 'other-place', consistently opposed in its character to the idealized Athens of, for instance, the Funeral Oration.[74] Having invented this 'other-place' (the equivalent of the sacrificial victim), Athens exploits it for the purposes of self-examination: 'In other words, Thebes, the Other, provides Athens, the Self, with the place where it can play with and discharge both the terror of and attraction to the irreconcilable, the inexpiable and unredeemable, where it can experiment with the dangerous heights of self-assertion that transgression of fixed boundaries entails ... Athens acts out questions crucial to the *polis*, to the self, to the family and society, but these are displaced upon a city that is imagined as a mirror opposite of Athens.'[75] The 'other-place' is also situated in other, mythical time: 'the city puts itself and its values into question by projecting itself upon the stage to confront the present with the past through its ancient myths'.[76]

One problem with Zeitlin's theory is its emphasis on Thebes: 'Thebes, we might say, is the quintessential "other-

---

[72] Burkert (1966); Girard (1977); Rudhardt and Reverdin (1981); Foley (1985), 46ff.; Gould (1985), 16ff.

[73] Zeitlin (1982a) acknowledges a debt to Green (1979).

[74] Zeitlin (1985b), (1986). Vernant and Vidal-Naquet (1988), 334–8 call Thebes an 'anti-city', the paradigm of *stasis* and transgression. For Athens as the ideal city in the Funeral Oration, see Loraux (1986). For a listing, and brief analysis, of Euripides' plays set in Argos and Thebes, see Chalkia (1986), 173–87.

[75] Zeitlin (1986), 117; see also Gouldner (1965), 110–11; Simon (1978), 143–8; Euben (1986), 24–8; Redfield (1990), 326.

[76] Zeitlin (1986), 116. See also Loraux (1986), 119: 'a Greek city was interested in its past only to justify or magnify its present and much preferred the mythical past which it could always reinterpret, to the more recent past'. In this connection note the difference in the number of representations of Theseus as against Cleisthenes.

scene", as Oedipus is the paradigm of tragic man and Dionysus is the god of the theater.'[77] The psychoanalyst André
Green states that the Argive and Theban cycles are fundamental, although there is nothing in the tragedians themselves to
support such a view. The reason, Green argues, is that the
exemplary tragic situation is the family, and that the Argive
and Theban cycles, as exemplary family sagas, have paradigmatic value.[78] One difficulty with Zeitlin's formulation of
the specialness of Thebes lies in overlooking the variety with
which it is represented in tragedy: the Thebes depicted in
Phoenissae is in some ways importantly different from the city
in *Bacchae*.[79] A second problem is the equation between
Oedipus and Dionysus. That the latter is the god of the theatre is a matter of fact; that the former is tragic man *par excellence* remains arguable. Indeed, if we follow Knox's listing of
the subjects of fifth-century tragedies (so far as we can know
them), the Theban cycle provided just under half the number
for the Trojan War (33 to 68).[80] So, statistical evidence – for
what it is worth – suggests that the tragedians were in disagreement with Green and Zeitlin. The extant tragedies also
indicate that to name Thebes the principal 'other-scene' is an
exaggeration which leads the critic to neglect the importance
of other dramatic sites.

In Sophocles' *Oedipus at Colonus*, after Creon has kid-
napped the daughters of Oedipus, Theseus first attacks the
Theban for underestimating Athens. He then says (*OC*
919–20):

> καίτοι σε Θῆβαί γ᾽ οὐκ ἐπαίδευσαν κακόν·
> οὐ γὰρ φιλοῦσιν ἄνδρας ἐκδίκους τρέφειν.

> And yet Thebes did not educate you to be evil;
> for it does not like to nurture lawless men.

Zeitlin's comment – 'Here we know better than this kind and
simple king of Athens'[81] – seems bland. Theseus may indeed

---

[77] Zeitlin (1986), 117.
[78] Green (1979), 36–7. In the privileging of Thebes which we find in both Green and
Zeitlin the influence of Freud is not unimportant, although that influence is not
the basis of my criticism of Zeitlin.
[79] Saïd (1989), 112–36. See also the section 'Tragic Space' in chapter four.
[80] Knox (1979), 9.   [81] (1986), 141.

have an Athenocentric and possibly idealistic view of the involvement of the *polis* in the education of its citizens, but it is that same Theseus who notes that Creon must have had accomplices within Athens (*OC* 1028–31). To see that the ideal status of Athens itself is not always unproblematic one only has to look so far as its ready acceptance of Medea or the split vote of the jurors in Aeschylus' *Eumenides*.

Zeitlin calls Argos 'the middle term' and urges that, although it is a city of conflict, 'the city, or more precisely its characters, can be saved'.[82] This may be true of Orestes and the Danaids but cannot apply to Agamemnon and Clytemnestra, or to the victims of Thyestes' feast. I submit that any city can become an exemplary 'other-scene', whether it is the Argos of Aeschylus' *Agamemnon* and *Choephori*, the Athens of *Eumenides*, *Oedipus at Colonus* or Euripides' *Supplices*, the Corinth of *Medea*, the Trozen of *Hippolytus*, the Thrace of *Hecuba*, or the Troy of *Troades*. This is because, in their status as fictional worlds, all these tragic cities are necessarily, though in various ways, 'other-scenes'. Also, the representation of Thebes, or Argos, need not be consistent from tragedian to tragedian, nor from one play of a tragedian to another. Within certain cultural constraints and generic conventions, a tragedian was allowed a certain freedom to invent his dramatic world: not every detail and significance was inherited.

Perhaps if we generalize Zeitlin's approach it will become more applicable. As in sacrifice, into which violence is diverted, tragedy provides Athens with a frame in which the searching questions about ideology, about the self, can be contained. The other – referring here to the various dramatic worlds produced by tragedy – serves the self because the sort of radical questioning which tragedy performs is possibly subversive, and its destabilizing potential is mitigated by being situated in the other: self-examination *otherwise*. The characters who inhabit the fictional other-place are in cultural terms themselves consistently other to an Athenian democrat: kings,

[82] (1986), 118.

heroes, transgressors, barbarians, slaves, powerful and seductive women and so on. So, spatially, temporally, ethnically, socially and sexually the world of tragedy is other, represented for the benefit of Athens, the self.

Even this formulation, however, is not careful enough with the notion of 'other'. Self and other are necessarily interdependent, and the theatrical experience dictates that the audience undergo a movement between the two terms. In an earlier work than the one I have been citing, Zeitlin makes this general point: 'In other words, theater requires from the spectator a capacity like that of the actors to take on different roles, to place oneself in the position of the Other.'[83] However, the recognition of otherness (within the other-scene of tragic space) is not always an easy matter. Goldhill, analysing the role of doubling in *Bacchae*, demonstrates that once the other becomes double, as when Pentheus confronts Cadmus and Teiresias or the two faces of Dionysus, one is left with the problem of recognizing sameness and difference: the other becomes a problem rather than a given.[84] We should also remember that if we were to be over-schematic and inflexible in our use of self and other, we might be led to think that certain tragedies – Euripides' in particular – undermined the entire didactic project. The argument would be as follows: if a tragedian, by the use of certain scenic effects, self-reference, anachronism and so on, were to invent an other-scene which was too close to home, too Oedipal if you like, anyway too like the world of the audience, then the distinction between the world of the self and of the other would be decreased. That would make self-examination *otherwise* less potent in its teaching, because the confrontation with the other, and thereby the self, would be minimized. Such a position is to be avoided for a number of reasons. First, fifth-century Athenian comedy could be didactic without depending on the creation of a dramatic world which, in its frame of reference, was very different

[83] Zeitlin (1982a), 179; cf. Arist. *Poet.* 1453a2ff.; *Rhet.* 1386a17ff.; see also Green (1979), 4; Vernant (1991), 204; Wiles (1991), 12.
[84] Goldhill (1988b).

from the world of the audience. Second, the elements which complicate the otherness of the other-scene are present in all the tragedians to varying degrees (note here the contemporary setting of Aeschylus' *Persae* and the comic intrusions into Sophocles' *Philoctetes*). What we are interested in are the different degrees to which those elements are present in the individual plays and individual authors. We are concerned with Euripidean dramatic worlds and how their particular construction relates to the questions they pose.

Bearing in mind these caveats about the use of self and other, we are still able to say, at least as a start, that tragedy performs its didactic function by examining ideology *otherwise*. This theory of the process of tragic didacticism is supported by a range of evidence. As I will demonstrate in chapters two and three, Athenian ideology is constructed against a series of others. Herodotus' work can be interpreted as a self-examination in that it is a history of Greek self-definition. Herodotus conducts his research by comparing the *nomoi* of various non-Greek cultures, and shows how the Greek self is constructed against those other cultures. There is also a universal human instinct for the other, which we might call an escapist tendency: elsewhere and formerly have stronger holds on our imagination than the here and now.[85] Or, as Pavel puts it, since we need an alien space in which to deploy the energy of imagination, there will always be fictional worlds (or representations).[86]

Examining the self through the other is also appropriate to a discourse produced in honour of Dionysus. His worship promotes the loss of self and the experience of otherness; as a divinity he represents an other way of thinking.[87] The mask – that deceptive medium through which tragedy teaches – allows the actor to become and the spectator to see the other.[88] But the carnivalesque qualities of the worship of Dionysus

---

[85] Bachelard (1969), 208.   [86] Pavel (1986), 148; see also Padel (1974).

[87] Daraki (1985), 28, 232.

[88] The mask is also associated with the goddess from the margins, Artemis, and that representative of extreme alterity, Gorgo; see Calame (1986); Vernant (1991), 111–38, 195–207.

and the festival in his honour make this self-examination *otherwise* of ambivalent value, for the inversions and transgressions of social order and social structures may more clearly define, may justify, those structures and that order: 'All this strengthens the status quo. And yet the opposite is also true.'[89] Tragedy seems to demonstrate the 'process of a developing city putting its own developing language and structures of thought at risk under the sway of the smiling and dangerous Dionysus'.[90] In Dionysiac theatre, tragedy can allow the violent, the irrational and the animal to manifest itself without causing actual harm to the society watching. But, like Dionysus himself, the spectating experience is bound to be an ambivalent one, a 'πόνον ἡδύν' ('sweet labour'), as the chorus of *Bacchae* say (66; cf. 280–3). Dionysus offers release, but also pain; he offers a fiction so that the audience may endure and understand reality; he offers a potent, but didactic deception. 'Tell a lie in a good cause,' as Cadmus says (*Bacch.* 334), or, as Reckford puts it: 'To follow Dionysus in dance is always somewhat mad, though this madness may avert larger insanity.'[91]

Tragedy, then, is a discourse, produced by the *polis*, which allows Athens to examine itself in a Dionysiac, other-worldly and transgressive manner, with the potential of teaching the citizens about themselves and their city. There follows an analysis of the processes of self-examination, as we find them in Euripidean tragedy and, more particularly, in *Troades*. But, to anticipate some of my argument, we will see that, in a spirit typical of Dionysus and under the pressures of war (both represented and actual), Euripidean tragedy complicates to an extreme degree the notion of self-examination *otherwise*.

But, first, what precisely is the object of tragedy's questioning? That which other critics have called the city's 'most cherished values and beliefs', 'the city's discourse', I have decided, out of a desire for economy of reference, to refer to as ideology. What we have now is a three-word description of tragic didacticism: tragedy questions ideology. Such a view of trag-

[89] Reckford (1987), 303.   [90] Goldhill (1986), 78.   [91] (1987), 52.

edy and its work is implicit in Vernant and in the scholars who have used his research. However, while various tragedies have been interpreted in the light of various aspects of Athenian ideology, no critic has explicitly related this questioning of ideology to tragedy's didactic function.[92]

But what is ideology? How do we now reconstruct Athenian ideology so that we may understand and identify the ideology as it is represented in tragedy? These are the questions which I consider in detail in the appendix. Here, I shall simply state that my working definition of ideology is: *the authoritative self-definition of the Athenian citizen.* With ideology thus defined, problems still remain with the tragic examination of ideology. Tragedy was an important part of civic discourse, being an ideological production performed at the Great Dionysia.[93] As civic discourse it potentially produces ideology. But, if tragedy teaches by examining ideology while at the same time itself being ideology, then it is likely that it will examine itself. Yet tragedy was performed after a series of ceremonies which seem to leave no doubt as to their character: they are overt celebrations of Athens and its ideology. Is tragedy similarly a celebration? It is, of course, possible that members of the audience could have taken most tragedies as affirmations of some aspect of their ideology. Aeschylus' *Oresteia, Euripides' Medea* and *Hippolytus* – to name but three – could all have been read by the (male) audience as confirming the view that women were properly excluded from the public sphere because of their subversiveness and seductiveness. Sophocles' *Oedipus at Colonus*, Euripides' *Supplices* and *Heracleidae* could all be reasonably interpreted as reaffirming the glory and piety of Athens and its ability to include out-

---

[92] Apart from the aspects of ideology which have already been considered and shall be in the next three chapters, prominent areas of concern have been: a) heroic vs hoplite values; see Knox (1961) on Sophocles' *Ajax* and (1964), as well as Bongie (1977) on *Medea*; b) exchange; see generally Dubois (1984); for violations of hospitality in *Alcestis*, see Buxton (1985); c) *nomos/phusis*; del Grande (1962); Arrowsmith (1963); Berns (1973).

[93] For Marxist analyses of the relationship between ideology and literature, which, like Marxist analyses of literary production and Marxist critiques of ideology, are difficult to apply to the fifth century, see Williams (1977); Macherey (1978); Larrain (1979), 211; Macherey and Balibar (1981).

siders. The same three plays could also be viewed as some sort of justification for Athenian interference in foreign states. Yet, when Medea proclaims that it is more difficult giving birth than standing in the hoplite phalanx (*Med.* 250–1); when the chorus, in the same play, assert the advent of a new sort of poetry, one not sexually prejudiced (*Med.* 410ff.); and when, in a society where 'l'*andreia* devient homme',[94] Alcestis dies for her husband, it is difficult not to see some questioning of ideologically prescribed sexual roles, or at least, a very provocative representation of them. The uncertainty which the audience would have felt in the face of tragedy may, though, be more helpful than we might at first imagine. For it suggests that tragedy had a special relationship with ideology. Though sponsored by the *polis* to be performed on a great civic occasion, tragedy questions as well as affirms ideology. The co-existence of these two positions in relation to ideology, and the uncertainty and fragmentation their co-existence would produce in the audience, point to the idea that tragedy's questioning of ideology lay in its ability to both question and affirm; in its ability, if you like, to split the audience, as the jurors in the *Eumenides* are split.

Yet we would probably assume that ideology prefers to affirm rather than question itself. Socrates said that a life lived without self-examination was wasted (Pl. *Ap.* 38a5–6). But to take Socrates as representative of the citizen body of Athens, knowing his ambiguous position within that group, would be a risky business. Yet Socrates did not just appear from nowhere – he was *Athēnaios* after all – and his statement may be taken as indicative of at least the possibility that his expressed value was shared by other Athenian citizens. Certainly, Athenian ideology, represented here by the Funeral Orations, claimed that Athenian education was of a very high standard (e.g. Thuc. 2.40–1; Lys. 2.69; Dem. 60.16). It also seems to have been the case that Athenians expected the institutions of the city (law courts, Assembly, palaestra etc.) to contribute to the education of the citizen.[95] From the point of

---

[94] Loraux (1978a).   [95] Ober (1989), 156ff.

view of ideology, if we may adopt that theoretical position, authoritative self-definition would seem to necessitate some sort of self-examination. If ideology is meant to maintain, stabilize and legitimate existing social relations, it will probably achieve its end by being perceived as stable and legitimate, both of which qualities might profitably be produced by self-questioning. It may be, then, that self-examination was a constituent of Athenian ideology, one which was developed in the law courts, by the sophists, under the pressure of military events and political decisions, and in the invention of historical writing, but one most impressively carried out by tragic discourse.

When I come to analyse *Troades*, two important (perhaps the most important) features of the ideology of Athens will be considered. The first is the process of self-definition, whereby the self compares himself to an other. Athenian culture established a series of such polarities, some in common with the rest of the Greek world (Greek/barbarian, free/slave, man/god), some more peculiar, at least in degree, to Athens (man/woman). The other ideological feature to be discussed is the *agōn* (contest, competition), which, as the principle of opposition, may be said to cover self-definition through difference. The *agōn* pervades Greek culture, from the Trojan War to the Funeral Games for Patroclus, from the Olympic Games to the Peloponnesian War, from debates in the Assembly to the staged rhetorical battles of the sophists. Indeed, throughout the analysis of *Troades* (but most especially in chapter three), we shall find that it is the *agōn*, as debate or war but always as a questioning, a testing, which informs the production of Athenian ideology.[96] I shall then proceed to discuss the relationship between ideology (and the questioning of it) and the particular spatial and temporal definitions of the Euripidean dramatic world. That is, the analyses of ideology and tragedy presented here all explore those never quite stable and interde-

---

[96] J. Thompson (1984), 13–15, following Habermas' use of speech act theory, argues that self-criticism is inherent in ideology. In arguing that Athens possessed a self-critical ideology I am making a historical rather than a philosophical point.

pendent terms: self/other, us versus them (culturally, ethnically, politically, socially and sexually); here versus there (spatially); and now versus then (temporally).

Troades is set in the aftermath of the Trojan War. I suggest that in the play we are confronted with a striking examination of ideology and that the power of Euripides' scrutiny is an effect of the setting of the play at the end of a war, perhaps the most fruitful site for exploring ideology.[97]

War and ideology

There are various ways of demonstrating this claim. One of the duties of an empowered member of the *polis*, i.e. a citizen, was that he must fight for his city. The dominant group is not only a civilian organization, but a group which, especially in the direct democracy of Athens, must fight the wars which it has itself decided to prosecute. The *polis*, then, was the unit of both political and military organization; and its citizens were all warriors. More particularly, however, the fifth-century citizen in most of the Greek world was a hoplite. The emergence of the classical *polis* and the hoplite warrior seem, as far as we can tell, to be contemporaneous.[98] The important fact here is that a collective practice sustained by the dominant group in war is almost certainly going to contribute to the values by which the *polis* is governed. The hoplite army was a community of equals, interdependent and interchangeable. As Vernant puts it: 'The army is the popular assembly in arms, the city out campaigning, just as conversely the city is a community of warriors.'[99]

[97] Winkler (1985), 37: 'Greek tragedies frequently examine moral issues that become acute under pressure of warfare.'

[98] However, attempts to make one the cause or effect of the other are prone to problems; see Detienne (1968), 120ff.; Garlan (1975), 124–5; Salmon (1977). Athens was different in that most of its warriors were sailors. And there is some indication that being a hoplite was already an ideological and nostalgic condition, looking, as it did, to ideal types, whether in Homer or Sparta. Of course, for my purposes it makes little difference whether Athenians were sailors or hoplites. All I stress is the new collectivity of war in the fifth century (the ship as phalanx, as it were). For more detailed treatment of the hoplite issue, see the appendix.

[99] (1980), 26.

While the equation of citizen with hoplite would seem to be true of most classical *poleis* (though we have insufficient evidence to make a conclusive statement), democratic Athens, which so frequently frustrates attempts to describe the Greeks as a whole, compromised the picture I have given of social and political organization. First, training of hoplites in Athens seems to have been fairly unsystematic: Pericles, displaying pride if not telling the whole truth, boasts of this (Thuc. 2.39.1–4).[100] Still, he is presumably asserting that, unlike Sparta, the political and cultural conditions of Athens were such that compulsory military training was unnecessary.

Second, the power of Athens depended less on her army than on her fleet. The predominance of the fleet undermined more oligarchically minded Athenians because the lowest of the Solonian classes, the Thetes, who generally manned the ships, were thereby empowered.[101] Naval warfare also required a degree of specialization which could very well have threatened the idea of a community of interchangeable equals. The predominantly naval strategy of Athens would seem to flout the hoplite ideal; certainly, the strategy for the Peloponnesian War championed by Pericles was one which stressed the undesirability of hoplite engagements for Athens.[102] Nevertheless, Athenian citizens were intimately

---

[100] See also Pl. *Laws* 830d; see Pritchett (1971–91) II.209–75. De Polignac (1984), 39, 87ff. demonstrates that, in the development of the Greek city, Athens is at almost every point exceptional.

[101] Athens may thus have offended against that aspect of the hoplite ideal which required that war was to be conducted by, and in the interests of, the landowner; see Garlan (1975), 89–90, 132–3; Vidal-Naquet (1986), 89; V. Hanson (1991), 5. For Themistocles' instigation of the naval policy, see Hdt. 7.144.2; Thuc. 1.14.3. Pericles is the heir of Themistocles in this respect (see Thuc. 1.142.6–7). Athenian naval skill is often referred to in Thucydides; see e.g. 2.84ff.; Edmunds (1975a), *passim*. For anti-fleet opinions, see Pl. *Laws* 706b–c, 707a–b. In 431 BC the numbers of Thetes and hoplites were probably about the same (20,000). The Thetes, however, suffered many more losses during the war; see Strauss (1986), 80–1, 179–82. As Strauss (ibid.), 173 says: 'If the *demos* were comparatively quiescent after 403, a major reason is that so many of its potential leaders were dead.'

[102] The Periclean strategy, along with the 'extreme ideology of non-professionalism', is sometimes characterized as anti-hoplite; see Lonis (1979), 17; Vidal-Naquet (1986), 90; Ober (1991), 188–9.

bound up with debating about and fighting war, whatever particular forms of war they adopted.

Third, in Athens' case, although the four Solonian classes have often been thought tied to particular warrior functions (Thetes man the fleet; the other three classes are mainly hoplites), the attribution of these functions seems to have been flexible: all the four classes served in both fleet and army.[103] And, as the fifth century progressed and Athenian expansion continued, both the hoplite army and the fleet grew more diversified, using metics, slaves and free barbarians.[104]

Athens adapts the hoplite–citizen equation. As Vidal-Naquet has said, the citizen was a warrior but not vice versa; we can add that the Athenian citizen was not only a hoplite and that not all hoplites were citizens.[105] However, for my purposes, whether the power of Athens was principally naval or not, it remains true that war and politics were structurally intertwined and that military action taken by the fleet betrayed the same collective characteristics as did the hoplite phalanx. Also, it is probable that Athens' flexibility in military organization stemmed from success. Put another way, the success of Athenian imperialism allowed the dominant group to define itself without relying totally on the conventional citizen–hoplite equation.

Yet, while Athens differed in the practical operations of war, in its civic discourse it represented the collectivity associated with the hoplite ethos in a very extreme way, using the Funeral Oration to meet its own ideological needs. While praising those who had died in combat, the distinctions between individuals were effaced; patronyms and demotic names were absent from epitaphs; familial, social and eco-

---

[103] Garlan (1975), 89, 129–30 disagrees but has no evidence. Hoplites in the fleet: Thuc. 3.16.1, 8.24. Thetes as hoplites, probably with state-provided armour: Thuc. 6.43.

[104] For the evidence, see Ridley (1979); Loraux (1982), 9; (1986), 32–7; Vidal-Naquet (1986), 88. For metics as a sort of lower Athenian, see Ar. *Ach.* 502–8. For metics at the battle of Delion: Thuc. 4.90ff.; slaves at Arginusae: Xen. *Hell.* 1.6.24.

[105] Vidal-Naquet (1986), 85.

nomic determinations disappeared. The Funeral Oration placed the individual under the sign of collective glory. The *polis* praised itself for creating a society for which individual members would gladly die. The Funeral Oration of fifth-century Athens marks war, always a fact of life, as a fact of and in civic discourse: a production of ideology. Those who were not Athenian but had fought and died nevertheless became *hoi Athēnaioi* for the day, appropriated in Athens' moment of self-praise.[106]

A second reason why war provides an appropriate frame for the examination of ideology is that war was for the fifth century already in discourse. It was the existence and authority of Homer's *Iliad*, a poem to which the Athenians, as other Greeks, were committed, which accounted for this fact. But the weight and influence of the first poem of western literature was not only general; specifically, it championed war as the ultimate human experience, where valour could be proved and everlasting fame won.[107] It has often been noted how both Herodotus (1.1) and Thucydides (1.23.1–2) bear the mark of Homer in their depiction of the wars they narrate as great, epic struggles. War, then, from Homer onwards, provided the most important material for both poetic and historical discourse, and an important way of evaluating the past and establishing standards, or ideology. But war was also discursive because it provoked discussion and decision-making in the assemblies of Greek cities: 'a speech can stop a war, a victory can settle a debate'.[108] War, then, is a privileged subject in discourse. As such, it is an important site of the production of ideology.

But war is also itself a test. War becomes the 'ultimate index of cultural superiority';[109] in war, ideology is put to the test. In democratic Athens, for instance, the decision to go to war was taken, after deliberation, by the Assembly. Such a deci-

---

[106] My brief remarks on the Funeral Oration owe much to Loraux (1982) and (1986); see also Bradeen (1969), Clairmont (1983). For discussions of the date of the introduction of the Funeral Oration, see Pritchett (1971–91) IV.106–24.

[107] Harrison (1960); Havelock (1972); Schein (1984), 67–88.

[108] Vernant (1980), 26–7.   [109] Havelock (1972), 51.

sion must represent either a perceived need to fight to defend one's *polis* (ideology) or the citizens' confidence in victory, or both. On the one hand, victory was necessary to sustain the self-definition (the self, even) which made the decision to fight in the first place; on the other hand, defeat was disaster. Wars – the most extreme example in the fifth century being the Peloponnesian War – had massive and catastrophic effects on the lives of citizens and their dependants.[110] Indeed, the hardship, pain, disease and poverty brought on by war were so extreme that we might think that the legitimacy of an ideology could become questionable. As Thucydides demonstrates in the Corcyrean episode (3.82–3), war is the best condition in which *stasis* (civil war, strife) can grow. Certainly, latent conflicts festered and flared up, as in Athens in 411 and 404 BC. An internal reorganization of the dominant group often issued from the external fact of war. However, war did not only have negative effects; it could be very profitable for the victor, a fact which partly explains the absence of any objection in principle to war in antiquity. War, indeed, was a fact of life, a frequent and inevitable occurrence, entirely natural and therefore unobjectionable.[111] As Finley has said: 'there were few years in the history of most Greek city states (of Sparta and Athens in particular), and hardly any years in succession, without some military engagements'.[112] It is significant that Plato, even as he constructs a utopia, insists that a *polis* should acknowledge that peace is merely undeclared war and therefore consider itself always at war (*Laws* 625e–626a).

The extremity and frequency of war meant that victory was crucial. It is no accident that the most stable of the classical

---

[110] Athenian reserves of wealth were consumed in the first years of the war, to such an extent that the Periclean strategy was reorganized in 425/4 BC; see Meiggs and Lewis (1969), no.69, pp. 188–210 (=Fornara (1977), 136). The population of Athens was directly affected by the plague of 430 BC and after; see Thuc. 2.47–54. The reduction in available manpower affected not only the armed forces but also the number of possible fathers. Socrates and Euripides may have had more than one wife each; see Pomeroy (1975), 66; cf. Thuc. 2.44.3–4; D.L. 2.26.

[111] Pl. *Laws* 626a–b, 628e–629a; Gouldner (1965), 142–5; Detienne (1968), 129; Havelock (1972), 23.

[112] (1983), 60.

Greek city states in the fifth century (which is not to say they were that stable) were Sparta and Athens, the most successful in war. Self-definition was always at stake in war: victory ensured reaffirmation and extension of one's ideology; defeat threatened it, leading to adaptation or outright rejection. Conversely, ideology could be seen to be the cause of victory or defeat, as in the case of the Greek victory over the barbarians (see below). War, therefore, put ideology to the test, just as, in a different way, tragedy did. Both war and tragedy are *agōnes* (see Dem. 18. 262). Tragedy (one *agōn*) represents war (another) in order to examine ideology. We should perhaps not be surprised at this collusion between tragedy and war, for in both areas of experience mortals come into contact with powerful and possibly destructive deities.[113] While it is true that the respective patron deities – Dionysus and Ares – can be absolutely opposed (*Phoen.* 784ff.), we find that the followers of Ares can be described as if they were a band of Dionysiac revellers (Aesch. *Ag.* 1189; Eur. *Supp.* 388–90; *Or.* 317–21), inspired and possessed by the god of war in the same way as Maenads were by Dionysus. On the other hand, Dionysus and his followers are depicted, in *Bacchae* for the most part, in military terms, as, for instance, at *Bacch.* 302 (see also 25, 762, 798–9, 1099–1100; Aesch. *Eum.* 24–5; *Ion* 216–18):[114]

Ἄρεώς τε μοῖραν μεταλαβὼν ἔχει τινά.

He [Dionysus] has some share of Ares.

But there is one principal method of self-definition, and therefore of the production of ideology, which was reinvigorated, if not invented, by the Greek victory in the Persian Wars. I refer to self-definition through difference, or, to put it another way, the construction of a self-image

---

[113] Note also that 'Socrates' says at Ath. 628ff.: 'οἳ δε χοροῖς κάλλιστα θεοὺς τιμῶσιν ἄριστοι ἐν πολέμῳ'/'Those who honour the gods most beautifully in dances are the best in war'. On gymnastic training for war, see Pritchett (1971–91) II. 213–16; Pleket (1976), 76; Poliakoff (1987), 94–9, 103. On the dance in antiquity, see Lawler (1964), especially 74–91 on dance and drama.

[114] I am indebted to Lonnoy (1985).

through comparison with an other. In common with the structures of Greek thought in other areas, the Greeks tended to think about themselves and their relationships with other people in terms of polarities, defining one entity in opposition to one or more other entities which then tended to be grouped by analogy.[115] That is, as Dubois puts it, the 'definition of the norm, the human subject, proceeds through a catalogue of difference'.[116] In Athenian terms of the fifth century, the self was the male adult citizen (i.e. the member of the dominant group), who could define himself as man against gods, animals and women; as free against the enslaved; and as Greek against barbarian. All the others can be grouped by the fact that they are excluded from the body politic, but, as was the habit of Greek polarizing thought, they could also be conflated into one single other. Thus, for example, barbarians can be effeminate and slavish.[117] Evidence of this form of self-definition is very frequent in fifth-century iconography and literature.[118] A couple of examples will suffice. The first is from Aeschylus' *Agamemnon* (918–25), where Agamemnon contrasts himself as male to women, barbarians and the gods. Another example, which is so explicit that it is worth quoting, has Socrates (or Thales: the attribution is unsure) counting himself fortunate:

πρῶτον μὲν ὅτι ἄνθρωπος ἐγενόμην καὶ οὐ θηρίον, εἶτα ὅτι ἀνὴρ καὶ οὐ γυνή, τρίτον Ἕλλην καὶ οὐ βάρβαρος. (D.L. 1.33).

First because I was born a man and not a beast, second a man and not a woman, third Greek and not barbarian.

---

[115] G. Lloyd (1966); Dubois (1984).

[116] Dubois (1984), 4; or Goldhill (1986), 61: 'the male subject defines himself through a sense of the other'.

[117] Each other also has its own subset of distinctions. For instance, barbarians are distinguished from Greeks by their language, their behaviour, their religion and their politics; see Hall (1989).

[118] For discussions of various iconographic items in these terms, see Dubois (1984), 13–14, who notes in general that 'the public art of the democratic *polis* is the realm in which the ideas of difference were played out, the space in which men learned to define themselves as male, Greek, human, as citizens in a community from which the other – female, barbarian, animal – was excluded'.

53

But the use of an other in self-definition was not new in the fifth century. However, as a process, it seems to have been emphasized by the victory in the Persian Wars, and by the rise of Athens as the principal Greek opposition to the Persian Empire after the end of the Wars, which had the consequence of, in Edith Hall's words, inventing the barbarian.[119] That the barbarian fitted happily into an existing system of self-definition through difference is attested in the way that the Amazons served as a mythical model of the defeated.[120] But our principal source for this new development in Greek self-definition is Herodotus, whose whole work can be seen as an exercise in cultural definition, an attempt to define what it was, what it meant, to be a Greek.[121] This is done, for the most part, through comparison of *nomoi*.[122] For instance, in Book 2 Herodotus notes that the Egyptians are, in some of their customs, mirror opposites of the Greeks (2.35.2: the different activities of men and women; referred to at Soph. *OC* 338ff.) and, in others, exactly the same (2.158.5: the linguistic definition of barbarians). But, ultimately, the description of Greek self-definition is most powerfully achieved in the narrative of the Persian Wars (Books 7–9). For, when Greek met

[119] Hall (1989), 54: 'The all-embracing genus of anti-Greeks later to be termed the barbarians does not appear until the fifth century ...'

[120] Or the victory over the Amazons was used symbolically, as in the Stoa Poikile; Hall (1989), 68–9. See also Loraux (1986), 67 on the use of the Amazons in the Funeral Oration; and see Lysias 2.4–5, Pl. *Menex*. 239d–240a; see also Shapiro (1983) on Amazons in vase-painting. For more detailed, and wide-ranging, discussions of the Amazons, see Dubois (1984) and Tyrell (1984).

[121] Hall (1989), 1: 'Greek writing about barbarians is usually an exercise in self-definition.' Hall, however, underestimates the difficulties of maintaining a secure distinction between Greeks and barbarians. This can be seen generally in the narrative of Herodotus, which, as it describes the construction of the polarity, very artfully shows its inherent problems; on which see especially Hartog (1980)/ (1988). It can also be glimpsed in the vague formulation of Greekness which Herodotus eventually comes up with at 8.144; see also 7.104. As Walbank (1951), 59 puts it: 'The idea of a Greek nation is alien to the thought of most Greeks at most periods throughout Greek history.'

[122] Hartog (1980)/(1988) is subtitled: 'The Representation of the Other in the Writing of History.' Hartog is mainly concerned to analyse the rhetoric of otherness which Herodotus constructs (especially in relation to the Scythians), but that rhetoric depends on and partly constructs the self. For Herodotus, see also Immerwahr (1966); Benardete (1969); Jouanna (1981); Laurot (1981); Hall (1989).

barbarian, it was a test of military valour, of tactics and strategy, but also of respective self-definitions, or ideologies. The Greeks triumphed and this, in the case of Athens, provided the impetus for almost a century of successful imperialism. Athenian self-definition – ideology – of the fifth century issued to some extent from the achievement of the Persian Wars. This, then, is a good reason why war serves fruitfully as a frame for examining ideology.

But there is a more particular reason. The Peloponnesian War, during which all but one of Euripides' extant plays were produced, was an especially rigorous test of the security of self/other, especially Greek/barbarian, distinctions. Dubois has argued that war clarifies difference: as 'the polar opposite of *philia*, of marital conjunction, [war] is a temporary *agōn* which must end by affirming difference'; 'war is the process and the occasion which illuminates the relationship of polarity'.[123] This may be true of wars in general but, as Dubois argues elsewhere, the Peloponnesian War was a special case. For, unlike the Persian Wars, where the threat of the other came obviously from outside the boundaries of mainland Greece, in the Peloponnesian War the other was no longer an alien invader but from within:[124] the Peloponnesian War set the Greek world against itself.

But there are yet other reasons for war's importance to ideology. Since ideology has been defined as the authoritative self-definition of the citizen body, and since one crucial method of providing self-definition is through polarity, war, the place where opponents meet, is an extremely appro-

---

[123] (1984), 88–9.

[124] Dubois (1984), 115; on pp. 56–7 Dubois charts this development on a series of public monuments built in the fifth century: the Athenian treasury at Delphi, the Theseion, the Parthenon, the temple of Apollo Epikouros at Bassae. I agree with the first part of Dubois' thesis, i.e. that self-definition based on polarity and analogy was put under extreme pressure during the Peloponnesian War, but not with the second part, which says that in response to the crisis, a new system of hierarchical thought about difference was established. For there is no reason to think that the polarities of the fifth century were not already hierarchical (e.g. man/woman). On the other hand, definition based on polarity did not cease with Plato; nor can he and Aristotle be taken as representative of the citizen body (as a tragedian more reasonably can).

priate frame for the examination of ideology.[125] Second, war is a principle of opposition and difference, expressed most famously by Heraclitus:[126]

πόλεμος πάντων μὲν πατήρ ἐστι, πάντων δὲ βασιλεύς, καὶ τοὺς μὲν θεοὺς ἔδειξε, τοὺς δὲ ἀνθρώπους, τοὺς μὲν δούλους ἐποίησε, τοὺς δὲ ἐλευθέρους.

War is father and king of all; and some he has shown as gods, others men; some he has made slaves, others free.

War, that is, has its effects precisely in the terms of polarities used in self-definition: free/slave, men/gods. And war as *agōn* is, in a sense, the final polarity, the one which produces a winner and a loser, one which is a matter of life and death.

Polemos and *logos*: the conditions of production

Within the cultural context (outside the more immediate context of the Great Dionysia), there are two main events or series of events which inform the drama of Euripides. First (as has already been noted), the Peloponnesian War, and second, that explosion of intellectual activity which we identify with a heterogeneous group of thinkers called the sophists. The increasingly brutal effects of the war and its unprecedented transgressions are traced by Thucydides, from the narrowly unsuccessful proposal of mass execution of citizenry at Mytilene (427 BC) to the breakdown of family relationships in the *stasis* at Corcyra (427 BC: itself just one instance of the pressure under which traditional *nomoi* came). It was

---

[125] Heraclitus (Kahn 82): 'εἰδέ⟨ναι⟩ χρὴ τὸν πόλεμον ἐόντα ξυνὸν καὶ δίκην ἔριν καὶ γινόμενα πάντα κατ' ἔριν καὶ χρεώμενα'/'one must realize that war is shared and conflict is justice, and that all things come to pass (and are ordained) in accordance with conflict' (trans. Kahn).

[126] Heraclitus (Kahn 83; see also 20, 75, 78, 81, 103, 124). For discussions, see Kahn (1979), *ad loc.*; Voegelin (1957), 336; Guthrie (1962), 403–88; Gouldner (1965), 145–6; G. Lloyd (1966), 96ff. For the difficulties in constructing a text for Heraclitus and the need to be aware of the ideological motivations of the authors who have preserved his work, see C. Osborne (1987). Foucault (1980), 90 and 114 argues that war, rather than language, should be our model for studying human societies; he also inverts Clausewitz's dictum: politics becomes war pursued by other means. For war as a source of slaves, see Thuc. 3.36.2; 5.32, 116.4; Arist. *Pol.* 1255a6ff.; Synodinou (1977), 16.

only a short journey from Mytilene to the massacre at Melos (416/415 BC), and from Corcyra to violent coups in Athens (412/411 and 404/403 BC).[127] In the chapters which follow we see how *Troades* similarly unmasks the devastation wrought by war. In both Thucydides and Euripides, and under the pressure of war, humanity and civilization are at risk.

The effect of the sophists may have been less obviously fatal but was still considered by some to be inimical to the very bases of Athenian society. While Thucydides describes the effects of war on families, Aristophanes' *Clouds* represents the harm a sophistic education can do to the relationship between father and son. Although the views of the sophists were not uniform and their interests ranged from theories of knowledge to language, from education to the nature and origins of society, from mathematics to astronomy,[128] it is evident both from the satire of *Clouds* and from the prosecutions which sophists faced (see chapter four) that sophists – when attacking the existence of gods, for instance – could be perceived as a threat to traditional values.

So, we have two things: a war and a particular intellectual environment. In the latter half of the fifth century one man presided over both: Pericles.[129] The Periclean legacy (war and the sophists) constitutes a cultural crisis – in the relation of its problematic rhetoric to the war, to rhetoric and language *per se*, to traditional *nomoi*, to the constitutive polarities of Athenian ideology, and to the democracy. In fact, the two features of the Periclean legacy are teasingly brought together

[127] Pritchett (1971–91) V. 218 provides a table of massacres of captives: even allowing for the state of the evidence, there is a sizeable discrepancy between the number of massacres in the 27 years of the Peloponnesian War (21) and in the other 73 years of the fifth century (7); the same holds true for mass enslavements (pp. 226–8) after battles or sieges (34 in the Peloponnesian War, 21 in the rest of the fifth century).

[128] Kerferd (1981).

[129] Pericles may have patronized Damon, Anaxagoras and Protagoras: Kerferd (1981), 18–22. Of course, Pericles was the *rhētōr par excellence*, a glowing testimony to the rhetorical education a sophist could provide; though see Macleod, 'Rhetoric and history' in (1983), especially p. 81 on the ambivalence of (the Thucydidean) Pericles' rhetoric.

in the description of Tydeus in Euripides' *Supplices* (902–6).[130] Tydeus' qualities in war (one part of the legacy) are described in terms of the other (sophism). He was not splendid (*lampros*) with words but, with a shield, he was a clever sophist (*deinos sophistēs*), inventing (*exeurein*) many wise things. Although he lacked the judgement (*gnōmē*) of his brother Meleager, he gained himself a similar reputation through his skill (*technē*) with the spear. He also invented (*exeurōn*) a precise (*akribē*) art or music (*mousikēn*) with the shield. The terminology – from invention to music (which are not usually applied to war) – is pervaded by sophistic associations.[131] It is this cultural crisis – war and sophists, the Periclean legacy – which Euripidean tragedy inhabits, reflects and examines.[132] That this is the case can be seen from a comparison between Thucydides' narrative of the events of 428–427 BC and two of Euripides' plays first performed around that time.

In Book 3 of Thucydides we find an analysis of the role and power of rhetoric in the running of empire and in the prosecution of war. The result is two notoriously complex debates (the Mytilenean and the Plataean) and the chapter on *stasis* at Corcyra. Both the debates show the 'historically complementary in the rhetorically contradictory';[133] both reveal a (sophistic) concern with the possibilities and limitations of

---

[130] Most editors bracket these lines; they may be interpolated. See Collard (1975a), 333–6 for a discussion.

[131] *Deinos* seems to have been first used to mean 'clever' by Herodotus (5.23; see also Soph. *Phil.* 440; *Hipp.* 921; Pl. *Prot.* 341a). For *exeuriskō*, see, for instance, Aesch. *PV* 459–60, where Prometheus talks of inventing for mankind number (or mathematics), which he calls the most excellent of skills (*sophismatōn*). On *akribēs*, see Gow (1950) on Theocritus 15.81. For *mousikē*, see Pind. *Ol.* 1.15; Hdt. 6.129; Pl. *Prot.* 340a; *Phd.* 61a; *Rep.* 403c; *Tim.* 88c; it is also significantly applied to Agathon at Ar. *Thesmo.* 159. It is worth remembering that the importance of *logos* in the Athenian democracy continues, on the one hand, the Homeric ideal of the skilful speaker (usually a warrior, e.g. Nestor; on which, see Martin (1989)), and, on the other, brings with it an increasing awareness that language is inevitably corruptible.

[132] For an eloquent expression of this not unusual view, see Arrowsmith (1963), 34–6; see also Gouldner (1965), 134; de Romilly (1986), 5–73.

[133] Macleod (1983), 64.

language;[134] both betray the idea that *logos* must deceive to be effective and that it is dependent on paradox and contradiction for its power. In a superb analysis of the Mytilenean debate, Macleod demonstrated the internal inconsistencies of the speeches of both Cleon and Diodotus (Thuc. 3.37–40, 42–8).[135] Cleon never escapes this basic contradiction: while he claims it is just and expedient to punish the Mytileneans because their revolt is unjust, he also admits that the Athenian Empire is itself unjust. Therefore he is only left with the expediency of punishment. This Diodotus questions in a manner that is difficult to gainsay: what is needed is rational deliberation based on the grounds of expediency rather than a legal judgement determined by anger. Even so, Diodotus agrees with Cleon that the Empire is oppressive and that consequently revolt by the allies is inevitable; he, again like Cleon, has no long-term solution for this outcome. In concluding that the truth is that sometimes all deliberation is futile, Macleod is perhaps too pessimistic (the mass execution is, after all, stopped), but there is no doubting the power of his reading.

The Plataean debate (Thuc. 3.53–67) is perhaps wrongly named; it is more like a parody of a trial. As is the case with Helen in *Troades* (see chapter three), no charge is brought by the Spartan judges against the Plataeans (3.52.4; see also Gorg. *Pal.* 4).[136] Instead they are asked a short question: have they in the present war ever aided the Spartans and their allies (3.52.4)? Given that the Plataeans are allies of the Athenians, such a question can only expect the answer 'no'. Although the Plataeans try to defend themselves, they are caught up in a series of inconsistencies. They tactfully answer the short question (3.54.2) by reminding the Spartans of the realities of

[134] Guthrie (1971), 219. A concern with obvious political implications in Athens, where 'Faith in public argument lay at the root of the democracy' (Buxton (1982), 1). See also Voegelin (1957); Goldhill (1986), 222–43; Ober (1989), esp. 104ff.; Ober and Strauss (1990).

[135] Macleod, 'Reason and Necessity' in (1983). For Thucydides generally I have found these critics most useful: Woodhead (1970); Cogan (1981); Macleod (1983), 52–159; Connor (1984).

[136] Macleod (1983), 118; M. Lloyd (1984).

alliance, but they assert a little later (3.55) that it was the Spartans who refused to have them as allies; in blaming the Spartans for the present state of affairs, the Plataeans abandon their earlier tact. They claim that they were right not to betray Athens (3.55.3), but that allies cannot be held responsible for their actions (3.55.4). Towards the end of their speech they say that they are well disposed towards Sparta, having been her enemies only by necessity (3.58.2). Their defence, in fact, only allows them to answer the Spartan question negatively.[137]

Still, the Thebans need to reply, fearing that the Spartan judges may have been swayed (3.60.1). The appeal they most have to counter is the Plataeans' invocation of their actions in the Persian Wars, when, alone of Boeotian cities, they did not medize (3.54.3, 56.4–5, 57.2–3, 58.4–5, 59.2). Although it is never explicit and they never use the word 'medize', the Plataeans contrast their former services to Greece with the treachery of the Thebans, who did medize. In reply the Thebans simply argue: however bad we were then, the Plataeans are much worse now. And the neologism they use to cover this decline in Plataean behaviour is 'atticism'. In one stroke this equates the heinous crime against Hellenic culture which the Persian invasion perpetrated with Athenian behaviour in the following fifty years, and the behaviour of treacherous Greeks then (medism) with allies of Athens now (atticism). Indeed, the Plataean use of their part in the Persian Wars had been an appeal to the Spartan memory of the liberation of Greece in 479 BC. Another liberation – from Athenian tyranny (see 2.63.2, 3.37.2) – is invoked by the Thebans in the word 'atticism'.[138]

The Plataean use of the Persian Wars in their defence was by 427 BC a conventional standard in judging the merit of a city. The Theban invention of atticism is also an invention of a new standard; and it is one which turns the full ideological power of a hierarchical polarity onto Greece. The Greek defeat of the Persians turned the latter into 'others': atticism – a

---

[137] I am indebted to Macleod (1983), 103–22.   [138] Cogan (1981), 68–9.

crime of the present replacing that of the past – invents a barbarian within Greece. The Thebans, speaking on behalf of a Greece they had abandoned fifty years before, reinvent Athens as other. This 'cruel rhetorical trope'[139] is all that the Thebans need (certainly their arguments are not consistent: compare 3.62.4 with 3.63.2). It provides Sparta with an ideological slogan under which to fight the war – not against a place, but against a culture.

In Euripides' *Hecuba*, in which Hecuba's situation betrays some similarities to that of the Plataeans[140] and which, like *Troades*, is set in the aftermath of the Trojan War, the chorus remark on how the context of war affects that fundamental polarity of all Greek society: friend/enemy (*Hec.* 846–9):

> δεινόν γε, θνητοῖς ὡς ἅπαντα συμπίτνει,
> καὶ τὰς ἀνάγκας οἱ νόμοι διώρισαν,
> φίλους τιθέντες τούς γε πολεμιωτάτους
> ἐχθρούς τε τοὺς πρὶν εὐμενεῖς ποιούμενοι.

> It is strange how for mortals everything comes together,
> and how the laws have determined necessity,
> turning bitter foes into friends,
> and making enemies of former friends.

So the Thucydidean description of war effecting an inversion in friend/enemy relations (whether between cities or on an individual level) is confirmed in generalized form in Euripides. The consequences of war are obvious throughout the play.[141] Hecuba sustains a life which is in fact more like death (431), suffers from both fall from power (284–5, 486, 496, 619ff.) and loss of *polis* (159–61). The most troubling effects of war, however, are the two murders (of Polydorus and Polyxena) around which the play is structured. The first is sanctioned as a ritual sacrifice, the latter is violently avenged. Polyxena dies a noble death, managing to be simultaneously decorous and erotic (558–61, 568–70), but the sacrifice remains troubling: why does Achilles demand a human sacrifice (258–63)? Is it just (263)? In communal terms, are its effects in any way bene-

---

[139] Ibid., 69   [140] Hogan (1972).
[141] Luschnig (1976); C. Segal (1990).

ficial?[142] Agamemnon acquiesces in the revenge Hecuba takes upon Polymestor, but it turns the Thracian into a rabid wild beast (1058, 1172–3; see also 1071–5), who prophesies that Hecuba will herself become a dog (1265). The sacrifice and the revenge are joined by one fact which is of interest here: as in Thucydides, and combining the two parts of the Periclean legacy, they both focus on rhetoric at work in the context of war.

Greek opinion about the sacrifice is divided. Agamemnon is against it; the sons of Theseus support it (*Hec.* 120–4). The argument continues until Odysseus, portrayed pejoratively as an eloquent demagogue, intervenes and persuades the army (130–3). When Odysseus comes on stage, his purpose is to report the decision of the Greek assembly, not to debate. The alternative he offers to Hecuba is one of compulsion or assent (225–7). Yet Hecuba, who thus finds herself – like the Plataeans – in a hopeless position, tries to persuade Odysseus. Her main argument is that she accepted the supplication of Odysseus when he was discovered in Troy by Helen and that, since a friendship or alliance (*philia*) has been established, he should return the favour (*charis*) and yield to her entreaties (239–53, 273–8). However, this plea, this attempted persuasion, is undermined by Hecuba's vitriolic criticism of Odysseus as a demagogue and, by implication, the powers of persuasion (254–7). But she concludes her speech by asking Odysseus to use his rhetorical skills again (287–8). In asking this, she acknowledges that a speech cannot be divorced from the status of its speaker: Odysseus, whatever his arguments, can persuade (has he not already done this?); she, as a victim of war, cannot (293–4). Odysseus' response is similar to the Spartan question in the Plataean debate. He asks, in effect, 'what have you done for the Greeks to compare with the services of Achilles?' He reminds her that their relationship, based on supplication, is a personal one (301–2); that *philia*

---

[142] Kitto (1961³), 219; Steidle (1968), 44; Vellacott (1975), 192. For the question of the cultural acceptability of the sacrifice, see Pearson (1962); Adkins (1966); Hogan (1972). For the possibility of human sacrifice outside myth, see the bibliography in chapter two, n. 16.

relations, the due observance of *charis*, are more important in the city's view, mainly because of the requirements of war (306–12). Anyway, barbarians do not observe proper *philia* relations (328–9), something already recognized as false by Odysseus himself.

Hecuba realizes that her persuasion has failed (334–5). Polyxena does not try to sway Odysseus but does persuade Hecuba to accept the decree: he has power on his side, after all (402–4). The only successful persuasion, then, is that of Polyxena: Hecuba fails and Odysseus has no need to convince any Trojans of anything. We witness a futile *agōn*, which can only demonstrate, as in the Plataean debate, that persuasion is affected by the relative power of the speakers and that constitutive polarities (friend/enemy here) can be distorted or ignored.

The complications in *philia* relations which the war has brought forth are extended in the debate between Hecuba and Agamemnon. Hecuba wants Agamemnon to take revenge on Polymestor. Polymestor, an ally (*philos*) of the Greeks, has killed Polydorus, the son (*philos*) of Hecuba, while looking after him as a guest (*xenos*, related to *philos*). Hecuba needs to persuade Agamemnon, who has become *philos* to her through his relationship with Cassandra (826–30). Hecuba uses arguments based on Polymestor's transgression of hospitality (792–7) and Greek notions of law (798–805). But she herself finds these pleas unconvincing: she has not learned to persuade, and Persuasion is a tyrant, the only vehicle for fulfilling one's desires (814–19; see Gorg. *Hel.* 6). Towards the end of her speech she laments that she is not a physical incarnation of eloquence (836–40), as if that could replace her lack of social status. Ironically, Agamemnon agrees with her arguments, although he does note the difficulties of the Greek alliance with Polymestor (850–63). Hecuba releases him from any involvement in the revenge, simply asking that he control the Greeks should the news of Polymestor's murder leak out (870–4). So, when her persuasion has worked, it has not really been necessary.

The final debate is between Hecuba and Polymestor, after his children have been killed and he himself blinded. By now

Hecuba has become a resourceful exponent of rhetoric. Her luring of Polymestor into the women's tents with the promise of gold, where the attack can take place, is a skilful piece of seductive persuasion (1145–71). Polymestor can only muster the argument in his defence that he killed Polydorus to save Greece from future trouble (1136–44; the same argument will be used of Astyanax in *Troades*). Hecuba, who is now in a position of strength, dismisses the argument; she now has the confidence, and the power, to attack rhetoric – in a highly rhetorical manner, of course (1187–94). She thus confirms the earlier insight that the effectiveness of persuasion is dependent on status.[143]

Represented in *Hecuba*, then, is the confusion engendered in the use of fundamental polarities by war. We also see that, when that confusion is grasped and the victims of war have recourse to *peithō* as their last hope, rhetoric is controlled by those in power, by those who have won, by war: rhetoric, as it were, is polemic.

An even more extreme account of war's effects is contained in Thucydides' section on Corcyra (3.82–3), where he makes some generalized remarks about the nature of *stasis* and the relation between language and morality.[144] The events at Corcyra appear to stand for the degeneration of the Greek world, the symptom being the subversion of language and morality, those two interdependent conventions.[145] As words are changed or perverted, so too are traditional ties and customary restraints (3.82.6–7). Narrating the events at Corcyra in the chapters before he analyses the *stasis* (3.70–81), Thucydides presents us with a series of failed persuasions, a series of failures of political discourse to inhibit violence.[146] The language of the revolutionaries expresses a new world: what was once called, for instance, an act of irrational audacity (3.82.4:

---

[143] I have found these critics useful: Buxton (1982), 170–86; Gregory (1991), 85–120.

[144] See especially Macleod, 'Thucydides on Faction' in (1983); also Edmunds (1975b); Hogan (1980).

[145] Macleod (1983), 125.   [146] Connor (1984), 96–9.

'τόλμα ... ἀλόγιστος') now has currency as the bravery of a good comrade ('ἀνδρεία φιλέταιρος'). The dichotomy justice/expediency, which had problematically informed the Mytilenean debate, is replaced by a self-referential quality: 'εὐπρέπεια λόγου'/'speciousness (or plausibility) of speech' (3.82.8; cf. Helen at *Tro.* 951). It is the conventional view that the disintegration of the community is being illustrated, even caused, by this subversion of language. While this is true, what is also depicted is the formation of a new semantics, which may be criticized by Thucydides himself, but which still inevitably conveys meaning. One interpretation of the chapter would be that Thucydides is realizing and lamenting the fact that language has no inherent moral quality and no control over the precise meanings it conveys. Rather, language is any particular combination of meanings and processes by which meanings are produced. Therefore, in Corcyra, it is not language itself which is subverted but an establishment, or an order represented and formed by a particular language. The crisis is of a new language succeeding the old, though the transformation is neither instant nor clean. But the important point is that both the old and the new languages can be seen as inadequate: the old failed to cope with the new political situation; the new contributes to its instability. Language, any language, is shown to be contradictory since it is problematically and simultaneously cause and effect. It is central in forming the character of political life, but at the same time, as the speed and apparent ease of its transformation shows, it is inherently neutral. In Thucydides, then, we read not only the troubling effects of war, through *stasis*, on language, but also his insight – paradoxical and caused by war – into the nature of *stasis*, 'the undoing of human progress by the very means of that progress'.[147] Thucydides was not alone in remarking on the problems of language, for we find a similar view in Gorgias' *On Not Being*, where language is argued to be fundamentally inadequate to its apparent task of expressing the

---

[147] Macleod (1983), 125.

world (DK 82B3).[148] Nor was Thucydides the only author to register dismay at the proliferation of new languages, for that, after all, is what lies behind the plot of Aristophanes' *Clouds* (esp. 1036ff.), in which new types of education, which involve the learning of new languages, new rhetorics, are offered against more traditional methods.

In Euripides' hands, this scrutiny of language appears in a number of ways. Euripides produces a rhetorical discourse. This it would be foolish to deny. But there is an inherent instability in *peithō*, stemming from its necessary relativism and its ability to be used opportunistically. Euripidean tragedy tends to represent the insecurity associated with *peithō*, as the various treatments of Odysseus all testify. To be more specific, it is also the case that Euripidean tragedy in general, and the plays set in the aftermath of the Trojan War in particular, betray the pressures of war. Under the sign of war the traditional and fundamental opposition of *peithō* to *bia* begins to break down; indeed, the outbreak of war signals the failure of *peithō* to inhibit violence.[149] What we so often see in Euripides – *Supplices*, *Hecuba*, *Andromache*, *Medea*, *Troades* are all good examples – is the violence of persuasion, a conflation of the opposed terms, more often than not as a result of war.[150] In this, Euripides shares his insight with Thucydides, who nonchalantly describes Cleon, the most aggressive prosecutor of the Peloponnesian War, as 'the most violent and the most persuasive' (Thuc. 3.36.6: 'βιαιότατος ... πιθανώτατος').

I will give one more instance: the examination of *sōphrosunē* (self-control; but see below) in *Hippolytus*. It should be said that this word touched on Athenian civic discourse in three important ways. First, the word played an important part in the political conflicts of late fifth-century Athens, as various interest groups tried to appropriate it for their own

[148] For very various views of this work of Gorgias, see Untersteiner (1954), 145–75; Voegelin (1957), 275ff.; Gomperz (1965), 1–35; Guthrie (1971), 194ff.; Newiger (1973); Robinson (1973), 56ff.; G. Lloyd (1979), 81–5; Kerferd (1981), 93–9.

[149] On *bia/peithō*, see Buxton (1982), *passim*.

[150] *Troades*, like *Hecuba*, represents the violent effects of Odysseus' persuasion: Astyanax is to die. *Supplices* represents the failure of political language to curb violence. Medea's persuasive skills are in the service of a gruesome end.

(ab)uses.[151] Gregory has read the play from this position, arguing that *sōphrosunē* was a vague term which concealed oligarchic or elitist attitudes. She sees the play as showing Euripides' attempt to redefine the word and make it available for the democracy.[152] However, because of the pressure under which *sōphrosunē* is put, and because the word is so ambiguous in the play, we shall see that such an interpretation is flawed. Second, *sōphrosunē* is an important term in personal morality. Goff reads the play 'as a series of articulations of desire in speech and of attempts to silence it'; *sōphrosunē* is one of the terms which 'most acutely focuses the problems of the relation between desire and speech'.[153] Third, *sōphrosunē* may help us to understand a developing intellectual discourse about the self. Gill wants to relate *Hippolytus* and Plato's *Charmides* as two instances of the examination of *sōphrosunē*.[154] *Hippolytus* tells the story of the struggle of Hippolytus and Phaedra against the irrational forces of the two goddesses, Aphrodite and Artemis (whose statements of divine power encircle the play), as well as against irrational human forces. Both characters depend to an important extent on self-images determined by their understandings of *sōphrosunē*. (Gill notes four different senses of the word in relation to selfhood: chastity or purity, virtue, self-control, good sense or prudence.)[155] But will either character survive the struggle? How effective do their values prove? Phaedra first thinks that she will be able to use her *sōphrosunē* to overcome her troubling passion (398–9); indeed she seems to see *sōphrosunē* as fundamental to maintaining her all-important *eukleia* (423, 489, 687, 717). Hippolytus' conception of the term is somewhat different, being more doctrinaire and rigid. Further, he tends to flaunt his possession of *sōphrosunē* (1100, 1365). Artemis even believes that he dies because of it (1402), a belief in conflict with

---

[151] For *sōphrosunē* used in connection with oligarchs: Ar. *Frogs* 721–30; *Knights* 334; *Clouds* 1006; *Birds* 1540; Thuc. 1.84.1–2; 3.58.1, 59.1, 82.8; 6.11.7; 8.24.4, 63.3, 64.5, 97.2. It is more difficult to pin down the democratic use of the word. For a general discussion, see North (1966).

[152] Gregory (1991), 50–84.   [153] Goff (1990), 32 and 39.

[154] Gill (1990).   [155] Ibid., 80.

Phaedra's view (731: 'σωφρονεῖν μαθήσεται'/'he will learn to be *sōphrōn*'). The Nurse is cynical about the whole notion (358–9), even though for rhetorical purposes it is she who calls Phaedra *sōphrōn* (494). Hippolytus contradicts this: women cannot possess *sōphrosunē* (667); it is given to only a few in nature (80). The profusion of competing claims to understanding or possessing *sōphrosunē* and the fact that, though both Hippolytus and Phaedra are motivated by *sōphrosunē*, they are unable to communicate with each other would suggest that it has proved ineffective in combating the wills of the two goddesses. It is precisely the failure of an ideology based on *sōphrosunē* in the face of divine power play which *Hippolytus* represents. Divine power, irrational power disables the non-contradictory use of ideology. At 1034–5 Hippolytus says:

> ἐσωφρόνησε δ' οὐκ ἔχουσα σωφρονεῖν,
> ἡμεῖς δ' ἔχοντες οὐ καλῶς ἐχρώμεθα.

> She practised *sōphrosunē*, without being *sōphrōn*.
> I possess it, but did not use it well.

What use is *sōphrosunē*, we might ask? And where is it, except in the space of language?[156] Hippolytus, privileging the term by paradoxical utterance ('one of the points of the play where desire renders language unintelligible'),[157] would seem to be undermining its efficacy, even questioning its existence. That which is central in the human tragedy is displaced by divine power. All this does not quite seem a successful democratic appropriation, as Gregory argues. The language of politics, of the self, of desire, becomes involved in the politics of language. We are shown crumbling definitions, slippery meanings and meanings deferred. At the heart of the play for the human characters is failure and want of power. Language is shown to be inadequate. It is only with language that the human characters can get to grips with their tragic predica-

---

[156] See Gill (1990), 81–2 on the ambiguity of these lines and how they fit into the recurrent dislocation in the play between outer act and inner mental state (e.g. famously at *Hipp.* 612).
[157] Goff (1990), 40.

ment; indeed, that is part of their tragic predicament. As in Thucydides and Gorgias, language is always other.

Both Euripides and Thucydides are involved in a questioning of language and its fundamental role in politics. That both were concerned with language, rhetoric, and rhetoric in war shows the centrality of these concerns in intellectual debate in Athens, and in civic discourse as a whole. That both authors present us with language as deception and paradox, as ambiguous and other, reveals the problematic status of that centrality in civic discourse and, therefore, the crisis of civic discourse itself. Civic discourse in such a condition, caused by the double strain of war and (some) sophists' arguments about language and rhetoric, is an important factor in the production of Euripidean tragedy.

In summary: tragedy performs its didactic function by examining ideology, defined as the authoritative self-definition of the citizens. War provides a rich source for this examination because, as Vernant says, 'politics can be defined as the city seen from the inside ... war is the same city facing outwards';[158] because war was both a frequent occurrence and extreme in its effects, one of which was putting ideology at risk; and because the Persian Wars were used to justify one process of self-definition. So, while Athenian ideology was tested in the fact of war and in places outside the bounds of the *polis*, Euripidean tragedy uses war as a site for looking inwards, for self-examination. And my chosen play – *Troades* – is arguably the most extreme war-play extant.

[158] Vernant (1980), 25.

2

POLARITIES

The first aspect of tragic teaching to be considered is the examination of constitutive polarities. Of course, not all tragedies deal with all the same polarities and with the same questioning force.[1] Here, men and gods, men and women, the free and the enslaved, Greeks and barbarians, and friends and enemies are discussed in turn. These are interdependent and mutually reinforcing (see chapter one), and what is different about the reading of the play offered here is that it is not confined to analysing one of the polarities.[2] For the sake of clarity, however, the polarities have been separated from each other, although interdependence is indicated whenever it is important. Finally, although this manner of questioning ideology is not uniquely Euripidean, there remains a certain difference about *Troades*, which is marked by an affirmation that the problems that the characters encounter when using the polarities are both very extreme and extreme because they are an effect of war. This has something in common with Euripides' other Trojan war-plays – *Andromache* and *Hecuba* – but also with some of the insights we find in Thucydides' narrative of the *stasis* at Corcyra.

Ritual disorder

Poseidon opens the play. He announces who he is and whence he has come (1–3). He makes clear the longevity of his love

---

[1] *Troades*, for instance, does not concentrate at any length on man/animal, which is a feature of both *Andromache* and *Hecuba* (see *Andr*. 630, 1141, 1169–70; *Hec*. 1058, 1072–3, 1172, 1265); on the latter play in these terms, see C. Segal (1991). As gods are in hierarchical opposition to men, so are men to animals; see Burkert (1966); Detienne (1981).

[2] Though now see C. Segal (1991), 109 on *Hecuba*: 'The play combines the familiar Greek polarity of marriage versus war with the Greek analogy between marriage and sacrifice; and it explores the otherness of the female by combining it (as in the *Medea*) with the otherness of the barbarian.'

for Troy (4–7). Then, with Hecuba prostrate on the stage, he describes the final defeat and destruction of Troy (9–12). The scene is set: the audience imagine the ruined city as backdrop. The material effects of war are not the god's only concern; he is also keen to inform us of the breakdown of religious practice. The war has left the temples desolate ('ἔρημα' at 15) and the shrines of the gods bloodied (15–16). Greek impiety has gone so far as to cut down and slaughter the Trojan king at the altar of Zeus the Protector (16–17). The irony of the place of the murder is not something which Poseidon acknowledges; he merely mentions that he is departing from Troy and his altars (25) because he has been worsted by Hera and Athene (23–4) and because war undermines religious practice (26–7):[3]

ἐρημία γὰρ πόλιν ὅταν λάβῃ κακή
νοσεῖ τὰ τῶν θεῶν οὐδὲ τιμᾶσθαι θέλει.

Whenever evil desolation takes hold of a city,
worship of the gods suffers (literally: 'is ill') and is not usually honoured.

The choice of words – the evil desolation, the disease – reveals that the breakdown is unambiguous; it is also obviously a consequence of war. The Greeks have murdered Polyxena at the tomb of Achilles (39–40: note that Poseidon does not use the vocabulary of sacrifice) and we are reminded obliquely that Agamemnon before the war sacrificed his own daughter, and thereby – a disastrous aberration – has abandoned religious worship and piety (43: 'τὸ τοῦ θεοῦ τε παραλιπὼν τό τ' εὐσεβές').

Poseidon's response, then, is to desert his beloved city; but Athene, who enters at line 48 and who had formerly been hostile to Troy, wishes to change her allegiance (65–6). This reveals a certain fluidity in gods' attachment to men, which Poseidon criticizes (67–8): gods, as well as men, order the world on the basis of a distinction between friends and enemies, and changing one's mind about these things upsets

[3] Except where indicated I have used the Oxford Classical Text of *Troades* (ed. J. Diggle). For fragments of tragedy, all references are to Nauck (1964²), unless stated otherwise. Translations are my own unless stated otherwise.

stability.[4] But Athene has a solid reason for her change of heart, one which Poseidon must understand: Ajax desecrated her temple by dragging off the prophetess Cassandra; and the Greeks have not punished him (69–70). So, it is not only the case that the Greeks have acted sacrilegiously in Athene's temple; it is also true that they have betrayed their alliance with Athene, an alliance which helped them to sack Troy (9–11, 67ff.). Athene wishes to teach the Greeks a lesson: they must respect her power and learn to worship the other gods (85–6). Poseidon agrees to help. He uses the adjective 'stupid' ('μῶρος') to describe those who plunder temples, cities and tombs (95–6). However, retribution for such acts will follow (97): the repetition of *erēmia* from line 26 (and see 15) reminds us that the Greeks are responsible for this impious desolation of Troy.[5]

---

[4] Euripides may have invented Poseidon's attachment to Troy (which we saw at lines 4–7; see also *IT* 1414–15), since in Homer he is an enemy of Troy (*Il.* 14.357ff.; 20.34; 21.435ff.), although he did build the city's walls (*Il.* 21.446–7; see 8.519; 21.526ff.). On the relation between the prologue and the rest of the play, see O'Neill (1941); but now, Erbse (1984), 60–72. On relations between Poseidon and Athene, see Fontenrose (1967) and (1968); Wilson (1968a). For lines 48–97 as interpolated, see Wilson (1967) and, against Wilson, Erbse (1984), 72.

[5] For the various uses of *mōros* in Euripides, see Denniston (1939), 59 ad *El.* 50. Diggle (1981), 59 and Kovacs (1983) both find lines 95–7 unacceptable grammatically. The latter proposes, after Blomfield, that the first 'τε' in line 96 be replaced with 'δέ', with a 'μέν' understood after 'ἐκπορθεῖ' in line 95. The lines are then translated as: 'He is a foolish man who, on the one hand, sacks cities, and, on the other, having laid waste temples and tombs and sacred places of the dead, then himself dies later (in the same way).' The foolishness therefore, according to Kovacs, is that of a man whose final failure is judged by earlier success. However, Kovacs' other arguments against the usual reading of these lines (which I follow) are questionable. He says that: a) the lines talk of abandonment, not desecration. Strictly speaking this is true. But the lines have a more general reference, pointing us back to lines 15–16 and 25–7, where sacrilege is more in evidence; b) the sacking of cities is not in itself sacrilegious. Again, this may be true – see Scully (1990), 36–9 – but Poseidon has made it clear (15–17) that sacrilege has occurred, as of course does Athene. It is the manner of sacking that is important; c) Poseidon is motivated to attack Troy not because his own temples have been desecrated but because Athene asks for his help. But if his own temples, though abandoned, have not been desecrated, is there any obligation for him to act against the Greeks? Athene is very clear that sacrilege in one's own temple demands an appropriate response, and Poseidon agrees. Also, Athene is motivated to attack the Greeks not only because of what they have done, but because she wants to teach them a general lesson about religious worship (85–6). Taking all these objections to Kovacs together, it becomes clearer that lines 95–7 can be interpreted as: it is a foolish person who, through possible sacrilege during the sacking of a city, runs the risk of provoking divine retribution. See also Biehl (1989), 122–4.

The prologue, then, draws a particular picture. The war has left Troy a city without proper worship of the gods. The Greeks have murdered impiously, desecrating temples; their behaviour after victory condemns them to suffering. The gods, fickle but powerful, eager for honour yet, as we shall see, quick to ignore particular offerings, bring about a certain equivalence between the victors and the vanquished. As they exit from the stage (this also marks their departure from Troy), Hecuba lifts herself from the ground and performs a monody (98–152). There seems nothing for her to do but lament (e.g. 106–7). This is itself a last recourse of ritual, a last attempt to impose order on a world looking increasingly chaotic and hopeless; and it is a consolation to which the Trojan women will return.[6] However, as the play progresses, we shall see from the point of view of the Trojan women how a range of ritual activity is affected by the war. We shall watch as they develop new, and occasionally startling, attitudes about human relations with the gods.[7]

The entry of Cassandra early in the first episode is heralded by Talthybius' alarm at torches burning off-stage, inside the women's tents (298–302). Hecuba tells him it is Cassandra in a frenzy (306–7). Cassandra's speech (308–40) shifts the play's focus on ritual. She surely employs ritual language, but she certainly does not lament; she even makes the comparison herself (315ff.). Cassandra sings her own wedding song, brandishing torches according to custom (322–5). She urges the women, including her mother, to lead a sacred dance (326–8, 332–4). She offers sacrifice in Apollo's temple (329–30), which has presumably been destroyed. For Cassandra, then, some form of ritual activity apart from lamentation is possible. Her song is characterized by exhortations to happiness (327–8, 336–7), by an inaccurate address to the 'beautifully dressed' (*kallipeploi*: 338) Trojan daughters (compare Hecuba at 496–7 on her tattered rags), and by whooping, Bacchic cries of '*euhan euhoi*' (326).[8] Amid the carnage and weeping,

---

[6] Gregory (1991), 161–2.

[7] For ritual crisis in Euripides generally, see Strohm (1957), 50–64; Foley (1985).

[8] See Lee (1976), 125 and Biehl (1989), 468 on the meters of Cassandra's song.

such delirious celebration seems grotesquely inappropriate. But Cassandra has her reasons: she is celebrating her marriage to Agamemnon because it will be the agent of his destruction (356–60). Just as a form of ritual continues for Cassandra, so does the war.

The worst result of this war for the Greeks, however, is the disturbance to proper burial rites, which they have been denied. They have not had the (necessary) benefit of their wives' ritual ministrations; their tombs lie in a foreign country (376–9); and their parents at home in Greece thus have no one to tend their graves (381–2). Agamemnon himself, according to Cassandra's prophecy, will have a dishonourable burial (446–7; see Eur. *El.* 323ff.). And the prophetess had previously asserted that the reward for fighting a defensive rather than an offensive war is that in death due funeral rites are observed. The dead Trojans, as against the Greeks, have been taken home by loved ones and buried in their native land (387–90). The chorus cannot agree: they call on their dead husbands, unburied and deprived of funeral lustrations (1085: 'ἄθαπτος ἄνυδρος'). Hecuba, also using two negatives, says something similar of Priam, for he is unburied and friendless (1313: 'ἄταφος ἄφιλος'), although she also indicates that, before the fall of Troy, Hector was buried (1233). Cassandra herself prophesies that her own experience of burial will be more akin to that of the husbands of Hecuba and the chorus than of those glorious Trojan heroes she had praised. She will be thrown out as a naked corpse, carried along by storm water to near Agamemnon's grave, where she will be food for wild animals (448–50). It is only after anticipating her death that she jettisons the marks of her service to Apollo and leaves the festivals she had so loved (451–2). And, just before her exit, she reaffirms a belief in the burial of her brothers and father, whom she will meet below the earth (459–60). But the important point is that to be unburied (or to be buried improperly) is so woeful a state that it can be the motive for, and the focus of, the action of a whole play (*Antigone*), and laments about unburied comrades or relatives echo down through Greek literature, from Achilles on Patroclus (Hom. *Il.* 22.386), to

74

Teucer about Ajax (Soph. *Aj.* 1307; see 1333), to Antigone on Polyneices (Soph. *Ant.* 21ff.). Here, in *Troades*, it is just another effect of war (many more are listed), its impact actually heightened not only by relative understatement, but also by the fact that, not for the first time, Cassandra's statements are contradicted by other characters. The validity of Cassandra's analysis of the war – its effects and the result – is the subject of the first section of the next chapter. Our interest here is in demonstrating that, as a result of war, one important aspect of the ritual order is in a state of some confusion.

Andromache reports to Hecuba that she has seen the corpse of the sacrificed Polyxena, and that she has given (at least minimal) funeral rites to her, covering her with clothes and lamenting over her (626–7). But the event is not dwelled on: Andromache is more keen to compare the relative contentment of Polyxena and herself (630–1). The burial of Astyanax is more complicated. Even before he has been murdered Talthybius orders Andromache to bear the unpleasant news without complaint, otherwise the Greek army may not allow the boy to be buried (735–6).[9] After the boy's death, narrated by Talthybius, Andromache is prevented from burying her son (she must leave for Greece) and begs that the corpse be handed over to Hecuba (1141–4). The Greeks, then, are quite willing to murder a child and leave him unburied. Yet, in this atmosphere of ritual impropriety, the Greek Talthybius declares to Hecuba that 'we' will bury the corpse (1147: 'ἡμεῖς'), and that he has already bathed the body (1150–2). He starts to dig the grave (1153). There is a glimmer of ritual order in this aid given by a Greek to a barbarian and an enemy, by one of the victors to one of the vanquished. The burial does indeed take place (1246ff.), but not as an easy sign of ritual order. For burial rites are supposed to indicate a sense of continuity within the community (indeed a sense of community itself), as Cassandra so firmly declared. But how can this be in the case

---

[9] Hom. *Il.* 11.451–5: Odysseus threatens Socus with the loss of his proper funeral rites; for the importance attached to such rites in Homer, see Vernant (1991), 50–74. And for the mutilation of corpses in the *Iliad*, see C. Segal (1971).

of Astyanax? He was the last hope for the survival of Troy: with his death, Troy dies. Hecuba, in what has become a cliché of war, remembers earlier times of stability when Astyanax promised to bury her and honour her tomb. Now the roles have been reversed (1182–6). Also, at the burial, the corpse of Astyanax is adorned in wedding robes (1218–20). This is strange, as such clothing of the corpse and the consequent association of marriage with death, or the experience of marriage in death, is more normally the domain of virgin girls.[10] Antigone laments how she will marry Acheron (Soph. *Ant.* 814–16), the tomb in which she is incarcerated is addressed and described as a bridal chamber (*Ant.* 891, 1205), and Haemon, in killing himself, finally wins his nuptial rites in Hades (*Ant.* 1240–1). Polyxena in *Hecuba* will never be married but will lie in the house of Hades (*Hec.* 416–18). In *Troades*, Cassandra says that she will be married in Hades (445). Alternatively, one finds in Euripides the distinctive figures of the virgin or the wife who sacrifice themselves to save their city or group: the former swaps marriage for death (Macaria at *Heracl.* 579–80); the latter rejoins her husband in death (Evadne at *Supp.* 1019–20, 1063). Although Andromache talks of her son as a sacrificial victim (747), given the complete destruction of Troy, the death of Astyanax can only be 'a parody of the traditional city-saving sacrifice'.[11] So, as soon as ritual order is suggested, those things

[10] Strohm (1957), 50–63; Foley (1982b), (1985), 84ff.; C. Segal (1991), 115–16. For more general studies of the similarities of marriage and funerary rites (rites of passage), see Alexiou (1974), 120–2; Seaford (1987).

[11] Burnett (1977), 315. On the possible reasons for the death of Astyanax in the *Iliad*, as seen by Andromache (and they are not so characterized by *realpolitik*), see 24.737–8; Schein (1984), 190. Bérard (1989), 97 notes that marriage and death were '"stagings" in which women have the primary roles'. For Euripides' plays of self-sacrifice generally, see Wilkins (1990); for the different manner of noble death for men and women, see Loraux (1982), (1987); Vernant (1991), 50–74, 84–91. The sacrifice of Polyxena in *Hecuba* is perhaps the most complete treatment of a virgin's sacrifice, though here too there is no city, or group, to save; see Pearson (1962); Adkins (1966); O'Connor-Visser (1987), 50–72; Michelini (1987), 158–70; C. Segal (1990), 111–19. Other Euripidean sacrificial heroines: Alcestis, who dies for her husband – see Nielsen (1976); Iphigeneia in *IA*, who dies for Greece – see Foley (1985), 65–105; and Medea, who, by sacrificing her own children (*Med.* 1054), commits a form of self-sacrifice (*Med.* 1361–2); see McDermott (1989), 75–8.

which burial rites support and promote (community, continuity) have their absence confirmed through the peculiarities of the burial of Astyanax.

Ritual disorder is also marked in the various representations of sacrifice, though these are not as pervasive in *Troades* as in the plays mentioned above, or as in Aeschylus' *Oresteia*.[12] Poseidon mentioned in the prologue how Priam was cut down at the altar of Zeus (17). Cassandra claims she saw the murder, but she uses a word from the vocabulary of sacrifice to describe it (483: 'κατασφαγέντ''), as do the chorus (1315–16: 'a sacred death amidst unholy sacrifices/murders'/ 'θάνατος ὅσιος ἀνοσίοις σφαγαῖσιν'). Using the same term ('σφαγαί') the chorus more generally describe the murders of Trojans at the altars (562). The central sacrifice, however, is that of Polyxena, as a gift to the dead Achilles (622–3). Hecuba's response is to call it an unholy sacrifice (628: 'σῶν ἀνοσίων προσφαγμάτων'). Polyxena is also sacrificed at Achilles' tomb in *Hecuba*, but in that play much is made of the event: Odysseus justifies the sacrifice on political grounds (*Hec.* 299ff.); Polyxena's acceptance of her fate, indeed her preference for freedom and nobility in death over servitude, is stressed (*Hec.* 342ff.); and, in Talthybius' messenger speech, the ritual atmosphere, the nobility and propriety with which Polyxena dies and the eagerness of the Greeks to give the girl due burial are all emphasized (*Hec.* 518ff.). The absence of similar detail in *Troades* is intriguing.[13] In the absence of any ritual context, we become more mindful of the fact that the sacrifice is to a dead hero and not a god. Without hearing Polyxena herself accepting her fate willingly (or some report of her so going), we are conscious that the fact that the sacrifice is voluntary in *Hecuba* frees the Greeks from any guilt.[14] We are also aware that it is not a self-sacrifice intended to save city or group, as neither still exists. The relation between gods and men rested, in part, on sacrifice; yet, in this sacrifice,

---

[12] On sacrifice in the *Oresteia*, see Zeitlin (1965).

[13] For a comparison between the two Polyxenas, see Petersmann (1977).

[14] Wilkins (1990), 183: consent freeing the killer from guilt is a normal feature of Euripidean self-sacrifices.

it is not gods but a semi-divine, transgressive hero who is honoured.[15] Lacking Polyxena's consent, the Greeks may be guilty of murder; and, because her sacrifice is not a city-saving self-sacrifice, the killing of a human is not culturally acceptable.[16] A further irony in the Greek desire to honour Achilles with a human sacrifice is that Greeks of the fifth century tended to think that only barbarians were capable of such wickedness (see *IT* 380–91).[17] So, the problems involved in the maintenance of one polarity (man/god) infect the security of another (Greek/barbarian). Even though Athene can found a ritual of human sacrifice (*IT* 1450ff.), such sacrifice can still be deemed to constitute a breakdown in ritual propriety. This is a war, then, which began with the 'rape' of Helen and the sacrifice of Iphigeneia. It ends with the sacrifice of the king, as well as of the king's daughter. As Foley says: 'to call murder sacrifice is to put an act of human violence into a social and religious context whose larger implications the spectator can begin to understand'.[18] The larger implications are that war brings with it a confusion between murder and sacrifice (both nouns can be translated by 'ἡ σφαγή'). Proper performance of sacrifice (and of other ritual) is a sign of civilization. In

---

[15] Foley (1985), 26.

[16] Wilkins (1990), 180 notes Lycurgus *Against Leocrates* quoting Euripides' *Erechtheus* (fr. 50A) as an exemplary tale of the self-sacrifice of Erechtheus' daughters and sisters. Wilkins states: 'The contribution of each sex is clear: sacrifice is required of all children of suitable age ... eligible boys must stand in the battle-line; eligible girls may be called upon for human sacrifice to promote victory.' O'Connor-Visser (1987) devotes a whole book to human sacrifice in five plays of Euripides (*Heracl.*, *Hec.*, *Phoen.*, *IT*, *Erech.*). On pp. 208–10 there is a discussion of sacrifice in Euripides and his attitudes towards the Peloponnesian War, where she claims, impossibly I would say, that the representation of sacrifice in Euripides betrays his increasing distance from Athens' leaders. For the possibility of historical human sacrifices, see Henrichs (1981); O'Connor-Visser (1987), 211–32; Wilkins (1990), 178–80; Hughes (1991). Burkert (1966) argues that behind every animal sacrifice lies the possibility of regression to the sacrifice of humans.

[17] Hall (1989), 146–7.

[18] Foley (1985), 41. The theory of sacrifice argued for in Girard (1977) has been influential. It can be summarized as follows: the community unites and purges itself of violence by a collective act of violence against a victim (animal or human), who has been arbitrarily chosen. This does not apply happily to Polyxena, as her selection has surely not been arbitrary (the Greeks have demanded that someone of appropriate standing be sacrificed to Achilles).

Troades the signs are not good, and that is critical for the relationship between men and gods.

As the play progresses we see the uneven but developing response of the Trojan women to this crisis. Unlike the audience, the characters have not seen the prologue and so, for the women, the role of Athene has been anti-Trojan and merely destructive. In the first stasimon, which, in common with Hecuba's first reaction, is announced as a lament for Troy (511ff.), the chorus attribute the eruption of violence from the wooden horse to Athene (560-1). Later, in the exchange of laments between Andromache and Hecuba (577ff.), Andromache sees the hatred of the gods as responsible for the pain she is now experiencing (596-7) and describes the bloody corpses lying at the feet of Athene (599). To this point, it might be argued that the Trojan women are observing a fact often experienced by the losers in war: the gods have not supported them. Still, Athene (it seems to Andromache) can now only be honoured with dead Trojans. And Hecuba simply abuses the gods for self-conscious demonstrations of their destructive capabilities (612-13), which, for the audience, have been evident since the prologue. More tellingly, in the second stasimon, the chorus deign not to criticize Zeus for failing to help Troy, even though he loved the Trojan Ganymede (845-6).[19]

The relationship between the women and the gods seems, then, to be one of complaint and criticism. Hecuba had at 469 invoked the gods as if in prayer ('ὦ θεοί') but then goes on to denigrate them as bad allies ('κακοὺς ... τοὺς συμμάχους'). The fact of defeat makes this a truism for Hecuba, but there is still something serious about calling gods *kakoi*; perhaps that is the luxury of the loser. But we should also note that, while Hecuba has been disappointed by divine support, we know from the prologue that the Greeks are going to experience the

---

[19] Burnett (1977), 306-7 calls the chorus here arrogant. Note how Zeus at Hom. *Od.* 1.32 laments that men always blame the gods for their own self-inflicted calamities; Gouldner (1965), 133.

same disappointment. The next couplet, almost comic in its resignation in an area where fear and reverence are normally appropriate, continues by saying that, even though the gods are useless, it remains comforting to invoke them (470–1). But Hecuba changes her mind. She begins her speech against Helen by allying herself with the three goddesses associated with the Judgement of Paris (969: 'σύμμαχος'). Although we should not ignore the role of rhetorical convenience (i.e. to persuade Menelaus to kill Helen) in Hecuba's change of mind, one wonders why, given her earlier criticisms of the gods (and there are more to come), she is so keen to show them to be in the right. But it is surely the war which has effected such a confusion: the gods have been responsible for the end of Troy; they have abandoned the city, yet how can one live in opposition to, or without, the gods?

This progressive understanding of the gods continues in Hecuba's famous prayer at 884–8. In form the prayer is conventional, calling on Zeus by alternative names.[20] But those names seem to deny Zeus anthropomorphic existence. He is difficult to understand, Hecuba says, and may be either 'the compulsion of nature' ('ἀνάγκη φύσεος') or 'the mind/intelligence of men' ('νοῦς βροτῶν').[21] What is the force of combining these abstract, and contemporary, characterizations with the more traditional view of Zeus?[22] It suggests a war-induced confusion about the nature of Zeus or, at least, a review of formerly held beliefs. If Zeus is an inflexible law of nature or the mind of men, can one really sacrifice to 'him' with any effect? And, inconsistent with her earlier protestations, Hecuba, at 887–8, seems to hold an exalted view of the goodness and the justice of the divine.[23] So, in more conventional anthropomorphic terms, does Andromache, at least in so far as she cannot believe that Zeus is the father of such a

---

[20] Barlow (1986), 209.

[21] For discussion of these two phrases, see Scodel (1980), 94–5; Gregory (1991), 171.

[22] For Euripides' use of fifth-century cosmological speculation here, see, for instance, Scodel (1980), 128ff.; Biehl (1989), 334–7; and, in general, Reinhardt (1960).

[23] M. Lloyd (1984), 310.

scourge as Helen. However, this comforting belief runs contrary to the poetic tradition and to the statements of Cassandra, who, as we know, always tells the truth (398/766–70).[24]

Just as Hecuba transforms the gods from bad allies into
good ones, so, before the *agōn*, she is willing to praise the
justice of the gods. Both are developments from earlier in the
play, and both are brought about by the rhetorical demands
of the *agōn*. In this debate, Helen depicts the Judgement of
Paris in anthropomorphic terms.[25] This rendition shows the
gods in their most human (i.e. most vain, egotistical, fallible)
clothes. Hecuba's reply is apparently a masterly *reductio ad
absurdum*, a superb piece of fifth-century rationalization. It
depends, in part, on seeing the gods as figures incapable of
human folly and irrationality (971ff.). No doubt, Hecuba's
argument does not quite ridicule the gods; perhaps it can
even be characterized as pro-Olympian (with the proviso that
Aphrodite becomes a disease). But the implication from the
prayer at 884–8 is that the Judgement could not have occurred, if the other gods, like Zeus and Aphrodite here in the
debate (989), have become abstract forces.[26] More telling, of
course, is that two very anthropomorphic gods have already
appeared in the prologue.[27] The gods, then, offer no clear
aspect to mortals, who, as a consequence, draw confused and
inconsistent pictures of divinity.

We have seen in the prologue Poseidon describing the impiety of man; but the women, in turn, search for answers about
the behaviour of the gods. The chorus ask Zeus whether he
has betrayed his altars in Troy, whether he has abandoned the
offerings he has received there (1060–70), and then proceed to
identify the effects of war on sacrifice (1071ff.):[28]

---

[24] Burnett (1977), 314; Scodel (1980), 135.

[25] On the Judgement of Paris, see Stinton (1965) and Walcot (1977). For Helen's
anthropomorphism, see Vellacott (1975), 142–3; M. Lloyd (1984), 307.

[26] M. Lloyd (1984), 311.

[27] Scodel (1980), 135 argues that Hecuba's position is compromised by the fact of
Helen's victory in the debate. However, such a victory is itself problematic; see
chapter three.

[28] On whether this passage may be referring to Phrygian ritual, see Bacon (1961),
142; on the distinctions made between Greek and barbarian religion, not one of
the key differences, see Hall (1989), 86–93, 143.

φροῦδαί σοι θυσίαι χορῶν τ'
εὔφημοι κέλαδοι κατ' ὄρ-
    φναν τε παννυχίδες θεῶν,
χρυσέων τε ξοάνων τύποι
Φρυγῶν τε ζάθεοι σελᾶ-
    ναι συνδώδεκα πλήθει.

Your sacrifices are gone and the sweet [or 'auspicious']
sounds of choirs and the all-night festivals of the gods
held in darkness,
and the figures of gold images
and the holy moon-cakes of the Trojans,
twelve in number.

The build-up of detail in the passage – the choirs, the gold
images and the twelve sacrificial cakes – demands that we
recognize that, even with all these offerings, there is a nagging
absence of the gods at Troy, except in so far as they contributed to its destruction. The gods, indeed, like their sacrifices,
have departed Troy ('φροῦδα', 859; 'φροῦδαί', 1071).[29] I do
not mean to suggest that the gods always responded to sacrifices, because they did not (see e.g. Hom. *Il.* 6.301ff.). However, the extremity of Troy's fall from grace is stressed in
the complete absence of divine support. Hecuba extends the
chorus' complaints. We have a scene where sacrifice is not
only abandoned, but also deemed useless (1242: 'μάτην δ'
ἐβουθυτοῦμεν'/'we sacrificed in vain'). If the relations between
men and gods have their focus in sacrifice, and sacrificial practice has been abandoned and condemned, then those relations
are in crisis. The gods, according to Hecuba, have not recipro-
cated the sacrificial offerings of men and are therefore to be
dismissed (1240–1):

οὐκ ἦν ἄρ' ἐν θεοῖσι πλὴν οὑμοὶ πόνοι
Τροία τε πόλεων ἔκκριτον μισουμένη.

There was nothing to the gods apart from my sufferings
and Troy chosen as the city to be hated.

[29] On the vocabulary of privation and desolation in the play, see Strohm (1957), 34;
Poole (1976). Euripides may be exploiting the often-stressed, though not unique,
sacredness of Troy in Homer: *Il.* 4.46; 6.96, 277, 448; 21.128; 24.27; *Od.* 1.2; 11.86;
17.293; see Chalkia (1986), 190–1; Scully (1990), esp. 16–40.

As Troy begins to burn, Hecuba finds herself calling to the gods in what seems to be an instinctive reaction. She cuts herself short (1280–1):

καὶ τί τοὺς θεοὺς καλῶ;
καὶ πρὶν γὰρ οὐκ ἤκουσαν ἀνακαλούμενοι.

But why do I invoke the gods?
For they did not listen when they were called on before.

And finally, while she watches the final and complete destruction of Troy, Hecuba addresses the temples of the gods and her beloved city (1317). As she sees the city for the last time, the suggestion is that, along with the destruction of the temples, the absolute departure of the gods is confirmed.

The women of Troy have made a painful discovery: 'The gods can receive worship and expect it, but men may expect no return for this.'[30] Years of religious practice have been undermined by the testing and destructive nature of war, as both gods and mortals make clear. Ritual practice as it appears in the play is either possibly improper (the sacrifice of Polyxena) or ironic (the burials of Polyxena and Astyanax), because the rite cannot perform its function when the ritual context, the city and the family, has been destroyed. Apart from the dubious consolation of lamentation, war has destroyed not only homes and husbands but also the possibility of women performing the one public function which Athenian ideology allowed, namely, the performance of ritual, probably, as Zeitlin says, 'the only legitimate reason for leaving the house'.[31] War, then, as Euripides represents it, even destroys the normal ideological ordering of society, which is, of course, Thucydides' insight in the Corcyrean episode. While ritual

---

[30] Havelock (1968), 116; see also Scarcella (1959), 70; Meridor (1984); *HF* 1307–8. Porphyry *De Abstinentia* 2.24 may help us to understand why this is so serious: one sacrifices to the gods to honour and thank them, but also to receive something in return; see Guépin (1968), 149; Parker (1983), 159.

[31] Zeitlin (1982b), 129 and *passim*. But the exclusion of women in fifth-century Athens from the public sphere except for ritual practice is a large and vexed topic; see, for example, Gould (1980), 50–2, 58; Just (1989), 13–25. It should be noted, however, that Solon instigated a law against excessive lamentation by women in public (Plut. *Sol.* 21).

and sacrifice have not guaranteed divine indulgence to the Trojans, the Greeks have acted impiously after victory. In ritual terms, the war for them also will have terrible consequences.

The Trojan women respond to this crisis by questioning the gods. No simple answers are forthcoming. Yet the gods can be seen as beings – very humanly – interested in the furtherance and sustenance of their power. *Troades* dramatizes how divine self-interest conflicts with the notion of reciprocity which conventionally governs divine–human relations. The mortals struggle to understand but are left floundering in the ambiguous aspect the gods seem to present: just, yet amoral; abstract, yet anthropomorphic. Although the power of the gods is apparent, it is not evident that that power can be worshipped and thereby brought over to the worshipper's side. But the play not only shows the women questioning the value of the gods to men; it also represents doubts about the difference of gods from men. If the gods are self-interested, if they can change allegiances at will, if they are subject to human flaws such as vanity and stupidity, then in what sense are they different from humans? Once their difference is questioned, or minimized, their use as an other in self-definition is necessarily problematic. And the agents of this questioning of divine otherness are the women of Troy, themselves other to men.

Aftermath of war: women on stage

As the statements made by Agamemnon and Socrates (or Thales) testified, women were grouped together with animals, gods and barbarians as other to the male citizen. Work by many scholars has enlightened us on various aspects of women's exclusion from most of what we now call classical antiquity. But woman as other was not only an inherited cultural phenomenon but also, more precisely, a literary one, most succinctly betrayed in the exchange between Hector and Andromache in *Iliad* 6. The authority of Homer, in this as in other respects, resonates throughout Greek literature, but nowhere more fascinatingly than in Greek tragedy: from the dreadful subversions initiated by Clytemnestra in Aeschylus' *Oresteia* through Sophocles' *Trachiniae* and Euripides' own early plays, *Alcestis, Medea* and *Hippolytus*.[32] *Troades*, in comparison with some of these plays, cannot be viewed as an especially rich text for the exploration of sexual relations, but, in common with the other polarities examined in the play, the special impact lies in the way that this polarity and its problems are highlighted by being set in the aftermath of the Trojan War.

War is the responsibility of men, but war also kills men.[33] The normal consequence of loss of men in war is that their wives, daughters and other female dependants will be enslaved by the victors. And that is the case in *Troades*. But Athens, in its tragic discourse, also allows these Trojan women, these male actors, who have lost their men, to speak, to enter a public sphere of rhetoric and argument. The war-scene, the special dramatic space which the play provides, allows 'women' to perform what has formerly been prohibited and it renders tragedy's ability to have women speaking that much more obvious and extreme.[34] Towards the beginning of her monody, in response to the terrible calamities which have befallen her, Hecuba says (110–11):

> τί με χρὴ σιγᾶν; τί δὲ μὴ σιγᾶν;
> τί δὲ θρηνῆσαι;

> Why should I be silent? Why should I not be silent?
> Why should I lament?

[32] On the meeting between Andromache and Hector at the Scaean Gates, see Arthur (1981). The bibliography on women – their legal and cultural status, their place in myth, etc. – is vast. Here is a small selection: Foxhall (1989); Gould (1980); Just (1989); Keuls (1985); H. King (1983); Lacey (1968); Loraux (1981a), (1982); Padel (1983); Pomeroy (1975); Rousselle (1988); Schaps (1978). On women in tragedy, see also Easterling (1987); Foley (1981), (1982a); Loraux (1978a), (1987); Shaw (1975); Slater (1968); Zeitlin (1985b). On Aeschylus' *Oresteia*, see Goldhill (1984); Zeitlin (1978); on Sophocles' *Trachiniae*, see Dubois (1984); on *Alcestis*, Buxton (1985); on *Medea*, Kuch (1984), 51–72; Pucci (1980); on *Hippolytus*, Goff (1990); Goldhill (1986), 117–37; Zeitlin (1985a).

[33] On the historical evidence concerning women during wartime, see Schaps (1982).

[34] The *locus classicus* of Athenian prescription of silence for women is Thuc. 2.45.2.

At various points in the play Hecuba will adopt all three strategies. But Hecuba's questions also direct us to the sense in which the destruction of Troy and its consequences are, for the women, so crushing that they are ineffable; yet, at the same time, it is part of their tragic predicament (as of the characters in *Hippolytus*) that their only recourse is language.[35] And the play presents us with a range of linguistic responses: from the lamentation of all the women (except Cassandra) to Cassandra's (manic) prophecies and arguments; from Andromache's affirmation of the male ideology of marriage to the fifth-century debating techniques employed by both Helen and Hecuba in the *agōn*. And all this is a result of war. Lamentation was always a public task of women, but tragic war, or rather its effects, allows the women to speak in other less ideologically appropriate ways. In this sense, the effects of war confront the norms produced by Athenian ideology.

Troades is a women's play, and I do not say that just in banal reference to its title. The chorus and Hecuba are ever-present; Cassandra, Andromache and Helen come on in sequence; Polyxena lurks in the background. Hecuba will lead the laments like a mother bird (146ff.), Cassandra depicts her future in terms of a bizarre marriage (308ff.), while Andromache reviews the past as exclusively the history of her marriage (645ff.). The cause of the war is seen to be one wretched marriage (498–9), and the end of the war is described by the chorus in a domestic context (542ff.).[36] Indeed, the play consists of three central scenes in which, in turn, two daughters and one daughter-in-law discuss, reflect on and argue about marriage with their mother, Hecuba. The explicit concerns of Hecuba and Andromache are the fates of their children, their husbands and their families (577ff.).[37] But, apart from the play's representation of women's concerns, the

---

[35] Gregory (1991), 155–60.

[36] This is unusual considering epic narratives of war; see Kaimio (1970), 90 and compare *Hec.* 905ff.

[37] Gellie (1986), 118. Poole (1976), 262 notes that the structure of the play is one of a series of partings between parent and child.

use of woman as an inferior other in male self-definition is examined in the treatment of the effects of war on marriage and in the contrast between Andromache and Helen.

In *Andromache* and *Hecuba*, but especially in *Medea*, there is a focus on the *lechos* (and on other words for bed, e.g. *lektron*). In all three plays the bed is featured as the most important aspect of a marriage, and the main determinant of a woman's behaviour. A wife's attitude towards it is also a sign of the state of the marriage. But difficulties arise over such an evaluation, because the term is ambiguous. *Lechos* can connote the place of reproduction, the site of *erōs*, and it can describe metonymically the institution of marriage itself.[38] A similar focus can be found in *Troades*.

Both the chorus (203) and Andromache (667, 745), in their different ways, lament the passing of their old *lektra* and fear the fact that war will take them to strange new Greek beds.[39] Cassandra, typically different, tells her mother not to pity her *lektra* (403–4). In all these examples the word *lektron* seems to refer to the place where a man and a woman are united, but without specifying the precise nature of the relationship (i.e. is it marriage or concubinage?). This confusion about the types of available relationships between men and women is demonstrated in the cases of both Andromache and Cassandra. At 660, describing her relationship with the son of Achilles – we presume that she is to be Neoptolemus' concubine – Andromache calls herself *damar* (derived from the verb *damazō*: 'I tame'), a word which usually means a legitimate spouse.[40] Cassandra's status is even more murky. When Talthybius reports that Agamemnon has taken Cassandra as a special prize (249), Hecuba asks whether her daughter will be a slave to

---

[38] See *Med.* 41, 286, 380, 568ff., 672, 999, 1290–1, 1338, 1367; Rohdich (1968), 59–66; *Hec.* 365, 635, 933; *Andr.* 30, 370, 465ff., 904–5, 909, 927–8. Loraux (1981a) examines the bed as a defining fact of a woman's life, noting especially the equivalences between war and birth.

[39] Craik (1990) argues that innuendo and imagery about the sexual violence the women will suffer pervades the play.

[40] Barlow (1986), 192; Seaford (1987), 130. Vernant, 'Marriage' in (1980) demonstrates that the distinction between the wife and the concubine was not clear cut in Athenian law.

Clytemnestra (250–1). Talthybius' reply is interesting (252):

οὔκ, ἀλλὰ λέκτρων σκότια νυμφευτήρια.

Barlow translates this: 'No, not so, but as concubine to share his bed.' Lee's version is this: 'No, but the unmarried sharer of Agamemnon's bed.' What Barlow translates as 'concubine' and Lee as 'unmarried sharer' is literally 'dark/unlawful ('σκότια') nuptials' ('νυμφευτήρια'). In the prologue Poseidon had said this about Agamemnon and Cassandra (44):

γαμεῖ βιαίως σκότιον Ἀγαμέμνων λέχος.

Agamemnon will forcibly marry the dark/unlawful bed [of Cassandra].

The word translated 'marry' ('γαμεῖ') can also mean 'have sexual intercourse with'; and the word for 'bed' ('λέχος') is, as we have seen, one which can connote a range of sexual relationships. In both descriptions of the relationship the speaker uses one word from the vocabulary of marriage, the same metaphor of illegality, and a word for bed. So, a relationship which is not a marriage can only be described in the qualified terms of marriage. That Cassandra should have to experience such a fate is another gruesome and transgressive effect of war: she is a virgin priestess (253: 'τὰν τοῦ Φοίβου παρθένον'), granted a life without sex or marriage by Apollo (254: 'ἄλεκτρον'). But Agamemnon has been struck by desire for her (255).

However, the two Trojan women, Cassandra and Hecuba, both look on the relationship as a marriage. Cassandra asserts this in the whole of her first speech, which is a hymn to Hymenaeus, the god of marriage (308–40). Although Hecuba is sure of Cassandra's insanity (349–50) in singing such a song, she also seems to accept that, even under threat of force, it is a marriage which is being contracted. But we can only note that acceptance in the use of the phrase 'γάμους γαμεῖσθαι τούσδ'' (347: 'this marriage would be contracted'), and we have already seen that words with the *gam-* root can refer both to marriage and other forms of sexual union. Cassandra reaffirms her belief that it is a marriage by comparing it to that of Paris and Helen (357; see also 405):

Ἑλένης γαμεῖ με δυσχερέστερον γάμον.

By marrying me he will contract a more disastrous marriage
than that of Helen.

It is a marriage, then, but one which also shows us that war
has unleashed a form of marriage totally at odds with the
'ideal' which Andromache will describe later. In a line which
it is difficult not to read ironically, Talthybius calls it a 'good
marriage' or a 'good match' (420: 'καλὸν νύμφευμα'); for Cassandra, though, it is a marriage in Hades (445). Just as Hecuba (at *Hec.* 1016–17) uses the area inside the women's tents,
unknown and ignored by men, in order to murder Polymestor, so Cassandra exploits the male-determined institution of
marriage to take revenge on the destroyers of her family, her
oikos and her *polis*. However perverse, the marriage will conform to Hecuba's dictum later in the play that the woman
who betrays her husband should die (1029–32), for death is
Cassandra's fate.

War also undermines one of the functions of marriage,
namely, to provide children who will maintain the patriarchal
oikos. Cassandra notes that the war has enforced on the
Greeks an absence of normal home life (371–2). And, although the chorus indicate that there are still Trojan children
alive (1089ff.), Hecuba bemoans the fact that the splendid
royal sons she has raised have been killed, and that the daughters she groomed for appropriate marriages have been taken
away and enslaved (474–8, 484–6, 581, 583, 603–4). We hear
of Polyxena's sacrifice, as we see Cassandra being taken away
(see 500–4). War has destroyed the prospects of Astyanax,
who, paradoxically for a patrilineal society, has become a victim of his father's nobility (742ff.). Andromache looks back
on her marriage with Hector (745: *lektra*) as unhappy because
it has produced a son who will be sacrificed to Achilles
(746–8). The nursing and the labour pains were all for nothing (758ff.). Medea threatened male supremacy by the murder
of her own sons, that is, by the destruction of the seed of the
continuation of the patriarchal *oikos*. No such drastic personal measures are necessary here, since the disturbing of the

89

security of the *oikos* is an effect of war, the most extreme test of an ideological construct. The woman (Helen) who in this play most represents a threat to men significantly has no children, as if, in her case, the steps which Medea had to take have already been performed.[41]

The confrontation with Athenian ideology is most overt, though, in the contrast between the (apparently) model wife, Andromache, and Helen, traditionally evil and dangerous. At 643ff. Andromache describes her marriage to Hector as one which neatly yields to the demands of (contemporary Athenian) ideology. She has aimed for a good reputation (643: *eudoxia*),[42] and she has striven in the house of Hector to act in accordance with what has been deemed appropriate and *sōphrōn* (645–6). She has avoided the scandal which follows from a woman staying outdoors, remaining inside the house (648–50).[43] She has also not allowed her house to be compromised by the clever gossip to which women, she implies, are sometimes prone (651–4). She has maintained respectful silence in the presence of her husband (654), and both husband and wife have lived in their appropriate spheres (654–5), knowing when to insist and when to yield (655–6). But this ideologically perfect union has been finished by the war. Taking her cue from Homer rather than Pericles, she is now outside and speaking. Still, her belief that her marriage to Hector had all the ideologically proper ingredients has not been undermined. Her view is perhaps echoed by Cassandra when

---

[41] For the importance of children in marriage, see Pomeroy (1975), 64–5; Keuls (1985), 110ff. For Medea's infanticide – worse precisely because she kills her sons – see Easterling (1977); McDermott (1989), 9–24. *Med.* 563, 669, 718: Medea kills the seed of Jason; see Pucci (1980). Rousselle (1988), 48 notes the evidence of women calling a pregnancy which led to the birth of a girl 'bad', of a boy 'good', and Simon (1978), 246 notes the prevalence of infanticide of female children, at least in the fourth century; see also Oldenziel (1987).

[42] Phaedra has a similar concern with *eukleia*: *Hipp.* 409, 423, 687, 717.

[43] For the ideological prescription that women should stay inside the *oikos*, see Thuc. 2.45.2; Xen. *Oec.* 7.30. Of course, see also Hom. *Il.* 6.390–481; Hector's reply to Andromache does put her in her place (441ff.). Cohen (1989) quite rightly argues that practice may have contradicted ideological prescription, women being outside a great deal. For gossips, see *Andr.* 931. For a marriage which works through lack of conflict, see *Med.* 15, and note Aesch. *Pers.* 864–6 for the good man being one who stays at home; and for, in contrast, the wandering hero who rarely sees his children, see Soph. *Trach.* 31–3.

she says that if the Greeks had stayed at home (397: 'εἰ δ' ἦσαν οἴκοι'), Hector would never have died (albeit gloriously) and the Greeks would not have experienced so much grief. Cassandra – difficult to believe, but dangerous to doubt – says that men should have chosen their homes and marriages before war.

Helen is portrayed in sharp contrast to Andromache. She is held responsible for the war and its effects (131ff., 498–9, 1114).[44] She is, in effect, accused by Andromache of promiscuity (667–9). More than that, Helen is not only responsible for the war but is also, in her problematic parentage, the child of a demon (768–9):

Ἀλάστορος μὲν πρῶτον, εἶτα δὲ Φθόνου,
Φόνου τε Θανάτου θ' ὅσα τε γῆ τρέφει κακά.

First of *Alastōr*, then of Envy,
of Murder and Death and all the evils which the earth nurtures.

The list of destructive demons is emphatic, to be sure. But some problems surround calling *Alastōr* the parent of Helen. *Alastōr* is a surname of Zeus in his capacity as avenger of evil deeds. But we know that Zeus is Helen's father (though Andromache denies it: 766, 770). More normally, the title is applied to any demon who avenges wrongs.[45] Avenging wrongs? Helen? Surely not. Perhaps Andromache uses the word in the same sense as Helen does later of Paris (941), simply to signify violent effects, righteous or otherwise. It is clearer that Helen is dangerous because of her famous eyes, which beguile men (Aesch. *Ag.* 418–19) and have destroyed Troy (*Tro.* 772; see *Hec.* 442ff.). In addition, the mere sight of her provokes a desire which overrides all other claims on men (892–3; see Aesch. *Ag.* 687–90):

---

[44] Vellacott (1975), 140. And note that Poseidon says that Helen is rightly held prisoner (line 35); Strohm (1957), 34. For anxiety over causes of the Trojan War in *Andromache*, see lines 103–16, where Andromache says the rape of Helen is the cause; lines 273–308, 1009–46, where the chorus blame the gods; see Aldrich (1961).

[45] On *alastōr*, see Fraenkel (1950), ad. Aesch. *Ag.* 1501; and see *Pers.* 354; Soph. *Trach.* 1092; *Phoen.* 1556. Though see Aesch. *Ag.* 749, where it may be Helen who is described as 'νυμφόκλαυτος Ἐρινύς' ('a fury hated by wives'); Goldhill (1984), 64.

αἱρεῖ γὰρ ἀνδρῶν ὄμματ', ἐξαιρεῖ πόλεις,
πίμπρησιν οἴκους. ὧδ' ἔχει κηλήματα.

She captures the eyes of men, destroys cities,
burns homes. These are her charms.

Most tellingly, and most in contrast to Andromache, Helen is
seen to possess no *sōphrosunē* at all (1012, 1027–8), because,
as Hecuba tells her, in her situation she should have committed suicide. By killing her, Hecuba hopes that Menelaus will
establish a precedent: women who betray their husbands will
die (1030–2). Menelaus agrees: Helen will become a negative
exemplum to women (1055–7; Helen can never simply be this:
see Hom. *Od.* 4):

ἐλθοῦσα δ' Ἄργος ὥσπερ ἀξία κακῶς
κακὴ θανεῖται καὶ γυναιξὶ σωφρονεῖν
πάσαισι θήσει.

And, having come to Argos, the evil woman
will die the evil death of which she is worthy
and she will put moderation [*sōphronein*] into all women.

Helen is castigated for her lack of *sōphrosunē*, but that term,
its attribution and the effects of possessing it are problematic.
Andromache, for instance, can only remark that her reputation as a model (*sōphrōn*) wife has become a source of pain.
For the very qualities which are supposed to ensure that a wife
remains silent and not talked about are possessed by Andromache to such a degree that word of her behaviour has spread
to the Greek camp, where, as a wife who conforms perfectly
with male ideological prescriptions, she has become an object
to be desired (657–60).[46] Andromache is caught in a dilemma:
proper wifely behaviour urges her to honour Hector, and thus
dishonour her new husband, and vice versa (661–4). More
remarkably, the *sōphrōn* wife admits the possibility that
Helen's defence by recourse to Aphrodite (in the *agōn*) is
correct (665–6):

---

[46] Havelock (1968), 122–3: it is a woman's problem in defeat that she must become
chattel childbearer to the enemy. Personal integrity is impossible. Andromache
exemplifies the problem: 'It is in her nature to identify with the man to whom she
is assigned.' A partial reading, of course.

καίτοι λέγουσιν ὡς μί᾽ εὐφρόνη χαλᾷ
τὸ δυσμενὲς γυναικὸς εἰς ἀνδρὸς λέχος.

And yet they say that one nice time [i.e. night] softens
a woman's hatred for a man's bed.

If one feature of the model wife is to hold a suitably contemptuous view of women (as Phaedra does at *Hipp.* 406–7), it is perhaps no accident that Andromache confirms the view that women are excessively attached to the bed (e.g. *Med.* 568–73). But she distances herself from ordinary women by an analogy with animal behaviour: even horses do not abandon their mates easily, and animals are inferior to humans (669–72). So, Andromache uses one hierarchical polarity (man/animal) to buttress her view of the proper marriage. But, in asserting the correctness of her position, she must deny that the ideological prescription is the norm in practice: she need only look to Helen for supporting testimony.

Helen as scourge, pest and insult to the good name of women: the picture is not new.[47] But is Helen's character being too easily defined and condemned? First, it is not obvious to, nor the opinion of, all the characters at every point that Helen can be blamed for the war. Cassandra – and she always tells the truth – would seem to make Agamemnon and the Greeks responsible for the war (368ff.). Andromache rejects this explanation by preferring to blame the war on the fact that Paris was not killed as an infant (597–600). There is some irony, some pathos even, in this choice: Andromache's own son will be killed in order to prevent a war in the future. The chorus, though their condemnations of Helen are otherwise forthright (e.g. 780), sing an ode to *erōs*, one of the deities who lie behind Helen's effects on men (840ff.). Indeed they confirm that *erōs* came to Troy long before Helen, Eos and Zeus desiring two Trojans, Tithonus and Ganymede respectively. Of course,

---

[47] For the treatment of Helen in this play, see Amerasinghe (1973); Vellacott (1975), 136–48; M. Lloyd (1984); Gellie (1986). On Helen in the *Iliad*, 'the woman who subjugates warriors instead of being subject to them', see Arthur (1981), 26. On various treatments of Helen, from Homer to Shakespeare, see Suzuki (1989). For women as by nature evil, see Hesiod *WD* 57, 702ff.; and Loraux's excellent article (1978b).

Helen's entry after the ode on *erōs*, all dressed up, is ironic.[48] Menelaus, before the *agōn*, states that he came to Troy not for Helen's sake, but to take vengeance on the guest who betrayed him (864–5). The problem of causation, of Helen's responsibility for the war, continues in the *agōn*, where it becomes even more difficult to identify exactly who is responsible for the war. Is it the fact that Paris was born, and then not killed (919–22)?[49] Is it because of the power of Aphrodite (945ff., 989ff.)? Helen 'neither evades responsibility, nor pretends that she had any alternative'.[50] Hecuba's response to Helen's defence is revealing, because of its problems and anomalies.[51] In attacking Helen she establishes a sort of unholy alliance with the man who, in one way or another, has been responsible for the catastrophe inflicted on her *polis* and her family.[52] So, as we consider the effects war has on sexual relations, we must also see its effects on *philia*. War is the violent response to those who are your enemies; yet here the formerly hostile ally themselves to each other. But, if Helen's reputation as the evil woman is dependent to an extent on her responsibility for starting the war and that responsibility is questionable, then we have reason to pause before condemning her.

The ideology, then, which demands that women be silent, stay inside, nurture *sōphrosunē* and obey their husbands (or rather their masters), comes under attack from all sides: from the inspired Cassandra to the apparently promiscuous Helen; by the famously moderate Andromache; and in the rhetorical manipulations which Hecuba employs in her attempts to secure Helen's death.

But in this demonstration of the difficulties attached to the depiction of Helen as evil, promiscuous etc., we must not rob her of all threat to male security. She is dangerously beautiful

---

[48] Strohm (1957), 34; Havelock (1968), 126.

[49] Helen confuses *post hoc* and *propter hoc*: Vellacott (1975), 140.

[50] Vellacott (1975), 143; for responsibility as a growing fifth-century concern, see M. Lloyd (1984), 305.

[51] I will be dealing with the *agōn* in the next chapter. Hecuba's response may also be said to be conditioned by the appearance of Helen, standing before her as wife and noblewoman rather than as suppliant (1025ff.).

[52] Vellacott (1975), 146.

and has been the wife of three men, two of them perhaps simultaneously. Although Cassandra had suggested that Agamemnon and the Greeks were responsible for the war, she also says that, had Paris not married Helen, events would have been different. Any other bride would have provoked no talk (398: 'σιγώμενον'), and thus would have conformed to the dictates of ideology.[53] Even if Helen herself is not responsible for what happens to her and those associated with her, she is a woman around whom the codes of hospitality are transgressed, a war is started, and a decision of the Greek army (her death) perhaps overlooked (see chapter three). In her marriages, she seems to have upset the rules and conventions of exchange which are so constitutive of Greek, as well as of Athenian, culture.[54] Andromache, we remember, said that Helen was the offspring of many fathers, not one; and she has a destructive and indiscriminate effect on Greeks and barbarians alike (766–71).

Vellacott claims that Helen is different in that she has chosen her own husband.[55] This is not quite the case, at least according to Helen herself. She was first coerced by the power of Aphrodite (935ff.) to marry Paris, who took her by force, as did Deiphobus later (959ff.); and now Menelaus has returned to win her back in war. Still, it remains the case that clustered around her person are all the problems which men perceive about female sexuality, i.e. how their desire for women turns into a problem to be blamed on women. We might say that Helen is a representative threat: 'la femme brouille tout'.[56]

Dubois asserts that war reveals stress and division, as well

---

[53] In referring to the marriage of Helen and Paris at 398–9, Cassandra uses the word *kēdos*, also used to refer to Helen at *Ag.* 699; see Seaford (1987), 126. This can mean 'trouble' (Hom. *Il.* 1.445; 2.69; 18.53); 'funeral rites' (*Il.* 5.156; Hdt. 2.36); an object of care or anxiety (*Ag.* 699); and, presumably by association, connection by marriage (Hdt. 7.189; Aesch. *Supp.* 331; *Phoen.* 77). Cassandra's use of the word in *Troades* seems to make use of all the possible meanings.

[54] On woman as a sign in marriage exchange, see Lévi-Strauss (1969), 496; Bergren (1983), 75–8. Culture could be defined as that which provides structures of exchange – in language, marriage, money, foreign relations. On *xenia*, see Benveniste (1973), 77–82; Baslez (1984); Herman (1987); Lonis (1988).

[55] (1975), 143; Arthur (1981), 26.   [56] Loraux (1978a).

as human nature. War also, she claims, clarifies difference
('the showing forth of difference').[57] In summarizing my analysis of the male/female polarity as represented in *Troades*, we
see that such a characterization of war is not one we can
apply. First, there is a disruption of those practices and prescriptions which determine the difference of women from
men. The sort of labour which keeps women inside the *oikos*
has been curtailed by war: no more weaving at Trojan looms
(199ff.).[58] Women forsake their places inside and come into
the public sphere and speak. Second, war has caused the upset
of the normal structures of exchange.[59] The three marriages
of Helen, that character's possible promiscuity, her transgression (willing or otherwise) of the conventions governing the
giving of a woman to a man – all these contribute to our
picture of structures of exchange in disarray. Also, Helen,
even if she is a dangerous and promiscuous wife, still manages
to stimulate in men a desire so strong that it makes them
ignore the subversion of their own ideology. The problems
associated with Helen, though, are matters of the past. Similar
problems are foreseen for the future, but these are connected
with Cassandra, who, through marriage, will cause devastation in the House of Atreus. Even when Andromache acts in
accordance with ideology, her reward is to become the concubine of the son of her husband's murderer.

War has also revealed the hazy and insecure status of the
Greek wife. I refer to the pseudo-marriages of Cassandra and
Andromache. The war, which is men's responsibility, destroys
children who have been raised to perpetuate the male domination of the structures of exchange, civic discourse and ideology. A war, which the Greeks embarked upon in order to
redress a transgression of the code of hospitality and a theft of
a wife, destroys the very status quo it is supposed to protect.
In this respect, war is a gamble and possibly self-defeating.

[57] Dubois (1984), 81 and 88–9.
[58] Women weave, often, as against speaking: see Bergren (1983), 71–5.
[59] As Pericles' citizenship law testifies, the Athenians were attached to endogamy; see
Davies (1977); Patterson (1981); Baslez (1984), 94ff.

So, the difference between, or the hierarchy of, men and women is not clarified in the context of war, nor is it collapsed. Rather, it is rendered questionable. Of course, the questions which *Troades* raises about this central topic are not precisely the same as those we find in other tragedies of Euripides. But there remains the same overriding concern: how secure is men's self-definition when that self-definition depends on a certain attitude towards, and a certain set of discursive practices concerning women? There is a basic problem with the characterization of women as other: as other, they would be perceived as outside the circle of equals that is men. But women are inside as well, used for sexual pleasure and for the perpetuation of the species. As the other inside, they must be marginalized internally. The occasional outburst of a male desire for reproductive self-sufficiency (*autarkeia*) and virulent misogynistic tirades (Jason at *Med.* 568–75; Hippolytus at *Hipp.* 616–68) are manifestations, in a way, of male recognition of the problem men have created in their partial exclusion of women.

But these women who speak on the tragic stage are, of course, men, actors with their lines written by a man to be performed in front of (mainly) men. The citizens examine themselves in this female other. Since the other is necessarily (and however problematically) excluded, and since the audience (the self) uses the other for self-examination (which is often subversive and challenging), the audience, gathered at this central event of civic discourse, sees its ideology affirmed (women are other) as well as questioned (women are very problematically other). Athenian civic discourse is male-controlled yet it also offers potent criticism of the procedures and practices which lead to such control.

No one is free

Men define themselves against women: the free (men) against slaves. As has already been demonstrated in chapter one, all groups placed in opposition to men (the self) are also equated, as other, by analogy.[60] Thus women become slavish, as do barbarians, who in turn can be characterized as effeminate (Arist. *Pol.* 1252b).[61] Slavery, among Greek peoples, was an accepted fact, although towards the end of the fifth century and in the fourth century there was some discussion as to whether slavery was conventional or natural (Arist. *Pol.* 1253b, 1255a), even as to whether it should be condemned on moral grounds (Alcidamas, the pupil of Gorgias: schol. ad Arist. *Rhet.* 1373b).[62] However, as was observed by both Heraclitus (Kahn 83) and Aristotle (*Pol.* 1255a), it was a fact of war that the victors could enslave the surviving losers: in 421 BC (six years after their change of heart over Mytilene), the Athenians enslaved the women and children of Scione, an allied city which had revolted (Thuc. 5.32), and five years later those of Melos (Thuc. 5.116). On the one hand, it is these familiar consequences of war which *Troades* represents. Poseidon describes the now enslaved Trojan women waiting to be allotted to their new Greek masters (28ff.). The chorus (185, 204–6, 230–4), Hecuba (140, 192, 489ff., 507, 1271, 1280, 1311) and Andromache (577, 614–15, 660) have all become slaves.[63] The yoke of slavery has, according to Andromache, been brought upon the whole city of Troy (600). On the other hand, while all the characters understand what it means to be

---

[60] Dubois (1984), *passim*; Hall (1989), 206 (one of the moments when the interdependence of the polarities is sufficiently stressed); G. Lloyd (1966), 434: 'Two types of oversimplification seem to be particularly common in early Greek argumentation. 1) Opposites of any type tend to be taken as mutually exclusive alternatives (i.e. polarity) ... 2) The relationship of similarity tends to be assimilated to that of complete identity (i.e. analogy).'

[61] Note also *On Ancient Medicine* 16, where it says that all who are free fight well; see also Hdt. 7.104–5.

[62] For lists of lines in Euripides concerning slaves, see Decharme (1893), 162–71; A. Thomson (1898), 93; Nestle (1901), 348–61. A more fruitful survey can be found in Brandt (1973), whose main concerns are to show the differences between Euripides and the other two great tragedians in this respect, as well as the appearance of the noble-slave type (pp. 12–14). Unfortunately there is no discussion of *Troades*. Yet Synodinou (1977), 96–110 is right to criticize Brandt for not seeing the implied attack on slavery as an institution in the appearance of the noble slave; see also Neuberger-Donath (1970); di Benedetto (1971), 212–19; Kuch (1978); (1984), 103.

[63] This is also true in *Hecuba* and *Andromache*. For the former, see Daitz (1971); for the latter, see *Andr.* 12ff., 29–30, 99, 110, 114, 155, 163–8, 433–4, 933.

a slave and while their legal status as slaves is not in doubt, the play presents us with a number of reasons why calling these Trojan women slaves – fact of war though it may be – is not a simple matter.

One complicating factor is that all the slaves we see and hear about on the stage are women. Their experience, both before and after the war, may in some respects be analogous to that of slaves. For, if we understand slavery not just as a legally enforced social and economic position but as a lack of control over one's own life, as powerlessness, then the experience of women in marriage has its similarities to that of slaves. Cassandra, already violated by Ajax (70), must submit to an enforced marriage to Agamemnon (44). Helen, in the *agōn*, talks of being sold (to Paris) for her beauty (935–6), and of being forced to marry both Deiphobus and Paris (959–60, 962). In all of these cases (except the selling of Helen) the same word, in some form or another, is used: it is the word for 'violence' or 'force' (*bia*). Of course, we should be careful about trusting the testimony of Helen, both because of who she is and because what she says must be seen as determined by rhetoric and by her need to avoid execution at the hands of Menelaus. Nevertheless, to assert that men forced women into marriage or to perform sexual favours would not have been exceptional in fifth-century Athens. And it has already been seen that it is not only Cassandra who will suffer a slavery that is a form of marriage, i.e. sexual servitude. Andromache will experience the same thing (66off.). Hecuba mourns the servile and domestic tasks she may have to perform (489ff.), but then she is an old woman. For Andromache at least, and perhaps for the chorus (their status and age are not precisely defined), the future will be a gruesome caricature of past experience: 'marriage' dominated by men.

But we must not underestimate the change of status the women are suffering. It is most evident in the fact that the Trojan individuals whom Euripides puts on stage are all of royal blood. Andromache refers to this transformation bluntly (614–15: 'nobility has come to slavery'/'τὸ δ' εὐγενὲς ἐς δοῦλον ἥκει'), and she tells Astyanax that the nobility (744: 'τὸ

99

δ' ἐσθλὸν') of his father cannot help him. This reversal of fortunes is a consequence of war and therefore must be seen as a
cultural rather than a natural fact. However, if nobility is no
defence against becoming a slave, neither is victory. For the
only two supposedly free characters who appear on stage –
Talthybius and Menelaus – are both compromised as to their
freedom. Talthybius, who is sympathetic enough to think that
Cassandra's mania (as he sees it) is the result of a free spirit
resisting slavery (302–3), is himself described by Cassandra as
servile in his function as a herald (424–6: she calls him *latris*,
which means 'servant').[64] And he himself admits this to be the
case (710–11):

οὐχ ἑκὼν γὰρ ἀγγελῶ
Δαναῶν τε κοινὰ Πελοπιδῶν τ' ἀγγέλματα.

Unwillingly shall I announce
the common message of the Greeks and the sons of Pelops.

For Menelaus we must look at the *agōn*, where Helen indirectly challenges his claim to be free. Helen herself had in
the prologue been described by Poseidon as justly a prisoner
of war (35). In her speech, employing a traditional argument,
Helen dares Hecuba to be more powerful (948: 'κρείσσων')
than Zeus, Zeus who has power (949: 'κράτος') over the other
gods. Helen says that this is impossible, because Zeus, like
everyone else, is enslaved by Aphrodite (950: 'κείνης δὲ δοῦλός
ἐστι'). By making even the most powerful being in the uni-
verse subject to the power of another, Helen questions the
confident use of the free/slave polarity. But Menelaus concludes after the *agōn* that Helen's introduction of Aphrodite
was specious. He claims that Helen left for the stranger's bed
willingly (1037–8: 'ἑκουσίως'); which is, of course, precisely
what is at issue. But, while Menelaus seems firmly to deny
Helen's far-reaching implication that it is impossible to say

[64] Although heralds had an important role in religious and political life throughout
antiquity, democratic Athens developed a certain contempt for them: see *Heracl.*
120ff.; *Supp.* 426ff.; *Or.* 888ff; Cassio (1985), 59ff. While Talthybius is a slave
though free, Polyxena in *Hec.* is free in her slavery (i.e. by the manner of her
death): see Daitz (1971), 222; Vellacott (1975), 213; Luschnig (1976), 232.

that anyone has really done anything willingly, we suspect, and the Athenian audience suspected, that Menelaus will not kill Helen: he will, instead, be overcome with desire, thus flouting Hecuba's warning (890ff.), confirming her statement that a lover always remains a lover (1051), and demonstrating the truth of Helen's assertion that all are enslaved to Aphrodite.

We are therefore compelled to agree with Scodel's assertion: 'Freedom does not appear in the tragedy.'[65] We are also reminded of the conclusion Hecuba reaches in the eponymously titled play (*Hec.* 864–7):

> οὐκ ἔστι θνητῶν ὅστις ἔστ᾽ ἐλεύθερος.
> ἢ χρημάτων γὰρ δοῦλός ἐστιν ἢ τύχης,
> ἢ πλῆθος αὐτὸν πόλεος ἢ νόμων γραφαὶ
> εἴργουσι χρῆσθαι μὴ κατὰ γνώμην τρόποις.

> No mortal is free.
> Everyone is the slave of either money or chance,
> or the mob in the city or the writings of the laws
> compel them to adopt methods against their judgement.

A startling list, to be sure; and occasionally paradoxical, as when the Queen claims that some are enslaved to written laws (*Hec.* 866), the very things which usually mark out the Greeks as free as against barbarians (Hdt. 7.104) and tyrannies (*Supp.* 433). But the essential point is the same as that implied by Helen: no one is free. Yet Hecuba, the slave, will set Agamemnon, the king, free (*Hec.* 869). In a sophistic context these lines concentrate 'a protest against any and all restrictions',[66] a protest which can be found in the Old Oligarch with reference to democracy's tyranny over aristocrats (Ps. Xen. *Ath. Pol.* 1.8), in Antiphon's criticism of all binding social institutions (DK 87B44), and in the power-hedonism advocated by Plato's Callicles (*Gorg.* 491eff.). In the extremity of her situation, Hecuba has learned that all are enslaved, but she has also discovered 'a marvellous resurgence of freedom and power. And this is the paradox. If there really is no law, and no order, then a person can do what she really wants ... Yet her triumph coincides with her full acceptance of slavery' (see *Hec.* 756–7).[67] The freedom Hecuba has acquired is the freedom to destroy others and herself. While slavery is impotent, this freedom-in-slavery is merely negative. In *Troades* there is no occurrence during the play which quite matches this paradox of freedom-in-slavery. But the women we see, each of them confronted with a new life of slavery, are not simply passive and resigned, as Steidle argues.[68] Cassandra, inspired, looks forward to taking vengeance on those who have killed her loved ones, just as Hecuba actually does in the play named after her. Andromache argues with herself about whether she should submit to her new condition and compares her position negatively to that of the dead Polyxena. She also insults Odysseus for engineering the death of her son (724), causing Talthybius to remind her of her powerlessness (730). Helen probably beguiles her way to freedom by proclaiming her slavery (although her 'slavery', *qua* wife, is a condition she can never escape). Hecuba, the barbarian slave, demands the death of Helen the Greek, and scorns the Greeks for the killing of her grandson (1159ff.). In contrast to Talthybius, then, who must against his will deliver the words of his masters, Hecuba and the other Trojan women, supposedly now slaves, have at least the freedom to speak frankly.[69]

The Trojan War plays of Euripides (*Andromache*, *Hecuba* and *Troades*) are the only extant tragedies with slaves as their leading characters. It can be no accident, then, that a sense of powerlessness, that words of privation and desolation dominate the play.[70] But that is not all: the distinction between the free and the enslaved is represented as a messy one. Among the free there already exist relations of servitude: woman to man, herald to master, men and gods to Aphrodite. Those who are enslaved betray characteristics of the free which the free themselves do not possess. As was the case with women, Euripides exploits war to allow those usually denied access to

---

[67] Reckford (1985), 123–4. Synodinou (1977), 24: *Hecuba* 'confuses the conventional distinction between free and slave'.
[68] (1968), 51.   [69] Scodel (1980), 108.   [70] Poole (1976), esp. 264.

civic discourse – slaves – to speak on the stage of the Theatre of Dionysus. Again as with women, the result is an examination of a constitutive polarity which leads to a complication of the other. Slaves – free-speaking and noble – may not produce a sustainable self-definition for the free.

Who is the barbarian?

The polarity free/slave most clearly implicates one other constitutive opposition of fifth-century Athenian ideology: Greek/barbarian. Aristotle (*Pol.* 1252b), Aeschylus (*Pers.* 241–4), Herodotus (7.135) and Isocrates (4.181) all tell us that Greeks equated barbarians with slaves.[71] The establishment of the Greek/barbarian polarity has already been considered in chapter one, but some of the points are worth reiteration. After the victory in the Persian Wars, the Greeks were able to define themselves against the defeated barbarians. The stressing of cultural difference – based on differences in language, religion, politics, behaviour – was also an assertion of Greek superiority, examples of which are scattered around fifth-century texts.[72] In doing this, the Greeks used an already existent process of self-definition against an other. More, though: so pervasive was the notion of barbarian that fifth-century authors used it to describe inherited figures from Homer and elsewhere. This is particularly the case in tragedy, which as a body of texts most strikingly betrays the fascination with this new other.[73] 'The time had come for the tragic poets, as witnesses to Athenian democratic ideology, to invent the mythical barbarian ... The Hellenocentric view-

---

[71] Many slaves in Athens were likely to have been barbarians: Garlan (1988), 46–7, 120–1; Hall (1989),196.

[72] For collections of such examples, see Bacon (1961); Baldry (1965); Synodinou (1977), 50–4; Kerferd (1981), 156–9; Hall (1989).

[73] Aeschylus' *Persae* is the first extant example of the polarization: see Hall (1989), 57; and for its depiction of the Persians as both hauntingly similar and radically other, see Goldhill (1988a). It is worth mentioning that although the polarity did not exist in Homer, i.e. his Trojans are not barbarians, so infected by barbarization had the interpretation of Homer become that he could be championed as the educator of the Greeks precisely because he demonstrated the superiority of Greek over barbarian; see K. King (1985), 47.

point of the tragic poets therefore led them to reinterpret myths by turning heroic characters of Hellenic or indeterminate ethnicity into barbarians, and by inventing other barbarian figures altogether.'[74]

But the important point is that the polarity can be seen to be established in and as a result of war. Euripides, though, writes about a different war, the Trojan War. Yet he inherited, from other tragedians and the public art of Athens, a concerted attempt to rewrite the Trojan War – and that means Homer – under the sign of the Persian War, in an analogous fashion to the reshaping of the Amazonomachy and Centauromachy.[75] In the fifth century, Homer's Trojans themselves are barbarized, becoming assimilated into a group which contained Phrygians, Persians and barbarians.[76] *Troades* is no exception to this general rule. Although Euripides is not as interested as either Aeschylus or Sophocles in giving particular details of barbarian customs, manners and culture, there is in the play explicit mention of the difference of barbarians (more of which below), as well as a rhetorical examination of the distinguishing signs of the barbarian.[77] Our questions must be: how will a tragic treatment of the Trojan War, written during the Peloponnesian War, represent these Greeks against these Trojans? In what ways are the Greeks distinguished from the barbarians? And will the Peloponnesian War, rather than the Persian War, prove to be the narrative that informs the play's treatment of the barbarian?

The first distinguishing signs are the names given to the

[74] Hall (1989), 102 and 113.

[75] Hall (1989), 102: Trojans became orientals and 'assumed defeated postures which echoed the sixth-century conceptualizations of Amazon Queens'.

[76] For this convenient, but ideological, tragic conflation, see Bacon (1961), 101–4; and now see Hall (1988) and (1989). In the fragments of Sophocles we get a much more foreign picture of the Trojans than we do in the extant plays. For examples of the conflation in *Hecuba*, see 4, 827, 1064, 1111, 1141.

[77] Bacon (1961), 168: in Euripides 'the actual concrete foreigner disappears, and we have instead the symbolic foreigner'; see also Aélion (1983) I.180–5. There is muddled criticism of this in Hall (1989), 160–2, which, oddly, amounts to an extended paraphrase of Bacon. On the play as a tragedy of groups, see Kitto (1961³), 213; Lee (1976), xxiv. Barlow (1986), 32 notes that Troy is occasionally seen as a person (e.g. 780, 1278, 1324). It is a nameless person, though; see 1278, 1319, 1322; Gilmartin (1970), 220.

respective peoples, armies and cities. The Greeks are most often called Achaeans (19, 86, 159, 305 etc.), as are their ships (81, 1017) and army (236, 863). They are also called Argives (167, 171, 179, 342 etc.), Danaoi (184, 230, 711, 1122; see also 447, 747) and Greeks (203, 267, 413, 900, 1019). Various Greek cities and kingdoms are mentioned: Argos (301, 313, 992, 1055, 1087), Sparta (994), Athens (803, 974), Phthia (187; see 575, 1125), Ithaca (277). These are the homes, of course, of prominent Greeks: Agamemnon, Menelaus, Neoptolemus, Odysseus. And Greece itself is often alluded to (125, 490, 566, 678 etc.). Although the panhellenic nature of the expedition is referred to (413, 721), the list of cities given above reflects the fact that Greece was not a country, but a collection of independent states. The chorus, as they list their prospective destinations – Corinth, Athens, Sparta, Thessaly, Sicily, Thurii (203ff.) – can distinguish between cities they would prefer and those they would find obnoxious.

The Trojans most commonly call their city Troy (99, 100, 130, 173 etc.) and themselves Trojans (143, 157, 166, 289 etc.), though they also use Ilium (25, 145, 423, 511 etc.) and other well-known signposts such as Mount Ida (199, 1066) and Pergamum, the citadel built on the mountain (556-7, 851, 1065, 1295-6). But the Trojan women are also identified as barbarian. This is achieved first by the use of references to Troy as Phrygian or Asian (the former is very much more pervasive than the latter). At the beginning of the play, Poseidon tells us he has come to the city of the Phrygians (7; see also 531, 567, 994), and throughout the play we hear of Phrygian spoils (18, 574), troubles, strength and so on (432, 754 etc.).[78] Andromache expected her son to be king of Asia (748), something which Helen claims Paris was offered at the Judgement: leading a Phrygian army he would conquer Greece and control Asia and the boundaries of Europe (925-8). To call Troy Phrygian (or Asian) is to barbarize it.

[78] The Trojans in *Hecuba* are normally called Phrygians; but they are also barbarians (see 328ff., 734). For Troy as *Phrugōn polis*, see *Hec.* 4; *Andr.* 194, 291, 363, 455; *Bacch.* 58; *IA* 682, 773, 1290; Chalkia (1986), 193.

Hecuba makes this more explicit when she laments the passing of Troy's greatness (1277–8):

> ὦ μεγάλα δή ποτ' ἀμπνέουσ' ἐν βαρβάροις
> Τροία ...

O Troy, who once among barbarians breathed forth
great things ...

But, even with names, the identification of Trojans as just barbarians is not a simple matter. Hecuba, as she mourns the loss of her sons, distinguishes between Phrygians, Trojans and barbarians (476–8); and, answering Helen in the *agōn* about the Judgement of Paris, she separates barbarians from Phrygians (973–4). Divisions can be made between the Greeks as well, between Achaeans and Greeks in fact (294). However, the names given to the two parties cannot be the focus of the difference (or the confusion of that difference) between them. After all, the English can call themselves English, British, European or western: each of the titles works within a different system of distinctions. Since the Greeks believed they differed from barbarians in cultural ways, it is to the information we are given about those areas that we must turn.

First, the Greeks. They have won this war (at least in conventional terms; see chapter three), but we know from the prologue that they are doomed to an unpleasant future. Whatever the reasons for this – it may be their hubris, it may be the whim of the gods, or both[79] – it is important that the victors are not painted in any glorious colours. It is important because it is part of the difference between Greek and barbarian that the latter is defined by immoral or cowardly behaviour.[80] We have already discussed in the first section of this chapter how the Greeks have committed sacrilege. Agamemnon sacrificed his own daughter in order that the war could be prosecuted (371). Hecuba's view of Odysseus is extreme and negative (278ff.). Cassandra criticizes the Greek expedition

---

[79] O'Neill (1941), 319; Kitto (1961³), 212; Erbse (1984), 60–72.
[80] Note Phrygian cowards (*Or.* 1351–2, 1447–8, 1483–5), the threatened cannibalism of Polymestor (*Hec.* 1070–3), the tendency to incest and polygamy (*Andr.* 168ff.), and to intrafamilial murder (*Med.* 1339–40); see Hall (1989), 124–6, 188.

in paradoxical but powerful terms (368ff.), implying that the Greeks have been stupid to start offensive action (400). Polyxena has been sacrificed to the ghost of Achilles – 'unholy' is Hecuba's description of this act (628). Odysseus has persuaded the army to kill Astyanax (721), a decision criticized again by Hecuba (1158ff.). The news of the execution is something which Talthybius claims he regrets to announce, feeling an excess of pity (786ff.), which may imply a general lack of that emotion among the Greeks.[81] But for most of the play, even though their influence hangs over it, the Greeks are absent.[82] Menelaus appears briefly, saying little, and (in one critic's opinion) acting as an advertisement for the stupidity of the war.[83] The representative Greek is really Talthybius.

Opinions differ over the herald. Conacher thinks him harsh and sinister. Barlow and Gilmartin offer more fruitful evaluations.[84] While he is alien to the Trojans, he is sympathetic to their predicament, a sympathy otherwise lacking. Hecuba goes so far as to call him 'friend' or 'ally' (267: 'ὦ φίλος'), which is strange given the normal characterization of barbarians as incapable of maintaining *philia*.[85] But we should remember that a little later Hecuba attacks the Greek Odysseus for perverting friendships and alliances (288). So, although the Greeks whom Talthybius represents are inglorious (and, incidentally, compare unfavourably with the Greek heroes of the Ganymede Ode), the herald is, as befits his function, stuck between the two groups, working for one, pitying the other.

What of the Trojans? The political distinction – freedom against tyranny, the independent states of Greece against the orderless hordes under Xerxes – was probably the most important of the differences which Greeks saw between themselves and barbarians.[86] The tyranny of Troy is referred to by

---

[81] B. Vickers (1973), 94.
[82] Poole (1976), 275; Scodel (1980), 73.   [83] Luschnig (1971), 11.
[84] Conacher (1967), 144–5; Barlow (1986), 34; Gilmartin (1970). Kitto (1961³), 212 notes that while Hecuba's presence is constant, Talthybius comes in 'like a series of telegrams'.
[85] Aesch. *PV* 224–5; *Hec.* 328–9, 1199–1201; *Hel.* 274; Pl. *Gorg.* 510b–c; Pl. *Symp.* 182b–c; see Hall (1989), 194–5.
[86] Hall (1989), *passim*.

Hecuba (474, 1168–70), by Andromache (748), and also by Helen (though coming from a Greek woman who is appealing to her Greek husband in difficult circumstances, her reasons for so doing must be deemed rhetorical (927–8, 934)).[87] The difference in political constitution is matched by differences in dress and behaviour. For instance, there are the splendid oriental robes of Paris, to which Helen is so attracted (991–2). Astyanax is buried in Phrygian gowns (1218–20). There is the chorus' description of the Libyan flute and the Phrygian songs which were being played and sung the night of the Greek entry into the city (541ff.).[88] The description of the festivities need not be accurate and may, in fact, be more Greek than barbarian, but the important point is that the Trojans are associated with Libya and Phrygia. The same can be said of Hecuba's aside about Phrygian education at 1209ff., and her prayer to the son of Cronos as 'Phrygian Lord' (1288).[89]

If the Greeks do not always act like Greeks, at least, we feel sure thus far, the Trojans are tyrannical, fond of expensive clothes, purveyors of exotic music; in short, they are barbarians. Helen herself confirms this when she says to Menelaus that she has brought benefit to Greece because the Greeks are not in the power of the barbarians (933). But it is around Helen that problems with the Greek/barbarian polarity are clustered, since she, like Talthybius only more so, tends to cross the boundary between Greek and barbarian. Andromache states that she is a pest to Greeks and barbarians alike (771), and Hecuba accuses her – this is ironically contemptuous coming from the Trojan queen – of being attracted by the oriental garb of Paris (991). Moreover, Helen has herself

[87] For Troy as a tyranny elsewhere, see *Hec.* 55–6, 365–6, 809; *Andr.* 3. Other barbarian tyrants: Thoas (*IT* 17, 1020); Polymestor (*Hec.* 979ff.).

[88] On Hecuba's *thrēnos* (98ff.) in contrast to the Greek paean (126), see Hall (1989), 132; see also Alexiou (1974), 83–5.

[89] There is possibly a reference to Phrygian gods at 151–2, but it rests on Wilamowitz's emendation. The manuscripts have the adjective agreeing with the beats of the dancers' feet rather than with the gods. It must anyway be acknowledged that the Greeks themselves did not always see religion as a crucial difference between themselves and barbarians, as Herodotus testifies.

an eastern proclivity for extravagance and opulence (994–5, 1022–8, 1107–9; cf. *Or.* 1368ff.), and is fond (it is claimed) of barbarian subservience (1020–1).[90] In her criticisms of Helen, Hecuba brings out some of the negative aspects of Troy as a magnificent barbarian *polis*. Indeed, as Burnett has shown, the former wealth and pride of Troy before the war are constantly reiterated.[91] When, in the lines quoted earlier (1277–8), Hecuba mourned the past power of Troy, she also betrayed some of the fatal hubris and self-importance supposedly typical of barbarians. So, in trying to attack Helen, Hecuba becomes, as it were, a contemptuous Greek. The *agōn* shows Hecuba being transformed before our eyes into a sympathetic Greek. How? Apart from her criticisms of luxury and extravagance (over which she must have presided), her speech is a model of Greek agonistic rhetoric. When confronting a barbarian in a debate, a Greek would surely be tempted to make use of the original linguistic distinction and cast doubt on the comprehensibility of his barbarian opponent.[92] This is Agamemnon's strategy in his debate with Teucer in Sophocles' *Ajax* (*Aj.* 1263; see also Gorgias' Palamedes at DK 82B2a). Helen does no such thing here (but how could she, being a 'barbarian' herself?); in fact, Hecuba persuades the Greek Menelaus. Connected with this sudden possession of a fine Greek skill is Hecuba's insistence on the rationality of the gods. Her attack on *amathia* (irrationality), another barbarian characteristic (see Ar. *Clouds* 492),[93] again marks her out as not quite a simple barbarian.

Statements of Greek superiority are legion in extant Greek literature (although the work of Herodotus is a complex and subtle treatment of such claims). But, in Euripides, there is

[90] Extravagant barbarian subservience at *Or.* 1507–9; and see Synodinou (1977), 46–50; Zeitlin (1980), 59.
[91] Trojan wealth (497, 506, 582, 991–6, 1253; cf. *Hec.* 923ff.); pride (152, 474–5, 748, 1020–1, 1169, 1277–8): see Burnett (1977), 310–12.
[92] Isocrates (*Paneg.* 50; *Antidosis* 293–4) states that the possession of *logos* is what distinguishes the Greek from the barbarian; and this is *logos* as both speech and reason: see Baldry (1965), 22; Buxton (1982), 58–9; Hall (1989), 199–200.
[93] Hall (1989), 122–3.

also a certain barbarian contempt for Greeks. In *Andromache* (243–4), Andromache rejected Hermione's implication that barbarian mores are inferior:

Ερ. οὐ βαρβάρων νόμοισιν οἰκοῦμεν πόλιν.
Αν. κἀκεῖ τά γ αἰσχρὰ κἀνθάδ' αἰσχύνην ἔχει.

Her. We do not live in a city with barbarian laws [customs].
And. Shameful things bring shame there and here.

In *Troades*, Hecuba attacks the Greeks, and uses the same adjective (*aischros*) to register her disapproval of Astyanax's murder (1190–1). And Andromache expresses this same evaluation explicitly in the terms of Greek/barbarian (764):[94]

ὦ βάρβαρ' ἐξευρόντες Ἕλληνες κακά.

O Greeks, who have devised barbarian evils.

We find ourselves in a confusing situation. Greeks are more barbarian than barbarians; barbarians show Greek tendencies; Helen oscillates between the two. It is perhaps no surprise that it should be Andromache who offers the most explicit statement of the confusion surrounding the Greek/barbarian distinction, as it is she – the captured Trojan princess rather then Helen, the transgressive Greek – who represents the perfect wife in the terms of Athenian ideology (643ff.). The extremity of Euripides' treatment of the Greek/barbarian distinction requires special attention.

In her recent book, Edith Hall has argued that the Trojan plays of Euripides 'come closer than any other extant fifth-century source to subverting the antithesis on a moral level of Greek and barbarian'.[95] How are we to explain the subversion of a polarity which, as Hall in the rest of her book is at pains to point out, was central to an Athenian citizen's sense of himself? Generally, it can be noted that Euripides' examination of Greek superiority lies in the representation of two interdependent types of character: the Greek who behaves like

---

[94] Cf. Soph. *Aj.* 1259–63; *IT.* 1174. On inward and outward barbarism in *Andromache*, see Synodinou (1977), 54–60.
[95] Hall (1989), 217.

a barbarian and the barbarian who is, in Greek terms, noble. In the first instance, 'barbarian' is used as a portmanteau term for outrageous behaviour regardless of the ethnicity of the perpetrator.[96] But, given Greek contempt for barbarians, it is not surprising to find the adjective employed in this manner. And such a use cannot explain the many examples in tragedy of the noble barbarian (apart from the Trojan women in *Troades*, mention should be made of Polyxena and Andromache in *Hecuba* and *Andromache* respectively).[97] Hall's attempts to explain the tragic phenomenon of the noble barbarian are worth examining.

When barbarians are the principal characters and the Greeks are by and large absent (as in *Troades*), it is inevitable, indeed necessary, that tragedy should allow the audience to identify with suffering protagonists. And that suffering will produce sympathy in proportion to the nobility of the character. Still, this first explanation is insufficient. The question is not only whether the Trojan women are sympathetic, because of course they are; rather, we should ask why Trojan women – barbarians – have been chosen as the principal characters in the first place. And however sympathetic the Trojan women are or become, they remain barbarians, subject to tyranny and subservience, two conditions that remained inimical to the Athenians. Thus, Euripides challenges the fact that, in the terms of ideology, the conjunction of nobility and barbarianism remained an oxymoron. And the question of the likely audience response is further complicated by the fact that the Greek/barbarian, slave/free and friend/enemy polarities are interdependent. The subversion of any of these polarities was often carried out by describing one term of one polarity with a culturally and ideologically inappropriate term from another. Such is the case when Talthybius notes that the enslaved Cassandra possesses a free spirit (302–3: 'τοὐλεύθερον') or when the barbarian, Hecuba, calls the Greek, Talthybius, friend (267). Thus, just as ideology demands that all the

---

[96] Hall (1989), 203–10; see also Grube (1941), 290.
[97] Hall (1989), 211ff.; see also Delebecque (1951), 406.

polarities I mentioned be mutually reinforcing, *Troades*, in complicating one, subverts the other. A more obvious test case, perhaps, is when Hecuba, during the *agōn*, begins to adopt Greek moral positions. The change could be explained in terms of the noble barbarian, but that would be to neglect the influence that the Greek, Helen, has on the transformation. For Hecuba's 'Greekness' is temporary, used only to scupper the arguments of Helen. How could the accuser remain barbarian and condemn Helen, the Greek who loved being barbarian? What would be the point, in front of a Greek judge, of criticizing barbarian transgressions of Greek (not to say Athenian) ideology from a non-Greek perspective? Hecuba's 'Greekness' is rhetorically determined.

A second possible explanation offered by Hall is that Euripides was, in this area as in others, influenced by progressive, contemporary thought. There may have been a late fifth-century perception that, although all mankind had formerly been divided into Greeks and barbarians, this division was both incorrect and unhelpful (Pl. *Statesman* 262d), and there were various attempts to argue for the unity of mankind.[98] Hippias (Pl. *Prot.* 337c–e) states that mankind is by nature one family (and he himself wore Persian clothes). Antiphon seems to assert that no natural distinction can be made between Greeks and barbarians, using biological arguments (DK 87B44b, 45–7, 63, 65, 67–71). Thucydides, though he scorns barbarians (1.18.2), also notes that the distinction is historical: in the past there were no barbarians (as against Greeks), for Greeks themselves were barbarian (1.5.1, 1.6.5).[99] But it is not from these sorts of contemporary thoughts that the Euripidean scrutiny of the Greek/barbarian polarity issues. Hall wants to argue that Euripides is being sophistic in a more specialized sense: Euripides' subversion of the polarity should not be seen as evidence that 'he or his contemporaries had disowned the usual belief in Hellenic superiority ... but that it was so fundamental a dogma as to produce striking rhetorical

---

[98] Baldry (1965); Hall (1989), 160.
[99] See Hall (1989),168ff. on the non-Greek parentage of many heroes.

effects on being inverted'.[100] As it cannot be denied that there were elements of showmanship in some sophistic subversion, this seems to be a more powerful argument. But two objections can be made. First, sophists who attacked traditions or conventions were often not received as playful entertainers striving for striking rhetorical effects, but as dangerous subversives who threatened the stability of society.[101] Second, as Hall herself says, no contemporary thinker was as extreme as Andromache in *Troades* (764).[102]

Finally, Hall is ready to see the importance of the Peloponnesian War: 'When the Peloponnesian or Theban characters turn into "enemies", the logic of the tragic narrative dictates that the barbarians imperceptibly turn into "friends", and assume the role of surrogate Athenians. *Andromache* and *Troades* fight the Peloponnesian War on a mediated poetic plane.'[103] No doubt, to some in the audience, this would be true. And to claim that the Athenian self identified with a tragic other is the basic model of tragic didacticism outlined in chapter one. But Hall's reading does justice neither to the complexities of the attribution and value of barbarianism and otherness represented by the conflicting voices in *Troades*, nor to the way in which, in the latter half of the fifth century and most especially during the Peloponnesian War, the idea of barbarian as other was complicated by events and experience. Our evidence about late fifth-century Athens seems to show that the rigidity of the distinction between Greek and barbarian, or at least its enforcement in ordinary life, was being eroded. The Athenians (like Helen) were noted for their attraction to barbarian clothing,[104] and Athens was a centre of trade for the world of the Aegean, the richest city in the Greek world, and the ruler of an empire which had its eastern limits

---

[100] Hall (1989), 222.

[101] For the prosecution of sophists (Euripides possibly included) in Athens, see chapter four ('Senses of time: the play').

[102] (1989), 221.

[103] (1989), 214.

[104] Ps. Xen. *Ath. Pol.* 2.8. The Greek/barbarian distinction may not have been the only one difficult to perceive from appearances: the same author (1.10ff.) remarks on how difficult it was to distinguish between slaves and citizens in Athens.

in Ionia, bordering on the Persian Empire. Athens was in contact with barbarians in both war and peace. A few years after the production of *Troades*, Alcibiades would defect temporarily to the Persian side. And the Persians became increasingly involved in hostilities as the war progressed (the war saw the introduction of the Persians – the original barbarian other – into Greek armies);[105] so much so, in fact, that the Spartan general Callicratidas lamented Persians coming between two Greek cities (Xen. *Hell.* 1.6.7). Besides, we know that there was plenty of contact and communication between Greeks and non-Greeks in the fifth century, and also that it was not always easy to maintain with confidence that there was a notional unity called *Hellas*.[106] Herodotus tells the story of the establishment of the Greek/barbarian polarity, achieved by the successful repulsion of the barbarian hordes under Xerxes. Its privileged force in the service of self-definition depends to some extent on distortion: the greater the numbers of the invading forces, the more powerful the fact of Greek victory. The numbers of the Persian army, as Herodotus gives them, are plainly impossible: in recording them, he tells the history of the invention of the barbarian other and its necessary opposite, the Greek self.[107] Thucydides, the historian of the Peloponnesian War, shows that self in a process of disintegra-

---

[105] On Persia's involvement in the latter stages of the Peloponnesian War, see Meiggs (1972), 351–74.

[106] Hall (1989), 178–9.

[107] Here are the figures of Xerxes' armed forces: army – 1,700,000 + 100,000 cavalry + 300,000 added *en route*; fleet – 1,207 ships (see Aesch. *Pers.* 341ff.) with 200 per ship = 241,400 + 30 marines per ship = 36,210; 3,000 penteconters with 80 men per ship = 240,000 + 120 European ships (200 per ship) = 24,000. So, the army is 2,100,000; and the fleet has 4,327 ships with 541,610 men on board. Put together = 2,641,610. Herodotus then doubles the figure by adding on 'camp-followers' = 5,283,220. Finally, Herodotus, no doubt enjoying all this, restrains himself from a further addition, that of cooks, concubines, eunuchs, beasts of burden and Indian dogs (see Hdt. 7.60.1, 87.1, 89.1, 97, 184ff.). These are all impossible figures. Here are some more recent estimates, mainly based on supply logistics: How and Wells (1912), *ad loc.*: army – 360,000; fleet – 800; Bum (1962), 326–32: army – 210,000; fleet – 533; Hignett (1963), 345–56: army – 180,000; fleet – 600. It is surely no accident that Herodotus is nearer to the figures given in the epitaph, which he himself gives (Hdt. 7.228), of the Spartans at Thermopylae: an insight into the creation of a paradigmatic myth. Hall (1989) does not consider this topic.

tion. No longer does war clarify and impose difference. The other is no longer an alien invader but a Greek from within. The principal difference between Greek and barbarian was that the latter did not speak Greek. (Interestingly, the Egyptian definition of barbarian has a similarly linguistic base, except, of course, that it refers to all those who do not speak Egyptian: Hdt. 2.158.5.) As we saw in chapter one, Thucydides, in his account of the *stasis* at Corcyra, refers to the invention of a new semantics, a new language. So, are these Greeks still speaking Greek? If not, are they still Greeks? Or have they become barbarians, as Andromache suggests at *Troades* 764–5? Euripides' Trojan War, like the Peloponnesian War, makes the identification of Greek as against barbarian problematic.

Friends and enemies

Euripides' polemic scrutiny of the Greek/barbarian polarity implicates the final polarity I am going to discuss – friend versus enemy, or *philos/echthros* – if only because the barbarian came to be other originally by being *echthros*. Benveniste, starting from Homer, has demonstrated that the word *philos* cannot be separated from the institution of hospitality, with its obligation of reciprocity. Still, even within Benveniste's own terms the word remains thoroughly ambiguous: 'beloved' (Hom. *Il.* 1.20); 'one's own' (*Il.* 5.480, 9.555, 22.408); 'friend, kith or kin' (*Il.* 14.256); husband (Hom. *Od.* 15.22); 'lover' (Xen. *Mem.* 3.11.4); 'nearest and dearest' (Aesch. *Pers.* 851, Aesch. *Eum.* 216, Soph. *OT* 366, Soph. *OC* 1110, *Med.* 16); 'ally' (Xen. *Hell.* 6.5.48, cf. *Med.* 898).[108] The institution of *philia* also describes a code which prescribes benefit to one's friends and harm to one's enemies; that is, a code of heroes, of politicians within domestic politics, and of foreign states.[109]

In *Troades*, the code of *philia* has already been transgressed:

---

[108] Benveniste (1973), 273–88; Fraisse (1974), 72ff.; Herman (1987); Schein (1988), 182–90; Blundell (1989), 26–50.
[109] Knox (1964); Connor (1971), 30–80, 99–108; Herman (1987); Blundell (1989); and see n.85 for barbarians as unable to maintain *philia*.

Paris, the host-deceiver (866: 'ξεναπάτης'), has stolen the wife of Menelaus, thereby justifying bellicose reaction. War, in a sense, means that a relationship of *philia* has broken down, that, as a network, it is no longer functioning.[110] Indeed, one sign of the Trojan women's depressed post-war condition is that they have lost their *philoi*. This is true of the chorus (1081) and of Andromache (661, 673). The attribution of *philos* to Hector's shield rather than to Hector himself (1222) indicates that the relation of *philia* which joined Hector to the women is no longer present: the same can be said of the reference to Priam as *aphilos* (1313). It is also true of the Greek women left back in Greece (376ff.). But the effects of war are not only seen in the loss of friends and relatives which each side experiences at the hand of the other; war makes both groups look inwards, finding enemies where there were friends, or harming their friends instead of their enemies. Agamemnon has killed his daughter for the sake of the expedition, an action which Cassandra describes explicitly in the language of *philia* (370).[111] Odysseus, in Hecuba's view, is an untrustworthy perverter of *philia* relationships (288). Hecuba, the barbarian, and Talthybius, the Greek, develop a friendship, both by direct address (267) and in the herald's assistance with the burial of Astyanax (1147ff.). Hecuba and the other Greek who appears on stage, Menelaus, form an alliance (see 912–13) against Helen, who is herself, as wife, a *philos* of Menelaus. Hecuba even pleads with Menelaus to kill Helen on the grounds that he will thereby not betray his allies (1044–5: 'συμμάχους') whom she has killed. Hecuba takes the Greek side against a Greek. Socrates says that it is generally thought wrong to enslave friends, but right to enslave enemies (Xen. *Mem.* 2.2.2), yet the Greeks, represented by Menelaus, are enslaving his (temporary) *philos*, Hecuba. As for Helen, she is both friend and enemy, and her fate is not clear (see chapter three).

Further problems issue from the ambiguity of *philos*. Paris breaks the code of *philia* (i.e. as friendship and hospitality) by

---

[110] Dubois (1984), 88–9.   [111] Cf. Euripides fr. 582; Scodel (1980), 72.

establishing another form of *philia* (marriage); this is an irony that pervades the play. The result of Paris' marriage is that Trojan women will be forced into marriages with those who were formerly their enemies, definitely not their *philoi*. Andromache expresses her disgust at women who can swap partners with facility (667–8), but she realizes that her own temperament, her own exemplary behaviour as a wife, leads her to expect a woman/wife to love (*philein*) the man she is given. And that, of course, is Hecuba's rejected advice to her (699–700). Once confronted by Helen, the woman who has had too many husbands (*philoi*), Hecuba's views are a little different: the woman who betrays her husband should die (1032).

Finally, *philos* does not just refer to a personal relationship; it has its place in the public sphere as well. Paris' transgression of the code of hospitality, which is a relation between individuals and families, brings about the public action of war. Ideologically, the public and the personal aspects of *philia* do not interpenetrate, but here, as in *Andromache, Hecuba* and Sophocles' *Antigone*, we are shown how the public and the personal can be in conflict in terms of *philia*.[112] Cassandra reveals her continuing loyalty to the fatherland by twice addressing it as 'beloved' (318, 458: 'φίλη πατρίς'). Hecuba advises Andromache to foster Astyanax so that he can return to live in Troy once again (699ff.), but now any action concerning Astyanax has become implicated in the public as well as the personal spheres, as the Greek execution of him testifies. We are in a war, and would therefore expect sides to be clearly delineated in terms of *philia*, which after all governs whom one fights. War, however, does not just make the public and the personal difficult to disentangle; it also renders identification of who is *philos* and who is not a problematic and unpleasant exercise.

[112] See Goldhill (1986), 79–106. Blundell (1989), 50–9 gathers together examples of conflicting loyalties of kin and city, and conflicts between the demands of *philia* and other moral norms. For problems in *philia* in the other Trojan War plays of Euripides, see *Andr.* 26–8, 138–9, 170–6, 376, 416, 516, 530, 610–12, 655ff., 706–7, 723–4, 733–4, 742, 974–5, 985–6, etc.; *Hec.* 120ff., 828–30, 846–9, 855–6, 953ff., 983–5, 1000, 1114, 1199–1207, 1251.

So, the proper relations of enmity between the warring Trojans and Greeks, and those of friendship within each group, are confused. The effect of the war on the Trojan women is that they no longer have their old *philoi* (in the sense of family and friends), who have been replaced by former enemies; they have also lost their beloved fatherland (*philē patris*). The Greeks, on the other hand, have gained new *philoi* (in the sense of possessions), who will cause disruption when they return to their families. The questions asked of the institution of *philia* revolve around its potential in both the public and the private spheres. War reveals how these two spheres can be in conflict. Using perfectly proper criteria one can deem an enemy of one's *polis* – a public enemy – a personal *philos*;[113] and, as the *Palamedes* of Euripides perhaps exemplified, a *philos* in the public sense can be a personal enemy. *Troades*, along with *Hecuba* (see chapter one), shows that war is the result of transgression of *philia* codes, which the prosecution of war further upsets and complicates in spectacular ways.

In common with the rest of Greek tragedy, Euripides questions a series of mutually reinforcing polarities which are fundamental in the self-definition, the ideology, of the Athenian citizen. But what is distinctive about *Troades* in this connection is highlighted when the polarities are considered as part of a system. Two things are revealed: first, the extremity of the questioning; and second, the fact that that, in turn, has been produced under the pressures of war. There is something disturbing about this latter feature in that war is itself a principle of opposition and polarity or, as Dubois puts it, war 'is a temporary *agōn* which must end by affirming difference'.[114] But war, in Euripides as in Thucydides, manifestly fails to perform this function. In the prosecution of the Peloponnesian War, Thucydides shows the other – the barbarian – within, the fragility of alliance between cities and the instability

---

[113] Sophocles' *Antigone* examines this same problem; but see Hom. *Il.* 6.212ff. for Glaucus and Diomede.
[114] (1984), 88.

within cities.[115] In *Troades*, Euripides represents the difficulties of attributing otherness, whether that be to gods, women, slaves, barbarians or enemies. The pressure of war sees to it that the other cannot quite hold as an easily definable entity; and, since the two terms necessarily depend on each other, the same must be true for the self. Such a representation complicates both Zeitlin's model of self-examination *otherwise* and self-definition against the other.

One can sense something of the poignancy of this for the Athenian audience. For they were members of a society that had committed itself to viewing war as a supreme human activity and the standard by which human achievement was measured. They were happy to accept and perpetuate (through, for example, the Panathenaea) the cultural authority of Homer, the poet of war, whose epic subjects remained those of their own tragedians. Yet their actual experience of war may have provoked very different and less worthy responses. But this, for the Athenians, was the agony of war. And that leads us into the one polarity which has not yet been considered. War produces a winner and a loser. War is an *agōn*.

---

[115] *Stasis* is itself the polarization of the *polis* – so Gehrke (1985), 245–9 – yet the polarization of the citizens could be said to be a manifestation of the failure of the polarities constitutive of ideology to perform their function (i.e. of stabilizing and justifying the various inclusions and exclusions practised by the dominant group). It is no accident that one of the features of the *stasis* at Corcyra was the freeing of slaves (Thuc. 3.73); see Fuks (1971), 49.

3

THE *AGŌN*

The *agōn*, which orginally meant an assembly or assembling, was a pervasive institution.[1] But all the assemblies in the classical era to which *agōn* could be said to refer have one thing in common: they are games, tests or competitions. As such, they are regulated and are supposed to deliver a winner and a loser.[2] The *agōn* describes activities as diverse to us as athletic competitions, set-piece rhetorical debates and war. The last of these perhaps looks strangest to us, but that war is an *agōn* can be gleaned from a number of sources. In the *Iliad* (23.667–75), Epeius perceives athletic victory as 'a surrogate to achievement on the battlefield'.[3] Herodotus tells us that, before the battle of Plataea, the Spartans were anxious to have a certain Tisamenus fight on their side. The latter had been informed by the oracle that he would win the greatest contests, which he interpreted as the heptathlon at the Olympic Games. The Spartans, however, believed that the *agōn* referred to war (Hdt. 9.33). And at 2.89.8 Thucydides has Phormio encouraging his troops for the forthcoming *agōn* (here a sea battle). The verbal form – 'ἀγωνίζεσθαι' – is also used for fighting in both Herodotus (1.76.4, 82.3) and Thucydides (1.36.3, 6.16.6).

As *agōn*, war endures a welter of prescriptions and rules. A famous instance of regulated war comes when a border dispute in 550 BC between Argos and Sparta is settled by an *agōn* between 300 troops on each side (Hdt. 1.82). The rules of war

---

[1] Rankin (1983), 102; see also Finley and Pleket (1976), 20–2.
[2] Lonis (1979), 25–7. On the importance of victory in classical antiquity, see Poliakoff (1987), *passim*. Victory is an important theme in Pindar: on this, see Gouldner (1965), 46–55; Lefkowitz (1976); Mullen (1982), 196ff.; Nisetich (1989), 34–49. However, for the ambiguities and dangers which arise out of victory, see Crotty (1982).
[3] Poliakoff (1987), 105.

cover the choice of locations, the time limit to be imposed, the setting-up of trophies, the treatment of heralds, the proper methods for agreeing to treaties and for declaring war in the first place.[4] Most of these concern conduct before and after an engagement, but the rules governing the battles themselves do, as Lonis argues, tend to disallow activities which interfere with hoplite tactics. In this way, the rules of war in the classical era stress the hoplite phalanx.[5] That is to say, even though there is fundamental continuity in agonistic principles and mentality between the Homeric and the classical era, the rules as well as the tactics of war have changed. There is some overlap in the use of heavy-armed infantry (see the appendix), but classical warfare is to be placed in between war fought predominantly by aristocratic individuals (Iliadic warfare) and war waged increasingly by professional mercenaries (one can see this developing towards the end of the Peloponnesian War).[6] Thus far I have, for the most part, been describing ideology concerning war: no doubt, in practice, this was compromised, whether through infringements of rules or through

---

[4] For the rules of war, see e.g. Pritchett (1971–91) II. 147–89; V. 203. On the custom of the burial of the dead after battle, see now the extensive discussion in Pritchett (1971–91) IV. 94–259; see Ducrey (1968) and Pritchett (1971–91) V. 203–45 on the treatment of the vanquished.

[5] Lonis (1979), 28–30. Some actions in war look distinctly odd unless we accept Lonis' argument, e.g. Cleomenes' refusal to take possession of towns (Hdt. 6.82; see also Plut. *Apo. Lac.* 231e). Of course, in agreeing with Lonis to the extent I do, I am not urging that the rules of war were invented for the purpose of producing outstanding hoplite performance, which was more likely a result of coercion and fear; for religious sanctions which surrounded the breaking of war rules, and which may have inhibited the use of *apatē* in war, see Pritchett (1971–91) I. 327–31. He notes in this connection the piety of some generals (Nicias, for instance) and the rage which followed the mutilation of the Herms in 415 BC.

[6] It might be thought that some conflict would have arisen over the avowed collective virtues of the hoplite phalanx (in one *agōn*) and the individual glory won in sport (another *agōn*). Poliakoff (1987), 113 goes so far as to say, and quite convincingly, that the concentration on athletics after the advent of hoplite warfare shows that games were meant to provide individuals with the sorts of rewards that war in its collective character could no longer offer. Yet this approach cannot quite deal with Alcibiades, who boasts of his Olympic victories, claiming that they are good for the image of Athens: Thuc. 6.16; Plut. *Alc.* 12.1. On the enigmatic relations between athletics and political leadership in fifth-century Athens, see Kyle (1987), 68, 154; Finley and Pleket (1976), 102ff.; Pleket (1976). Also, it must not be forgotten that sport could be seen as an entirely proper training for war: Xen. *Mem.* 3.12; Poliakoff (1987), 96–103.

both sides claiming victory. Still, it was the Peloponnesian War, with its brutality and longevity – both unprecedented – which posed problems for war as *agōn*. Euripides' depiction of the Trojan War in *Troades* reflects and extends those problems.

The importance of looking at war as *agōn*, and of using that perception in analysing *Troades*, is that we are no longer looking at war as a frame, context or metaphor in which ideology is to be examined. We are now considering the examination of war itself. My interest here is in analysing the ways in which *Troades* dramatizes this examination. It does so in a scrutiny of victory, the necessary result of an *agōn*. Is there a winner in the Trojan War? What criteria could be used to make such a judgement? What is the value of victory? These questions apply both to the war and to another *agōn*, the rhetorical contest between Helen and Hecuba.

The ends of the war

Set in the aftermath of war, the play is most obviously concerned with its victims, who dominate the stage. But the play returns frequently to the question of the status of the victor.[7] Traditionally, it would seem, a victor is only agreed to be such by virtue of divine assistance (see e.g. Pind. *Pyth.* 8.73–8). Although we know from the dialogue between Athene and Poseidon that the Greeks have indeed received such assistance (see e.g. 72), there is something disturbing about the Greek victory. For, by their sacrilegious behaviour (15–17, 69–70), the victorious Greeks have turned the formerly friendly Athene into an enemy. So the Greeks, in the manner of their divinely assisted victory, have brought about an inevitably negative divine response. Victory allows no right of transgression.[8]

The challenge to the nature and value of Greek victory

---

[7] Kitto (1961³), 212; Vellacott (1975), 164; Barlow (1986), 27.
[8] Greek suffering because of victory: Kitto (1961³), 212; Conacher (1967), 136; Luschnig (1971); B. Vickers (1973), 94; Vellacott (1975), 164–6; Lee (1976), xvi–xvii; Poole (1976).

comes from the prophetess Cassandra. In the passages I discuss below Cassandra does not much talk of the future as one might expect; instead she engages in what might be called historical revisionism. She 'tells the truth' about the past (and the present). In the first passage she disputes the Greek victory; in the second, she eulogizes the Trojans.

368–85. First to be criticized is the Greeks' motivation for the war, i.e. the recapture of one woman: is Helen worth the death of thousands (368–9)? The problem with Helen is that she has been willingly abducted (373: 'ἑκούσης κοὐ βίᾳ λεληϲμένης').[9] So Agamemnon has fought for a woman whom he must despise and whose very sexuality is a threat to a social order established by, and in the interests of, men. Cassandra sums up Agamemnon's dilemma in a rich and complex couplet (370–1):

> ὁ δὲ στρατηγὸς ὁ σοφὸς ἐχθίϲτων ὕπερ
> τὰ φίλτατ' ὤλεσ'.

The wise general has destroyed what he loved
on behalf of what he hated.

War can be a response to a transgression of the complex system of *philia* (and the Trojan War certainly is). In these terms, after Paris' disregard for hospitality (*xenia*), Menelaus and Agamemnon have had no choice but to wage war in order to restore a wife to her proper master, i.e. to her proper *philos*. But Cassandra shows that Agamemnon's war is not properly based on the restoration of *philia* relations; it is rather the opposite since it undermines those relations. Then she defines 'what he loved' (*ta philtata*) in terms of the pleasures which come from the *oikos* (she refers, above all, to Iphigeneia). Cassandra can be seen as taunting Agamemnon and the rest of the Greeks when she says this, for she uses the word *hēdonas* (372: 'pleasures'), a word which quite normally has the connotation of sensual or physical pleasure (Pl. *Rep.* 328d; Arist. *Eth. Nic.* 1151a13). So, from the point of view of

---

[9] Such criticism of Helen was standard: for other instances, in both Homer and tragedy, see Seaford (1984), 157 (at *Cyclops* 280–5).

both family and *erōs* this could perhaps be seen as a peculiarly female challenge, a view borne out by the vocabulary,
which suggests the acquisitive and destructive natures of men
(369: 'hunting down Helen, they killed thousands'/'θηρῶντες
Ἑλένην, μυρίους ἀπώλεσαν'). The second point to be made
about this criticism of Agamemnon at 370–2 is that the adjective *sophos* is very artfully placed. It could be ironic: i.e. this
general who thinks he is wise but obviously is not because ...
Or it could, on the other hand, be interpreted as saying 'the
wise general did such and such a thing', as if the cause of the
deed were the fact that he was wise. But what has this clever
man (*sophos*) done but to overturn a traditional and normative polarity (friend/enemy; *philos/echthros*), the sort of thing
sophoi are known for and castigated for doing in the late fifth
century?[10]

The second criticism of the war is that it was not a worthy
war to have fought since it was not a war of defence. The
effect of prosecuting an offensive war (offensive in both
senses) is twofold. Like Agamemnon, all those who have died
in the war have substituted this supposed glory for the benefits
of a happy home life (377: 'they did not see their children'/'οὐ
παῖδας εἶδον'). But not only have the warriors lost the benefits
of the *oikos* (house, household) by being absent from it; the
oikos has been undermined by their absence. While some warriors have left their children and given up the chance of burial
at home (378: 'they lie in a foreign land'/'ἐν ξένῃ δὲ γῇ κεῖνται')
with all proper ceremony and by the proper hands (377–8),
others have left their wives childless (380: 'ἄπαιδες'), some of
whom have died as widows without even their husbands to
mourn them (380: 'χῆραί γ' ἔθνῃσκον'; see also 381–2).[11]

---

[10] Protagoras claims to make the weaker argument win: DK 80A1 (= D.L. 9.50); DK
80B6b (= Arist. *Rhet.* 1402a21; see the satire of the claim in Aristophanes' *Clouds*);
see Kerferd (1981), 83ff.

[11] 381–2 could refer either to the men who were away, who thus missed out on
proper burial, or to their wives left at home. It is an interesting feature in Pindar
that victorious athletes are, in part, defined by their successful *nostoi* (e.g. *Nem.*
2.24; *Pyth.* 8.81–6; see also Hom. *Il.* 13.222–30); see Crotty (1982), 104–37.
Crotty, ibid., 109, says: 'To lose one's *nostos* is synonymous with defeat.' See, in
this connection, Hom. *Il.* 16.81–2; 17.239. For the insecure return home as a
recurring theme in Euripides, see Bernand (1985), 344ff.

The effect of this extraordinary piece of rhetoric is doubly disturbing. Cassandra's observation of the consequences of war is not from her point of view concerned with anything so metaphysical, so ideological as man's self-definition. It is more directly concerned with the material effects upon women and children (these forlorn possessions of men) and upon all the performances associated with the life of the *oikos*, such as the joys of children, burial by family members, and an implied stability and continuity. It is true that the *oikos* has a central place in the *Odyssey*; that fifth-century Athenians employed children (male children, at any rate) as part of their self-definition; that Athenian ideology saw war as an activity designed to preserve the security of the *oikos*; and that, in fifth-century Athens, the effects on the family could be depicted as the principal horror of war.[12] It is also true that Athenian ideology could be presented partially, stressing the activities of men outside the *oikos* – military and political achievement – as crucial to self-definition. Cassandra, from the point of view of the victim, attacks this partial ideology of war as one which has pernicious effects on the home and the family. Her challenge is to war in this limited sense as both product and producer of ideology, and, because of the setting in the Trojan War and the continuing pre-eminence of the *Iliad*, to the link between militarism in fifth-century Athens and the model of the Homeric hero.[13]

With the backdrop of a city razed to the ground, such a challenge to Greek victory would be extraordinary whichever character made it. But the effect is heightened by the fact that it is Cassandra who utters these paradoxes. Why? Because the Cassandra of the tragic tradition, if not in Homer, was a prophetess who always told the truth but who, because she refused the advances of the god Apollo, was doomed never to

---

[12] At Ar. *Lys.* 476ff. Lysistrata laments that war causes domestic strife and a lack of men (and therefore of husbands). It should also be stressed that war seen as a glorious activity because it involves defence of *oikoi*, women and children is a feature of the *Iliad* (8.57; 16.830ff.; 17.220–4). As Scully (1990), 54–7 and 106ff. says, the concentration on the individualistic hero in the *Iliad* is distorting: it neglects the hero who fights for his *polis* (Hector is the most prominent example).

[13] Goldhill (1986), 166; see also Delebecque (1951), 444.

be believed.[14] Everyone knew – the whole mythical tradition
authoritatively asserts it – that the Greeks won the Trojan
War, yet Cassandra, speaking the truth, denies this fact. Gil-
bert Murray thought that we must believe Cassandra but, if
we do, we deny another part of the mythical tradition.[15] We
seem to have reached an impasse: how can we believe Cassandra? But how can we not, when disbelieving her, as the Trojans have discovered, normally leads to disaster? Euripides
confronts a mythical *donnée* (Greek victory in the Trojan
War) with a mythical figure who speaks the incredible truth.
Whose truth is questioned? That of Cassandra? Of myth? Of
Euripides? We cannot finally be sure. It is possible, of course,
that Cassandra's questioning of victory may have induced
agreement from some; but it is also possible that to imperial-
ists in the audience the voice of truth was quite wrong.[16] Although Cassandra, as the voice of truth, offers a powerful
critique of war as and in ideology (man's self-definition
through war), the second part of her speech, in its descriptions
of why the Trojans have won glory in this war, offers some
qualifications of the radical criticism we have seen in the first
part.

386–402. The Trojans are not quite seen to have won, but
they have acquired the greatest glory (386: 'τὸ κάλλιστον
κλέος'), because they have died for their country (387: 'ὑπὲρ
πάτρας ἔθνῃσκον'; cf. 376).[17] Already, in these first two lines,
we possibly have a slight compromise of Cassandra's earlier
position. The word for glory is *kleos*, a concept at the very
centre of the Homeric warrior's self-definition.[18] It is true that
Cassandra may be appropriating and reinterpreting the word,

---

[14] Cassandra is only mentioned twice in the *Iliad* (13.365–6; 24.699), where she
is merely the most beautiful of Priam's daughters. In the *Odyssey* (13.421–4)
Agamemnon describes her death. Her status as an incredible prophetess seems to
have come from the epic cycle; certainly by the time of the *Oresteia* she is a
prophetess; see Aélion (1983) I. 217–33.

[15] (1946), 142. Stinton (1986), on the scope and limits of allusion, does not consider
the example of Cassandra's extreme rewriting of the literary tradition.

[16] Goldhill (1986), 166.

[17] On this aspect of Athenian ideology, and the Funeral Oration, see Loraux (1986).

[18] See, for instance, Redfield (1975).

but the dangers of such a strategy are that while it may be neat rhetorical practice to make an opponent's terminology one's own,[19] there is a possibility that traces of the meanings and positions to which one is objecting may linger in the word one has stolen. At first this does not seem to be the case for Cassandra, for, consistent with her criticisms of the Greek army, she says that the Trojans were fortunate because they were able to maintain their home lives, and if they died they could be buried in their own soil (389: 'ἐν γῇ πατρῴᾳ'; cf. 378: 'ἐν ξένῃ δὲ γῇ'), handled properly (390: 'χερσὶν περισταλέντες ὧν ἐχρῆν ὕπο'; cf. 377: 'οὐ δάμαρτος ἐν χεροῖν') and by their own families (387–90; cf. 374–9). And surviving Trojans were able to live with their children (391–3, see 371–2, 374–9; Poseidon agrees, see 19–22). However, as soon as Cassandra starts to tell the truth about Hector, the word *patras* (fatherland) is revealed as part of the same set of warrior values which she herself had criticized the Greeks for adhering to. Hector is described as 'the best man' (395: 'ἀνὴρ ἄριστος'), a phrase with powerful heroic resonance. More than this, the glory that the Trojan hero has won in war has rendered the Greek expedition in some sense worth while (396–7). Cassandra's criticism of the Greeks, which amounted to a criticism of war in general (see 400), becomes qualified by her praise of the Trojan men. For in both cases the language of praise and blame is the same.[20] Nevertheless, it remains true that the emphasis of Cassandra's speech as a whole is that, paradoxically, the Trojans have not lost the war, indeed that they have benefited in a sort of metaphysical and ideological way that Cassandra will not allow to the Greeks, while the Greeks, supposedly victors, are really losers.[21]

Something like this last point has been observed by a

[19] E.g. Alcibiades' appropriation of Nicias' use of 'youth' (*neotēs*) in the Sicilian debate: Thuc. 6.12–13, 17.

[20] On the tension between 386ff. and 400, see Steidle (1968), 55–6.

[21] Medea also criticizes male self-definition through war in the famous couplet (*Med.* 250–1) where she compares fighting unfavourably to giving birth; see Loraux (1981a). Medea, however, goes on to appropriate some key aspects of (male) heroism: see Bongie (1977); Knox (1977).

number of critics. Usually the formulation is that the victors and the vanquished have been made equivalent.[22] By this two things are meant: that the Greeks will suffer as much as the Trojans have; and that they deserve to. The equivalence, then, is between the future of the victors and the past and present of the vanquished.[23] Let us examine this position.

We are told of some trouble back home in Greece in lines 1126–8. Neoptolemus has set sail because Peleus has been exiled from his own country by Acastus. More gloomy prophecies, or rather promises, come from Poseidon, Athene and Cassandra. Athene has changed her allegiance and wishes to give the Greeks 'a bitter return home' (66: 'νόστον πικρόν'), and 'to damage them' (73: 'δρᾶσαι κακῶς'); the Greek fleet will be ravaged with rain, hailstones, thunderbolts and so on (77ff.). Cassandra's promise is pithy, her contribution to Agamemnon's future bloodthirsty (359–60; and see also 404–5):

> κτενῶ γὰρ αὐτὸν κἀντιπορθήσω δόμους
> ποινὰς ἀδελφῶν καὶ πατρὸς λαβοῦσ' ἐμοῦ.

> For I shall kill him [Agamemnon] and I shall ravage his house,
> taking revenge for my brothers and my father.

Cassandra also prophesies the travails of Odysseus (432ff.) and makes an explicit comparison between his misfortunes and those of Troy (432–3):[24]

> ὡς χρυσὸς αὐτῷ τἀμὰ καὶ Φρυγῶν κακὰ
> δόξει ποτ' εἶναι.

> As gold shall my troubles and those of the Phrygians
> seem to him.

So it would appear as though there is indeed much suffering in store for the Greeks, just as the play presents to us the manifest suffering of the Trojans. But, while there may be comparable suffering for the Greeks in their future to that of the Trojans in the past, in the present of the play the fortunes of the two groups are contrasted. Troy is both metaphorically

---

[22] Mead (1938–9); O'Neill (1941), 319–21; Voegelin (1957), 265; Scarcella (1959), 63ff.; Sartre (1968); Luschnig (1971); Vellacott (1975), 164; Waterfield (1982), 142.
[23] Luschnig (1971), 8.   [24] Ibid., 10.

and literally down (37, 1263),[25] whereas the Greeks have achieved their goal and, in every traditional sense of the word, won. But the present is qualified by both past and future: the past reveals to us the possible folly of the motivation for the war (at least in Cassandra's speech), while the future makes clear that victory will not bring contentment to the Greeks (see the prologue). But is it right to name victory itself as the cause of the Greeks' future misfortune? It is quite explicitly stated by Athene and Poseidon that they are angry with the Greeks because of their desecration of the temples (69–70). We have to ask whether such desecration is a condition of, or particular conduct in, victory. Cassandra's challenge is that the wrong criteria are employed to judge the application of victory, not that the Greeks have not won because they have been impious. While critics have latched onto the common enough notion that victory itself is the cause of excess, that the victors are corrupted by victory, the real villain of the piece,[26] all the critical efforts to question the fact of Greek victory are flaccid compared to Cassandra's.[27] Although, as Professor Easterling reminds me, it is an irony of Cassandra's arguments that, in order to criticize war, she is necessarily a victim of it, the prophetess is well aware of the havoc which the Greeks have wrought on Troy. She fully recognizes that in the traditional sense the Greeks are deemed victors. It is not unknown to her that the manner of victory and its aftermath are separable from its fact. That the Trojan suffering of the past and present and the Greek suffering of the future could be seen to be equivalent ignores the degradation the Trojans will experience in the future. Nor does the apparent equivalence of Greek and Trojan (in this sense) affect the fact that in war, as it is traditionally constructed and represented, there is a

[25] Ibid., 10. Compare the stumbling Hecuba in *Hecuba* (52, 64ff., 170, 438ff.), symbolic of Troy's condition; Conacher (1967), 155–6; de Romilly (1986), 86.

[26] Explicitly formulated in this way by O'Neill (1941), 320; see also Ebener (1954); Voegelin (1957), 265.

[27] One must also remember that the shocking nature of her claims would no doubt be compounded by her demonic appearance. Mason (1959), 91 reads Cassandra's speech simplistically, describing her paradoxical utterance as 'the vapidly sophistic calculus of profit and loss'.

winner and a loser. It is not the Greeks' misfortunes in the future that determine their status as victors. Cassandra's attack is on the criteria used to judge victory and the value that should be attached to it.[28] Cassandra understands that the statuses of victor and vanquished are mutually exclusive. And we should remember that she seeks victory too (and most certainly revenge: 360), and that it will be as bloodthirsty and catastrophic in its effects upon the House of Atreus as the Greek victory has been on the Trojans. One way to view this is to say that *Troades* questions not victory *per se* but a notion of war which is ideologically constructed so as to require a certain sort of victory and certain types of terrible effects: war, that is, is questioned as *agōn*. One strategy for questioning an ideological product like war is to represent its deleterious consequences (desecration of temples, various impieties, slavery, death, destruction etc.). This *Troades* performs with great power. Another strategy is to make explicit the assumptions, the apparently self-evident or unstated principles which inform the traditional construction of war. In the Greek world (and notably in fifth-century Athens) these principles are agonistic: war as the contest which responds to transgressions of cohesive social structures; as determined by certain rules; as requiring victory; as having certain criteria for judging that victory; as allowing and/or expecting certain behaviour on the part of victors. While Cassandra accepts that war is sometimes inevitable (cf. Thuc. 2.61.1), she takes these submerged

---

[28] Scodel (1980), 117–18 shows that the value of victory is a topic of all the plays said to constitute the 'Trojan Trilogy'. We have the evidence of Aelian (*VH* 2.8) and of a scholiast on Aristophanes (sch. on *Wasps* 1326; *Birds* 842) that *Troades* was produced in a 'trilogy' of tragedies in 416/415 BC, followed by the satyr play *Sisyphus*. It is unfortunate that the two tragedies which preceded *Troades*, *Alexander* and *Palamedes*, have come down to us in such a fragmentary state. Although, from what one can tell, there may have been some thematic interests shared by the three plays, it seems unlikely that *Troades* was part of a trilogy in an Oresteian sense. None of the arguments used to support trilogic status (see Conacher (1967), 128ff.; Wilson (1967); Lee (1976), x–xiv; Scodel (1980), *passim*; Barlow (1986), 27–30) are in themselves sufficient. For arguments against trilogic status, see Koniaris (1973). For attempts to reconstruct *Alexander*, see Snell (1937); J. Hanson (1964); Coles (1974). For *Palamedes*, see Conacher (1967), 132; Koniaris (1973), 89–90; Lee (1976), xii–xiii; Barlow (1986), 29. For *Sisyphus*, see Koniaris (1973), 89–90; Scodel (1980), 124ff.; and on doubts about its authorship, Dihle (1977).

agonistic imperatives and renders them naked by extracting them from the smothering context of the *agōn* and putting them into the framework of the material life of the *oikos*. Cassandra challenges the *agōn*, then, with that which it would seek to exclude.

But we should not portray Cassandra as merely a radical critic of war. Her discourse is more complex and self-defeating than that. It has been noted that her eulogy of Hector is based on the very heroic terminology and notions which she criticizes elsewhere. There is also the fact that, in so far as she is setting off from Troy to become a victor herself, she too enters into the agonistic spirit. Yet, by her own criteria, she cannot be a victor, since she will die in a foreign land removed from the comfort of her family. She tells us that once in Greece she means to introduce mayhem into the House of Atreus. But this threat is couched in the language of victory: she will be triumphant (353: literally, 'bringing victory'/'νικηφόρος'; see also 460–1). And, speaking in general terms, Cassandra implies that her death will not be an inglorious one (401–2):

εἰ δ᾽ ἐς τόδ᾽ ἔλθοι, στέφανος οὐκ αἰσχρὸς πόλει
καλῶς ὀλέσθαι.

And if it comes to this, it is not a shameful crown of glory for the city to die nobly.[29]

Stephanos ('the crown of glory') is the wreath given to a victor. However, considering the criticisms Cassandra has offered of the Greek victory, her aggressive claims to her own victory and her prophecies of her own violence (e.g. 405: 'I shall destroy'/'διαφθερῶ') are somewhat disquieting. Given that Cassandra has questioned the Greek victory by introducing formerly excluded notions into the criteria used for judging victory, how should we take her own victory? First, we could see it as an appropriate and ironic revenge, for

[29] Cassandra speaks ambiguously here. I have translated the dative of *polis* as 'for the city': this could be seen as casting the city as a person, or even a warrior-hero. But the death of the hero is normally meant to ensure the survival of the city rather than its final destruction. Alternatively, and in an elliptical manner, by 'for the city' Cassandra means 'for anyone in the city'.

Cassandra says that the instrument of her destruction of the House of Atreus will be marriage (404–5). Appropriate because it was a marriage that caused the war in the first place (see 357); ironic because the life of the *oikos*, that which Cassandra would champion as being not responsible for war and violence, revolves around marriage. Alternatively, we could perhaps see it as furthering what she sees as evidence of Greek defeat, namely, the collapse of *oikos* life. Still, the point remains that, if only in revenge, Cassandra has been affected by a certain enthusiasm for the agonistic, a proclivity whose effects and principles she has criticized; and that qualifies her criticism. Even if she is not herself part of the *agōn*, her actions will cause 'matricidal *agōnes* [struggles]' (363: 'μητροκτόνους τ' ἀγῶνας').[30]

We have seen, then, that the value of victory has been questioned by the catastrophes of the war which preceded victory, by the ruinous excesses which victory can effect, by the fact that divine support has been ambivalent, and most radically by Cassandra's critique of the criteria by which victory is deemed to have been achieved. War as *agōn* has been questioned by the paradoxical prophetess of truth; and moreover, as she criticizes war, she herself is transformed into that which she attacks. Thus not only is war questioned by the voice of truth, but the voice of truth becomes questionable in its own terms. Certainly the characters pay little attention to her. The chorus, lamenting the fall of Troy and the loss of their men, describe how the Trojan women were raped, bringing a prize (*stephanos*) which was to bear children for Greece (564–6). The use of *stephanos* tells us that the chorus are talking of the consequences of Greek victory. Similarly, in the *agōn* between Helen and Hecuba, Helen argues that she should be spared from execution because she has been of service to the Greeks. Moreover, she asserts that she should receive a crown (937:

---

[30] The murder of Aegisthus is also treated as an *agōn* in Euripides' *Electra*, which uses the terminology of victory (*kallinikos, stephanos*) as well as the athletic imagery associated so strongly with *agōnes* (*El.* 883–5); see Zeitlin (1970), 655–60. On epinician aspects of *Hercules Furens*, see Foley (1985), 178–88; for *kallinikos*, see *HF* 49, 961; *Med.* 45, 765; and see Buxton (1982),165.

stephanos). Once again, a Greek victory is indicated. Finally, Hecuba addresses the shield of Hector as once victorious (1221–3: *kallinikos*); it is now the Greeks who have the prize. But it is not just the simple fact of Greek victory which the other characters believe confounds Cassandra's criticisms; it is also the mental state in which she makes her claims. Just before Cassandra emerges onto the stage, Hecuba says that her daughter is raging mad (307: 'μαινὰς θοάζει'). But the most interesting terms in which her 'madness' is described are those of Dionysiac or Bacchic delirium.[31] Hecuba and the chorus both use a participial form derived from the name Bacchus to say that Cassandra is frenzied (169: 'ἐκβακχεύουσαν'; 341: 'βακχεύουσαν'); Talthybius refers to the fact that Apollo has 'maddened' her mind (408: 'ἐξεβάκχευσεν'); and, finally, Hecuba addresses Cassandra as a fellow bacchant of the gods (500: 'ὦ σύμβακχε').[32] The other characters are attempting to marginalize Cassandra, by making her utterances irrational. Cassandra does not accept this. In order to begin her criticism of the Greeks Cassandra says (366–7):

> ἔνθεος μέν, ἀλλ' ὅμως
> τοσόνδε γ' ἔξω στήσομαι βακχευμάτων.

> I may be possessed by god, but nevertheless
> to this extent I shall stand outside my madness.

The word translated as madness is *bakcheumatōn*, once again from the vocabulary of Dionysiac delirium. If Cassandra always tells the truth, what difference does it make if she is

[31] On Cassandra and demonic possession, see Padel (1983), 15.

[32] For 'βακχεύω' meaning 'I am mad', see Hdt. 4.79, Soph. *Ant.* 136; as 'I am inspired', see *Ion* 1204; *Or.* 411. The verb is also used to describe Heracles' slaughter of his children: see *HF* 966–7, 1084–5, 1122. On the significance of Dionysiac vocabulary in tragedy (and for a list of instances), see Bierl (1989), who is, however, mainly concerned with *Antigone*. It might be thought bizarre that Talthybius, at 408–9, should have Cassandra being afflicted with Bacchic madness by Apollo, but it could be argued that this is appropriate because it was Apollo who gave Cassandra the gift of prophecy. On the complex relationship between Apollo and Dionysus, see Bruit Zaidman and Schmitt Pantel (1992), 197–9; also Mason (1959), 92, who notes Aeschylus fr. 341: 'ὁ κισσεὺς Ἀπόλλων, ὁ βακχεύς, ὁ μάντις'/ 'Ivy-crowned Apollo, the bacchant, the seer'. See Aélion (1983) I. 228–30 on the different relationships of Cassandra to Apollo and Dionysus in Aeschylus and Euripides.

afflicted with the Dionysiac or not? Or does it amount to saying: 'well, now I shall speak in plain Greek'? Does the pun on standing outside and ecstasy (*exō stēsomai*) suggest a new or different form of Dionysiac possession? Does it suggest that, at the very moment Cassandra denies being affected by Dionysus, she paradoxically confirms that she is possessed by the god? Or is it that, in order to tell the truth, Cassandra must abandon the Dionysiac? Not only does Euripides confront a mythical truth with a mythical teller of the truth. Not only is the voice of truth internally inconsistent. The framing of Cassandra's arguments also raises questions about the truth value of the representation performed under the aegis of Dionysus.[33]

Many tragedies deal with the ravages of war, but what is distinctive about *Troades* is this concentration on war as *agōn*, on the value of victory as well as its effects. It is perhaps no accident, then, that *Troades* also contains one of the most celebrated rhetorical *agōnes* in extant tragedy. The paradoxes and inconsistencies of this superb set-piece cannot help but reflect on the nature of the *agōn* as institution. The debate between Helen and Hecuba examines rhetoric at work, under the pressure of war. It also represents a war of languages, or rhetorics, where the result demanded by the institution of the *agōn* may be as specious and questionable as that of the war itself.

The causes of the war

The *agōn* in tragedy has exercised much scholarly attention.[34] It is helpful to remember the words of Vernant: 'Tragedy is contemporaneous with the city and its legal system . . . the true

---

[33] Murray (1946), 142 seems to give up in the face of these problems: 'I think, however, that certain speeches in certain situations must generally be taken as expressing the truth.'

[34] The basic work remains Duchemin (1968[2]); see also Strohm (1957), 3–50; Conacher (1981); P. Arnott (1989), 105–31. On the *agōn* in Euripides, see now M. Lloyd (1992).

subject matter of tragedy is social thought and most especially juridical thought in the very process of elaboration.'[35] The *agōn*, more than any other separable element in tragedy, represents this aspect of social thought. It is also the element which reminds us that tragedy shared with the law courts, the epideictic displays of the sophists and the Assembly of Athens itself, a fundamentally rhetorical nature.[36] Much energy has also been expended over the question of the dramatic relevance of *agōnes*. Euripidean scholarship has found the Euripidean *agōn* wanting in this respect. Bond, for instance, finds the *agōn* in *Hercules Furens* quite ungermane[37] and Collard has this to say in general: 'the poet [Euripides] is guilty of self-indulgent digression for the sake of rhetorical display, at the cost of dramatic continuity and relevance'.[38] And even an apologist for the *agōn* in *Troades* can only muster three slimly argued defences: it is emotional relief, a crystallization of some of the intellectual issues of the play; and, anyway, the cut and thrust of debate is good dramatic spectacle.[39]

In *Troades*, the *agōn* is certainly pertinent. One could argue, as Gellie does, that the debate scene is the culmination of the play's concern with marriage;[40] or, as Amerasinghe does, that the debate comes at the climactic point of the play;[41] or, as Ebener does, that the Helen scene brings together most of the important motifs of the play, especially those of responsibility

---

[35] Vernant (1970), 278–9; and see Vernant and Vidal-Naquet (1988), 23–8.

[36] Buxton (1982); M. Lloyd (1992), 19–36.

[37] *HF* 159ff. contains what Bond (1981), 108–9 believes to be an irrelevant and undramatic attack on archers. It is, of course, quite to the point, being part of the play's treatment of ephebic and hoplite themes.

[38] (1975b), 59. M. Lloyd (1992), 18 says something similar: 'The relationship of the agon to the action is often obscure and Euripides often seems to go to great lengths to detach it from its immediate dramatic context.' Lloyd, however, wants to argue that this, in part, is the function of the *agōn*, namely, to say something about the futility of rational discussion of tragic conflicts. (More will be said on this later in the chapter.) Conacher (1981), along with Duchemin (1968²), 124ff., believes that Euripidean debates become less relevant in the later plays; see also Strohm (1957), 37–8, 44–6.

[39] Stinton (1965), 39. Of course, I too am arguing, in part, that the *agōn* is a crystallization of some of the play's themes; but Stinton, having offered the insight, makes very little use of it.

[40] (1986); see also Erbse (1984), 68f. [41] (1973), 99.

and man's relation to divinity.[42] But, apart from being important in the examination of war as *agōn*, the debate between Helen and Hecuba concerns itself with the question which also causes vexation in *Andromache* and *Hecuba*, namely, who is responsible for the war, and what sort of justice the guilty party should receive. Finally, just as Cassandra opposes the fact of Greek victory, the *agōn* employs fifth-century argumentative techniques for the purpose of debating a mythical problem. All this will be discussed in more detail in this and the next two chapters. For the moment, let us quote Vernant again, in summary: the *agōn* shows tragedy confronting 'heroic values and ancient religious representations with the new modes of thought that characterize the advent of law within the city-state'.[43]

Helen's entry at 895 places before the audience a new spectacle.[44] All the women we have seen so far have been Trojans and therefore their appearance (within the formal confines of tragic costume) has betrayed their calamitous situation (note Hecuba's rags at 496–7).[45] Helen, however, appears in her finest garb (1022ff.). The arrival of Helen, whose physical appearance is unaffected by the ravages of war, represents a break in the emotional mood. That we are about to witness a debate is indicated by Helen asking Menelaus whether it is possible to argue in a speech (903) against the justice of her (already decided) execution.[46] An exchange of speeches (*logoi*) suggests the procedure of the law courts or the Assembly. Although Menelaus is initially unwilling (905), he is per-

[42] (1954); see also Strohm (1957), 34–5; Desch (1985–6), 81–90. Collard (1975b), 61 notes that most Euripidean debates occur before the climax of the play: they talk about the past (*Hipp.* 902ff.; *El.* 998ff.) or expose an already fought conflict (*Hec.* 1129–1292). Both of these descriptions can apply to the debate here, but whether the debate marks the climax or not is more difficult to prove. The debate here also fits into the category which has two speakers performing before a third person who acts as arbiter (*Heracl., Phoen., Andr., Hec.*); see Collard (1975b), 63.

[43] Vernant and Vidal-Naquet (1988), 26; see also M. Lloyd (1992), 104.

[44] Lee (1976), 225.

[45] On Euripidean rags, see Ar. *Frogs* 1063–7; Macleod (1983), 47–9.

[46] Euripidean debates are often introduced in a similar way, being preceded by such words as *agōn, agōnisma, agōnisdomai*; see *Supp.* 427; Collard (1975b), 61; M. Lloyd (1992), 4. Here, at 895, Helen uses the word *phroimion*, i.e. both simply 'beginning' and the technical rhetorical term.

suaded by Hecuba that, if he allows a full-blown debate (909: 'ὁ πᾶς λόγος'), the only possible result is that Helen will be found guilty (906–10), indeed that a full debate will kill Helen (910: 'κτενεῖ'). A serious *agōn*, then, not only with the result which the *agōn* requires, but with one which is a matter of life and death, just like that other *agōn*, the war, for which Helen will be held responsible. Menelaus allows the debate very emphatically because of Hecuba's arguments (912–13), which is odd for three reasons. First, in those Euripidean debates which take place before an arbiter, it is normally the arbiter who asks for the debate in the first place, as do Demophon at *Heracl.* 132ff. and Agamemnon at *Hec.* 1129–31.[47] Second, Menelaus allies himself with an enemy and a barbarian rather than with a Greek and a *philos* (albeit errant). An effect of war, no doubt. Third, Menelaus allows the debate on condition that the outcome is already determined, i.e. he allows the debate only in so far as it is not really a debate (an exchange of *logoi* leading to a conclusion based on those *logoi*). A specious *agōn*, then? Perhaps Menelaus, having endured and won the ten-year-long *agōn* of the war, has no desire to become involved in another. But a disturbing question is raised: are all *agōnes* already determined? It is possible. But Menelaus' reluctance and insecurity lie in the fact that he is permitting a contest not of strength but of words. Rhetoric can have a mysterious, magical power; hence the attempt to control it.[48] Menelaus may believe that the result is predetermined, but such certainty is out of place in the world of *peithō*.

It is Helen who speaks first. This does not follow the practice of the law courts, where the defendant always spoke second. But, given that Helen has already been thoroughly attacked in the play, it would perhaps have made little sense to have another speech of accusation.[49] In fact, only in *Electra* and *Troades* does the defendant speak first: all the other debates follow the forensic order. Most scholars have

[47] M. Lloyd (1992), 110–11.
[48] Gorgias is the great exponent of rhetoric as magic; see e.g. *Helen* 8ff.; C. Segal (1962); de Romilly (1973), (1975); Walsh (1984).
[49] M. Lloyd (1992), 17, 101.

been keen to note that in Euripidean debates the 'winner' is the defendant, who normally speaks second,[50] a fact which has been presumed to be important here in determining victory. But, unlike Menelaus, the audience – Cleon's 'θεαταὶ τῶν λόγων' ('spectators of speeches') – does not have to hear the arguments with the result already determined. As we might expect, the question of who wins this debate is a vexed issue. And it is difficult to come to a particular conclusion in this matter by arguing from a set of conventions gleaned from other Euripidean debates. One could say that the winner speaks second and thereby presume that we know the result from the convention rather than from the content of the *agōn*. But one could also claim that the normal sequence in Euripides (and in the law courts) is that the defendant speaks second; and that the defendant is normally the winner.[51] Since Helen is the defendant and speaks first, the *agōn* here, certainly in one sense and potentially in the other, does not comply with the perceived convention. Some critics have assumed that Helen loses, and that she is guilty, because she speaks first. But one could just as easily argue, from the convention, that because she is the defendant she is innocent and that she should be adjudged the winner. It should also be said that Helen's guilt, i.e. her responsibility for the war, is not self-evident. Indeed, one of the purposes of the *agōn* – for the audience, if not for Menelaus, Hecuba and the chorus – is to establish whether she is guilty or innocent, and to do this surely as much by the substance of the arguments as by the *agōn*'s form. And, as with the Plataeans in Thucydides and Palamedes in Gorgias, no specific charge is levelled against her.

Helen's prooemium is conventional (see *Andr*. 184ff.).[52] She stresses the notion of exchange, as she did to Menelaus at 903 (915: 'you will not reply'/'οὐκ ἀνταμείψῃ'; 917: 'I shall reply'/'ἀμείψομαι'), and rhetorically considers that the debate is not possible because of the hostility of Menelaus (915:

[50] Duchemin (1968[2]), 139; Collard (1975b), 62; Barlow (1986), 210.
[51] Lee (1976), 227–8.   [52] M. Lloyd (1984), 304.

'thinking of me as an enemy'/'πολεμίαν ἡγούμενος'), although an opponent, even an extremely hostile one, is what one might expect to confront in an *agōn*. Alternatively, the use of *polemian* at 915 suggests that war may have made further *agōnes* impossible, that its confusion and destabilization of important polarities has somehow made the idea of an *agōn* with two contestants obsolete. Helen's use of *polemian* also brings into focus the strangeness of the (temporary) alliance of Menelaus and Hecuba. Nevertheless, Helen asserts her own intention to argue (916–17) and expresses the hope that her opponent will respond in the proper manner.

Helen begins to talk of the causes of the war (she mentions three), which she does in straightforward and orderly fashion (919–20: 'first ... and second'/'πρῶτον μὲν ... δεύτερον δ''). The first is expressed briefly: the birth of Paris (919–22).[53] The second cause amplifies the first: the failure to kill the infant Paris leads to the ruin not only of Troy but also – in a nice rhetorical identification – of Helen herself (921: 'Troy and me'/'Τροίαν τε κἄμ''). At this point at least, and as a rhetorical device no doubt, Helen appears pathetically to accept the result of the debate, if not the justice of that result (see 904), as a foregone conclusion, thereby implicitly parading the sort of humility which most commentators find so lacking in her physical appearance.[54] A sleight of hand, then, to identify herself with Troy while their physical differences were presumably so manifest and while she has been accused (throughout the play) as the destroyer of the city. Also, we have here a rhetorical and convenient use of the common Greek confusion between *post hoc* and *propter hoc*.[55]

---

[53] Cf. *Andr.* 293–300. *Andromache* is indeed much concerned with causes, on which see Aldrich (1961).

[54] Havelock (1968), 127; Scodel (1980), 96 believes that Helen shows no sense of shame; Lee (1976), 225 agrees. Such a sense of shame is only necessary, though, if Helen is guilty. Scodel, Lee and Sienkiewicz (1980) seem, like Menelaus, to think that the verdict has already been decided. Desch (1985–6), 77–90 believes Helen to be an opportunist; Gregory (1991), 182 n.39 thinks her 'the most self-serving of all the tragic protagonists who use "l'excuse de l'invincible amour"'.

[55] Vellacott (1975), 140. Though, as Lee (1976), 229 points out, it was traditional to regard the Judgement of Paris as 'the origin of troubles', or 'ἀρχὴ κακῶν' (*Andr.* 274ff.; *Hel.* 23ff.).

The third cause (924–31) is a further amplification of the first two: once Paris was born and had not been killed, his next significant action is the judgement he gives between the three goddesses (924). Helen's description of the Judgement is more or less traditional, especially in its anthropomorphism.[56] Even before the Trojan War had begun, the three goddesses were aware of some enmity between the Trojans and the Greeks: Pallas and Hera both offer Paris victory over the Greeks. While Pallas merely offers Greece to Paris (926), Hera, more expansively, offers tyranny – the sort of rule a barbarian would fancy – over Asia and Europe (927–8). Aphrodite promises the possession of beauty (i.e. Helen) if she is adjudged the winner (929–30). The pitfalls of beauty are suggested, for Aphrodite's promise leads to a different transgression, that of *xenia* (hospitality) and *philia*. And there is a sense in which self-reference is at work. The argument over the details of the Judgement of Paris – a judgement about beauty – suggests that we remember that we may be watching another such judgement in the *agōn*. Will it be Helen's beauty, or her words, which might convince Menelaus?

931–37. Paley thinks that 931, like 923, is inane, allowing Helen to invent her next argument. Lee agrees. However, inane or not, the line accentuates the rhetorical nature of the speech, and also makes a bow to (so-called) fifth-century rationalism (931: 'consider the argument'/'σκέψαι λόγον'). The line also hints that the audience, especially Menelaus, may not be considering Helen's *logos* as the most powerful and obvious part of her persuasion, but rather her beauty. Helen now addresses herself to Menelaus. Like Oedipus (Soph. *OC* 72, 92, 287–8, 432, 462–3, 486–7, 576–7), she has brought *onēsis* (benefit) to the Greeks (933):

> καὶ τοσόνδ' οὑμοὶ γάμοι
> ὤνησαν Ἑλλάδ'

> And to this extent my marriage
> benefited Greece.

---

[56] See Stinton (1965); Walcot (1977); M. Lloyd (1984).

Oedipus was supplicating a foreign city (Athens), trying to persuade the Athenians to let him stay in Colonus to die. He was an exiled hero with a powerful presence, which, even in death, he could offer to the Athenians as protection against invasion in return for acceptance. Helen has no such status or power; indeed she has nothing to offer for the future. Her claimed benefit lies in the past, and we are startled because Helen says that it is her marriage – the very thing so often derided (see 357–8, 398–9) – which has aided the Greeks. Gone now is the grandiose terminology of Asia, Phrygia and Europe. Helen's benefit lies in the fact that the Greeks have avoided defeat at the hands of the barbarians (933). In arguing this, she directly appeals to Menelaus' assumed Greek disdain for barbarians as well as to the conventional association of barbarians with tyranny (934). But the benefit to the Greeks has been catastrophic for herself. Perhaps her beauty has some part in this, she 'innocently' suggests (936), as she tries to evoke pity for her position by calling attention to her lot as wife (936: '[I was] sold for my beauty'/'εὐμορφίᾳ πραθεῖσα').[57] Instead of receiving the *stephanos* for her part in the Greek victory, she has been reviled. Cassandra's powerful critique of victory does not seem to apply in the world of Helen, since, apart from being an anomaly – she is a Greek barbarian, a semi-divine human, a woman at the centre of a series of transgressions – for Helen the fact of Greek victory is plain: she would not otherwise be in this position of arguing against a slave and her husband allied together.

938–44. Helen now moves on to her actual departure from Menelaus' house (938–9). Her humility slips. Menelaus is roundly abused (943: 'ὦ κάκιστε'), surely rather an astonishing attack (and also possibly comic), given the relative situations of Helen and her husband. Paris becomes an *alastōr* of Hecuba (avenging fury, bane, curse, evil genius) aided by a powerful goddess (940–1). This is a remarkable rhetorical

---

[57] Medea complains that women must buy husbands (*Med.* 232–4). Hippolytus, from the male point of view, laments the fact that you have to bribe potential husbands with dowries in order to get rid of your female relatives (*Hipp.* 628–9).

reversal. Earlier (768), Andromache had called Helen the child
of *Alastōr* (amongst other demons); no one had demurred. The
implication of Helen's remark is that Paris is the avenging
demon of both Hecuba and Aphrodite, and thus Helen clev-
erly associates the queen and the goddess. The sarcastic tone
of the reference to Paris' polyonymity (941–2: 'whether you
want to call him Alexander or Paris'/'εἴτ' Ἀλέξανδρον θέλεις
ὀνόματι προσφωνεῖν νιν εἴτε καὶ Πάριν'; see 925) suggests that
whatever name Paris is given he is merely the instrument of
the will of the goddess on the one hand and of the queen
on the other.[58] For once, then, Paris is not blamed. Since the
fatal attraction of Helen's beauty has already been implied,
Helen can reasonably assert that the fault for the transgression of Menelaus' hospitality lies with Menelaus himself (because he left the house: 943–4; cf. *Andr.* 592ff.). Given the
normal opprobrium attached to Paris in this connection, and
given that she is appealing to Menelaus, Helen's claim is
rhetorically dextrous but startling.

945–50. Helen now gives two reasons why she is not to
blame for leaving her husband's house. The first is an argument from probability (*eikos*) at 946–7:

> τί δὴ φρονοῦσά γ' ἐκ δόμων ἅμ' ἑσπόμην
> ξένῳ, προδοῦσα πατρίδα καὶ δόμους ἐμούς;

> What was I thinking of when I followed the stranger [guest]
> from home, betraying my fatherland and my house?

This is particularly neat, as some key ideological concepts are
present. The first part of the question could be paraphrased:
would I have transgressed the code of hospitality (*xenia*)? The
use of *patris* cannot be accidental, appealing as it does to the
patriarchal notion of what a country is. Helen once again
turns the tables on Menelaus. But her question is also part of
a *reductio ad absurdum* which, having asked the question, she
completes with her own answer. Without explicitly stating

---

[58] Stinton (1965), 36: 'Helen is deliberately needling Hecuba by using the name Paris
and then correcting herself in mock apology.' See Lee (1976), 229; Biehl (1989),
352.

that she was coerced by Aphrodite,[59] Helen refers to the power of the goddess, and compares her own human weakness with the strength of Zeus, who is himself enslaved to the goddess of Desire (948–50), a point stressed by the emphatic use of antithesis ('μὲν ἄλλων ... κράτος/κείνης δὲ δοῦλός'). Helen had earlier implicitly excused herself on the basis that this goddess Aphrodite, to whom all are enslaved, is taken with her beauty (929): if Aphrodite cannot resist Helen, what human can (see Gorg. *Hel.* 6, 19; Eur. *Hipp.* 447ff.)? The *reductio* is completed with a brief plea for forgiveness (950), nicely adding humility to the otherwise trenchant ridiculing of her accusers.

951–60. Having considered why she was not able to resist being taken away to Troy, Helen proceeds to why she was not able to escape once she got there (952–4). Human rather than divine agency is at work here. She tried but could not escape, both because she was caught during an attempt (955: she has witnesses) and because she was forced into another marriage, this time with Deiphobus, and against the will of the other Trojans (960). Helen tries to strengthen her point by liberal reference to the force used to compel her to marry again (959: 'having seized [me] with force'/'βίᾳ ... ἁρπάσας'; see 936–7, 962) and by a slyly included description of her own first marriage to Paris as divinely decreed and therefore unobjectionable (953: 'my marriage [bed] prepared by the gods'/ 'θεοπόνητά μου λέχη').[60]

961–5. In her final passage Helen reiterates some of the claims she has already made. But she first appeals to Menelaus in the name of justice, an appeal strengthened by verbal

[59] M. Lloyd (1992), 103–4.

[60] Wilamowitz deleted 959–60 and Diggle, followed by Barlow and Biehl, brackets them. The consensus is that they are interpolated. Certainly, by introducing Deiphobus here, Helen makes it difficult to know to which husband she refers in 962; see M. Lloyd (1984), 309; (1992), 105–6. Barlow (1986), 211–12 accepts that the lines may refer back to Deiphobus' rivalry with Paris in *Alexander*, but she also insists that the introduction of Deiphobus muddies the sequence of thought. According to Barlow, Helen wants to stress the force (*bia*) of Aphrodite (see 964–5) and mention of another sort of force is not helpful. However, one might argue that Helen wishes (or needs) to make use of any situation in which she is forced by another person to act against her will; see Lee (1976), 233.

repetition (961–2: 'rightly . . . justly'/'ἐνδίκως . . . δικαίως'). She then implicitly refers back to the fact that she has been instrumental in bringing about Greek victory in noting again that she has not been accorded, as would be appropriate, the status of victor (963; see 937). To her claim that she has not been a free agent in any of her marriages, which is repeated here (962: 'he married with force'/'βίᾳ γαμεῖ'; cf. 936–7), she adds that she has been actually enslaved (964; this matches and extends the 'I am abused'/'κὠνειδίζομαι' of 936). Then, referring back to 940 and 948–50, she warns again of the power of the gods, attributing *amathia* to Menelaus should he wish to overcome that power.

Helen denies responsibility for starting the war, and demands instead the right to be hailed as victor. Then, rejecting blame for going to Troy, she argues that humans cannot resist the gods, especially Aphrodite. She should therefore be pardoned. And, once in Troy, she was not able to leave. Vellacott claims to find in Helen's defence the notion of mixed responsibility: 'she knows that on the day when she obeyed Aphrodite there was nothing else to do . . . She neither evades responsibility nor pretends that she had any alternative.'[61] This sounds neat, and we may agree with the first part of the quotation. Nevertheless, there is no suggestion that Helen takes responsibility for anything that has happened. Instead, she blames Hecuba, Priam, Paris, the three goddesses (Aphrodite in particular), Menelaus, Trojans, Deiphobus. Like the speaker of Gorgias' *Helen*, Helen makes use of traditional cultural and religious notions to demonstrate that she is not responsible (Priam, for instance, speaking to Helen in the *Iliad* (3.164), blames the gods rather than her). Throughout her speech she has recourse to elements which control her and disallow the possibility of individual responsibility. Her fate has been determined by force or *bia* (men, gods, situations), by slavery (to men in marriage), and by naked power (men and gods again). Helen uses her womanhood – normally, of course, an inferior

---

[61] Vellacott (1975), 139. See Hom. *Il.* 19.86–8, 137–8; Aesch. *Ag.* 218ff. for other statements of mixed responsibility.

position in the social hierarchy – to show that the abnormal events which she seems to inspire do not in fact issue from her. Yet, at the same time, by debating at all, she contrasts her own willingness to engage in the exchange of *logoi* to the *bia* employed by men and gods.[62] As she exploits her ordinariness *qua* woman, she rhetorically usurps the male function of public speaking. Yet she stands before us, beautiful, challenging Menelaus (and us) to resist this powerful, but non-verbal, form of persuasion.

Before the debate had begun, Hecuba had warned Menelaus not to gaze at Helen, lest he be seized with desire (891). Throughout Helen's speech it is not clear which might be the more effective, her looks or her words. The truth is that it is probably both, and that this is emphasized by the way in which the word for desire in 891 (*pothō*) is picked up and punned on by the chorus at 967. The chorus recognize the disquieting quality of Helen's rhetoric: her *peithō* (persuasion) is destructive and must itself be destroyed. Helen's speech is thus framed by the Trojan women's fear of her erotic and rhetorical power.[63] Also, we see in the chorus' remarks that Menelaus' already determined outcome has begun to look a little fragile. Unlike Helen, the chorus do not even pay lip-service to the language of the *agōn*. There is no advice to exchange *logoi* here; instead, Hecuba is told to crush Helen's *peithō* (967: 'destroying her persuasion'/'πειθὼ διαφθείρουσα τῆσδ''). Helen, according to the chorus, is an eloquent villain (968), who speaks well (967–8) but is too clever (*deinon*, that choice description of the sophists). For the chorus, Helen has a sort of Protagorean quality, because she can make the guilty position sound innocent. Lee has a curious remark on the chorus' criticisms: 'Euripides guards against the persuasiveness of his own rhetoric.'[64] But how? By answering with more, of course. Hecuba begins her reply by responding to Helen's description

---

[62] On Helen and *bia*, see Donzelli (1985), 395–6; Gregory (1991), 172. On the various forms of constraint in *Troades*, see Saïd (1978), 253–6.

[63] Craik (1990), 8. For the relationship between eroticism and persuasion, see chapter one, n.63.

[64] Lee (1976), 235.

of the Judgement of Paris (924ff.), which was her third argument against the charge that she was the principal cause of the war. We already know that Hecuba's attitude to the existence of the gods as anthropomorphic entities is ambivalent (884–8). Here, however, she seems to accept the anthropomorphic tradition. She does this first by allying herself to the goddesses (969). The use of the metaphor of alliance is interesting as it comes from the military and political sphere, thus keeping before us what is at stake (who caused the war). It also alerts us to the fact that the war pervades the experience of the women so thoroughly now that it does not sound strange to hear Hecuba describing her relationship with the gods in these terms.[65] And, while Hecuba's use of the word ally (*summachos*) is an appropriation of male values, it also demonstrates that we are witnessing an *agōn*, here a war of languages, of arguments. Second, Hecuba seems to accept that a judgement may have taken place; at least that is one possible understanding of the force of 'I do not think they [Hera and Pallas] came to such a pitch of irrationality (972: ʽοὐκ ἐς τοσοῦτον ἀμαθίας') that one sold Argos to the barbarians, and Pallas Athens to the Phrygians to be enslaved' (973–4). That is, Hecuba seems to be saying that something may have happened but not as Helen described it. What Hecuba objects to in Helen's rendering is that it makes the gods look stupid (972: *amathia*). That is, she does not believe in the Judgement *per se*, even though she does not offer any alternative details. She disbelieves the Judgement of Paris as Helen tells it because of the promises which the goddesses make (971–4). It is interesting, though, that she does not repeat Helen. Rather than Paris being given tyranny over Asia and Europe, in Hecuba's account Hera's gift is barbarian rule over Argos. And Pallas' offering is not military victory over Greece but, very strangely, the enslavement of Athens. We might detect here an Athenocentric attitude, or an oblique reference to the Persian Wars, with Paris as Xerxes. Both interpretations

---

[65] Though see Sappho 1.28, where Aphrodite is called on as an ally (*summachos*) in an erotic context.

are possible, but more importantly Hecuba tones down
Helen's rhetorical exaggeration at 927–8 (if it is an exaggeration). Helen, Hecuba implies, had used hyperbole to frighten
Menelaus into being grateful that the Greeks had avoided the
consequences of Paris' other possible judgements. Hecuba
attempts to remove that gratitude by specifying and diminish-
ing the promises of Hera and Pallas, and also by asserting that
such offers would have represented the height of folly. She
appeals to a hellenocentric attitude: it would have been folly,
again, for the gods to have supported barbarians over Greeks,
tyranny over freedom. This attitude historically issued from
the Persian Wars (firm divine support for the Greeks: Hdt.
7.178.1, 189; 8.37, 65; Plut. *Thes.* 35) rather than from Homer's
Trojan War, but it is one to which Hecuba could reasonably
expect the tragic Menelaus to subscribe. But Hecuba's reli-
ance on the absurdity of Athene promising to hand over her
own city of Athens is misplaced. For we have seen from the
prologue that Athene is quite willing to abandon Greeks she
has previously helped. The rebuttal of divine *amathia* is most
evident, however, in the two *reductiones ad absurdum* which
follow.

975–82. Hecuba not only dismisses the story about the offers at the Judgement (971–4);[66] she also rejects the notion
that the goddesses could be motivated by the desire to be
recognized as beautiful (977: 'ἔρωτα καλλονῆς'). Such an attitude would mean that the gods were irrational (*amatheis*), or
so it is implied by the use of 'desire' (*erōs*). Helen had, of
course, given no such description. Aphrodite fits unhappily
into this picture, but she is to be dealt with later. Hecuba
constructs the rhetorical questions of her *reductio* in a very
particular way. For she can only conceive of beauty as a quality which qualifies a woman for a good match in marriage.

---

[66] I have followed Diggle and Barlow in keeping Hartung's emendation 'οὐ' for the
MSS 'αἳ' at 975. Both readings imply that the goddesses went to Ida. Lee's reason
for preferring the MSS reading ((1976), 236) is that it is not the fact of the Judgement which Hecuba finds incredible, but the extravagant nature of the bribes; see
also Biehl (1989), 361. However, one might also argue that the aim of Hecuba's
speech would seem to be a denial of the frivolity of the gods: the 'αἳ' would
contribute to such frivolity.

Unlike Helen, Hecuba seems to accept, on behalf of the goddesses as well, the ideology which offers only marriage and
childbirth as definitions of woman's self. But then she has not
provoked outrageous and transgressive desire, as Helen has.
Hecuba thinks that Helen's portrait of the Judgement makes
the gods irrational (981–2: *amatheis*). But Hecuba's view of
the gods is problematic as well (see 884–8). While she dismisses the persuasion of Helen and allies herself with the gods
as wise (982: *sophoi*; see 969), her appeal to the wisdom of the
gods is marked by a certain desperation. Hecuba is throughout trying to come to terms with the gods' role in the (sense-
less) destruction of the war. Hecuba's question is, on the one
hand, 'what have we done to lose the support of the gods?'; on
the other, 'what is wrong with the gods that they should support the Greeks?' Later in the play, the Trojan queen will
come to some firm conclusions (see 1240–2).

983–6. What is at stake for Hecuba is both the power of
Helen's persuasion and the status of the gods as *amatheis*.
Hecuba cannot agree with Helen, for in so doing she would
have to admit the irrationality, or the stupidity, of the gods.
Note the sarcasm of 'γέλως' ('laughable') at 983. Then,
Hecuba denies that Aphrodite, great and powerful as she is
(cf. 940) and emphatically placed at the beginning of the sen-
tence (983), would need to go – in numinous person – to
Sparta (985–6). This misses Helen's point somewhat and is, in
fact, directly contradicted by Hecuba herself when she accuses
Helen a few lines later of becoming transformed into Cypris,
as well as by the appearance and comments of the gods Poseidon and Athene in the prologue. In saying this, Hecuba
accepts that Aphrodite can be everywhere in some way or
another.

987–90. This passage corresponds to Helen's claim (945–
50) that she was not responsible for her own abduction because of the power of Aphrodite. Hecuba begins by transfer-
ring the quality of beauty to Paris (987: 'my outstandingly
beautiful son'/'οὑμὸς υἱὸς κάλλος ἐκπρεπέστατος').[67] Given

---

[67] Note Hom. *Il.* 3.39, where Paris is evil, beautiful and woman-crazy; see Arthur
(1981), 23.

Helen's reputation and the fears the chorus have about her effect on Menelaus, it is startling that it is now Paris' (Helen-like?) beauty which drove Helen mad with desire, her mind (*nous*) inhabited by Cypris (988). In the next, celebrated, line Hecuba removes Aphrodite from the pantheon of wise divinities and makes her instead a principle of intemperance (989):

τὰ μῶρα γὰρ πάντ᾽ ἐστὶν Ἀφροδίτη βροτοῖς,
καὶ τοὔνομ᾽ ὀρθῶς ἀφροσύνης ἄρχει θεᾶς.

For all stupid (or 'intemperate') human acts are Aphrodite,
and the name of the goddess rightly begins with folly [*aphrosunē*].

This not only dismisses Helen's rhetorical question at 946 ('what was I thinking of?' – *phronousa* – 'would I have been sane ...?'); it is also a judicious selection of who is to be counted as truly divine. Yet removing Aphrodite in this way also necessitates her removal from the Judgement of Paris, which in turn removes one of the traditional causes of the war. The etymological pun which concludes this new exclusion is clever, but it is not an argument of the same rational character (however spurious) which Hecuba has elsewhere been at pains to produce.[68] In adopting what we might call an extra-rational argument, Hecuba is trying to rebut the effects of Helen's non-verbal persuasion, i.e. her beauty.

991–7. Hecuba must move on before the effects of her wit fade. She proceeds, therefore, to blame Helen's notorious penchant for extravagance and her very un-Hellenic attachment to barbarian culture (991–2):

ὃν εἰσιδοῦσα βαρβάροις ἐσθήμασιν
χρυσῷ τε λαμπρὸν ἐξεμαργώθης φρένας.

Seeing him [Paris] in barbarian clothes
and shining in gold, you went completely out of your mind.

The verb used here ('ἐξεμαργώθης') is both rare and extreme. Apart from inverting the Greek/barbarian polarity, Hecuba is also attempting to replace the irrationality of the gods (which

---

[68] I understand the difficulties of using the word 'rational' here, as it may be claimed that Hecuba's pun is only non-rational in our terms. Also note that it is unusual to deny that desire is caused by external factors; Waterfield (1982), 141.

she thought Helen promoted) with the madness of Helen herself. One can note Hecuba's rhetoric at work in two other
ways. First, in order to gain the fullest force from the picture
of Helen's hedonism, Hecuba minimizes the wealth and luxury available to her in Sparta (993: 'having little in Argos'/'ἐν
μὲν γὰρ Ἄργει σμίκρ' ἔχουσ''; see Hom. *Od.* 4.43–6, 71–5 for
the splendour of Menelaus' palace; cf. lines 996–7, quoted
below). Second, she exaggerates Helen's extravagance by
comparing it to the wealth of Troy itself (994–6):

> τὴν Φρυγῶν πόλιν
> χρυσῷ ῥέουσαν ἤλπισας κατακλύσειν
> δαπάναισιν

> the city of the Phrygians,
> flowing with gold, you hoped to overwhelm
> with extravagances

One should also note here the repetition of 'χρυσῷ' ('gold'; cf.
992 above) in relation to Troy: in order to establish Helen's
tastes as blameworthy, Hecuba must also demonstrate the
same faults in her own city. Finally, she reaffirms her very
Greek scorn for the barbarian taste for the sybaritic lifestyle,
again by comparing it with the poverty of Argos (996–7):

> οὐδ' ἦν ἱκανά σοι τὰ Μενέλεω
> μέλαθρα ταῖς σαῖς ἐγκαθυβρίζειν τρυφαῖς.

> Nor was the palace of Menelaus enough
> for you to revel in your fondness for luxuries.

998–1009. Hecuba begins this next passage by picking up
the use, if not the point, of *bia* (force) by Helen (998; cf. 959,
962). She attributes to Helen a plea which she did not make,
i.e. that she was forced to leave Sparta by Paris. As Vellacott
puts it: 'she [Hecuba] sarcastically refutes what she [Helen] did
not say'.[69] The hoped-for force of this refutation of nothing is
to undermine the claim that Helen did make about trying to

---

[69] (1975), 146; see also Amerasinghe (1973), 102. As M. Lloyd (1992), 109 points out,
in other versions the problem is less one of why Helen failed to escape from Troy;
it is more why the Trojans did not hand her back to the Greeks (see e.g. Hdt.
2.120).

escape from Troy. Hecuba then accuses Helen of opportunism and fickleness (1002–9), noting that, although she claims to be a victim of force, she is in fact a very sharp observer of relative power (1004–7).

1010–14. Hecuba now deals with Helen's description of her attempted escape (955–8) and of her unwillingness to stay in Troy (1011). The delay between the rebuttal of the claim Helen did not make and this refutation probably works in Hecuba's favour, especially when, sandwiched between the two, there is a potent description of Helen the prudential, scheming, fair-weather wife (1005–9). But Hecuba's advice on what Helen ought to have done is not really an answer to Helen's claim of attempted escape. She asks why Helen did not kill herself (1012–13). Her choice of appropriate deaths is in tune with our knowledge of the required manner of suicide for noble women, but sits unhappily with her claim a few lines earlier that Helen lacks the male quality of *aretē* (women more usually strive after *eukleia*, as Phaedra, or *eudoxia*, as Andromache). Again, Hecuba has recourse to the ideology in which *gunē* only means 'woman' when it also means 'wife', and in which, in circumstances like Helen's, the only noble course of action (1013: *gennaia*) is suicide.

1015–19. Another answer to 955–8. Hecuba herself offered to assist Helen's escape. She quotes the advice she gave (1016–19). This is an interesting passage which makes Helen's departure from Troy and therefore the end of the war an effect of the reaffirmation of proper marriages (1016–17: 'my children will make other marriages'/'οἱ δ᾽ ἐμοὶ παῖδες γάμους ἄλλους γαμοῦσι'), or rather of the dissolution of that marriage, born out of transgression, between Helen and Paris (1018–19). Yet Hecuba addresses Helen as daughter (1016: Ὦ θύγατερ'), thereby accepting – if only sarcastically – the marriage between Helen and her son.

1020–1. Hecuba explains why her advice was ignored. This is a repeat of 991ff., where Helen's attraction to barbarian luxury was also derided. Again, Hecuba adopts a Greek position of scorn against Helen's taste for the barbarian life. Here that is associated with transgression (1020: 'you ran riot'/

'ὕβριζες'), subservience and animality (1021: 'to prostrate themselves'/'προσκυνεῖσθαι'; the *kun-* part of the verb comes from *kuōn*, which means 'dog'), and desire (1021: 'you wanted'/'ἤθελες'). In so doing, she not only demonstrates once again her temporary Greekness; she also attempts to strengthen her criticism and appeal to Menelaus by virtue of the extremity and completeness of her derision for Helen.

1022–8. Here, some ironic reversal. The Greek Helen, who was so attached to barbarian attire, but came from dowdy Sparta, stands resplendent in fine vestment (1022–3), though we only have Hecuba's word for it (but see 1107–8). The Queen of Troy, however, wears clothes appropriate to her new servile status (496ff.). In addressing Helen, Hecuba once again uses strong language (1024: 'O abominable [literally 'to be spat upon'] woman'/'ὦ κατάπτυστον κάρα') and tells Helen what she should be wearing and how she should be acting (1025–6). There is something absurd about Hecuba's suggestion that Helen should dress down, precisely because she is Helen, as if the righteousness of Hecuba's attitude were being mocked by the inherited associations of Helen's appearance. There is also something inconsistent in Hecuba's implicit fear of Helen's appearance (about which earlier she had been more explicit; see 892), for she had tried to argue that it was not Helen's looks that swayed Paris but vice versa (987, 991). She also recommends to Helen the quality which men prescribe for women: *sōphrosunē* (1027–8). Possession of this would have allowed Helen to do the decent, the *gennaios*, thing and kill herself.

1029–32. The final address to Menelaus reaffirms male ideology. A *nomos* should be established (1031–2) whereby treacherous wives are killed by their husbands. Hecuba recommends this as a sort of victory for Greece and, implicitly, for men (1030: 'crown Greece'/'στεφάνωσον Ἑλλάδ''). Lee's comment (*ad loc.*) is singularly inappropriate: 'Hecuba simply means that it would be a credit to Greece that her warriors had captured and slain an abominable woman.' Is it so simple? Given the complications that the notion of victory is prone to in this play, Hecuba's advice sounds more like an explicit affirmation of one aspect of male ideology, the transgression of which led to the war (another aspect of male ideology) and her own current calamities. It also emphasizes the differences between Hecuba and Cassandra: Hecuba not only shares male ideology in defeat, but positively asserts it.

Hecuba's response, then, is as slyly rhetorical as Helen's defence. While we saw some slick moves in Helen's speech, Hecuba is very slippery indeed.[70] Some of Helen's points are not answered, while replies are made to arguments which have not been offered. Hecuba also arrogantly appropriates Greek attitudes towards barbarians. Indeed, Helen is depicted as a barbarian, with all the usual pejorative associations. Such inversions play a key part in Hecuba's persuasion. And although, in her dismissal of the Judgement of Paris, she is even more fifth-century and rationalistic than Helen, by deferring to male ideology she is less radical (even if in some of the advice Hecuba gives to Helen, e.g. to commit suicide, one senses something beyond rhetorical manipulation of ideology: it sounds as though she 'really means' it). This is an appropriation of that which is most likely to convince Menelaus: Hecuba betrays the good orator's skill of knowing her audience. Most critics have been impressed by Hecuba's rhetoric but without noticing that part of its appeal lies in the fact that it is a barbarian who is speaking. Barbarians, even when they speak Greek, are defined as lacking the Greek *logos*. Yet here, the barbarian stands up to Gorgias.

Hecuba convinces us, then, that she is a smooth practitioner of the rhetorical art. Her persuasion after all tries to persuade Menelaus that it is not persuasion at all, but the truth. But, in flexing these rhetorical muscles, Hecuba reveals some significant inconsistencies. Although she accuses Helen of opportunism, her temporary alliance with Menelaus demonstrates that very same quality. Her depiction of the gods is flawed, though that is in part because of statements she makes before and after the *agōn*. We should note that, although

---

[70] For a discussion of the rhetorical sophistication of Euripidean debates generally, and of the *agōn* in *Troades* particularly, see M. Lloyd (1992), 19–36.

Poseidon says that Helen is rightly being held as a prisoner of war, he is otherwise neutral (35). Hecuba, without any evidence, calls Helen 'hated by the gods' (1213: 'θεοστυγής'). Furthermore, some of her criticisms of Helen reflect on herself. For instance, her advice to Helen directly contradicts that which she gave to Andromache: Helen bewitches men (892–3) but should have committed suicide (1012–14); Andromache should prefer life to death (632–3) and should act in such a way that her new Greek husband will love her (699ff.).[71] Of course, the situation of the two women is entirely different. Gregory distinguishes in the sharpest moralistic way: 'Andromache is an authentic, Helen a simulated victim of force.'[72] But this is to miss the fact that Hecuba's condemnation of Helen is conducted in terms which are supposed to be applicable to all women (1031–2):

> νόμον δὲ τόνδε ταῖς ἄλλαισι θὲς
> γυναιξί, θνῄσκειν ἥτις ἂν προδῷ πόσιν.

> Establish this law for other women.
> The woman who betrays her husband should die.

Finally, the ferocity of her response to Helen is, as some critics have noted, entirely out of keeping with the picture of the pathetic, downtrodden and lamenting victim of war we otherwise receive. There is some force, therefore, in Burnett's remark that once Hecuba has herself 'called for blood, she can no longer be read as a pathetic anthology of war's atrocities'.[73]

Given that the nature of rhetoric lies in its association with the non-logical, the contingent and the non-rational, and given the inconsistencies I have shown in Hecuba's speech, it is odd to find in an otherwise powerful analysis that Goldhill

---

[71] Burnett (1977), 296.   [72] Gregory (1991), 172.

[73] Burnett (1977), 296; see also Fitzgerald (1989), 218. There is a general problem with this position, however. Following Dale (1954), xxv–xxvii, it is not clear that in Euripidean tragedy consistent character controls situations. Dale's celebrated formulation is that 'the rhetoric of the situation' determines character scene by scene. M. Lloyd (1992), 101, 109 argues that rhetorical sophistication might be said to have been used as a mark of character in early Euripides, but not in a play produced in 416/415 BC.

thinks that Helen is 'defeated by Hecuba's superior reason, superior rhetorical manipulation'.[74] Certainly, Hecuba manipulates the Greek/barbarian polarity and male ideology concerning women. But we should perhaps attempt a more balanced assessment of both the reason and the rhetoric of the two women's speeches. We should also ask: in what sense has she defeated Helen? What sort of victory is it?

Gorgias' *Helen* offers four possible reasons why Helen went to Troy with Paris: because of divine necessity or fate, because Paris compelled her, because she was persuaded and because she was overwhelmed by the power of love. If any of these reasons is true, then Helen cannot be blamed. In *Troades*, Helen, 'as if she had used Gorgias for her rhetorical training',[75] uses the first, second and last of Gorgias' arguments (as well as some of her own). It was Aphrodite who offered her to Paris (929–31), thus making her abduction a decision of the gods (Gorg. *Hel.* 6); Paris married her by force (962/ *Hel.* 7); and Aphrodite, the goddess of love, is a powerful divinity who cannot be resisted (940, 945–50; *Hel.* 19). Hecuba, using a rationalizing approach, attempts to debunk Helen's anthropomorphism. Both, therefore, employ contemporary

---

[74] (1986), 237. (Goldhill has since retracted this position publicly.) Grube (1941), 293: 'Hecuba's reply is vigorous and direct, in splendid contrast to the artificial rhetoric of Helen's performance.' Most critics have been sympathetic to Hecuba, which, also in most cases, has been equivalent to seeing her as winning the debate. For exceptions, see Scodel (1980), 99 (Helen wins the debate, a victory whereby the dangers of sophism are highlighted); Barlow (1986), 206–8 (the arguments of neither Helen nor Hecuba are right); Fitzgerald (1989). This testifies to the power of the rhetoric Euripides has given her, but does not do justice to the play's concern with the attribution of victory; see also Gellie (1986), 116, who claims that the scene shows the 'hollowness' of Helen. On the problem of the rhetoric of rationality in Greek thought, see G. Lloyd (1988), esp. 336.

[75] Goldhill (1986), 237; see Saïd (1978), 252ff., 268ff.; Donzelli (1985). The attempt by M. Lloyd (1992), 100–1 to demonstrate no direct relationship between Gorgias' *Helen* and Helen's speech in *Troades* is beside the point. The question is not one of priority, or even influence, but of similarity. There are, of course, some differences between the two speeches (the narrower focus in Gorgias, the absence in *Troades* of an argument that Helen was persuaded to leave Sparta and thus is not responsible), but, as I show in the main discussion, three of Gorgias' four arguments are employed by the Euripidean Helen. For a different perspective on Helen in Gorgias (based on Helen as exemplary female sign which the male author must appropriate in the manner of Zeus swallowing Metis), see Bergren (1983), 79–86.

fifth-century argumentation. Indeed, there is something of a Euripidean joke in that the ultra-modern Gorgianic discourse is answered by a set of arguments perhaps even more contemporary and avant-garde. The effect is analogous to Cassandra's criticism of Greek victory. Here the confrontation is not between a mythical fact and a mythical truth-teller, but between a mythical problem (who is responsible for the Trojan War?) and fifth-century techniques of argumentation.[76]

Helen, to start with, explicitly admits that she is talking about the irrational: like Gorgias, she allows for the existence of a power called desire. As Vellacott says: 'She is rational enough to know that she is dealing with the irrational.'[77] Hecuba, however, finds desire, or the irrational, a problem. Her response stresses the wisdom and rationality of the gods: they are not *amatheis* (975–6, 981). This seems to be of particular importance to Hecuba but, in order to maintain the position, she has to overcome some serious obstacles. The first of these are the offers each of the goddesses makes to Paris at the Judgement. Although Hecuba describes the promised gifts of Hera and Athene as *amatheis* (972), she does not even consider that of Aphrodite. One suspects that her lack of consideration in this respect is based on the fact that she finds it disturbing that a woman can be offered as a gift at all. It is true that possession of a woman, especially one as universally desirable as Helen, could be seen as a sign of status. But the possession of Helen is one which offends against ideology in two ways: to have her, Paris must transgress the code of hospitality; and having her will be adulterous behaviour. The alternatives to Helen offered to Paris, conquest and dominion, are, after all, valid male goals, in a world where most of the goals are created by men: how can a woman, even Helen, be offered in competition with such aspirations? Worse, how could her son have made the irrational and subversive choice of adultery over power? Hecuba has no answer, apart from

---

[76] Goldhill (1986), 236–8; M. Lloyd (1992), 104. More will be said on this topic in chapter four.

[77] (1975), 139. See Saïd (1978), 424ff. on the relation between desire and culpability in Euripides.

outright denial. She tries hard to absolve Paris from blame: he becomes a sort of Helen, not dangerous, but nevertheless endowed with a magnetic and irresistible beauty (987). Hecuba is now free to condemn Aphrodite and Helen.

But this is also a move fraught with problems. Since Aphrodite has made the offer of a woman, and because she has inspired the choice Paris makes, she is turned into a principle of desire, a force of irrationality. This complicates Hecuba's attitude to the other gods as well as to Aphrodite. She ridicules Helen's story of Aphrodite's presence, *qua* anthropomorphic entity, at Sparta (983–6), but she also seems to accept that as a principle of irrationality Aphrodite can be present anywhere and everywhere (987–9). And, while the wording of 975ff. suggests that Hecuba is willing to accept that there was such an event as the Judgement, she disagrees with all the details and can give no information herself as to what the Judgement could be about. Furthermore, once Aphrodite has ceased to be an anthropomorphic divinity, Hecuba still has to show that Helen should be blamed. But Helen could very easily reply that it makes no difference whether Aphrodite is anthropomorphic or not: the point is that she exists, as a powerful even irresistible force. Hecuba tries to show that Helen was attracted to Paris rather than vice versa, but she offers no arguments as to why or how Aphrodite can be resisted. The punning of 990 is no substitute. In trying to blame Helen, Hecuba makes the extreme rhetorical move of generalizing her attack into one on irrationality, sexuality, desire and woman (Helen and Aphrodite are taken as representative of these disturbing factors). But Hecuba cannot explain them, only condemn them.

From the substance of the arguments themselves, it would have been difficult for the audience to decide whom to favour as a winner of the debate (something they may have been able to do with Medea, or Andromache, or Hecuba). But the play could possibly present the victory of one of the speakers as a matter of fact (as in *Heracleidae* and *Hecuba*). In these terms, then, who has won this debate? When Menelaus enters, he tells us that Helen has been handed to him by the Greek army either to be killed or to be taken back to Argos (873–5). He has decided to do the latter, and to kill Helen on arrival in Greece (876–8, 883). Hecuba approves of his intention (890), but warns him to avoid looking at Helen, as that may change his mind (891–4). When Helen enters, Menelaus announces his decision to kill her, although he does not say where (901–2). Helen asks for the opportunity to argue against her fate, but Menelaus rebuffs his wife: it was for death, not arguments, that he came (903–5). It is only because Hecuba persuades him that the debate will have no effect on his decision to execute Helen that Menelaus allows the debate to go ahead (906–15). However, after the debate, Menelaus, contradicting his earlier stated intention to take Helen home to Argos (876ff.), apparently agrees to stone her immediately (1036–41), judging that her introduction of Aphrodite into the argument was specious. Helen then supplicates Menelaus (1042–3), and Hecuba urges him not to be duped (1044–5). In asserting that he is not being deceived, Menelaus already betrays that he has shifted position: now Helen is to be taken back to Argos before being stoned (1046–8). Hecuba, unpersuaded, complains that Menelaus has also been overwhelmed by the irrationality of desire which she so fears (1051). The episode concludes with Menelaus giving a wholesome but not entirely convincing affirmation of male ideology and a statement of his intention to kill Helen on returning to Argos (1052–9). What is to happen to Helen? Some scholars think she will survive,[78] some that she will be killed.[79] But there is no firm evidence in the text for either position, although Menelaus is the judge and he does say that Helen is guilty. However, the two options between which Menelaus hesitates alert us to the absence of a third, which is that he will take Helen back to Argos and live happily with her as his wife. This is Homer's account in *Odyssey* 4. It will not really do simply to assert that the audience will remember Homer and

---

[78] Scodel (1980), 98–9; Craik (1990), 14 n.12; see also Grube (1941), 294; Havelock (1968), 127.

[79] M. Lloyd (1984), 303.

therefore assume that Helen has won, nor that we can ignore Homer altogether.[80] As with Cassandra's criticism of the Greeks, the Euripidean version must necessarily and permanently grate against the mythical and literary traditions, leaving the question unresolved.[81]

Michael Lloyd, in his recent book, agrees on the lack of the resolution, but for different reasons.[82] He argues that, in all the Euripidean debates, only in *Heracleidae* and *Hecuba* does one side clearly gain its ends. He says (p. 16): 'In no other agon in Euripides does any character gain a meaningful victory in the sense of achieving his ends by means of what he says.' The reason for this difference from debates in the law courts, Lloyd argues, is that Euripides is telling the audience that talking will not resolve tragic conflict. This failure of debate is stressed by the obscure nature of the relationship of the Euripidean *agōn* to the action of the play around it. Such an apology for the dramatic irrelevance of the *agōn* will no doubt be attractive to some. But there are two problems. First, while Lloyd is keen to study the *agōn* in its 'full dramatic context' (p. 18; see also p. 2), he tends to prefer to understand each *agōn* in relation to other *agōnes* in other plays (e.g. p. 2: 'Variations can be understood only in terms of the norm'). He thus misses the relation of the *agōn* in *Troades* to Cassandra's questioning of victory and the distinctive nature of the debate's failure to secure a victor. Second, it is inconsistent to claim of the *agōn* in *Troades* that, in common with other debates, no character achieves his ends by what he says and also that, while Menelaus is resolved to kill Helen at the beginning of the debate (with some reiterations at the end), the matter of Helen's death is left unresolved. From Helen's point of view at least, a significant result (i.e. possible life rather than certain death) has been achieved.

Hecuba's victory, then, is not clear cut or certain. It may be that it is analogous in its questionable and ambivalent status

---

[80] Gregory (1991), 174 makes the first point.
[81] Goldhill (1986), 238 n.42. Steidle (1968), 54 sees Hecuba's victory as only apparent; see also Strohm (1957), 36.
[82] M. Lloyd (1992), 15–17, 110–12.

to the victory of the Greeks. Both these victories fulfil the terms of the *agōn*, but since both results are challenged, the *agōn* itself is questioned as an institution which can properly produce a victor. That is the essence of Cassandra's criticism. The world of her undefeated Trojans is, as far as is possible, traditional but not agonistic. But the critique is inconsistent as well, for the criteria and values she offers in opposition to war as it is traditionally conceived are similar to those which issue from Paris' choice of Aphrodite and, therefore, of Helen. Paris chooses, as Cassandra might have done, woman, over the honourable goals of conquest and dominion.[83] But Paris' choice is of woman associated not only with the home and the family but also with desire and sexuality, non-rational elements which Cassandra neglected to consider. That the values which inform Cassandra's criticism of the war and its victors should have something in common with those which played their part in starting the war is a delicious Euripidean irony.

In the next two chapters I will discuss in detail the effect of the anachronistic appearance of sophistic discourse in *Troades*. But I want to stress one general aspect of sophism which Guthrie summarizes as the observation that the sophists demonstrate that there are no criteria, no clearly defined ways of judging.[84] *Troades* offers many conflicting criteria, but none are secure. The *agōn*, the principle of polarity which informs war, might be expected to remain intact while war effects the confusions and transgressions of all the other constitutive polarities. But no, for the *agōn* itself has become a problem. Whether in war or in debate and even if played by the rules, it does not in this play provide certain victors.

There is more than a hint of self-reference in *Troades'* representation of the difficulties of the *agōn*, for tragedy is itself a dramatized *agōn*. And its judge is the audience. The play throws the responsibility for deciding who won the war and who won the debate onto the audience, stealing from them

---

[83] It is difficult to evaluate the role of the promised gifts in Paris' decision to choose Aphrodite: was Aphrodite really the most beautiful, or did Paris like the idea of possessing Helen? Obviously, my argument prefers the latter.

[84] (1971), 196.

any confidence they might have in traditional knowledge. Who should they believe? The epic cycle or Cassandra? Homer, Menelaus or Euripides? A second point of self-reference is that each poet, protagonist and chorus competed for the first prize – tragedy as *agōn* in a different sense. Euripides is sometimes thought not to have won the author's prize as often as he should.[85] But could he expect victory when he so powerfully demonstrates the difficulties of judging it? And, given those difficulties, can victory itself be judged important? And what implications could the problems of victory have for Athens, the imperial *polis*, at the time of *Troades*' production still engaged in a long war, seemingly without end or result?

Vernant has described war not only as agonistic but as discursive: 'A speech can stop a war, a victory in war can settle a debate.'[86] But, bearing in mind our difficulties with judging a winner, perhaps we might say that if war is discursive, it is because discourse is polemic. Barthes has described culture/ discourse as a war of languages.[87] *Troades* contains such a war. Some characters, like Menelaus and, more strangely, Hecuba, may speak from apparently authoritative positions of ideology (which Barthes calls 'encratic'); others, such as Cassandra and Helen, speak from marginal and disturbing positions ('acratic' in Barthes' terminology).[88] But on the tragic stage both positions are contained within Athenian ideology. And it is in recognizing this that we confront a possibly unstable aspect of Athenian ideology, namely, that it is constructed agonistically. It provides self-definition through comparison with designated others, but it is, especially in tragedy, forever examining those self-definitions by confronting them, in *agōnes*, with discourses that subvert some of Athens' most cherished values. Barthes may be right to say that a discourse's ability to mix languages gives it a certain 'festive

---

[85] Of course, Euripides won the first prize fewer times than Aeschylus and Sophocles, but we have no reason to think that he was ever denied a chorus; see Stevens (1956) and now Michelini (1987), 52–94.

[86] (1980), 27.

[87] 'Pax culturalis', 'The war of languages', 'The division of languages' in (1986).

[88] (1986), 107.

dimension';[89] and that is certainly appropriate at the Great Dionysia. But we cannot help but be struck by the quirky nature of Athenian ideology when, at the potent central event of civic discourse called the Great Dionysia, at the very moment when Athens' power is most celebrated, it seeks to affirm itself by putting itself at risk.

[89] Barthes (1986), 110.

4

SPACE AND TIME

The most distinctive features of *Troades* are those which can be grouped under the title 'tragic space'. I include in this category the spatial characteristics of the play (the scene, references to other places, the various discussions of space), the temporal characteristics of the play (the Trojan women's views about time, the balance between mythical and contemporary features), and, finally, the relation between the world of the play and the world of the audience (does the former acknowledge the latter?). All these three aspects of the play can be called 'tragic space' since they play a part in defining the world of the play, or the space of the stage, for and against the world of the audience (the space of the auditorium). But in order to provide a context against which the distinctiveness of our first category, the spatial characteristics of *Troades*, may be seen, it is necessary to broaden our investigation by considering the political and cultural importance of space in fifth-century Athens and by surveying the variety of the tragic representation of space.

The space of Athens

The invention of the *polis* was the invention of its space: spatial and political organization were mutually reinforcing. But to produce a description of the space of Athens involves recording two separate but often merging histories: first, of the political organization of space in Athens and other cities; and, second, of the discussion and representation of space.

De Polignac has traced how the birth of the *polis* coincided with the establishment of non-urban, monumental sanctuaries

163

in the eighth century BC.[1] In this way, a new space was invented. The sanctuary, situated on the margins of a territory, first acted as a marker of that territory and who controlled it.[2] Second, the monumental nature of the buildings presupposed the ability to make decisions collectively. Third, and most important, the new sacred space of cult (distinguished from indeterminate Dark Age religious space)[3] allowed for the creation of a unifying social space, namely, that which we would call the *polis*. It was in this new sacred space that the whole community was brought together. It was in religious terms that integrations into and exclusions from the community were managed. It was in the same terms that the new cohesiveness of the *polis* was expressed. Sacred space thus lies at the root of civic space. More particularly, the space of the polis was organized around two poles, the political at the centre and the sacred at the margins: ritual processions from centre to margin, from city to sanctuary, mark the unification of the two terms into the *polis*.[4]

This association between sanctity and the *polis* is reiterated throughout both the *Iliad* and the *Odyssey*. In fact, as Scully has reminded us, the *polis* – and its walls, temples and agora – receives the epithet 'sacred' more frequently than anything else so described in the Homeric poems.[5] It is also interesting that Homer's Troy has its important temples – of Athene (*Il.* 6.87) and Apollo (*Il.* 5.446) – inside the city walls. Athens, like other Greek cities, was also founded on a link between its sacred space and its political institutions, but their spatial relationship was organized in a manner comparable to Homeric Troy rather than to actual contemporary cities: the most important sanctuary of Athens was that of Athene, which was situated on the Acropolis in the centre of the city. Athens was therefore what de Polignac calls a 'monocentric' city. The rit-

[1] (1984), esp. 41–92. [2] Ibid., 42–9.
[3] Ibid., 27–8 notes the example of the sacrifice to Poseidon at Hom. *Od.* 3.1ff., which takes place on the beach: appropriate for the god of the sea, but not a well-defined sacred space.
[4] Ibid., 154–6. De Polignac notes (p. 48) that the only good roads in classical Greece were between urban centres and sanctuaries on the periphery of the territory.
[5] (1990), 16–40.

ual processions of other Greek cities from urban centre to peripheral sanctuary are replaced in Athens by the Panathenaic procession from margin to centre.[6]

In Athens, then, the civic order itself was based on the spatial and hierarchical model of centre and margin. The city stood as a centre for the surrounding territory, and at the centre of the city was the acropolis and the agora.[7] Detienne traces how the classical *polis* used the prevalent idea in Homer of putting prizes for games and objects of plunder 'into the middle/centre' (*es meson*).[8] It is especially true of democratic Athens that this was used to convey the idea that when one spoke in public one spoke from the centre: one walked *es meson* as a precondition of discourse.[9] So, while the territory is centred by the *polis*, and the *polis* by the acropolis and the agora, we can see that the demes which extend outwards from the main city are also themselves, on the model of city, centred spaces.[10] And while the acropolis and the agora stand at the centre of the city, the *oikos*, sometimes opposed to *polis*, itself has the hearth (*hestia*) at its centre, a model appropriated by the *polis*, with its public hearth (*koinē hestia*) at the political centre (Arist. *Pol.* 1322a26ff.).[11] The significance of all these facts is that Athenian political space was centred space, where authority and power stood at the centre and, as it were, radiated outwards to the margins.[12] And, although Cleisthenes

[6] De Polignac (1984), 87–90.

[7] See Thuc. 2.15.6 on the equivalence of the acropolis and *polis*; see Lévêque and Vidal-Naquet (1973), 16–17; Humphreys, 'Town and Country' in (1978); Loraux (1981b), 42ff.; Vernant (1982), 125–8; (1983), 220–1, 228, 232.

[8] See also Theognis 677–8: social order breaks down when fair distribution of objects is no longer directed *es meson*.

[9] For power *es meson*, see Hdt. 3.142; 4.161; 7.164. For the idea that one puts proposals *es meson*, see Hdt. 1.207; 3.80; 7.8. For political discourse *es meson*, see Hdt. 3.83; 4.118; 8.21, 73. One finds similar expressions in Euripides at e.g. *Supp.* 439 in defence of the democracy; *Hel.* 1542; *Tro.* 54; *Erechtheus* fr. 65.90 (Austin). See Detienne (1965) and (1967), 83–102.

[10] De Ste Croix (1981), 9–19; R. Osborne (1985).

[11] Gernet (1981), 322–39.

[12] Note the story of Thales demanding one centre for Ionia: Hdt. 1.170; see Pl. *Laws* 745bff.; Vernant (1983), 221, 231. On the agora as a political and religious centre, see Hom. *Il.* 18.497ff.; Soph. *OT* 161; *Or.* 919; see Kolb (1979), 507ff. See also Loraux (1981b), 41ff. for other expressions of space, e.g high/low. On sacred land and space (and thus sites of potential transgression), see Parker (1983), 160–70.

divided Attica into coast, plain and city, the idea of a centred space was also an important feature of the Cleisthenic reforms. Noting the influence of geometrical speculation and the politicization of the goddess Hestia, Vernant summarizes the reforms in this way: the Cleisthenic *politeia* was an undifferentiated civic space where 'all the citizens would be on the same level and would occupy symmetrical and reversible positions in relation to one common central point' (i.e. the common hearth).[13] Indeed, the public art, the civic discourse of Athens uses the idea of the self included at the centre, and the other outside.[14]

Athens was also the centre of an empire. The empire, subject to power from the centre,[15] generated income, displayed tellingly before the performance of the plays at the Great Dionysia. Athens was also the centre of trading in the Greek world, which, because of the number of foreign traders, meant that Athens was obliged to invent the status of metic. Also, in the fifth century Athens became the self-proclaimed intellectual capital of Greece (Pl. *Prot.* 337d; Ath. 5.187d; Plut. *Per.* 3–6.2). Athenians, renowned for their intelligence and speed of thought, engaged in what Aristotle calls an indiscriminate search for knowledge after the defeat of Xerxes, expanding their minds as well as their empire (Arist. *Pol.* 1341a28–32). That this education was partly achieved by interaction with those foreign intellectuals, the sophists, did have problematic consequences for Athens conceived as a spatial unit.[16] Tragedy, as will be seen later, represents some of those problems.

The Homeric poems depict cities in a variety of ways. Troy in the *Iliad*, on the one hand, is a citadel reminiscent of the Mycenean era, yet it still has some features (e.g. free-standing,

[13] Vernant (1983), 212ff.; see also Lévêque and Vidal-Naquet (1973).

[14] Dubois (1984), *passim*.

[15] Athens also brought in certain lawsuits from the empire to be tried in Athens: Ps. Xen. *Ath. Pol.* 1.16; Meiggs and Lewis (1969) 45.4, 46.31–41, 52.70–6; Ar. *Birds* 1041.

[16] Pericles boasted that Athens was an education to the rest of Greece (Thuc. 2.41.1); cf. Voegelin (1957), 267: 'in order to become ... the school of Hellas, Athens had to be its schoolboy for two generations'.

communal temples) more readily associated with the Ionian cities of the eighth century. Scheria in the *Odyssey*, on the other hand, situated on a low-lying peninsula, has a dominant Ionian influence. What unites the the Mycenean and the Ionian models of the city is that they are walled.[17] In the *Odyssey*, however, civilization is perceived more in the existence of cultivated fields than of walls (*Od.* 5.63ff., 10.147ff.; cf. *Cycl.* 115–16).[18] Ithaca itself has no walls, nor any public buildings, and Odysseus is amazed at the walls of Scheria (*Od.* 7.43–5). But since the Troy of *Troades* is to be our focus later, it is worth while observing the spatial features of Homeric Troy. It will also become clear that it is an important presence behind Euripides' representation of the city.

In the *Iliad*, the walls of Troy are its most marked feature, frequently used in adjectival form to describe the *polis*.[19] They are divinely built and, like the *polis* as a whole, sacred (*Il.* 4.46, 164; 6.96, 277, 448; 8.519; 21.128, 526ff.; 24.27; see *Od.* 11.86, 17.293); their effectiveness and beauty is commented on (*Il.* 1.129, 7.71, 8.24). It is at, on or around the walls that many of the most important events of the poem take place, for example, the discussion between Helen, Priam and the Trojan elders in Book 3, or the scene between Hector and Andromache in Book 6, or the duel between Achilles and Hector in Book 22. And to compare groups of men, or individuals, to walls is to stress their strength (e.g. *Il.* 4.462; 11.485; 12.40–6, 373; 15.617–20; 24.499–501). The walls of Troy enclose and define the community of Troy.[20] The close connection between walls and *polis* is underlined by the fact that founding a city is, in Homer, to build its walls (*Il.* 7.452–3; *Od.* 6.9–10;

[17] Scully (1990), 81–99.
[18] Vidal-Naquet (1981), 84–5; Scully (1990), 45–6.
[19] Scully (1990), 41–53.
[20] Garlan (1968), 255: 'la notion d'enceinte urbaine est inséparable du concept de la cité.' Scully (1990), 3: 'Both for the polis at war [Troy] and the polis in a remote land of ease [Scheria], the circuit wall is crucial for definition as it encloses the entire urban community.' And ibid., 47: 'For Homer, the polis is essentially a spatial and architectural entity which nurtures, by enclosing, civilization with its prize of women and children.'

11.260ff.), and that walls can stand metonymically for the city (Thebes, in this case: *Il.* 2.691).[21] In classical antiquity the equation between walls and cities provoked different reactions. Thucydides was keen to note how civilized cities were able to flourish in the early history of Greece only on condition that they had walls (1.8.3) and also the relation between the Athenian democracy and Themistocles' Long Walls (1.107.4).[22] But the historian can also have Nicias telling his troops that men are the *polis*, not walls and empty ships (7.77.7; cf. Aesch. *Pers.* 349; Soph. *Aj.* 158–9; Soph. *OT* 56–7). Plato allows that people may prefer to have walls, but if they do: 'the whole city should be one wall' (*Laws* 779b: 'πᾶσα ἡ πόλις ἓν τεῖχος'). Lycurgus was said to have dismissed walls as well, preferring that they be made of men rather than brick (Plut. *Lyc.* 19). Later, Aristotle was firm in his rejection of the distrust of walls (*Pol.* 1330b–1331a).

The idea that the *polis* is an enclosure, a sort of bounded space, which protects those who are inside from the dangers and uncertainties of the outside, is a feature both of the Homeric poems and the myths which were used by tragedy. Hector in the *Iliad* stands as the hero who must protect those inside his city from the terrible fate that awaits them should what is outside be let in. Myths of wandering heroes – the *Odyssey* is the most celebrated – who journey through outlandish places without cities and with different customs, reinforce the idea of *polis* as civilization enclosed. Indeed, the model of the transgressive hero who goes into the wild outside in order to protect his community but in so doing becomes, as it were, infected with the outside, bringing destruction and madness to the very people he tries to protect on the inside, is used, sometimes obliquely and sometimes more overtly, time and again in fifth-century tragedy.[23] And the *Bacchae* dramatizes the advent of the god from outside, Dionysus, to the centre of the

---

[21] For *polis* as originally meaning 'walls', see Heraclitus fr. 65 (Kahn); Chantraine (1968), 926.

[22] On walls as giving a city bargaining power, see Thuc. 1.93; Lawrence (1979), 113.

[23] Knox (1964). Bernand (1985), 15 calls the tragic hero 'un vagabond'.

polis from the wild outside of the mountains: the music of the god is a threat to the spatial integrity of Thebes. The Great Dionysia is itself the result of the god's advent.

Walls were as important to Athens as they were to Homer's Troy. They allowed Pericles, at the beginning of the Peloponnesian War, to urge on his fellow-citizens a strategy of abandoning the territory of Attica to seek refuge inside the impregnable fortifications of the city. So, Athens was not only a centred space; it was also a well-defined, enclosed space. The sense of belonging to which a citizen aspired was firmly constructed in spatial terms. At the level of ideology, to be included was to be empowered; excluded, impotent. That is the reason why exile was such an extreme punishment (see e.g. Eur. *El.* 1314–15; *Phoen.* 388ff.). In overtly political terms, the importance of Pericles' citizenship law of 451 BC has often been commented on. But its definition of Athenian citizenship shares with the institutions of hospitality and supplication the notions of inclusion and exclusion as its basis (Arist. *Ath. Pol.* 26.3; see appendix one).

But, in defining the citizen as an enfranchised male adult, as one included at the centre, Athens produced an internal civic order prone, at least in one respect, to inconsistency. For, within Athens, gender politics were also in part constructed spatially.[24] Women, lifelong legal minors with no political rights except from their associations with male citizens (father, brother, husband), were excluded from all explicitly political activity, and their appearances in the public sphere were limited officially to involvement in ritual. Their place, prescribed by ideology, was inside the *oikos*; their duty, similarly prescribed, to be silent and to bear children (Thuc. 2.45.2; Xen. *Oec.* 7.30). But women were also supposed to be secluded inside the *oikos*, having separate living quarters from the male members of the family, associating with domestic

---

[24] For the methodological difficulties of writing a history of this gender politics based on the evidence of men alone, see Goldhill (1986), 107–12; Just (1989), 1–12. On women as nameless, see e.g. Schaps (1977); Keuls (1985), 20, 90ff., 124.

slaves (Xen. *Oec.* 9.5).[25] In this way ideology prescribed an indoor life for women and, in so doing, it constructed a gender-based conception of space: women – inside/men – outside.

Women, however, as has been seen in chapter two, were also defined as other to men. As such, they were grouped by analogy with barbarians and slaves: this meant that they were depicted as outside the circle of men. Yet the wives, sisters and daughters of Athenian citizens were Greek and free; they were also, as a matter of fact, inside the city. Therefore, women were, so to speak, excluded within. The tension between these two spatial determinations is frequently exploited in the tragic representation of women.

So far, then, Athens – centred and enclosed by its walls – has been seen to have had a spatial organization similar to that of Homer's Troy. But in one respect Athens was distinctive. For, unlike other Greeks, the Athenians did not perceive themselves as having come from elsewhere (*Erechtheus* fr. 50, 7–10 [Austin]).[26] They had instead the myth of autochthony, a story of a special relationship with space. The myth states that Athenians were originally Athenians; they had always been who, what and where they were, because they were born from the soil of Attica.[27] Of course, this myth served many purposes, convincing Athenians of their superiority to other Greeks in countless imaginary victories, marking out, therefore, both the hierarchies within Athens (men and women) and without (Athenians and others).[28] Thus the originary myth of Athens is constructed in spatial terms. Membership

---

[25] Keuls (1985), 100ff.; Just (1989), 105–25. On the archaeological evidence for separate quarters for women in fifth-century Athenian houses, see Walker (1983); and, against her, M. Jameson (1990). Cohen (1989) argues that the seclusion of women was maintained only at the level of ideology. In practice, and in common with other Mediterranean women, the women of Athens spent much of their time outside (in the fields, in the market, at ritual processions etc.).

[26] It should be noted, however, that the homogeneities in language and culture which constituted the Greek world were the product of Greek mobility and of the contacts Greeks had with other peoples; see Purcell (1990).

[27] Ar. *Wasps* 1075ff.; Hdt. 7.161; Thuc. 2.36; Dem. *Epitaphios* 4–5; Pl. *Menex.* 245d; Arist. *Rhet.* 1360b31ff.; see Loraux (1981b), 197–253 [=(1990)], which concentrates on *Ion*.

[28] Autochthony was an appropriate myth for the *logos hēgēmonikos* that was the Funeral Oration (see Thuc. 2.39.2, 41.2, 41.4, 42.1).

of a *polis* was always crucial to the Greeks: from Homer on, the first question a new often arrival is asked is often 'where are you from?' Athens, however, through the myth of autochthony, tightened the connection between ethnic identity and spatial origin.

The development of the space of Athens was not, however, only a matter of Cleisthenic reorganization, or of adapting the Homeric model of distributing spoils of war. The influence of geometry on the Cleisthenic reforms has already been noted, as has the similarity of Athenian space not to other contemporary cities but to Homeric Troy. Increasingly in the fifth century there arose new discourses of space – geometry, geography, the relationship between place and (political and personal) constitution – which coincided with and reinforced the organization of civic space. For instance, Greek maps of the sixth and fifth centuries, as far as they can be reconstructed (mainly from Herodotus), show us that the Greeks represented themselves as at the centre of the world with Celts, Scythians, Indians and Ethiopians, for example, all placed at the edges.[29] The idea of Greek centrality was further stressed in the identification of Delphi as the centre of the whole world (see *Med.* 668; *Or.* 333, 592). And the Hippocratic work, *Airs, Waters, Places*, in its discussion of how climate and quality of land affect health and character, places Greek Asia Minor in the middle between the extremes of climate to north and south (*AWP* 12).

It is in the work of Herodotus, however, that the most complicated examination of space can be found. Herodotus the ethnographer elaborates and extends the mythical inheritance of wandering heroes (such as Odysseus), whose journeys into fantastic places confirmed the nature and desirability of Greek space.[30] With Herodotus, the geography, as well as the culture, of the other receives systematic treatment. As with the

---

[29] See Heidel (1937); Myres (1953), 32–60; Vernant (1982), 127; Dilke (1985), 22ff.; Jacob (1988). Helgerson (1988) is an interesting piece concerned with the relationship between maps and authority in renaissance England.

[30] On the *Odyssey* as the story of Odysseus' return to normal civilization, see Vidal-Naquet (1981). For other myths of wandering heroes, see Davison (1991).

examination of the customs of other peoples, so the definition
of the space of the other assists the understanding of Greek
space. Hartog has recently demonstrated the complications of
this enterprise in his analysis of Herodotus' account of the
Scythians.[31] Scythia, already celebrated as a land at the edges
of the earth (Aesch. *PV* 416ff.; Ar. *Ach.* 702–3), uncultivated
and with an extreme climate (Hdt. 4.28–30; see *AWP* 19), is
inhabited by nomads (Hdt. 4.1–44; *AWP* 18). Unlike Greek
cities, which bury their heroes in the centres or walls of their
cities, the Scythians bury their kings on the edge of the territory.[32] In all these respects Scythia and the Scythians display
an essential otherness to the Greeks. But this otherness is variously complicated: Scythia is shown to have its own frontiers
and margins and it is between Asia and Europe (Hdt. 4.45; see
AWP 12, 17); the Scythians think of themselves as cultivators
of land (Hdt. 4.5–7); Scythian nomadism, in the encounter
with the army of Darius, is represented as a military strategy
(similar, in some ways, to that of Pericles in the Archidamian
War);[33] and, oddly, these nomadic Scythians worship the
goddess Hestia, a divinity who normally stands for fixity and
permanence (Hdt. 4.59, 127).

These complications are sometimes a wish to curb the
polarizing zeal of the Greeks (Scythia is not simply nomadic
space; it is divided into plots (*nomes*) just like Egypt: Hdt.
4.62, 66); on other occasions, Herodotus reveals something
about Greek perceptions of space (nomadism is inconceivable
except as a strategy). Herodotus is also a surveyor, measuring,
giving dimensions and boundaries (e.g. Hdt. 2.127; 4.85). He
even goes so far at one point as to turn Scythia into a geomet-
rically acceptable square (Hdt. 4.99–101).[34]

[31] Hartog (1988).
[32] Greek heroes buried in the centre: Adrastus in the agora of Sicyon (Hdt. 5.67);
Theseus in the Theseion in Athens (Plut. *Cim.* 8; *Thes.* 36). Heroes buried in the
walls: Aetolus in Elis (Paus. 5.44). In both cases the heroes are supposed to assist
the defence of the city: note the story of the struggle for possession of Orestes'
bones at Hdt. 1.67–8; note also that Oedipus in Sophocles' *Oedipus at Colonus* will
act after his death as a defence of Athens. For the burial of Scythian kings, see
Hdt. 4.71; Hartog (1988), 134–8.
[33] Hdt. 4.46; cf. Thuc. 1.143.5; Hartog (1988), 200–6.
[34] See Hartog (1988), 340ff.

Herodotus is an important contributor to fifth-century considerations of space. His importance to a study of tragic space lies in his description and definition of the space of the other and, thereby, of the self. Tragedy had a similar role to play in examining civic space and it performed that role by representing spaces of various degrees of otherness. Tragedy, however, is distinguished from Herodotus by the fact that it was performed in a central civic space, the Theatre of Dionysus, near the Pnyx and under the Acropolis.[35] And for the Great Dionysia at least, Greeks (including representatives of Athens' allies) came from all over to watch the plays. Vernant is right to state that tragedy occupies the same civic space as assemblies and courts, even as it opens up the 'space of the imaginary'.[36] The authority of tragedy issues not only from a traditional reverence in which poets were held but also from its authorization by the *polis*. The traditional function of poetry was reaffirmed by the *polis* granting tragedy the right to be performed at the centre. Tragedy's authority has its source in the centre, because it is one of those discourses placed, as it were, *es meson*.

The motivation for examining space was that, as has been seen, spatial and political organization were mutually reinforcing, or, to put it another way, space played a crucial part in determining civic, individual and gender identities.[37] It is the tragic representation of these identities (together with their problems) and their relationships to space that will be the main interest of the next section of this chapter. The survey conducted there will not only show how tragedy picked up

[35] On this and the relations between the Agora, the theatre and the *orchēstra*, see Wycherley (1949), 50–1; Webster (1970²), 5; Padel (1990), 337; but, for a detailed treatment, see Kolb (1979), especially at p. 514: 'daß einerseits das Theater in Gestalt der Orchestra der politische Kern der Agora und andererseits der Volksversammlungsplatz die Geburtstätte des Theaters war'.

[36] Vernant and Vidal-Naquet (1988), 187.

[37] The connections between space and power are much in evidence in the twentieth century, mainly because they so often seem to be in crisis. For instance, Lenin rejected Einstein because he did not want to lose the objective reality fundamental to Marxism-Leninism; see Kern (1983), 134. Frederic Jameson (1984) has advanced a notion of cognitive mapping as a sort of spatial politics designed to cope with the groundlessness of the late twentieth-century experience.

and used the spatial features of the *polis* outlined above (city as walled enclosure, the importance of the centre); it will also act as a context against which the unique space of *Troades* can be mapped.

Tragic space

The fact that theatre requires expression in space has led some scholars into an examination of the 'stagecraft' of tragedy.[38] This has involved considerations of the different uses of the various acting areas (*orchēstra*, *logeion*, *theologeion*, *mēchanē*; occupied by chorus, actors, actors/gods, gods respectively) and the distinctions between entrances and exits using the two *parodoi* and the *skēnē*. Entrances and exits from different *parodoi* could signify an entrance from or an exit to different places. The *skēnē* could represent a house, a tent, a palace, a cave, and permitted the imagined possibility of events happening not only off-stage somewhere else but off-stage indoors, often revealed by the doors opening and the *ekkuklēma* rolling out with a corpse or a fatally wounded character on it. The use of the *theologeion* and of the *mēchanē* allowed hierarchical distinctions between the divine and the mortal to be made visual.

Most of the potentials of stagecraft were established by the *Oresteia*.[39] That they were exploited to the full in Euripides can be seen from the use of all available exits at *Or.* 1246ff. and of all the levels on the vertical axis at *Or.* 1561ff.[40] Euripides also develops the use of scenic devices. At the end of *Medea*, Medea appears on the *mēchanē* above the house; she therefore occupies a position which is normally reserved for

---

[38] Hourmouziades (1965); Taplin (1977); Seale (1982); Halleran (1985). Descriptions of *mēchanē*, *ekkuklēma* etc. can be found in any of these books. On the merits of stagecraft criticism, see especially Taplin (1977) and (1978), who is criticized by Goldhill (1986), 265–86, who is in turn questioned by Wiles (1987), to whom Goldhill (1989) responds.

[39] Taplin (1977), 434–51.

[40] Saïd (1989), 109–10. It is possible to see Euripides joking about the restrictions the conventions of stagecraft impose on his dramaturgy: see e.g. *Hipp.* 575ff.; Winnington-Ingram (1969), 130–1.

the appearances of divinities. Through this characteristic transgression of a stage convention Euripides stresses first Medea's superiority over Jason and, second, that her act of infanticide has taken her out of the human realm altogether.[41] By contrast, the gods Apollo and Dionysus, in *Alcestis* and *Bacchae* respectively, enter from the *skēnē* rather than on the *theologeion* or *mēchanē*.[42]

The tragic stage had no scenery which signified precise location; what scenery there was seems to have been multi-purpose and decorative.[43] But the fluidity of scene which this permitted was rarely exploited.[44] From play to play, however, the dramatist was relatively free to invent the details of the dramatic world. The Thebes which is the scene of *Hercules Furens*, *Phoenissae* and *Bacchae* is a city of various character-istics. The same famous landmarks are regularly mentioned in all three plays (the seven gates, the rivers); Thebes in the first two plays is framed between Athens and Argos, in the last between Delphi and Asia. The Thebes of *Phoenissae* is, like that of *Septem*, a besieged city which is trying to keep invaders out; the same city in *Bacchae* has Pentheus attempting to keep the women in. Thebes in these three plays is always an other-scene, but its details are determined by distinctive dramatic requirements.[45]

An important development after Aeschylus is that of an imaginary off-stage area, i.e. the introduction of other places apart from the scene into the imagination of the audience. In Aeschylus there is certainly an interest in the geography of the world beyond the scene of the play (*PV* 407ff., 700ff., 786ff., 823ff.; *Ag.* 281ff.); a similar interest continues in both Sopho-cles and Euripides, as the lists of alternative destinations in

[41] Cunningham (1954); Collinge (1962); Gredley (1987), 39.
[42] Saïd (1989), 111.
[43] P. Arnott (1959), 38; Baldry (1971), 46–9.
[44] There are three examples of scene changes: in Aesch. *Cho.*, somewhere between lines 584 and 653, the scene moves from Agamemnon's tomb to the palace; there is a striking shift from Delphi to Athens at Aesch. *Eum.* 234–5; see also Soph. *Aj.* 654ff., 805ff. See Taplin (1977), 103–5, 338–9, 377; Knox (1979), 7; Seale (1982), 163.
[45] Saïd (1989), 112–36.

Philoctetes and *Troades* testify.[46] But the use of off-stage scenes to dominate the imagination of the audience is more frequently a feature of Euripides. It is true that in Aeschylus' *Septem* the events around the city walls determine the responses of the characters and the chorus on stage. It is also true that two off-stage areas are crucial to the appreciation of Sophocles' *Antigone*: one is the site described by the guard (*Ant.* 249ff.), where the body of Polyneices lies unburied outside the city walls; the other is the rocky tomb of Antigone. But, apart from being more frequently used, the off-stage area is referred to more often and described in more detail in Euripides. Three examples will suffice. At *Phoen.* 109–92 Antigone and the Pedagogue watch the movements of the Argive army beyond the city walls, reporting to the audience on what they are seeing rather than, as in messenger speeches, on what has been seen or heard.[47] A more striking instance of the struggle of the off-stage with the on-stage can be found in *Hecuba*, in which the site of destroyed Troy – a civilization in ruins – competes to hold our attention with the actual scene in Thracian Chersonese, a border zone which lacks any signs of civilization. Especially important here is the description of torch-bearers making their way to Troy to burn the city down (*Hec.* 1260–4): at this point in the play we seem to have travelled back to the ruined city.[48] (As we shall discover in the next section, *Troades* also makes rich use of the imagined backdrop of Troy destroyed.) Such a multiplication of scenes is also apparent in *Hippolytus*, which is set in Trozen. Crete, however, is frequently introduced, mainly as the home of Phaedra (*Hipp.* 372, 719, 752, 757), but also as a sort of determinant of the action which the audience see occurring in Trozen. The 'pull-backward'[49] is most clearly seen in the ref-

---

[46] For the former, see Taplin (1987), especially p. 72: 'This [*Phil.*] is perhaps the most "geographical" of all surviving tragedies ... the locality of Philoctetes' place of exile gains in strength from being set within a sort of mapping of the entire span of the northern Aegean.' For the latter, see the next section.

[47] Hourmouziades (1965), 123–4. Hourmouziades also discusses the off-stage area in *Ion* (pp. 113–15).

[48] Hourmouziades (1965), 121–3; C. Segal (1991), 42–4; Zeitlin (1991), 53–6.

[49] Reckford (1974).

erences to Crete as the site of improper sexual behaviour (e.g. *Hipp*. 337–9). In a sort of heroic sexual extension, the mother and sister of Phaedra have consorted with beast and god respectively. And Phaedra herself, in her desire for a third marginal figure – Hippolytus – depicts herself in a direct line beginning with Pasiphae and continuing with Ariadne (*Hipp*. 341). Phaedra's 'tragic heredity' is from Crete; her passion, it is hinted, is as much caused by 'inherited sexuality'[50] as by Aphrodite or herself, 'as though Crete were the spiritual location of an atavistic criminality'.[51]

This brief survey demonstrates that Euripides used and developed the conventions of stagecraft established by Aeschylus. But to talk of tragic space is not merely a matter of stagecraft. For the extension of what may be included within the other-scene, of what spatial characteristics it may bear, should be seen to have effects on the process of self-examination *otherwise*. One could say that the increased complexity of the dramatic world inevitably produced a more complex, at least a more detailed, self-questioning. Alternatively, one could avoid general statements of this kind and attempt to evaluate developing spatial sophistication in relation to the peculiar qualities and themes of each play. For instance, in the case of *Antigone*, one could argue that the treatment of Polyneices' corpse and the confinement of Antigone in a cave are abuses of spatial propriety which are examples of, and underline, Creon's misunderstanding and misuse of authority: the spatial features here confirm one interpretation of the politics of the play.[52] In *Hippolytus* the movement back to Crete (and also to Athens) stresses the powerlessness of the characters over their present predicament unravelling in Trozen. But there is a disturbing sense in which the human drama we are watching in Trozen has been robbed of any import. Such a use of the

---

[50] Both phrases are from Winnington-Ingram (1960), 175.
[51] Reckford (1974), 324; and see his (1972). Barrett (1964), ad *Hipp*. 1253–4 is insistent that there is no reference to Crete in the messenger's mention of Mount Ida. Given the frequency of reference to Crete elsewhere in the play, it seems restrictive to limit the ambiguity of reference at this point. Crete is also kept in mind by the use of Artemis' Cretan title 'Diktunna'.
[52] Easterling (1987), 22.

elsewhere to cast doubts on the here and now seems to demonstrate that, with Euripides, we confront a more ironic, even a self-defeating, organization and use of tragic space.

To discuss tragic space is also to raise the question of how tragedy represented space; space, that is, as fundamental to the organization of the *polis* of Athens (see 'The space of Athens' above). Tragedy examines the relationship between a person's position within the space of the *polis* and gender identity, and between individual identity and knowledge of spatial origin. It also probes the connection between possession of civic identity and being inside the *polis*, and the dangers which can issue from those who pass from inside to outside, or vice versa. The space of the *polis*, defined and enclosed, is represented as under threat and centredness is put at risk by heroic transgression. All these aspects of tragic space – treated in turn below – represent spatial crisis as part of the otherness of the dramatic world. And that otherness is itself complicated: Athens, the space of the self, is put on the tragic stage, the space of the other.

It was argued earlier that women, although other to men, were not simply excluded from the city, but excluded through seclusion. Their place was inside the house; men occupied the outside within the city. When this ideological equation of women/inside and men/outside is compared to the tragic representation of women – and tragedy, after all, is itself an ideological product – we confront a problem. Shaw argues that the very appearance of women in the public space of the stage was a transgression of their prescribed role.[53] This rather simplistic notion has been criticized by Easterling on three grounds:[54] it confuses tragic women with 'real' women and underestimates the fact that drama is 'make-believe' (male actors were used to play women); it presumes that we always know that tragedies are set outside;[55] and it overestimates

---

[53] Shaw (1975), 255–7.   [54] Easterling (1987).
[55] Easterling (1987), for example, notes inside scenes in Sophocles' *Trachiniae* (see 203–4) and Aeschylus' *Persae* (140–1); see also Dale (1969), 259–71; Taplin (1977), 65; Padel (1990), 337.

the transgression because in actuality, even in Athens, women pursue ritual activity outside. The important point, however, is not so much whether women are represented as being outside in tragedy (which, of course, they frequently are), but why they are outside and what they do when they are. For instance, when outside, women are not merely represented as performing ritual, but as engaging in conflict between the public and the private spheres, between the *oikos* and the *polis*. Our question must be: what could be the reason for a male author, for male actors, for a patriarchal society to put the powerful and transgressive women of tragedy on stage?[56]

A recent approach to this problem is that the procedures and functions of tragedy are tightly bound up with the cultural definition of the feminine.[57] Rather than seeing the relationship between men and women as one which is just powerfully inverted – there are a large number of feminine men and masculine women in tragedy – women often act as agents in men's discovery of their own otherness.[58] Women can perform this function because, as an other excluded within, they can speak with authority about the inside and they stand for ever on the threshold between the inside and the outside.[59] This liminality provides a good reason why women should be

---

[56] Slater (1968), 3–74 argues that tragic women were psychological projections originating in the psychosexual experience of men. The representation of women as dangerous and subversive figures and the desperate misogynistic response which some characters are driven to stem, Slater argues, from the mother/son relationship. While a father exercised himself in the political and military world outside, a son would stay at home with his mother, in a world of women and slaves. The father, because absent, becomes idealized and resented; the ever-present mother, on the other hand, becomes seductive and therefore hostile and repellent. The powerful creations of the tragedians, then, are a result of the ambivalence towards women with which all men grow up. For criticism of Slater, see Foley (1981), 137–9; (1982a), 21; Goldhill (1986), 112–14.

[57] Zeitlin (1985b); see also (1982b), 147 on the male curiosity about the hidden, and Vernant (1989), 224 on the male self being directed outwards. Zeitlin (1985b) is a more nuanced study of self and other than her (1986), precisely because it allows more flux between the two terms.

[58] Zeitlin (1985b), 67 (for feminized men, see p. 65); Gould (1980), 56; Foley (1981), 135. Padel (1983), 16 says nicely that tragic women were 'a natural site for inner pain'.

[59] Note Alcestis, described as *othneios* (strange, foreign) and *thuraios* (outside the door, abroad, liminal); see *Alc.* 532–3, 646, 778, 805, 810–11, 1014; see *Med.* 244–5, 397). See Buxton (1985); Zeitlin (1985b), 75, 80; Chalkia (1986), 245; Luschnig (1992), 19–33.

so important in the tragic questioning of ideology: for it is in its liminal spaces, on the margins, that a structure of ideas – an ideology – can become vulnerable.

In *Hippolytus*, the eponymous hero refuses to honour Aphrodite. This failure to integrate desire into his self is paired with Phaedra's secret desire in a particularly potent exploitation of both the scenic conventions of tragedy and the cultural definition of the feminine. While Phaedra remains inside the closed space of the *oikos* her desire stays secret, finding shelter in its dark recesses; but at the same time it stands in opposition to the social values for which the *oikos* stands (what Zeitlin calls the 'cultural oxymoron of the chaste wife').[60] When Phaedra is wheeled out onto the stage (on the *ekkuklēma*) from the house, she deliriously and obliquely reveals her desires, which the audience know from the prologue concern Hippolytus. But the object of Phaedra's desire is also suggested by her self-projection into the open spaces, the mountains, meadows and woods, which are Hippolytus' favoured habitat (*Hipp.* 198ff.). Her speech 'demonstrates how far from domestic territory is the site assigned to female desire': it has been contained within herself and the house but yearns to be outside the city.[61] It is only in the open, outside the house on the stage, that Phaedra's secret is revealed to the Nurse and the chorus. Phaedra states that she had at first wanted to hide her secret in silence (*Hipp.* 393ff.). That is now impossible. Language – associated with men and the outside – has intervened. The Nurse, less bound by the need to maintain a good reputation, has persuaded Phaedra that Hippolytus should be told.

So, desire – the problem of women – was to be suppressed by men's prescriptions for the malady: silence and concealment inside. But the Nurse's efforts to persuade Hippolytus, i.e. her breaking of the silence, occur inside, the place more often associated with silence, the place where Hippolytus might be thought to be least comfortable. Hippolytus, dis-

---

[60] (1985a), 65.
[61] Zeitlin (1985a), 74–5. See also Zeitlin (1985b), 70; Goldhill (1986), 123–4.

gusted but perhaps not surprised by the sort of words he has heard inside, comes out to declare the awful news to the world (*Hipp.* 601ff.). But his desire to speak is constrained by an oath of silence which he has already sworn. Frustrated, he condemns all women, demanding their removal from the reproductive process and, most especially, recommending that women live among dumb beasts, removed from language altogether (*Hipp.* 616ff.). Phaedra's distress at having her secret illuminated and discussed in this way leads her into what seems to be a correction of the apparent disorder in the pairings of silence (inside the house) and speech (outside). The dangerous nature of what can happen inside the house – and inside a person – is fully revealed when Theseus, on his return, demands that the doors of the house be unbarred to see his hanging but apparently silent wife (*Hipp.* 808ff.).

But it is only apparent. For, in seeming to conform to one of the dictates of male ideology (concealing desire within), Phaedra transgresses another. She leaves behind the letter, a false account of her relations with Hippolytus: her body – inside the house but still visible – is silent, but she still communicates. For Theseus the document howls (*Hipp.* 877). His response on learning the terrible information contained in the letter is to invoke a special form of language, a curse, against his son (*Hipp.* 885ff.). Such is the confusion produced by the intervention of desire into language that Theseus, attacking Hippolytus, demands that humans be given two recognizably distinct voices, one truthful, one deceptive (*Hipp.* 928–30) – what he needed, we might think, for the voice emanating from Phaedra's letter. He now prefers the evidence of Phaedra's corpse (*Hipp.* 958ff.). Hippolytus, when his actual speech fails to convince his father, impotently calls on the words he could have used had he not sworn the oath (*Hipp.* 1060ff.), and hopes for the vocal witness of the walls of the house (*Hipp.* 1074–5). However, unlike Phaedra but appropriately for the inside of the house, they remain silent. So, both language (speech and silence) and the ideology ruling spatial organization (inside and outside) fail to cope with desire. The male characters do not recognize the dangers of the failure to accommodate, to find a space for otherness and desire, which instead pollute their space. Aphrodite has her say; desire is not silenced or managed; spatial order is undermined; and Hippolytus is dead. However, for the men in the audience – who were not bound to follow the misrecognitions of the characters – the failures of the two leading men could have been enlightening.[62]

Women, then, command the relations between the inside and the outside. In addition, men can never quite ignore the inside. Sometimes they need, as Orestes does, to reclaim it from a transgressive female. But in order to do that, they need the help of those who have experience and knowledge of the inside, which means that they must depend on women, as Orestes depends on Electra. Should they not have feminine assistance (or support), men go inside at their peril, as the examples of Hippolytus, Agamemnon (in Aeschylus' *Agamemnon*) and Polymestor (in *Hecuba*) testify.[63]

The men of the audience also use tragic women to teach them about the inside. The cultural fact of women being (in the name of ideology) excluded within merges with the theatrical strategy of exploiting the flux between inside and outside, off-stage and on-stage, the seen and the invisible. Along with the god of the theatre, Dionysus (himself of ambivalent sexuality), tragic women accomplish for men the recognition of something hidden inside (the house, the self) which men would seek to repress (contain), but which they should accommodate (contain). That effect is partly achieved by women's involvement in the spatial movements of tragedy, whether they be physical or metaphorical.[64]

The relationship between individual identity and certainty

---

[62] In this section I am indebted to Knox (1952); Zeitlin (1985a); Goldhill (1986), 107–37; Goff (1990).

[63] Zeitlin (1985b), 73. P. Arnott (1989), 133 expresses the point somewhat simplistically: 'What is good, honest and open tends to happen outside; what is sly, furtive and malicious, inside.'

[64] Zeitlin (1985b), 66, 80. See also Padel (1990), but especially p. 364: 'The inside and outside of the theatre's space offers the watching imagination a way of thinking about the inside and outside of other structures important to tragedy: city, house, self.'

of spatial origin (womb, *oikos*, *polis*) is one through which Sophocles' *Oedipus Tyrannus* can profitably be read.[65] Vernant, in a celebrated article, reminds us that the original unanswered question of the play – 'who killed Laius?' – is transformed into another question, namely, 'who is Oedipus?'[66] The latter question could be rephrased as 'where is Oedipus from?' At the beginning of the play Oedipus obviously thinks he originates from somewhere other than Thebes. But what would normally be conventional entrances from and exits into the *skēnē* exploit stagecraft to mock his certainty with dramatic irony: this *skēnē*, the audience know, was his original home. Throughout the play he is confronted, as it were, by a map of his past: Creon returns from Delphi, the old man from Corinth, and the shepherd from Cithaeron.[67] Furthermore, Oedipus' first recognition that he may not be who he thought he was comes at the point of the description of the crossroads at Phocis, where he killed Laius (*OT* 726ff.).[68] Trying to recover his past, and thus his origins and identity, Oedipus retraces his past journeys, as if the map will sort out who he is. Accused of being a bastard (of uncertain origin), Oedipus makes his way to Delphi, where he is told of the prophecy concerning his fate (*OT* 779ff.). He then recounts the story of the murder at Phocis and his subsequent arrival in Thebes (*OT* 800ff.). Having discovered that he is not Corinthian and that he was exposed on Cithaeron (*OT* 1025ff.), he wants to discover how he arrived on the mountainside in the first place (*OT* 1164): the woman indoors will know the truth (*OT* 1171–2).[69] Having fully recognized himself, and after his self-blinding, Oedipus calls on three markers on the map of his

---

[65] It is also possible to detect in tragedy a connection between space and knowledge. In Sophocles' *Ajax* the chorus and Tecmessa discuss where they have looked for Ajax: the fate of the hero is uncertain until such time as they have located his body (*Aj.* 867ff.). In another example, the truthfulness of the news of the Greek victory at Troy is underlined by the lengthy description Clytemnestra gives of its transportation across the Aegean (Aesch *Ag.* 281ff.).

[66] Vernant and Vidal-Naquet (1988), 113–40.

[67] Taplin (1982), 167.

[68] For the religious significance of crossroads, and their appropriateness in the play, see Halliwell (1986b).

[69] Taplin (1982), 168–9.

existence: Cithaeron, Corinth and the crossroads at Phocis
(*OT* 1391ff.). The manuscripts for the end of the play are
corrupt, but one possible interpretation is that, after Oedipus
has demanded exile, it is refused him by Creon: thus, instead
of exiting by *parodos*, Oedipus once again returns into the
skēnē.[70] The question of who Oedipus is, then, is tightly
bound up with space: the error concerning his identity is an
error concerning his origin, and his successive attachments to
places. The identity of the hero is recovered along with his
spatial history.

In contrast, Euripides represents a more uncertain relationship between identity and space. We have already seen how
Phaedra's movement between the inside and the outside complicates what it means to be a woman (and, therefore, a man);
what, in fact, it means to be an individual. To take another
instance, Medea's move into the outside world of men seems
to have dehumanizing as well as degendering effects. Both
Phaedra and Medea are at first determined by the rigidities of
social space and then, in their different ways, exploit those
same rigidities to recast themselves, either through suicide or
murder. An even more extreme example is *Bacchae*, in which
the very idea of a stable, consistent identity is confronted by
the irresistibility of Dionysiac release. That release is, again,
characterized by particular movements in space: out of the
city into the mountains, from the civilized inside to the wild
outside (e.g. *Bacch.* 32ff.). When Pentheus, who stubbornly
attempts to resist the exodus of the women from the city, is
eventually tempted to go outside himself, he returns a frag-
mented person; and this is a fate which has been bestowed on
him by women who, outside the city, have ceased to be themselves. It could be argued that, as in *Oedipus Tyrannus*, the
relation between identity and space has once again been confirmed, that civilized and consistent behaviour requires spatial
security. But the play also suggests that movements between
the inside and the outside, beween selfhood and recognition
of otherness, are inevitable, even desirable, especially in the

[70] Taplin (1982), 170–2.

Dionysiac medium of the theatre; but also that these movements are problematic and can be dangerous.

It has been shown that the membership of a *polis* was for
Athenian citizens very much a matter of originating from the
appropriate place, whether that be the soil of Attica (autochthony) or two Athenian parents (Pericles' citizenship law).
Civic identity was, therefore, fundamentally related to space.
It follows that to be outside the *polis* – to be *apolis* – was
a catastrophic condition for anyone. Such a catastrophe is
represented in Sophocles' *Philoctetes*, in which the hero's
lamentable social and political status is exemplified by his
occupation of what seems to be a completely deserted and
uncivilized island. The *skēnē* here represents not a house or a
palace, but a cave, without women's quarters, and perhaps
even without doors.[71] Yet the aporia of Philoctetes' position
will be resolved one way or another by the end of the play.
And it is precisely one way or another: will he go to Malis in
the west, or to Troy in the east? Heracles, arriving at the end
of the play, orders Philoctetes to head for Troy, help sack the
city and then return to Malis with the spoils of war (*Phil.*
1423ff.). And this is seen as the first step of Philoctetes' return
to civilization and to his proper place in the spatial order.[72]
Comparison with Euripides' *Hecuba* is interesting. Again, the
scene is one where the signs of civilization are absent: no
temples or citizens; the Trojan women are in transit, living in
tents. Nevertheless, the interior spaces of the tents (the *skēnē*)
are still, as in a city, associated with women.[73] But one important difference remains. The Trojan women are not, like
Philoctetes, to have their former space restored: Troy has,
after all, been razed to the ground. For them the future holds
a spatial order, houses and cities, but it is one where they will
be demoted to the status of slaves.

Those who are outside the *polis* need to get in. But if the city
is to be a bounded space, it must decide whom to include and
whom to exclude. Anxiety about this decision is manifested in

[71] Taplin (1987), 72.   [72] Taplin (1982), 164–6; (1987); Seale (1982), 26ff.
[73] C. Segal (1991), 42–4; Zeitlin (1991), 53–6.

those tragedies which deal with outsiders supplicating for inclusion (Aeschylus' *Supplices*; Sophocles' *Oedipus at Colonus*; Euripides' *Heracleidae* and *Supplices*).[74]

In Euripides' *Supplices* Adrastus and the Argive women entreat Theseus to allow them into Athens. Athens often represents itself as the city which prides itself on acceptance of suppliants (e.g. *Heracl.* 329–30), but in this play the self-image of Athens as sacred protector of suppliants confronts other aspects of Athenian ideology and elements of *realpolitik*. Throughout the play the acceptance of the supplication is seen as involving *ponos* (toil, labour).[75] Although Adrastus appeals to Theseus on the basis of Athens' unique capability of 'undertaking the task' (*Supp.* 188–9: ὑποστῆναι πόνον'), Theseus at first refuses his request (*Supp.* 195–249).[76] Adrastus laments that Theseus judges him: all he wants is protection (*Supp.* 253–6). It is only after the appeal of Aithra, Theseus' mother (*Supp.* 297–331), who asserts that the undertaking of *ponoi* leads to expansion (*Supp.* 323), that Theseus accepts the supplication. Even then, his reasons for so doing are personal rather than ideological: he wishes to maintain his reputation as a 'punisher of evil men' (*Supp.* 341: ʼκολαστὴς τῶν κακῶν') and he cannot refuse a *ponos* (*Supp.* 342). So, the supplication is not accepted simply because Athenian tradition and ideology demand it, but because territorial expansion and maintenance of personal reputation – we should note glory (*Supp.* 373) and good fortune (*Supp.* 576–7) as well – result from undertaking *ponoi*. The supplication, Theseus adds, will be accepted by the city of Athens, but only because it will follow his wishes (*Supp.* 393–4). Finally, the effects of Athens' *ponoi* are not those which their supposed beneficiaries might have desired. At *Supp.* 950–2 Adrastus laments the effects of *ponoi* and advocates quietism ('ἡσυχία')

---

[74] On supplication, see Gould (1973), especially p. 101.

[75] *Ponoi* can be related to *polupragmosunē*. Ehrenberg (1947) rightly calls the latter the psychological base of Athenian imperialism; see e.g. Thuc. 1.70.8; 2.36.2; 2.40.2; 2.63.2ff.; 6.18.2.

[76] On Theseus' reply to Adrastus, see Zuntz (1955), 7; Fitton (1961), 430; Burian (1985b), 31.

instead, thereby urging on Theseus a mode of behaviour which is inconsistent with his earlier protestations.

By comparison, the representation of Athens' acceptance of Oedipus' supplication in *Oedipus at Colonus* is rather different. Although military action is required against Creon's men (who have abducted Antigone and Ismene), it is an effect rather than a cause of accepting Oedipus' desire for inclusion; and no imperialist tendencies are present. It is true that Sophocles' last play is much concerned with limits, and that the nature of Oedipus' integration into Athens is never quite clear.[77] That says much about limits in general, but does not, as Euripides' *Supplices* does, question Athens' motivation to act in accordance with its self-image.

It is because space and civic identity are intimately related and because Athens portrayed itself as a city which could include outsiders that Athens features in plays about suppliants. But its ability to include extends to the offer of sanctuary to otherwise uncontainable divinities or heroes. Thus, in the *Eumenides*, it is Athens which finds a permanent place for the Eumenides, the chthonic deities of revenge; and it is Athens which accepts Oedipus, the transgressor who has made every inclusion and exclusion problematic (*Oedipus at Colonus*). There are similar instances of the acceptance of heroes in Euripides. In *Medea*, the arrival of Aegeus from Athens allows Medea to plan her escape there (*Med.* 719ff.). In *Hercules Furens*, Theseus appears towards the end of the play with offers of a home for Heracles in Athens (*HF* 1322ff.). The representative of Athens is able to offer asylum to a figure whose place at the scene of the play is, or will be, no longer tenable. Heracles has just murdered most of his family, and Medea is about to kill her children. Here, then, we seem to have a bold claim about Athens' capacity to include even the most transgressive hero. The inclusion, some critics claim, is managed by the performance of tragedy itself. Athens, that is,

---

[77] Allison (1984); Burian (1974); Jones (1962), 214–34; Seale (1982); C. Segal (1981), 362ff.; Vernant and Vidal-Naquet (1988), 301–60; Winnington-Ingram (1980), 248–79.

transforms and reorders the transgressions of the past by representing them, and by representing itself as the only place where the menacing potential of the hero can properly be contained.[78]

But there are problems with this idealistic portrait of Athens. First, as with Theseus' acceptance of the supplication in *Supplices*, both Medea and Heracles are invited to Athens for the king's personal reasons. Aegeus believes that Medea will help him have children (*Med.* 703ff.); Theseus stresses his friendship (*philia*) with Heracles (*HF* 1154–6, 1234, 1398, 1400).

Second, if Athens examines itself in the other-scenes which tragedy creates, then Athens, as represented in tragedy, is itself an other-scene. But its otherness will necessarily be different from that of tragic Thebes or Argos because it is the city of the audience. And a different type of self-reflexivity is possible, one which is more often than not characterized by extravagant praise.[79] That praise, however, is qualified not only by the manner in which suppliants or heroes are included; it is also questioned by the risky nature of the inclusion. Does Athens contain tragic heroes, or is it infected by them? The particular flux between self and other which the representation of Athens sets in motion contributes to the complexity of tragic space. Assertions that the appearances of Athens on the tragic stage are simply self-reflexive miss the way in which the city is rendered other to the city of the audience (through, for

---

[78] Pucci (1977), (1980); Foley (1985); Zeitlin (1986).

[79] E.g. *Med.* 824ff.; see also *Heracl.*: Athens is free (198; see 287, 957), a land which allows free speech (181–2); it is powerfully aided by Athene, a goddess more puissant than the bride of Zeus (349–52); it is the city accompanied by the Graces (379–80); it is great and beautiful in the dance (358–60); it is just (901); it is *sōphrōn* (1012), and it can be loved (975). On the representation of Athens in *Hercules Furens*, see Tarkow (1977). P. Arnott (1989), 8ff., in a discussion of xenophobia and parochialism in Attic drama, notes that the only play where Athenian worthies are really shown in an unflattering light is *Hippolytus*. One might want to remark on how compromised a figure Theseus is in *Supplices* (see below: 'Euripidean time'). Butts (1947) argues that the glorification of Athens in tragedy was motivated by the tragic poets' desire to win the first prize. Such a view would sit unhappily with the probable controversiality of Euripides (who was nevertheless still a very popular poet); cf. Kuch (1984), 88.

example, the presence of kings, heroes etc.).[80] Notions of the otherness of tragic space which are excessively dependent on the representation of cities apart from Athens are simplistic.[81]

Tragedy, then, represents in various ways the connections between space and gender, individual and civic identity. It also examines the space of the *polis* itself, which in Athens' case was characterized by centredness, on the one hand, and enclosure by walls, on the other.

One of the most extreme scrutinies of the idea of the centre is to be found in *Medea*. Medea has a marginal status in Corinth: she has no husband, no land, no home (*Med.* 30–3); she is *apolis* with no family (*Med.* 255–8; see also 643–5). She also lacks a *kurios* (*Med.* 441ff.) and has lost her friends (*Med.* 502, 513, 604). Though her *oikos* is in Corinth, it is 'in a foreign land' (*Med.* 434–5: 'ξένᾳ χθονί'). Before she has even come onto the stage and while she is still inside the house, the Nurse tells the children that they should go inside but that they should avoid their mother. As Luschnig says, such an admonition is a 'spatial and cultural oxymoron'.[82] The fact that the inside in this play is dominated by a woman from the edges of the earth (see *Med.* 1261ff.) suggests that this inside is also, and more than usually, alien.[83] Jason tells her that if she still lived at the edges of the earth, she would have no *logos* (*Med.* 540–1). But her past relationship to space is as problematic as that she is enduring when the play begins. For the Medea who has come from the edges of the earth (*Med.* 1263) and who lives on the margins of Corinth has a habit of striking her enemies at the very centre: she has murdered her own brother 'at the hearth' (*Med.* 1334: 'παρέστιον') and she has outraged the 'royal hearth' (*Med.* 1130: 'τυράννων ἑστίαν'). This is not to say that *hestia*-as-centre/Medea-as-marginal is a secure opposition. Far from it: Medea prays to Hecate as a goddess who lives in the recesses of the house at the hearth (*Med.* 397).[84] The placing of Hecate at the centre of the house

[80] Pucci (1980), 117.
[81] I refer principally to Zeitlin (1986), who concentrates on Thebes.
[82] (1992), 35.
[83] Williamson (1990), 18.   [84] On the *hestia* in Euripides, see Chalkia (1986), 294–6.

constitutes another disturbance to the security of the centre: Hecate is normally a divinity placed at the door – *thuraios*.

In Medea's immediate world there is no centre, although it should be remembered that she is, as she herself says, different from other mortals (*Med.* 579). The centre is deferred to Delphi on the one hand (*Med.* 668: 'ὀμφαλὸν γῆς') and to Athens in the future on the other, where Medea hopes to live at the hearth of Aegeus' home (*Med.* 713; see also 1385). Whether she reaches Athens is uncertain. What is clear is that she comes outside to do battle with men and on male terms, namely, with persuasion and violence, but that she murders her children inside the house. When Jason arrives and, in conventional manner, asks that the doors of the house be opened (*Med.* 1314–16), Medea appears above the house, on her chariot, as if the inside has now disappeared.[85] It is also as if her scrambling of the terms of spatial organization has been so thorough that she has only one place to go: upwards into the heavens, out of the realms of discourse (*Med.* 1317ff.); which, in splendid Euripidean irony, also marks her entry into myth and the discourse of Athens.

The *Iliad* describes the threat of war to the *polis* as enclosed space. The same issue is treated in Aeschylus' *Septem*, where the walls and towers of Thebes receive an emphasis similar to that of the walls of Troy in Homer (*Sept.* 30, 63–4, 87–8, 109, 118, 153, 202, 219–21, 282, 291ff., 413, 621, 782). But the walls of Thebes are not only vulnerable because of war; they are at risk because on either side of them stands a son of Oedipus, progeny of the transgressor. The last lines of the messenger declare that Eteocles and Polyneices are dead. Immediately afterwards the chorus thank Zeus for saving the towers of the city (*Sept.* 805–9). The play suggests, therefore, that the walls avoid being broached only because Eteocles and Polyneices, whose family history is bizarre enough to undermine any notions of inclusion and exclusion, kill each other. Thereby the distinctions in space, which the walls provide, cease to be in jeopardy.[86]

---

[85] Luschnig (1992), 38.   [86] See Zeitlin (1982a).

The *Bacchae* represents an even greater threat to the integrity of Thebes. The play tells us that the boundaries of the *polis* are not secure; certainly, they are unable to resist the invasion of Dionysus, an invasion which is achieved by breaking the bounds of the city from the inside.[87] Those who are most imprisoned within the city, the women, will be sent to the mountains, the wild outside (*Bacch.* 37–42, 116, 165, 191, 219 etc.). Pentheus, the king who thinks that the *polis* exists to exclude irrationality, will himself be driven mad and to the mountains, where he will be torn apart by his mother and the other Bacchantes. As Dionysus says, the barbarian drums invented by himself and Rhea will be played at the centre of the city (*Bacch.* 58–61). The play enacts, therefore, precisely the subversions of the spatial definition of the *polis*, both concretely and metaphorically. But this could be said to apply to tragic Thebes and to Athens, since the agent of subversion – in a self-referential sense – is tragedy itself, representing Dionysus and his invading companions at the Great Dionysia, at the centre of Athens. Tragedy represents the alien and foreign sounds of the other; and the *Bacchae* seems to tell us, through its use of Dionysus, the god of the theatre, that the centre of the *polis* is constituted by otherness.

Tragedy was interested in how positions in space determined status or identity, and how the definition of the space of the *polis* was crucial to Athenian ideology. Euripides, however, can be distinguished from Aeschylus and Sophocles in that, in Euripidean tragedy, space is not only the frame in which (or the background against which) ideology is examined; it is itself held up for scrutiny. That is the case with Medea's effects on space, with the representation of Dionysus' threat to the *polis*, and – in an example not covered above – with the removal of Electra (in *Electra*) to the margins of the city away from the centre, where she was placed by both Aeschylus and Sophocles. *Troades* picks up and uses the various ways in

---

[87] Ironically, there is frequent reference to the walls and gates of Thebes: *Bacch.* 172, 653–4, 780–1, 919, 1145, 1202; see Chalkia (1986), 279 and 301.

which the space of the *polis* was defined and the relationships between positions in space and identity. But, as will be seen, its tragic space is unique.

Past, present and future: the space of Troy

The backdrop of *Troades* is the result of the Trojan War, an effect of the past. The fact that Troy has been destroyed is frequently mentioned. At the beginning of the play Poseidon recalls the stone walls which he and Apollo built around Troy (4–6; 1174); the city is now burning (8). Although Poseidon mentions the walls again (46), the emphasis is on the destruction of the city: the god refers to the burning ruins again at line 60; Hecuba (145, 586, 1274, 1279) repeats the description. The queen also uses the same word twice to lament the passing of her city (107: 'ἔρρει'; 173: 'ἔρρεις'). Andromache blames Paris for bringing down the towers of Troy (598) and the chorus recall the tens of thousands who have been lost (780–1); Hecuba asks what stops complete destruction (798: 'ὀλέθρου διὰ παντός'). While this frequent reference to manifest destruction alerts us to the distinctiveness of the dramatic space in *Troades*, there is also an emphasis not only on the material end of Troy, but also on the death of Troy as a place, or as a cultural entity which made civilized life possible. The temples have been razed (15–7, 1317ff.), the altars are ruined and sacrifices and festivals have been discontinued (1060ff.). Most extreme, however, are the closing scenes. Concrete references to Troy, most especially the walls, are ironic: built by Poseidon (5), described as 'square' (46: 'ξεστόν'), mentioned as marks of Troy's former glory (844), they have been destroyed once by Heracles (814ff.), and then penetrated by the wooden horse (12). Before their complete demolition, the only use for the walls of Troy is as a place from which to throw Astyanax, the last hope for Troy's continuation (701–5, 725–6, 783–6, 1134–5, 1173–7).[88] Thus, the former signs of Troy's

---

[88] Though we should not forget that Astyanax is threatened with the same fate in the *Iliad* (24.728–35); see Schein (1984), 190.

spatial definition, of the city's existence, become involved in the Greek attempt to ensure that Troy will never exist again. After Talthybius has ordered his fellow Greeks to raze the *polis* of Troy to the ground with fire (1260–4), the final fifty lines are dominated by references to the disappearance of the city. The glory of Troy has vanished for ever, manifest in the loss of its name (1278: 'τὸ κλεινὸν ὄνομ' ἀφαιρήσῃ τάχα'; 1319: 'τάχ' ἐς φίλαν γᾶν πεσεῖσθ' ἀνώνυμοι'; 1322: 'ὄνομα δὲ γᾶς ἀφανὲς εἶσιν').[89] The city burns for the last time (1295–1301, 1318); in fact, the *megalopolis* has become *apolis*, dead and no longer Troy (1291–2, 1323–4). The end of the play has the walls finally razed (1322–5; see also 1060ff., 1291ff.):

> Χο.　ὄνομα δὲ γᾶς ἀφανὲς εἶσιν. ἄλλαι δ'
> 　　　ἄλλο φροῦδον, οὐδ' ἔτ' ἔστιν
> 　　　ἀ τάλαινα Τροία.
> Εκ.　ἐμάθετ', ἐκλύετε;　　Χο.　περγάμων ⟨γε⟩ κτύπον.

> Cho.　The name of the land will be lost. Everywhere
> 　　　things are gone, and wretched Troy
> 　　　no longer exists.
> Hec.　Did you understand, did you hear?　　Cho.　Yes, the
> 　　　　　　　　　　　crash of the towers.

The emphasis on walls makes the Troy of *Troades* significantly similar to the Troy of the *Iliad*, where, as was seen in the first section of this chapter, the walls are frequently mentioned and the idea of the *polis* as walled enclosure is pervasive. Also, Troy, as a space which permitted and sustained civilization, is a feature of the representations of both Homer and Euripides. But the sacredness of Troy and its walls, so often reiterated in the *Iliad*, is only referred to once in *Troades* (122). This confirms the departure of the gods from Troy and the fact that the city has been destroyed. But it is in the fact of Troy's destruction that the distinctiveness of Euripides' city is established. Homer's Troy is not destroyed during the *Iliad* and, as with Aeschylus' *Septem*, the war raging outside the walls highlights the protection and the definition which the

---

[89] Compare Hom. *Od.* 19.260 and 597, where Troy is not to be named ('οὐκ ὀνομαστήν').

walls provide. In *Troades* war has moved on to the next stage: the city and its walls neither protect nor define; what is highlighted is their demolition.

The destruction of Troy is also frequently mentioned in *Hecuba*, but significant differences remain in the scene of *Troades*. *Hecuba*, like Aeschylus' *Prometheus Vinctus* and Sophocles' *Philoctetes*, is rare in that it is set in a region away from a city, where there are no buildings, no temples and no citizens, although, like Sophocles' *Ajax*, the scene is that of a Greek camp. *Troades* uniquely conjures up as its setting a city presently and completely destroyed. The destruction of Troy is not a fact of the past, as in *Hecuba*, or of the future, as in the *Iliad*; it is present before us. Easterling is probably right to say that to represent a city in this condition was possibly unpropitious, and that it could only be carried through if the city was not a real surviving one.[90] Troy was for the Athenians the mythical city (the fictional city) *par excellence*; even so, Euripides' war-scene powerfully and uniquely offers the audience a dramatic setting of a city razed, a *polis* no longer existing: there is no space, except elsewhere, left to define.[91] The effects of war have been brought home – wrought on homes – in the most compelling and distressing manner.

Nevertheless, the memory of Troy persists in lamentation and nostalgia (both gods and mortals indulge). Indeed, it is remembered as a bounded space, as we have already seen with Poseidon's mention of the walls (4–9, 45–6). There is also Helen's testimony that the warders and watchmen on the walls of Troy were witnesses to her attempted escape (955–7); and Cassandra's criticism of the Greeks, in which she describes them as dying even though they were not losing (as the Trojans were) 'the boundaries of their land' (375: 'γῆς ὅρια'; cf. *Hec.* 16ff., 650ff.). The Trojans, on the other hand, fought

---

[90] (1989), 15–16.

[91] See Poole (1976) on the images and the vocabulary of emptiness which pervade this play. Perhaps the fall of Troy is rendered more emphatic, more pathetic because the city is addressed as if a person (780, 1278, 1324); see Barlow (1986), 32. Cf. *Hec.* 159–60, 280–1, 475–83, 494, 547, 619ff., 668–9, 905–14, 1109–13.

to defend their city, and when they died they were brought home (386ff.).

But it is not as if, before the Trojan War, Troy had always been secure in its boundaries.[92] And the immediate past is not the only past referred to. Troy has a history and a habit of having its boundaries being transgressed. At 799ff. the chorus tell the tale of the sacking of Troy by Heracles. The function of this ode is difficult to evaluate, but it would seem that the chorus refer us back to a romanticized past as a sort of escape from the awful present. Such escapism is not untypical of Euripidean choruses,[93] but, on its own, it is not a sufficient explanation here. What is important is that the chorus, while romanticizing the past, suggest a sinister similarity between the circumstances surrounding the sackings, both past and present. For the chorus choose to concentrate on the delicate and Parislike Ganymede, who enjoys a life of beautiful servitude to the gods (819–24). While Ganymede complacently goes about his service, Troy, then as now, has been destroyed by the Greek spear (837–8). The chorus continue with an apostrophe to *erōs*. Zeus, in choosing Ganymede, had honoured Troy especially. But we cannot help but remember that it was *erōs*, Paris' for Helen, that led to the present destruction of Troy.[94] Ironically, the luxuriance of the poetry, by apparently distancing the past attack from the present one, only serves to stress the recidivist nature of the transgression of the boundaries of Troy. Nor should it be forgotten that the present sacking of Troy was preceded by other transgressions. In the Judgement of Paris as Helen describes it (925ff.), Paris is offered victory over the Greeks, domination over Asia and Europe, or Helen herself. While he refuses the first two offers, which would have amounted to a radical spatial reorganization of the political world, in taking the third, he prepares for

[92] Euripides' tragic Troy thus manifests a similar insecurity to the Thebes of the *Bacchae*, as described in 'Tragic space' above.
[93] Padel (1974). On *Hippolytus* as peopled by characters who 'live in worlds of their own creation' (which are then destroyed), see Luschnig (1988), 19–32.
[94] Strohm (1957), 34; Burnett (1977), 297ff.

the transgression of the code of *xenia* which is a prime cause of the war.

The beginning of the end for Troy is when the Wooden Horse makes the final and devastating entry into the space of the city (first referred to by Poseidon at 11–12). When the chorus narrate this invasion (521ff.), it is interesting to note how they list the various spaces which the city accommodated (cf. *Hec.* 905ff.).[95] With the appearance of the Wooden Horse at the gates, the Trojan people stand on the Trojan rock – presumably the Trojan acropolis where Trojan Athene's temple stood (see 522–6)[96] – and from this central vantage point they confidently declare that the Greeks have gone and the war is over. In happiness, they all run outside their houses (528) to the gates where the horse stood (531–2). Like the music of Dionysus in the *Bacchae*, the horse is brought to the centre of the city, to the temple of Athene (539–41). While imminent disaster waits at the centre the Trojans are described as partaking of various joyous activities, all of which are spatially defined: young girls dance festively outside (543–7), while, inside the houses, torches flicker (547–50); the chorus themselves are dancing in the temple of Artemis (551–5). It is into this ordered space that the bloody shout erupts, eventually taking hold of all of Troy (or at least the acropolis: 555–7). War emerges from his hiding place (560) and the altars run with Trojan blood (561–7). In the placing of important temples on the acropolis, in its centredness, the Troy of *Troades* is again similar to that of Homer. But the ordered and centred space, which the Greeks inside the Wooden Horse penetrated, has now gone for ever.

In *Andromache*, the scene of the play is marked by 'a monument to Peleus' marriage with the Nymph of the sea' (46: 'ἑρμήνευμα Νηρῇδος γάμων'): *hermēneuma* is an ambiguous word but, however we translate it, it has the connotation of a reminder, something concrete (present) in case you forget

---

[95] Kaimio (1970), 90; Barlow (1971), 31; Bernand (1985), 277–8.
[96] Bernand (1985), 278.

(the important absence).[97] *Troades* also seems to be defined in terms of those who are absent: the problematic present which Hecuba and the chorus inhabit has been determined by the representative loss of Hector in the past, and by the Greeks who will take them away to slavery in the future. Hector obviously never appears; the Greeks are represented only by the messenger Talthybius, and the brief appearance of Menelaus.[98] It is true that some measure of continuity issues from Hecuba's constant presence on stage, but that too is only temporary. (In *Hecuba*, Hecuba is present all the time, except at the beginning of the prologue.) Furthermore, her constant presence allows her to rail against the destruction of the ordered space of the city more frequently. But Hecuba not only laments the destruction of Troy; she is also engaged in an attempt to understand the role of the gods in bringing about the chaos she is now experiencing and the fragmentation that she is about to endure. Part of that attempt consists in denying the traditional anthropomorphic representation of the gods which Helen exploits for her defence (see 969ff.). One feature of the traditional representation is that gods move around in space in a similar way – more effectively, more magically, of course – to mortals. Hecuba rejects this when she ridicules Helen's suggestion that Cypris actually went to Sparta (983–6). The chorus, some lines later, seem to answer Hecuba (1077–8):

> μέλει μέλει μοι τάδ' εἰ φρονεῖς, ἄναξ,
> οὐράνιον ἕδρανον ἐπιβεβώς.

> It concerns me, lord, it concerns me whether you are
>   thinking about these things
> as you sit upon your heavenly throne.

---

[97] The opening lines of *Medea*, said by the Nurse, and the lines said by Jason just before the end of the play, both express a desire that the events of the play and those which preceded them should never have happened. At beginning and end, then, the play desires its own absence.

[98] On the importance of absent figures in the play, see Poole (1976). And see de Romilly (1986), 84 on Astyanax as 'personnage muet, mais central'.

The chorus portray Zeus as they described Ganymede (see 821ff.), i.e. as aloof, separate and complacent. In response to the total destruction of the ordered space that was Troy and to the dispersal of the surviving Trojans which is about to occur, Hecuba creates an alternative description of the gods, whereby their absence from the scene corresponds to their lack of responsibility for the events which have determined this dreadful situation. While the chorus point out one problem with such a description, namely, that it may mean a lack of divine interest, the words of Poseidon and Athene at the beginning of the play testify to the fact that, as much as anyone else, the gods are responsible for this carnage.

When the scene of the play is not determined by those who are absent, it is characterized by places which are temporary. It has already been seen that the remains of the city of Troy dominate our sense of scene, that the remnants of the past overshadow the proceedings. Apart from knowing that we are near a city destroyed, there is not much information about location. Poseidon talks of the Trojan women waiting to be allotted in tents, which he refers to as being here on the stage (32–3: 'ὑπὸ στέγαις ταῖσδε'); and he refers the audience to Hecuba lying in front of the entrance to the tents – literally 'gates' (37: 'πυλῶν πάρος'). Hecuba herself says she is close to the tents of Agamemnon (139: 'σκηναῖς ... Ἀγαμεμνονίαις'). Athene remarks to Poseidon in passing that they are walking in Troy (57), but this is a loose reference. Hecuba is more accurate a little later. 'This,' she says, 'is no longer Troy' (100–1: 'οὐκέτι Τροία τάδε'). In the absence of a city, it is perhaps not surprising that mention of the Greek camp and ships is fairly frequent (camp: 342; ships: 108, 159–60, 180, 686ff., 1050). But what the camp and the tents have in common is that when the play ends they will all be gone; allusions to the ships only serve to stress that fact. Indeed, the entrances and exits which the play enacts further accentuate the transient nature of the scene. Only one figure possibly exits by the *parodos* to the city and that is the goddess Athene at 97. And, although the chorus (split into two: 153, 176), Cassandra (308) and Helen (896–7) enter from the *skēnē*, no character returns to it.[99] Instead they all leave by the *parodos* which leads to the Greek ships and to final departure. Of the Trojans only Astyanax returns to the city, and that is for execution. The women of Troy are in transit. In the context of past and future destruction the immediate scene of *Troades* is characterized by temporariness.[100]

While inhabiting their temporary accommodation the chorus look back nostalgically to their former existence inside the *oikos* (199–201), where they spent their time weaving as required by ideology. Andromache remembers how she conformed to the presciptions of Athenian ideology both by staying indoors herself, unlike women with bad reputations (648–9), and by not allowing dangerous gossip inside the house with her (651–2). But nostalgia should be paired with anxiety about the future, which is also expressed in spatial terms: Hecuba asks whether she will have to stand guard at her new master's door (194); the chorus and Andromache both fear the inside space they will occupy in the future (203, 660). As usual, Cassandra's response to her plight is distinctive: she expresses no fear of new spatial arrangements, rather she predicts her own destructive effect on the House of Atreus (461). The nostalgia for the former spatial arrangements may be in part explained by the fact that one's status in society is produced not only by achievements and the possession of property but also by the place from which one speaks. The temporary nature of the Trojan women's living quarters – these women who used to inhabit palaces – stresses the parlous state they now find themselves in.

But, given the nostalgia and the concern about the future, what of the present? Could it be that the feelings expressed about the past and the future are the way they are because now, in the present, there is no authentic inside? Since the *polis* has been completely destroyed – it stands before us as

[99] Hourmouziades (1965), 24–5; Craik (1990), 4–5. The latter argues – wrongly, I believe – that the split chorus enter from the *parodos* from the city.

[100] Poole (1976), 270: the characters are caught between a past that has been totally destroyed and a future unpleasantly determined. The situation is similar in *Hecuba*, as is argued by Zeitlin (1991), 55.

such – is it not also true that the *oikos* has gone with it? And if both *oikos* and *polis* have vanished, in what sense can there be a spatial order based on the inside and the outside? Hecuba refers to her forced departure from her home (141: 'ἐξ οἴκων'), but otherwise we can imagine only tents, and they are temporary. Still, the first half of the chorus to enter have heard Hecuba's laments from inside (154) and describe the rest of the chorus as lamenting inside (157). The first half of the chorus eventually order the second half to come out of the tents, though here they are referred to as *oikōn* (166), an effect no doubt both of the flexibility of the Greek vocabulary for domestic spaces and of nostalgia. Hecuba begs that Cassandra not be allowed outside (170), but is instead confronted by the appearance of the second half of the chorus, entering from Agamemnon's tents (176: 'σκηνάς'). As already noted, Cassandra (294, 308) and Helen (880–1, 896–7), as well as the chorus, both enter from the tents. Hecuba is different: on stage throughout, forever outside. But, although Talthybius fears what is happening inside the tents (299ff.) and orders the gates of the *skēnē* to be opened up (304), there is no use made of the mysterious recesses as there is in *Hecuba*, when Polymestor is lured inside to his death (*Hec.* 979–81, 1014–19, 1044–6, 1109–13, 1148ff.).[101] Indeed, apart from the references to the past and the future insides, little is made of the idea of the inside and the outside in the present of the play. Or, rather, much is made of the fact that the inside has little significance in the present. When the women enter from the tents, they are never to return to them; the inside in Troy has been left behind for the last time.[102] All the women are waiting for the final exit, to the ships and to Greece. It is as if, in the here and now of the play, the normal spatial determinations have themselves died; as if they are, for the moment, absent and will be reformed only in revenge or in slavery.

So, the normal problems with the inside and the outside are

---

[101] P. Arnott (1959), 42; Baldry (1971), 51–3; Zeitlin (1991), 55.
[102] Craik (1990), 4.

missing from *Troades*. As with the idea of the public space
(*polis* as walled enclosure, as centred), the private closed space
of the *oikos* has been destroyed. One effect of war, that is,
is that it destroys the conventional organization of space,
at least temporarily. War means that its surviving victims,
women, are necessarily outside in a way which they are not
in tragedies which are not set in the immediate aftermath of
war. So much can be gleaned from a quick comparison with
Aeschylus' *Septem*, where, with a war still raging, Eteocles
can confidently assert that matters of the outside are men's
business (*Sept.* 182–3) and that sacrifice during war is the
concern of men (216–17). By contrast, the women of Troy
have witnessed the destruction of the ordered space of their
city and they therefore can no longer occupy the inside. And,
having lost their men they must speak for themselves, since
they have no one else to speak on their behalf. Not only that:
these women, who occupy this distinctive space, talk distinctively as well, in late fifth-century rational terms, in direct
criticism of the gods, in paradoxical rewritings of poetic tradition. At the centre of Athens, *es meson*, the extraordinary
nature of the space of *Troades* and of the discourse produced
there seem significantly interdependent. The fact that women
are talking at all, let alone in the manners they variously
adopt, is something of an irony (if not quite transgression)
when we remember these words of Hector from the *Iliad*, the
poem of war (6.490–3):

> ἀλλ' εἰς οἶκον ἰοῦσα τὰ σ' αὐτῆς ἔργα κόμιζε,
> ἱστόν τ' ἠλακάτην τε, καὶ ἀμφιπόλοισι κέλευε
> ἔργον ἐποίχεσθαι. πόλεμος δ' ἄνδρεσσι μελήσει
> πᾶσι, μάλιστα δ' ἐμοί, τοὶ 'Ιλίῳ ἐγγεγάασιν.

> But go home and attend to your own work.
> the loom and the spindle, and tell the maidservants
> to get on with their work. War will be the concern of all men,
> of all men born in Troy, especially me.

A statement of Telemachus is word for word the same (*Od.*
1.356–9), except that he substitutes *muthos* (speech, discourse)
for *polemos* (war). Like Eteocles in *Septem*, Telemachus and

Hector stress that war and discourse are the concern of men and that women should go inside.[103] In *Troades*, there is no inside to go to: the space of the *polis*, and those who inhabit it, has been turned inside out by war. For the women of Troy war and talking are the primary concerns.

What does the future have to offer? The answer, in short, is this: dispersal, and for everyone. The Greeks will experience wide-ranging suffering, since Athene wants to give them a painful return home (66: *nostos*; 77ff.); Poseidon promises corpses littering Mykonos, Delos, Skyros, Lemnos and Caphareus (89–91). Odysseus' journey, Cassandra predicts, will take him not only all over the world, but also down to Hades (433ff.).[104] And the chorus wish just as painful a *nostos* for Menelaus (1110ff.; and see *Hec.* 950–2, where the chorus wish the same on Helen). The fact that the future will be a time of travel for the Trojans (and no *nostoi* for them) is stressed in the prevalence of the imagery of sea and ship. So much can be seen, if only with re-reading, from the opening lines of the play, where Poseidon tells us of his home in the Aegean, the very sea over which the Trojans will be travelling. Also, we can imagine how the ships, waiting to take the prisoners away, become, for the Trojan women, an unpleasant reminder of a travelling destiny they wish to avoid. Ironically, the Wooden Horse is referred to as a ship (537–8).[105]

But we are given more precise details about the fates of the scattered Trojans. Cassandra predicts her own end. Significantly, she will be thrown out into the wild outside, food for beasts (448–50); and while she now has no *polis*, in death she will lie outside the city (she will be *apolis*), which effectively means that her spatial definition is merely negative (like that of Polyneices in Sophocles' *Antigone*). For the chorus and Hecuba, on the other hand, the problem is whether they are to be taken away (159–62, 180–1), to which *polis* they will be allotted (32–3, 187ff., 246ff., 296–7, 570–1; see also 300–1,

---

[103] Lysistrata ironically alludes to these lines from Homer (Ar. *Lys.* 520).

[104] Lee (1976), 149.

[105] Note also how Hecuba speaks of destiny in maritime terms at 686ff.; see Barlow (1971), 30, 57; Bernand (1985), 394.

1087ff.), and to which individual Greek (659ff., 1271, 1285). Andromache's first words are that she is being taken away by the Greeks (577) and the final words of the play, said by the chorus as the walls of Troy fall, are an order (to Hecuba and to themselves) to go to the Greek ships (1332). In their anxiety the women fasten onto a large number of possible places: in one passage they refer to Salamis and Corinth (1096ff.); in another, Hecuba names Thessaly and Thebes (242–3); Poseidon has already aired the possibility of Arcadia, Thessaly and Athens (30–1). The atmosphere of uncertainty surrounding their respective destinations is increased when Cassandra – confounding expectations again – denies that Hecuba will go to the palace of Odysseus (427–30). But the women's concern is especially prominent in the second strophe of the first stasimon (197ff.), where, in turn, they mention Corinth, Athens, Sparta, Thessaly, Sicily and Thurii.[106] The possibility of references to contemporary events in the passage is considered below (see 'Senses of time: the play'). What is the significance of the passage for the spatial concerns seen elsewhere in the play? First, as Kitto points out, the passage reminds us that the tragedy of the Trojan War concerns not just the characters we see on stage, but the remnants of a whole people.[107] But second, and I think more important, is the fact that the chorus envisage at length the dispersal of the Trojan people. This reading is supported by the vague and allusive qualities of the references.[108] The dispersal of the Trojans is a consequence of the destruction of their city, their bounded space. While the spatial ordering of the past has disappeared, the future holds only the prospect of fragmentation: the centre has not held. While the present is defined by the absence of conventional inside/outside distinctions, the future will reaffirm them, but in a radically different situation for the Trojan women, and in places all over the Greek world.[109]

---

[106] *Andromache* also refers to the dispersal of the Trojans (see lines 12–15, 126–7, 135–40, 141–2).

[107] Kitto (1961³), 216.   [108] Lee (1976), 102.

[109] Bernand (1985), apart from seeing uprooting ('déracinement') as a major concern of all three tragedians (p. 325), sees 'le Grec errant' as a central figure in Euripides

So, the past, the future and the present all offer a terrible transformation in spatial organization and definition. But what, then, of the presence of Athens in the list of destinations the chorus give? It has been observed that Athens seems to represent itself as the place of remedy, the place which can contain even the most transgressively tragic figures. Such is the case here, we might think, for Athens is 'renowned' (207: *kleinos*) and the 'sacred country' (218–19: *hiera chōra*; see *Med.* 825–6). But the separation and fragmentation which the Trojans will experience, the wide spaces which open up for them as a result of defeat (i.e. the loss of their own space) – all this is perhaps emphasized by the fact that in this play Athens is not the place which will remedy their suffering. It is mentioned as the most desirable destination, but they will not be going there. In *Troades* Athens represents itself as a futile hope, a fragile other-place desired but never reached.

The dramatic space of *Troades* is remarkable, then, in these ways. First, the space inhabited by the Trojan women, and its meaning in terms of social status, has been produced by figures who never appear on stage. Second, the normally important signs of space, and of differences in space (and therefore of status and power), have been destroyed. There is no *polis* to refer to and no *oikos* from which it can differ. Third, the space of the play is marked by its temporariness. The scene we see on stage will last only for the duration of the play itself. At the end of the play, it, too, will be gone. No palace, temple or city here, as in other tragedies, which we watch for an hour and a half, but which we can imagine existing both before and after the events we see represented. Fourth, the extraordinary space which the combination of the three features above produces poses problems for the way we should view the fact of tragic 'women' talking on the public space of the stage of the Theatre of Dionysus. Is it transgression or the inevitable product of war? Has war inevitably produced such a transgression?

(pp. 344–62; e.g. the soldier leaving for war, the sailor lost, travellers – all with uncertain *nostoi*). Chalkia (1986), 286 nicely says: 'C'est ainsi que l'espace qui prédomine dans la tragédie d'Euripide est celui du seuil, espace mouvant et instable ...'

Shaw's argument that it is transgression can be dismissed as simplistic; not on a theoretical and cultural level (Easterling's criticism), but dramatically, in the very constitution of the scene placed before the audience. Finally, the space of the *polis* receives a peculiar commentary in *Troades*. The Trojan women, having lost their own city, cannot supplicate for entrance into and membership of another; they will instead be dispersed as slaves throughout the Greek world. Nor do they have heroic stature with which to bargain for inclusion. Now that they have lost their homes and their husbands, their presence inside houses in the future will be affected by their changed status. The walls of Troy are mentioned only to confirm that they have ceased to enclose and define the city. And, in contrast to the problems of centredness which are represented in *Medea*, in *Troades* there seems to be no centre as Troy itself has been destroyed.

The distinctiveness of the war-scene in *Troades* complicates the use of Zeitlin's model of the dramatic site as other to the space of the audience. Normally, of course, the other-scene had elements of both sameness and difference as far as the Athenian audience were concerned. Hence, a certain mixture of Homeric and contemporary, palaces and *polis*. But the scene enacted before us in our play evokes a unique and troubling world, where the recognizable spatial signs of the city are conspicuous by their absence. Certainly, however, the space of what was formerly Troy can only be defined as stage space, for there is nothing else there.

Perhaps, for these reasons, the scene of *Troades* is excessively other; perhaps, for an Athenian audience, it was too close to home. For, in the emphasis on its walls, its centredness and its sanctity, Euripides' Troy is not only a rewriting of the city inherited from Homer; it also shows marked similarity to the space of Athens. And, for an Athenian audience experiencing the increasing brutality of war, the sight of space so catastrophically disrupted may have been disturbing. War – the city facing outwards, to use Vernant's phrase – is precisely a threat from the outside, and it has fundamental effects on space, as the facts of invasion, siege and conquest all testify.

War also has a tendency to change spatial organizations, to redraw boundaries, reconstitute the criteria for inclusion. For Athens the first years of the Peloponnesian War saw four invasions of Attica with the consequent destruction of property.[110] The Periclean strategy of bringing everyone in from the countryside betrayed confidence in the invulnerability of the centre (i.e. inside the walls of Athens), but all our evidence suggests that it put unbearable pressure on the centre, in both financial and human terms.[111] After the Sicilian catastrophe, Athenians had to live with the constant threat of invasion, in the form of the Spartan fort at Decelea (Thuc. 7.27). As the war progressed, with mixed fortunes for the protagonists and with no clear end in sight, there were increased efforts by both sides to persuade the Persians – very much a former other – to aid them.[112] For Athens the war was an experience in ruling an ever-changing empire, as territories fell out of their hands, were recaptured, and sometimes revolted again.[113] The crisis of the centre in Athens is manifest in the status of the fleet between 411 and 407 BC. Refusing the authority of Athens, the fleet became an alternative *polis*, a mobile centre.[114] But that is precisely the difference: the idea of a mobile centre was foreign to Athens. During the Peloponnesian War, the entity problematically defined in Herodotus – the Greek world – went through a crisis of new limits being imposed, of former

[110] Spartan invasion of Attica in 431 BC (Thuc. 2.11ff.); in 430 (Thuc. 2.57); in 427 (Thuc. 3.26ff.); in 425 (Thuc. 4.2ff.). On the impregnability of Athenian fortifications, see Thuc. 1.91, 142.

[111] For a strategic Periclean statement, see Thuc. 1.142 (see also 1.81.1; 2.13); Meiggs (1972), 306–39. For the expense of the strategy, see Meiggs and Lewis (1969), 68 and 69 [=Fornara (1977), 133, 136]; for the consequent plague, see Thuc. 2.47ff.

[112] Thuc. 4.50; 8.18, 37, 54, 58.2, 87; Xen. *Hell.* 1.6.7–11; see also Ar. *Lys.* 1133–4; Gorgias DK 82A1. See Meiggs (1972), 352ff.

[113] In the Peloponnesian War the earliest secession was that of Mytilene (Thuc. 1.50), followed by various cities in Thrace (Thuc. 4.75–5.15). After the Sicilian debacle there was another rash of secessions: Chios (Thuc. 8.5–15), Lesbos (Thuc. 8.32ff.), Euboea (Thuc. 8.95ff.); see Meiggs and Lewis (1969) 82 [=Fornara (1977), 152].

[114] Andrewes (1953), 2: 'The history of the years 410–407 BC is much more easily intelligible if we assume some sort of separation, even political tension, between the fleet in the Hellespont and the democracy in Athens.'

spatial certainties being undermined. *Troades* puts that crisis on stage.

Euripidean time

Given that tragedies were conventionally set in mythical time, the most obvious way of suggesting a different temporal character was by using anachronism. On this subject Easterling argues that, while it would be impossible to exclude the obvious and insistent contemporary reference in Greek tragedy, the tragedians made efforts to avoid certain more glaring anachronisms. There is, for instance, only ambiguous and fleeting mention made of coinage and books; and the theatre itself is not mentioned as such.[115] The tragedians, in short, were highly conscious of the 'dignity, distance and adaptability of the heroic setting'.[116] Easterling, then, has identified a convention which enabled tragedy to maintain a delicate balance between mythical and contemporary time, preserving the integrity of the mythical world yet at the same time reflecting on modern issues without offensive disharmony. However, while Easterling does note some (I think potent) exceptions to the convention, she is not concerned with their function; she is more interested to show how successfully the tragedians coped with portraying the time of myth in front of a fifth-century Athenian audience, or rather how they represented fifth-century concerns in a mythic world. But Euripides often seems to flout the convention.[117] We have already seen (in chapter three) how Euripides confronts myth with contemporary rhetoric in the *agōn* of *Troades*; below there is a fuller examination of the particular temporality of the same play. First, though, in order to demonstrate how overt Euripides' use of anachronism could be, the focus will be on *Supplices*,

[115] Easterling (1985), 4ff.
[116] Ibid., 1.
[117] See e.g. Arrowsmith (1958), 107: 'Euripides uproots a myth from the cultural context of a remote and different time and intrudes it forcibly into a contemporary world, thereby altering its motives, its characters and its meaning.'

where the temporal tension is caused by the constitutional differences between Athens and the heroic past.[118]

In common with a number of Euripides' plays, *Supplices* lacks a central hero; but it does have Theseus, that star of Athenian myth. From about the middle of the sixth century Theseus was an important ideological figure in Athens. First, he offered Athens an exemplum of energetic foreign policy: prowess on the sea, opposition to marauders and barbarians, and righteous interference in external states in the name of justice or panhellenic law. Second, he is associated with patriarchy. It was he who warded off the matriarchs *par excellence*, the Amazons, and it was he who helped the Athenian army overcome the effeminate barbarians at Marathon (Plut. *Thes.* 35). Both these victories were privileged in the iconography of fifth-century Athens: the Stoa Poikile, sponsored by Cimon, had a picture of Theseus at the battle of Marathon; the Theseion was decorated with a depiction of Theseus' victory over the Amazons.[119] Third, Theseus was perhaps connected with the more or less institutionalized *ephēbeia* – an institution which may have been revitalized or at least emphasized by Cimon, following the recovery of Theseus' bones on Skyros.[120] All of these aspects appear in *Supplices*. Theseus, having accepted the supplication of Adrastus and his dependants, must undertake to wage war with the Thebans on their behalf. Such an action is stressed as a *ponos*, but one which will lead to expansion (*Supp.* 323; see also 373, 576–7). The idea of *ponos*, and the *polupragmosunē* (meddling, busybodiness) with which it is associated, lies at the root of Athenian imperialism (see n.75). Less stressed, but still present, are Theseus' relations with women (294, 334ff.) and his youthful-

---

[118] In another play, *Heracleidae*, anachronism is stressed in the military differences between the Homeric and the contemporary worlds. This is most apparent in the use of the word *hoplitēs*. It is true that its use need not itself be jarring since it can have the non-technical meaning of 'one who carries arms'. However, most technical language has non-technical uses and origins. Given that *hoplitēs* is a rare word in tragedy and that it occurs more times in this play than any other (694, 699, 729, 800), we may have here an overt anachronism. Why? Because, in a single word, it suggests all the differences between the contemporary world and the world of myth, at least as those two entities are constructed in war.

[119] Merck (1978); Tyrell (1984).   [120] Podlecki (1971).

ness (190, 232, 250, 282). However, we must also remember that Theseus was the mythical founder of the democracy and as such he became a valuable and conveniently adaptable figure for the purposes of propaganda. Pheidias possibly used the features of Pericles for his depiction of Theseus on the shield of the *parthenos* (Plut. *Per.* 31). No doubt the appropriation of the exemplary mythical figure was intended to convince the *dēmos* of exemplary democratic inclinations. This is the most important feature of Theseus' mythical assocations for three reasons: a) democracy is not a value which would have seemed in Athens to have been always there; b) in the fifth century it was not universal in the Greek world; c) it was a very Athenian phenomenon and fundamental to Athenian self-definition. That is, unlike, say, military vocabulary in the fifth century, the word 'democracy' could not be used *without* referring to the contemporary era; there was no possibility of it being easily adaptable to the heroic setting.

In an extraordinary passage at *Supp.* 349–55, Theseus begins by saying that he desires the approval of the whole *polis* for any action taken on behalf of the Argives (349). Such an emphasis on all of the *polis* is itself unusual in tragedy. One can compare the *Supplices* of Aeschylus, where, it is true, there is also an emphasis on the *dēmos* and the *polis*. But the particular passages which can be compared in Aeschylus' play (368ff., 397ff.) have the king, Pelasgus, asserting that he cannot act without the approval of the *dēmos*: there is not quite an equivalent of Theseus' 'it [the people] will agree if/because I want it to' (350: 'δόξει δ' ἐμοῦ θέλοντος'). Pelasgus also claims that he will make the people benevolent, just as Theseus does (351). But again there is a significant difference. While Pelasgus will advise Danaus (the father and the suppliant) on what he should say and prays for the assistance of persuasion and chance (*peithō* and *tuchē*), Theseus will take Adrastus along to the Assembly merely as an example or support (*deigma*) for his own arguments (354–5).[121]

---

[121] On the figure of the king in early Attic tragedy, see Podlecki (1986), especially 82–6 on Pelasgus.

The anomaly of Theseus' authority within the democracy is stressed further in the statement on the foundation of the democracy (352–3):

> καὶ γὰρ κατέστησ᾽ αὐτὸν ἐς μοναρχίαν
> ἐλευθερώσας τήνδ᾽ ἰσόψηφον πόλιν.

> For I established it [the people] as sole ruler,
> having freed this city and made it equal-voting.

We might wonder how the *dēmos* is *monarchos* (an idea found at e.g. Ar. *Knights* 1330) when it always follows the wishes of one man. In what sense is a *polis isopsēphos* when one man's vote is more equal, more important than another's?[122] Collard, in his commentary, has this to say: 'Euripides dramatizes in an archaic setting a constitutional relationship analogous to that of contemporary Athens, where the *dēmos* was formally in sole control but was generally agreeable to direction by individual leaders.'[123] The play seems, in fact, to be making a more particular comparison, namely, between Theseus and the Pericles whom Thucydides describes as the single leader of Athens (Thuc. 2.65.9–10). For Collard, it would seem that the comparison with Pericles is supposed to demonstrate Theseus' reflection of a constitutive and continuous paradox of Athenian democracy, namely that, as Thucydides says, it is democracy only in name. But Thucydides' observation is restricted to the Periclean period and is not necessarily generally applicable to the fifth century before or after that particular statesman; that is, the exceptional authority of Pericles within the democracy was (for Thucydides) an exception. The anachronism of these lines, then, is all the more telling because it has a specific as well as a general referent.

But the anachronistic elements (and the comparison with Pericles) are most evident in the *agōn* (403ff.). (Of course, the rhetorical *agōn*, under the influence of the law courts and the sophists, pervades fifth-century texts.) The debate in *Supplices* is between the democratic and autocratic positions and as such is conducted in the language of contemporary politics

---

[122] On the ambiguity of *isopsēphos*, see de Ste Croix (1972), 331–40.
[123] (1975a), 199.

(see e.g. Hdt. 3.80–2). In this sense it is already, but not distinctively, anachronistic. Before Theseus begins, the herald arrives asking who the tyrant of the land is. Theseus responds by saying that he is not tyrant (403–4); he continues (404–5):

οὐ γὰρ ἄρχεται
ἑνὸς πρὸς ἀνδρός, ἀλλ' ἐλευθέρα πόλις.

For this city is not ruled
by one man; it is free.

The confidence of this assertion is somewhat undermined by the less ideological statement at 349ff., where he claimed that this *dēmos* which is not ruled by one man will always follow his wishes. Theseus' arguments in general are themselves highly conventional ideological apologies for democracy. A section from the Funeral Oration of Pericles, in its stress on the integration of all (whether rich or poor) into the deliberative process, matches Theseus' observations at 408 and 433–41 (Thuc. 2.37.1). The Periclean echo enhances the anachronistic flavour of the play. One critic even makes the interesting but unprovable suggestion that the mask worn by Theseus in the play bore the features of Pericles.[124]

The most explicit anachronism, though, is the 'clear reference to the Athenian system of elective annual magistracies and council' (406–7).[125] Later Theseus mentions written laws as benefits which Athens provides (433). Both of these features refer *specifically* to the Athenian democracy. References to fifth-century Athenian laws are quite common in tragedy (see *Hec.* 291–2), but not to the body of written law.[126] Easterling admits that these two references may be a little extraordinary: 'one cannot help feeling that Euripides is going beyond the traditional representation of Theseus'.[127] But what, then, is the effect of Euripides' anachronism? Easterling

---

[124] Podlecki (1975–6); see also Goossens (1962), 436; de Romilly (1986), 185ff., 205ff.

[125] Collard (1975a), 218–19.   [126] Gregory (1991), 100.

[127] (1985), 11. Bain (1977), 210 attempts to minimize the effect of the anachronism by saying that there is a council of sorts in Homer. But it is precisely the sort of council (whether democratic, oligarchic, peopled by aristocratic warriors etc.) which is the issue. Goossens (1962), 417 is overzealous in wanting these lines only to refer to the rise of oligarchic sentiment in the 420s BC.

says: 'It is interesting to see how freely Euripides can use the heroic setting, extending it to incorporate ideas which are strictly irreconcilable with it.'[128] This is true, but more can be said. Greek tragedies – excepting Phrynichus' *Capture of Miletus*, *Phoenissae*, Aeschylus' *Persae* and Agathon's purely fictional tragedy – use stories (*muthoi*) from a long and diverse tradition for their material. These stories have common features: they are set in a heroic past peopled by kings, their families and, of course, heroes. In this sense we could say that the tragedians and their audience knew what myths were. They also knew that tragedy and myth had a didactic function. It has been argued by anthropologists that myth is a mode of communication which tends to have a normative, naturalizing function, an effect achieved in part by its timeless and unspecific qualities.[129] Myth should persuade the citizen that the arbitrary and artificial structures of his society are in fact natural and should present a cultural construct as a self-evident truth or, as Bourdieu puts it, 'that which goes without saying'.[130] But it is not clear that such a description of myth fits at all happily with tragedy's questioning of ideology. Nor is it clear that the purpose of *Supplices*, and Theseus' defence of democracy in it, is to make democracy 'go without saying'. For democracy was always being fought for, and fought over, in Athens. In this connection, we should notice that Theseus is in one way very different from Pericles. For the latter, in Thucydides, offers many affirmations and descriptions of Athenian ideology, most especially in the Funeral Oration, in speeches to which we hear no reply.[131] Unlike Theseus' pronouncements in *Supplices*, Pericles' assertions are not part of an *agōn*. Just at the moment when Theseus gives his most explicit and detailed defence of democracy, he is confronted by a *logos* which is, in principle, as authoritative as his own (it is certainly more traditional, whence it derives much authority). If Theseus is supposed, *qua* mythical figure, to naturalize

---

[128] (1984), 40.
[129] Lévi-Strauss (1963), (1967); Barthes (1973); Bourdieu (1977).
[130] (1977), 164–70.   [131] Loraux (1986), 214–17.

the arbitrary, to make democracy 'go without saying', the placing of his defence in a debate is an odd way to go about it. Who is to say that the audience would not have been divided in their sympathies, like the jurors in *Eumenides*? Who is to say that there were not some incipient oligarchs in the audience who would have warmed to the herald's argument? And who is to say that the questioning power of tragedy has not overcome any naturalizing function which Theseus might be supposed to perform? On the other hand, it could be argued that Athens could only represent itself as a democracy in an *agōn*, since that was the rhetorical framework which characterized the democracy. There is some truth in this. But putting your best ideological foot forward in debate still runs the risk of self-inflicted defeat. The *agōn* may be the exemplary form of Athenian democracy but, in a way, it is also the one most prone to abuse, most likely to allow the very self-image it represents to be contradicted.

Furthermore, the specific contemporary references in *Supplices* are so insistent that a Lévi-Strauss might not even call the play a myth.[132] Of course, it is a general problem that tragedy and myth have different relations to temporality. As de Romilly puts it (though, I think, too neutrally): myth is non-temporal, suggesting permanency and repetition, but 'Greek tragedy describes an acute crisis of a temporal nature belonging to a world which, in many ways, remains non-temporal'.[133] *Supplices*, with its peculiar temporality, could be said to be taking a myth and making it unmythical in order to exemplify the problems of using myths for didactic purposes. At most, we could join together Lévi-Strauss' model of myth and Zeitlin's model of tragedy as self-examination *otherwise*. This would require saying that the represented world could be timeless, or at least temporally vague, as long as it maintained its difference from the world of the audience. But even this could not be applied to *Supplices*, for its criticisms

---

[132] Easterling (1984) might argue that the utterance of contemporary political arguments by Theseus is further evidence of the convenient adaptability of the tragic king. But does not Theseus' adaptability reveal a certain excess of convenience?
[133] (1968a), 31; and see ibid., 41.

and defences of democracy are, so to speak, too close to
home, too specific, for the necessary degree of difference to be
maintained.[134]

If Athenian society believed that tragedy did not work as a
sort of charter (as some other forms of myth did), overriding
differences with the past to provide authorizations for the present; if it believed, in fact, that tragedy taught that social
structures were arbitrary by involving the audience (as self) in
the other-world of the representation, then *Supplices* also presents problems. For the dramatic time and space of the play is
other mainly by virtue of its fictional status: it is set on the
margins of Athens, the home of the self, and one of its main
themes is the value of democracy, which was precisely a specific contemporary concern. Sophocles' *Oedipus at Colonus* is
also located on the edge of Athens, but it does not couple this
setting with an interest in Athenian democracy: it is concerned, instead, to dramatize Athens' ability to incorporate
even such troubling outsiders as the transgressive hero Oedipus. It is also true that we should compare *Supplices* with
Aeschylus' *Eumenides*, which sets itself in the centre of
Athens, at the moment of the constitution of the first law
court. In Euripides' play, however, there is no divine valida-
tion of democracy, as there is of the law court in Aeschylus.
Aeschylus represents Athens, recognizably the city of the audience, but with the necessary degree of difference provided
by the appearance of the divinities, Athene and Apollo. Furthermore, the debate on the principle of the introduction of
the law courts is conducted by an Olympian, on the one hand,
and chthonic divinities on the other. The participants in the
debate, in their divine majesty, are suitably different from the

[134] If Athenian society did indeed use myth in the Lévi-Straussian way to naturalize
the arbitrary – which I do not believe it did – *Supplices* would seem to suggest
that *these* sorts of myth can no longer do the job. Myth has failed to adapt to a
'hot' society; it has not retained its significant timelessness. Such a reading suggests that *Supplices* exemplifies a crisis of myth. Out of that crisis new forms of
myth and new forms of timelessness (the stock characters and plots of New
Comedy) may have emerged. For intimations of such a crisis elsewhere in
Euripides, see *El.* 737ff.; *HF* 1314ff., 1340–6; *Hipp.* 197; see Kamerbeek (1960);
Pucci (1980), 177–9; Foley (1985), 163; Goldhill (1986), 256ff.

audience. In Euripides, however, the tone and the vocabulary of the *agōn* is so insistently fifth-century – even with Theseus as one of the debaters – that we are forced to recognize that it is precisely Athens which is being defended and attacked, and an Athens less mediated by mythical narrative and divine personae. The representations of *Supplices* inhabit two different worlds simultaneously, bringing them together in a theatrical other-world from which the audience is not so distanced as it would normally expect to be when watching a tragedy. New degrees of similarity and difference between the represented world and the world of the audience are invented; and that complicates self-examination *otherwise*.

Senses of time: the characters

Does *Troades* produce a similar effect? Here, there are two approaches. *Troades* is a highly self-conscious play, but that self-consciousness is not only an attribute of the author; it is also possessed by the characters in the drama, who are understandably anguished about the end of their former world and the beginning of a new life of suffering. The Trojan characters are undone by the destruction of the glorious past; they are dislocated by the evanescence of the present, both because of its sad reflection on the significance of that glorious past and because it points to a future that can only distress. But this is our topic: is *Troades* a pure narrative of the negative, the nihilistic? Are the past, present and future all as nothing?[135]

We start with Cassandra. Her entry comes at a point when Hecuba and the chorus have already been heard vehemently lamenting the past (98ff., 197ff.). The entrance of Cassandra marks a break in the atmosphere. In lines 353–405 she announces, in a flurry of future tenses, a prophecy which predicts her role in the death of Agamemnon (357–60). But then she claims that she will pass over her own death and that of Clytemnestra (361–4). Indeed, though a prophetess and

---

[135] For this section I am much indebted to Labellarte (1982), especially 52ff.; see also Ebener (1954); de Romilly (1968a); Desch (1985–6).

therefore keenly alert to time in general and the future in particular, Cassandra states that her desire is to show that Troy *is* more blessed than the Greeks (365–7). Cassandra would seem to be interested in some extra-temporal moral and spiritual condition which Troy possesses. But we know: there is no Troy. And Cassandra's arguments about the respective conditions of the Trojans and the Greeks stress that fact. For her arguments, ironically for a prophetess, are historical (367ff. on the Greeks; 386ff. on the Trojans). The iconoclasm of Cassandra's interpretation of the Trojan War has already been commented on. In her attitude to time, she is similarly removed from any consensus or tradition. For, while Hecuba sees the past as glorious and the present and the future as thus even more distressing, and while Andromache now finds the past as depressing as the present and the future (though, with the death of Astyanax, there is worse to come), Cassandra makes the past still present: for her Troy still exists. She finds in the past neither absence nor futile splendour, but the meaning for her present and her future.[136]

We find different perceptions and conceptions of time with Hecuba and Andromache. At 618ff. Hecuba learns of the death of Polyxena from Andromache. Her initial reaction that it has destroyed her is not surprising (628–9). Andromache offers no comfort: what has happened is inexorable. Face the facts, she urges bluntly (630):

> Av. ὄλωλεν ὡς ὄλωλεν.
>
> Andr. She died as she died.

Following this, Andromache gives an account of time which is at odds with that of Cassandra. The awful fact of Polyxena's death, which has hurt Hecuba so grievously, is for Andromache a further concentration on the problems of her own present. Twice she asserts that Polyxena has fared better in death than she has herself in life (630–1, 636–40). And

---

[136] Simon Goldhill reminds me that the prophetic present tense is an important feature of Cassandra's language in *Agamemnon*. Still, my point remains: Cassandra barely prophesies in *Troades*.

216

Hecuba's response that death means nothing while life offers hope is simply brushed aside (632–3). Andromache stresses the superiority of death to life by picturing it as a denial of time (636):

τὸ μὴ γενέσθαι τῷ θανεῖν ἴσον λέγω

I say that not to be born is the same as death.

The exemplum of Polyxena's death captures this point for Andromache, for it is as if she had never seen the light of day (641). All that past, all that living was for nothing, was as nothing. That, Andromache asserts, is the benefit of death and the reason for preferring it to life. The argument is strengthened by a lengthy description of the propriety of Andromache's former existence and the futility, even the harm, which propriety has caused her. While married to Hector she had acted in accordance with the prescriptions of male ideology (645ff.), but the praise her actions might have been expected to bring has been grimly perverted. Her reputation precedes her to the Greek camp (657–8): ironically, the son of the hero who killed her husband is the man who wishes to take her back to Greece as his slave and concubine (659–60). In some horrible way, then, Andromache sees the ideological soundness of her past as the basis of her disastrous future. Furthermore, that future is divided into two equally undesirable options (both with important relations to the ideological status of women, especially as perceived by Andromache herself). She can either repeat her former behaviour with another man – a murderer she calls him (660) – and thereby betray her dead husband (661–3); or she can refuse to co-operate with her captor, making her prospects a good deal more unhappy than they might be (663–4). Respecting her past and her husband, she chooses the former option. And the reasons why Andromache makes this choice are based, as was her behaviour in the past, on ideology rather than on perceived emotional benefits for herself (665–76). But she is aware of the consequences of her choice. The present now consists in nihilistic questions and attitudes: 'is not death better than life?'; 'I have neither hope nor delusion' (680–2). Andromache's final attachment to her past determines the emptiness of the present and then the negativity of the future. Death and her life in the future have this in common: both are no futures, but the former is preferable by virtue of the completeness of its negativity. Andromache's (no) future would still have to be endured.

Hecuba's response to the nothingness of Andromache's attitude is immediately forthcoming. The old queen, in contrast to her daughter, uses the hopelessness of the present as a sort of consolation, as a time in which at least she does not have to say anything (694-5):

> οὕτω δὲ κἀγὼ πόλλ' ἔχουσα πήματα
> ἄφθογγός ἐιμι . . .
>
> And I have so many troubles
> that I am speechless . . .

Following this, however, and taking on Andromache's rhetoric, Hecuba tells her daughter to face the facts: Hector is dead, and no tears can save him (697-8). Hecuba urges Andromache to repeat her past and to honour her new husband (699-700). Andromache had already objected to this on the basis of her past attachment to Hector, but Hecuba asserts it not only because of the hopelessness of the present but also, bizarrely, on the basis of the potential of the future. If Andromache accepts her lot, the family will be united (703-4) and Troy might still exist (704-5). The fragility of the hope is poignantly expressed in the optative mood of the verbs ('ἐκθρέψειας ἄν, 702; 'κατοικίσειαν/γένοιτο', 705). In an especially extreme reversal, this potential, this hope is removed. The entry of Talthybius brings with it the news that Astyanax, the seed of the future, is to be destroyed. The Greeks, therefore, seem to agree with Hecuba that Astyanax could perpetuate the Trojan name and threaten Greece again at some point in the future.

In the exchange between Andromache and Talthybius which follows, Andromache reveals that she too had retained some sense of, and some hope for the future. There is some power in this revelation if we see it caused by further repetition of woe. The destruction of Troy, the death of Polyxena, the prospects of life with the son of Achilles – all these Andromache can somehow cope with. But the death of her son is beyond endurance (722: 'οὐ μέτρια'). The optimism is short-lived, indeed it dies in the moment of its revelation. But Andromache stresses this further in her next long speech at 740ff. She makes no attempt to console her son and the past is now seen as some sort of cruel joke, unsympathetic and deceptive (747–9):

οὐ σφάγιον ⟨υἱὸν⟩ Δαναΐδαις τέξουσ' ἐμόν,
ἀλλ' ὡς τύραννον 'Ασιάδος πολυσπόρου.
ὦ παῖ, δακρύεις; αἰσθάνη κακῶν σέθεν;

Not as a sacrificial victim to the Greeks did I give birth to my son,
but as a king of fruitful Asia.
O my child, are you crying? Do you perceive your troubles?

Hector will not return to help (752–4) and thus Andromache paints the picture of her son's desperate future and her own condition as defined by absent men. The present, though, gives assurance for the future, certain only in its promise of final closure: 'you shall die' (741: 'θανῇ'), 'Hector shall not come' (752: 'οὐκ εἶσιν Ἕκτωρ'), 'you shall break off your breath' (756: 'πνεῦμ' ἀπορρήξεις'), 'now, never again' (761: 'νῦν, οὔποτ' αὖθις').[137] The past now only offers futility (758–60: 'all for nothing ... in vain'/'διὰ κενῆς ... μάτην'). The end of Andromache's speech perhaps testifies to the fact that all the prospects, all the chimaeras, all the attempts at consolation and strength have become too much for her. The vanity of the past culminates in a present which is merely destructive (775–6: 'for we are destroyed by the gods'/'ἔκ τε γὰρ θεῶν διολλύμεσθα') or impotent (776–7: 'we cannot keep my son from death'/'παιδί τ' οὐ δυναίμεθ' ἂν θάνατον ἀρῆξαι'). Labellarte here is probably right to say that, for Andromache, the present has become an appendix to the past rather than a premise of the future.[138] We could add that Andromache sees the future as a continuation of the characteristics of the

[137] On the tenses in this speech, see Labellarte (1982), 87–9.
[138] (1982), 90.

present as she describes them at 776–80. That is, the present and the future are undifferentiated, characterized together by their hopelessness.

One might expect there to be a progression in the views expressed, and the attitudes conveyed, about time, but such an expectation would necessarily be based on a misunderstanding of the upheaval which the attitudes of the characters go through. It has been observed that the principal characters offer conceptions of time which are in marked conflict; there is no progression from one to the other either. It has also been noted that all the characters express a confusion (or madness in Cassandra's case?), a dismay and an anger at the fact that their former notions of time – of progression, of order, of narrative – have been shattered. The destruction of Troy has not only consisted in the burning down of walls, in sacrilege and transgression, but also in the devaluation of some of the values and beliefs by which the characters lived; and their beliefs about time are no exception. The reactions of each of the individuals put together constitute a general depression about time and its privileged place in each person's understanding of the world. It is all the more ironic, then, that towards the end of the play Hecuba should revert to a pessimistic yet conventional view, in its assertion of insecurity and randomness, of the way time operates (1203–6):

> θνητῶν δὲ μῶρος ὅστις εὖ πράσσειν δοκῶν
> βέβαια χαίρει. τοῖς τρόποις γὰρ αἱ τύχαι,
> ἔμπληκτος ὡς ἄνθρωπος, ἄλλοτ' ἄλλοσε
> πηδῶσι.

> Whoever thinks he is secure in his good fortune
> is a fool. For our fortunes, like a capricious man,
> tend to leap about in different directions.

Whereas Andromache had implicitly identified the present and the future, Hecuba speaks more in terms of the consequences of past Greek actions in the future. They have killed their fear of the future by murdering the person believed to represent it (Astyanax); Hecuba points out their presumption (1188–91).

So, as with distinctions between opposed classes or groups, *Troades* represents, in the attitudes of its characters, a blurring of differences between past, present and future. In all their various characterizations, these three parts of an apparently orderly progression become involved in a troubling flux from one to the other, or they are caught in disturbing identity when they should be different and are found to be inconsistent with traditional expectations. 'The time is out of joint' (a title of an article by Luschnig): time, that is, both in and of the play. Better perhaps to quote Euripides himself, here from *Bellerophon* (fr. 291.3):

ὁ γὰρ χρόνος δίδαγμα ποικιλώτατον.

For time is a a most intricate [various] lesson.

Having considered the various attitudes to time expressed in the play, we should continue by examining how the play is related to contemporary civic discourse. It is indeed one of the important facets of tragedy that it is able to appropriate, represent and question other contemporary, non-tragic discourses (including various parts of what we might call the literary or mythical tradition). Some comparison to Periclean rhetoric has already been seen, as has the rhetorical/legal structure of ideas which stands behind the *agōn*. Now I shall concentrate on anachronistic or temporal elements (sophistic thought; Cassandra's relation to the literary tradition; the possible equivalence of the Trojan and Peloponnesian Wars), noting how the juxtaposition of the contemporary with the mythical enables us to reflect on the distinctive dramatic world of *Troades* and on the didactic function of tragedy.

Senses of time: the play

Contemporary thought appears in various ways and attached, as it were, to three different characters in *Troades*. Cassandra at 368ff. adopts a position with no traditional basis to question a traditional fact, i.e. that the Greeks won the Trojan

War. One has only to look as far as Gorgias' *Helen* to see that paradoxical arguments of this nature are one of the characteristics of sophistic thought.[139]

Also obvious in its modernity is Hecuba's prayer at 884–8. Though traditional in that Hecuba searches for the correct name of the god invoked (885–6: 'whoever you are ... whether ... whether'/'ὅστις ποτ' εῖ σύ ... εῖτε ... εῖτε'), the prayer undoubtedly has connections with some of the cosmological speculation current in Euripides' time. Hecuba seems to deny Zeus an anthropomorphic existence. It was mentioned (in chapter two) that the combination of abstract, modern characterizations with the more traditional view of Zeus suggests a confusion about the gods. That the prayer is remarkable is noticed in the text of the play itself, when, immediately after its utterance, Menelaus asks the meaning of these new prayers (889: 'how strange and new are these prayers to the gods'/ 'εὐχὰς ὡς ἐκαίνισας θεῶν').[140] Hecuba's prayer seems to question the sort of existence which the divine figures of its mythical subject-matter conventionally lead. It produces, therefore, a certain disquiet: about religious belief surely, but also about the particular contract tragedy has forged with its audience, a contract based on its ability to teach through the otherworldly figures of myth. That the play has already presented the audience with anthropomorphic gods in the prologue – thus undermining Hecuba's doubts in advance – only serves to confirm the view that, in Euripides, sophistic scepticism can be challenged (in a sophistic manner) like anything else.

The confrontation between the mythical and the contemporary (especially the sophistic) is most obvious in the *agōn*.[141] What is the significance of the presence of Gorgianic rhetoric

[139] M. Lloyd (1992), 101. Labellarte (1982), 56 detects in Cassandra's argument (it is better to defend than to attack) a correspondence with the Socratic ethic that it is better to be harmed than to harm (Pl. *Crito* 49c). See di Benedetto (1971), 5–24 and Snell (1964), 56ff. on what they call Euripides' polemic against Socrates at *Hipp.* 373ff.; for a contrary opinion, see Barrett (1964), 227–9; Michelini (1987), 297–310. See also Whitman (1974), 106; Moline (1975); Irwin (1983); Kuch (1984), 92.

[140] McDermott (1991) argues that Euripides calls attention to his own mythic innovations by the use of the adjective *kainos*.

[141] For this generally in Euripides, see Kamerbeek (1960); Eisner (1979).

in Helen's speech?[142] Scodel thinks that, in using Gorgias, Euripides is making a point about the dangers of sophism. She thinks that Helen has won the debate and asserts that the criticism of sophism occurs in the dramatization of its triumph rather than its demise: 'to accept the Gorgianic defence is virtually to abandon the right to judge any human act whatsoever'.[143] There are a number of problems with this position. It assumes that Gorgias can be equated with sophism, defined as a unified phenomenon;[144] that only Helen's speech is sophistic; and that Helen wins. Scodel has not learned from the play that evaluation, of precisely the sort she makes, is difficult. Yet she is no doubt right when she says that Euripides 'simultaneously presents the difficulties of judging human motivation and causality and the chaos that arises if they cannot be judged'.[145] The substance of the Gorgianic argument is, of course, important. My concern here, however, is to evaluate the effect of the presence of such an anachronistic argument in the tragic representation of myth. For together Cassandra, Hecuba and Helen – the voice of paradoxical truth, the untraditional worshipper and the apologist for desire respectively – constitute an important sophistic presence in tragedy.

The appearance of, so to speak, a Gorgias on the tragic stage is not simply a problem of anachronism; it can also be construed as having a destabilizing effect on tragic space. The discourses of the sophists share none of the authorization and centrality of tragedy. Sophists were not culturally validated; they had no sacred space from which to speak. As champions of a troubling and unprecedented agonism, as producers of a baffling proliferation of discourses, and as promoters of what must have seemed like a threatening war of languages, the marginal, sophistic voices of the fifth century presented a challenge to traditional Athenian values. Occasionally, however, a sophist received a positive response, as when Gorgias stunned his Athenian audience in 427 BC (DK 82A4). More

---

[142] Scodel (1980), 94–104; Donzelli (1985); Barlow (1986), 206–7; Goldhill (1986), 166–7, 236–8; cf. M. Lloyd (1992), 100–1. On the *Helen*, see Kerferd (1981), 78–81; Saïd (1978), 193–8.
[143] Scodel (1980), 99.   [144] Kerferd (1981), 1–42.   [145] (1980), 99.

often, sophists in Athens faced derision, fear and even punishment. Although Protagoras claims that the intellectual's life had always been somewhat insecure, we have no evidence that anywhere else in the Greek world were so many thinkers penalized. Athens claimed to be a city of free speech, yet Damon was perhaps ostracized, and Protagoras was probably tried for impiety.[146] It is possible that even Euripides suffered the same treatment as Protagoras (*Life of Euripides* fr. 39.10; Arist. *Rhet.* 1416a28ff.).[147] The point is summarized by Goldhill: 'Tragic theatre is performed in a civic festival and is constituted in terms of dramatic or religious licence – a delimited freedom to transgress ... Sophists ... have a less prescribed and more dangerous allowance. Euripides may have shocked, but it is Socrates who is prosecuted and put to death.'[148]

The anomalous position of sophists within the spatial organization of the *polis* further underlines their marginality. For sophists are errant and ungrounded. Travelling from city to city, they never quite belong to one *polis* alone, even though Athens attracted them more frequently than others.[149] Not unsurprisingly, this rootlessness is most marked in the figure of Gorgias (DK 82A18 [= Isocrates 15.155ff.]: 'πόλιν δ' οὐδεμίαν καταπαγίως οἰκήσας'/'He never settled down in any city'). He had no wife, no children, and paid no taxes. As a sophist, 'he

---

[146] For the general insecurity of an intellectual's life, see Pl. *Prot.* 316c5ff.; *Ap.* 33c4ff.; *Meno* 91eff.; *Theat.* 149a7; Arist. *Rhet.* 1397b24; generally, see Dover (1975); Kerferd (1981), 21; Baumann (1990), 37ff. For free speech in Athens, see. Pl. *Gorg.* 461e2. For Protagoras being prosecuted by Euathlos, see Aristotle fr. 67 (Rose); for having his books burned because he was an agnostic, and being condemned to death but escaping, see Timon of Phleious fr. 5 (Diels); D.L. 9.52; as prosecuted by Pythodorus, see D.L. 9.54; see Baumann (1990), 67–8. Damon ostracized: Arist. *Ath. Pol.* 27.4; Plut. *Arist.* 1.7; *Nic.* 6.1; *Per.* 4.1–3. Diagoras outlawed for *asebeia*, see Ar. *Birds* 1071ff. Anaxagoras accused of the same: Ephorus FGH 70, fr. 196. See Derenne (1930), esp. 13–71. For Diopeithes' decree outlawing atheism, see Plut. *Per.* 32.2.

[147] See Kerferd (1981), 19; Rankin (1983), 136; Baumann (1990), 47. On atheism and impiety in Euripides' plays, see Lefkowitz (1989); on *Sisyphus*, see Dihle (1977); Scodel (1980), 122ff.

[148] (1986), 242.

[149] Travelling around: Pl. *Ap.* 19e; *Prot.* 313d, 316c6; Marrou (1956), 49; G. Lloyd (1988), 98. Gorgias (DK 82A1; Pl. *Gorg.* 449b–c; *Meno* 70c; Arist. *Rhet.* 1414b29ff.) and Hippias (Pl. *Hipp. Mai.* 281aff.; *Hipp. Min.* 363c–64a, 368a–369b) were conspicuous at festivals all over the Greek world; see G. Lloyd (1988), 91.

belongs by nature to the tribe of nomads: vagrancy and parasitism are his birthrights'.[150] The nomadic qualities of Gorgias reflect the relativism traditionally recognized in his work; they also stand in opposition to the Platonic, and absolutist, position that the errant, the fluid, the homeless are all dangerous and subversive: 'The Socratic word does not wander, stays at home.'[151] The problems arising from the idea of centred space in *Troades* have already been discussed (see above: 'Past, present and future: the space of Troy'). Those problems are stressed by the inclusion of the marginal voices of the nomadic sophists in Euripides' tragic discourse at the centre of Athens. And, by looking to the marginal and the nomadic, Euripides introduces into tragedy qualities which are troublesome for the centralized *polis*. Yet ironically all this is perfectly in the spirit of Dionysus, the travelling god (*Bacch.* 13–24).[152] Michelini, perhaps without realizing the implications of her imagery, says: 'Euripidean plays present no central idea and persuade to nothing; but they irritate, disturb, constantly recreating the intellectual and emotional experience of the Sophistic war game with arguments.'[153]

The relationship between Euripides and the sophists has been discussed very fully – and in various ways – by other scholars.[154] The argument here, as with the other peculiarities

---

[150] Huizinga (1955), 147. Yet Hippodamus, a sophist, planned the grid system of the Peiraeus: see Haverfield (1913); Lévêque and Vidal-Naquet (1973), 124ff. Although it is hard to determine its value for interpretation, it remains a fact that Euripides lived out his life beyond the boundaries of Athens in self-imposed exile (though Aeschylus did the same). Tedeschi (1978) argues that Euripides was not *misodēmos* but politically engaged.

[151] Derrida (1981), 124. Pl. *Soph.* 230b: the disorderly in soul are wanderers; see Salkever (1986), 282. For a provocative and difficult study of 'nomadology' as a political strategy in the contemporary western world, see Deleuze and Guattari (1987).

[152] Daraki (1985), 19–44.

[153] (1987), 120; so Walsh (1984), 93: 'The lack of a communal centre in Euripides is radical.' On the lack of central heroes in Euripides, see Knox (1952); Arrowsmith (1963), 40; Michelini (1987), 63. The point, however, can be overstated: a central hero was a Sophoclean feature, rather than one conventional to all tragedy.

[154] Decharme (1893); Voegelin (1957); Detienne (1967), 119ff.; Rohdich (1968); Guthrie (1971); Scodel (1980), 99ff.; Kerferd (1981); Rankin (1983), 122–34; Walsh (1984), 98–10; Goldhill (1986), 222–43; de Romilly (1986), 117–84; Michelini (1987).

of Euripidean tragedy, rests on observing that Euripides makes more, and more extreme, use of these sophistic discourses. It should be remembered that tragedy, as it developed through the fifth century, became increasingly suffused by elements of sophistic thought. Sophocles' *Philoctetes*, for example, displays a concern with rhetoric and its abuse, with the differences and confusions between appearance and reality; it can be taken as a criticism of certain values – relativism, hedonism, cleverness – normally associated with the sophists.[155] In Euripides, however, sophistic presence is not only perceptible in particular arguments or criticisms (although of these there are plenty of examples); it can also be measured in the way features generally believed inadmissible in tragedy intrude. I refer, for instance, to an eroticism and to a naturalism which is uniquely Euripidean. There are also the appearances of the sorts of characters ('Tyrants, usurers, cowards and other villains, all shamelessly flaunting their immorality')[156] which form the basis of the complaint of the Aristophanic Aeschylus against Euripides at *Frogs* 1013ff. But it would be hard to prove that such elements were, in content, inspired by sophistic thought. It is more their tone, their very inappropriateness, their shock value, their polemic qualities, and their lack of respect for convention which betray sophistic tendencies. In fact, the sort of sophism which is most apparent in Euripides is one which can be associated with two sophists, Protagoras and Gorgias, most especially the latter.[157] There are in Euripidean tragedy suggestions of the absence of truth, sometimes gloomy, sometimes comic; of the inadequacy and

[155] Rose (1976); Craik (1980); Greengard (1987), 68–86.
[156] Michelini (1987), 88; see also p. 77 for inclusion of erotic elements, and p. 68 for riff-raff; Macleod (1983), 47–9.
[157] Cf. Michelini (1987), 64: 'Euripides turned for his support in many directions ... he also went outside the established lines of the genre, finding a fruitful, abundant and peculiarly appropriate source in the prose genres ... that might perhaps be grouped together under the title "critical thought". By opening tragedy to material that had been for good aesthetic reasons [*sic*] confined to its periphery, Euripidean drama offered a considerable challenge to the integrity of the genre.' And at p. 127: 'In Euripidean plays, and there alone, contemporary discourse appears in its full range and complexity ... richly elaborated in all its cultural implications.'

fallibility of reason; of the bewildering complexity of the necessary instrument of political dialogue, language. All of this is reminiscent of Gorgias' *On Not Being*.[158] Nietzsche accused Euripides of being a proponent of aesthetic Socratism; but a more appropriate description of this bizarre discourse called Euripidean tragedy is aesthetic Gorgianism (what Michelini calls an 'aesthetics of dissonance', and Arrowsmith 'turbulence').[159]

The second way in which the temporal character of *Troades* is complicated depends on playing off earlier literary representations. Now, in many cases, tragic figures make their first appearance in Homer and for that reason first of all it is right to assert the importance of studying tragic texts in relation to Homer. Apart from the valuable studies of Knox, Winnington-Ingram and Vernant on the relation of the tragic to the Homeric hero, Goldhill has recently analysed in detail the connections between the *Odyssey*, the *Oresteia* and the *Electra* plays of both Sophocles and Euripides.[160] It would be impossible to be exhaustive in this area of study, and for all the admirable detail of Goldhill's discussion, it is intended to be exemplary rather than complete. Here I wish to analyse the

[158] On the *On Not Being* as worth taking seriously for all its ironic and playful character, see Dupréel (1948), 63; Voegelin (1957), 275; Gomperz (1965), 1–35; Newiger (1973); G. Lloyd (1979), 82–4; Kerferd (1981), 93ff.; Rankin (1983), 95–9; Loraux (1986), 241; and Guthrie (1971), 25: 'It was subversive stuff, both morally and epistemologically ...' For the same work as merely stylistic innovation – whether that is praised or not – see DK 82A1, 3, 4, 7, 29; Kennedy (1963), 64; as embarrassing, see Robinson (1973). On Gorgias as a sign of the deterioration of culture, see Huizinga (1955), 151. See Scodel (1980), 100ff. on the relation of the *On Not Being* and tragedy.

[159] Nietzsche (1967), 86–7; Michelini (1987), 71; Arrowsmith (1968),13. Rohdich (1968), 20–1 argues that Euripides includes sophistic elements in order to undermine their threat to the tragic world-view, but that he fails. Attempting to minimize a threat by including it is a conventional, but potentially self-defeating, strategy of institutions under threat, but it is not clear that we can know Euripides' intentions in this connection. For criticism of Rohdich, see Michelini (1987), 40.

[160] Knox (1964); Winnington-Ingram (1980) and Vernant and Vidal-Naquet (1981); Goldhill (1986), 138–67. Zeitlin (1980) is a splendid piece which in part concentrates on *Orestes'* playing off inherited texts and roles. K. King (1985) interprets *Hecuba* against the *Iliad*. See also Jouan (1966) for a study of Euripides' use of non-Homeric epic and mythical material.

Euripidean Cassandra. This involves something rather different from a study of tragedy compared with Homer, as Cassandra is only mentioned three times in Homer, twice as the most beautiful of Priam's daughters (*Il.* 13.365–6; 24.699), and on the other occasion her death is described by Agamemnon (*Od.* 11.421–4). It is possible that the figure of Cassandra as a prophetess who was doomed never to be believed because she resisted Apollo's advances was inherited from the epic cycle. But that, for the obvious reason of lack of any evidence, is difficult to prove.[161] Pindar mentions her as a prophetess (*Pyth.* 11.33), but that may be either before or after Aeschylus' *Oresteia*, which is the most detailed representation of Cassandra before that of Euripides. It is in the *Agamemnon* (1202ff.) that Cassandra relates to the chorus how she has spurned Apollo and how he, in retaliation, has ensured that no one will believe her prophecies.

It is this figure which Euripides has inherited. Lack of evidence prohibits the assertion that Euripides was using only Aeschylus' Cassandra but, given the fame, influence and authority of Aeschylus, and of the *Oresteia* in particular,[162] and given Euripides' obvious awareness of his illustrious predecessor – demonstrated in the most spectacular fashion in the rewriting of the recognition scene from *Choephori* in *Electra* – it will be difficult to resist the temptation of comparing the two representations (and they are the only two we have in tragedy).[163] If we compare the two Cassandras, there are some interesting differences.

Agamemnon 1076ff.: Cassandra's prophecy. Here, Cassandra predicts the fortunes of Agamemnon and Clytemnestra, herself and Orestes; she foretells the events, in part, of the latter stages of *Agamemnon*, as well as of *Choephori* and

---

[161] Aélion (1983) I.217–18.

[162] It is possible that the plays of Aeschylus were revived at the Great Dionysia sometime in the 420s; see Pickard-Cambridge (1968²), 100.

[163] Aélion (1983), I.217–33 simply asserts that Euripides had Aeschylus' Cassandra in mind for both *Alexander* and *Troades*; however, no evidence is produced for this claim, although there are some interesting insights on the differences between the two Cassandras (to which I am indebted).

Eumenides. There is a concentration, then, on the future, proper for a prophetess. Indeed, her mantic status is stressed throughout the scene (*Ag.* 1098, 1105, 1195, 1202, 1215, 1241, 1275). It is true enough that Cassandra utters her predictions by pointing to the past fortunes of the House of Atreus. Nevertheless, her indication of the recidivist tendencies to intrafamilial murder in that house does not obscure the fact that the past is used as a precedent and a cause of events in the future, which is the matter at hand. And, although the prophecy is immediately followed by the death of Agamemnon, and although on one occasion Cassandra refers to the imminence of the events she predicts (*Ag.* 1301), there is a sense in this passage of an unspecific but nonetheless powerful and gloomy future, underlined by a density and obscurity of language quite different from the Euripidean version. Such an impression is perhaps emphasized by the chorus' ability to understand Cassandra's references (even if not the precise significance of those references) to the past and Thyestes (*Ag.* 1242–3), but not her predictions (*Ag.* 1251–2; see 1133–5). The Cassandra of the *Oresteia* is a prophetess properly predicting future events amidst an atmosphere of gloom and of impending and, in fact, immediate doom. She also prophesies in a delirium produced by Apollo (*Ag.* 1209: *entheos*/ 'possessed by the god'). In *Troades*, by contrast, Cassandra's first entrance has her proclaiming her own marriage festivities and general joy (308ff., 331–7); and, before she starts to talk at length, she promises to stop being *entheos* (366–7).[164]

At *Tro.* 353ff. Cassandra looks forward to her role in Agamemnon's death; but she does so with some glee and with admiration for her own responsibility in the matter. At 361ff. she states that she will not sing of her own death and, as she moves into her justification of the Trojans' superior condition (365–405), she seems uninterested in prophesying at all. Oddly,

---

[164] See Aélion (1983) I. 221–2 and 226 on Cassandra's inspiration; and see di Benedetto (1971), 55ff. on the differences between the Aeschylean and Euripidean Cassandra in terms of rationalism.

her arguments are historical and ideological; they refer to conditions and states, rather than futures. At 428ff. she does begin to prophesy, but with some impatience (see 444), and she shows some eagerness to get on with her new role as agent of revenge, as one of the three furies (456–7: 'μίαν τριῶν Ἐρινύν') and someone who will reach Hades as a victor (460: 'ἥξω δ᾽ ἐς νεκροὺς νικηφόρος').

There is an immediacy about Cassandra's speeches in *Troades*, even though – if we rely on the mythical tradition – there is some time to go before she achieves what she so ardently desires. This contrasts with the vagueness of the future prophesied in *Agamemnon*, where the prophecy is immediately followed by one of the events it foretells.[165] Aeschylus' Cassandra does prophesy, and is thus concerned with the future. Her Euripidean counterpart talks more of the present and the past, generally referring to the future only to celebrate her own role in it and the death of her enemies. Such a celebratory tone is entirely absent from *Agamemnon*. Indeed, her prophecies in Aeschylus speak of facts which are unfortunate and depressing; Euripides' Cassandra predicts some of the same events, but it is not the predictions themselves that seem to matter but what the other characters take as her mad joy in predicting death (see e.g. 341–2; 406–7). The chorus in *Agamemnon* cannot understand the facts; in *Troades* they are incredulous in the face of Cassandra's behaviour. The audience would probably have shared both the incomprehension and the amazement.

The main difference between the two representations, however, is that, in Aeschylus, the truth of Cassandra's (prophetic) assertions is immediately confirmed. In Euripides, on the other hand, where Cassandra talks, as we have seen, about the past, it never is and never can be clear whether she is telling the truth. Cassandra was passed down with the authority of myth (and then of Aeschylus) as the prophetess who told the

---

[165] It should be noted that Cassandra seems to sing her own funeral lament at *Ag.* 1279ff. The paradox (a funeral lament is not normally sung by the future corpse; it looks backwards, not forwards) may have alerted Euripides to the potential of Cassandra in the representation of time.

truth. How, then, can we explain the fact that Euripides' Cassandra denies a mythical fact normally accepted as given? Whose truth is being questioned? Cassandra's? That of Aeschylus? Of myth? Of Euripides? Euripides would seem to be exploiting the authority of Cassandra as utterer of truth in order to challenge the mythical tradition. Euripides confronts the myths and narratives he has inherited with what, after Aeschylus, may have been one of their most inflexible and unadaptable figures. In so doing he challenges Aeschylus', Cassandra's and his own claims to be 'masters of truth', for all of them cannot be right. A mythical character, whose one great attribute is her inevitable production of the truth, becomes in Euripides implicated in the sophistic problematics of the late fifth century and a critic of mythical truth. In Cassandra, then, we can observe the uneasy relation of Euripides' *Troades* to its literary and mythical past: newly equipped with (sophistic) paradoxical instincts, she exploits her main mythical characteristic to question the truth of myth.

Troades depicts with great power the effects of war: enslavement of the losers; confusions in *philia*, in the distinctions between Greek and barbarian, man and god, and man and woman; sacrificial violence, horrible revenge, doubts about the value of victory, the problems and paradoxes of rhetoric. The play depicts the cultural and ideological crisis brought on by war. That crisis is comparable, and perhaps not surprisingly, to that effected by the Peloponnesian War. It is interesting to note that, by the time *Troades* was performed, the Trojan War may have been used, in comedy at any rate, as a way of talking about the Peloponnesian War. This is most apparent in the use Aristophanes makes, in *Acharnians* and *Thesmophoriazusae*, of Euripides' lost play *Telephus*. Although reconstructions of fragmentary plays are always hazardous, it has been possible in this instance to piece together what for us is the most important part of *Telephus*. This is the speech Telephus makes disguised as a beggar (fr. 703) in an attempt to persuade the Atreidae not to fight the Trojans. Given Aristophanes' other protestations against the war, some critics have taken the parody (at *Ach.* 496ff.) of this anti-war speech as an Aristophanic criticism of the Peloponnesian War.[166]

Some scholars have been led by this use of another, past war to examine the problems arising out of a present one to detect in *Troades* veiled, but nevertheless specific, references to the events of the Peloponnesian War. This form of criticism has been much attacked for paying too little attention to the supposed integrity of a literary text, and as being over-ingenious in its fanciful interpretations.[167] However, put in the context of a Euripidean discourse which has a tendency to create a distinctive temporal definition, attempts at finding detailed anachronistic references take on a new and more interesting aspect.

Delebecque, who writes the most on this matter, first argues that Euripides was a pacifist and that *Troades* was his great anti-war statement.[168] Delebecque thinks that the play refers to the anticipated Sicilian expedition of 415 BC, the outrage in Melos and the dangerous ambition of Alcibiades.[169] Other scholars do not always agree about the details: Maxwell-Stuart states that the play is about Sicily, not Melos;[170] West-

---

[166] The parody of *Telephus* performs other functions as well (the appropriation of tragic prestige to defend comedy against the charges of Cleon); see Foley (1988). For reconstructions of *Telephus*, see Handley and Rea (1957); Webster (1967); Heath (1987b). For Aristophanes and peace, see *Ach.* 524–9; *Peace* 603–14; Dover (1972), 84–8, 136–9.

[167] The most strident attack is by Zuntz (1972). Giles (1890), with a refreshing disrespect for what we now sonorously call Literature, ignores the literary problems of form, structure and meaning in his analysis of *Supplices* and takes the Funeral Oration in that play as a transparent description of the five leading political figures in Athens at the time of production. For a survey of possible contemporary allusion in Aeschylus' *Septem*, Sophocles' *Antigone*, *Oedipus Tyrannus*, and *Phoenissae*, see Diano (1969). For *Philoctetes* as referring to events in Athens in 409 BC, see Calder (1971); as representing Alcibiades in the figure of Philoctetes, see M. Vickers (1987).

[168] Delebecque (1951), 245–6. Goossens (1962), 520–7 agrees.

[169] Delebecque (1951), 245–62.

[170] (1973). Van Erp Taalman Kip (1987) argues that the play cannot *originally* have been written as a response to Melos for these reasons: a) the massacre occurred in the middle of December, but the play was performed in March; b) this leaves too little time to train a chorus, let alone write a play; c) the plays were probably selected in September. However, we should not forget the possibility that Euripides could respond to events as he was writing, and that he could have changed elements of the play at a late stage. Most important, though, is the fact that the writing of the play is not really the issue: it was a matter for the audience to decide in March whether they saw the play as a response (as *their* response) to Melos.

lake thinks he can find references to an Athenian alliance with Thessaly (*Tro.* 214–17);[171] and Goossens sees it as both a response to Melos and a prediction of the catastrophe in Sicily.[172] However, it is not the details which are important, but the validity of such a criticism. Can a play about the end of the Trojan War really refer to the Peloponnesian War? Some decades ago this question was at the centre of an acrimonious debate between Zuntz and three representatives of the contemporary reference school (Delebecque, Goossens, Grégoire). Zuntz bases his objections on an extreme and tendentious definition of an allusion: 'It can only be in the essential and evident bearing of an utterance upon particular facts or persons outside the drama, to the exclusion of its relevance to the context.'[173] Such a position implies that a line in a play cannot refer to more than one thing at once, and that only segments unexplained in other ways can properly be examined as allusions to contemporary events.[174] Of course, all that Zuntz does here is usurp the role of the contemporary audience in the construction of a play's significance, ironically a position shared by those who want to affirm the existence of contemporary allusions.[175] The point is simply this: we, in the twentieth century, are in no position to deny the possibilities

---

[171] (1953).   [172] (1962), 527–34.

[173] (1972), 58. A similar definition is adopted by Westlake (1953) and, oddly we might think, by Delebecque (1951), 34: 'le signe d'une digression politique, accentuée encore par l'absence de toute source mythologique directe'. Delebecque believes such a thing can be found; Zuntz does not. I have no need to adopt either of these exclusive positions. For wiser approaches, see de Romilly (1965); Conradie (1981); and especially Redfield (1990), 325–6.

[174] Zuntz (1972), 58: 'True: every and any word spoken by any person on the stage could make anyone in the audience think of anything. This infinite and indefinite possibility of association is irrelevant.' Of course, no one is talking about any and every association. I am arguing that we are in no position to legislate against very probable audience reactions based on important current events. Stinton (1986) argues that we must accept limits on the scope of allusion, though he is concerned with variations on myths.

[175] All the scholars I have mentioned also make the mistake of thinking that you can glean the authentic views of Euripides from statements made by his characters. For Delebecque (1951), 245, 261–2, Euripides is a pacifist and a patriot; in the opinion of Westlake, Euripides makes no attempt to guide public opinion, but his play is a desperate reflection of people's concerns at the time of production. In arguing for the possibility of contemporary allusion I in no way align myself with all the arguments and positions proposed by Delebecque, Maxwell-Stuart and Westlake.

of a contemporary audience finding – in many different ways, no doubt – references to the war they were engaged in as they watched the play. To insist otherwise is to claim that an audience should forget about the events which were determining each of their lives in an extreme and thorough way. There is no reason to think that a play obviously concerned with the effects of war should not make its spectators think of a war, in the same way as Sartre used *Troades* as an anti-nuclear-war fable.[176] Along with other less overt references to contemporary situations, we must allow for the possibility that the audience saw in *Troades* fairly detailed allusions to the Peloponnesian War (including Sicily, Melos and Alcibiades). This allowance must be made for all tragedy, but at the same time it should not be forgotten that the possibility of contemporary allusion is that much more obvious in *Troades* than in some other plays (hence the academic debate about it).

The presence of sophistic thought, the representation of Cassandra and the degree of possible contemporary allusion in *Troades* all serve to emphasize that the play, in common with other Euripidean tragedy, flows between the fictional world of myth, which tragedy uses, and the contemporary time of which tragedy itself was a product. By introducing a more extreme and explicit degree of anachronism, Euripides produces an other-world, a dramatic world, distinctively constructed in a conflation of the mythical and the contemporary, the other-worldly and the (political, rhetorical, ideological) here and now. A distinctive other will pose distinctive questions to the self.

There is one final area, however, in which the distinctiveness of the Euripidean world is apparent: it is again a question of spatial definition. The internal spatial and temporal definitions of *Troades* are fluid and insecure, but they nevertheless depend on the distinction between the world of the stage and that of the audience, which is perhaps the most important distinction for any theatrical performance. It is to this distinction that we now turn.

---

[176] Sartre (1968).

Self-reference: the audience and the play

The distinction between the worlds of the audience and the play (fiction/reality) has often been demonstrated to be neither easy nor comfortable.[177] This is the case whether we say that social interaction and interpersonal communication are marked by the adoption of personae, roles and masks;[178] or that much communal activity seems theatrical;[179] or that the semiotic systems of representation can be used as guides for signifying in the real world;[180] or that fictional discourse provides the models for so-called ordinary language;[181] or that both the real and the fictional are possible worlds.[182] Vernant has said that, with tragedy, we witness the city 'playing itself'.[183] But, as has been seen, the city represents itself by playing the other (to use Zeitlin's phrase). The balance and the flux between the self and the other, or between the actual self and the self represented *otherwise*, is important, since the tragic scrutiny of ideology seems to depend on the represented self being recognizable as self, but, mediated by the other, not too close to home. That balance is most likely to be affected by the use of a play's acknowledgement of itself as play, for in this way a different movement between the space of the stage and of the audience is created. What follows is a consideration of how Euripides exploits the uneasy distinction between the fictional and the real and how, in so doing, he forges a new and peculiar relationship with his audience.

It is in the relationship with the audience, one critic has recently argued, that one of the crucial differences between comedy and tragedy in fifth-century Athens can be identi-

---

[177] For a survey of opinion, see Pavel (1986).

[178] Cixous (1974), 386; Goffman (1974), 496–576.

[179] Goffman (1974), 186; Turner (1982), (1986). Connected with this point is the work of Huizinga (1955) and Caillois (1962) on 'play' and culture.

[180] Eco (1977), esp. 113: 'It is not Theatre which is able to imitate life; it is social life which is designed as a continuous performance.' See also Goffman (1969), 78: 'All the world is not of course a stage, but the crucial ways in which it isn't are not easy to specify'; but cf. (1974), 124: 'All the world is like a stage.'

[181] Generally, see Waugh (1984), 87–114; Pavel (1986), 18–25. However, my reference is to the debate between Derrida (1976) and Searle (1975), (1976).

[182] Elam (1980), 108; Pavel (1986), 136.

[183] (1970), 279.

fied.[184] And these relations are understood to be the types and degrees of self-reference present in the two genres. Taplin defines five categories of self-reference, which are listed and briefly explained below.

(1) *Audience*: the acknowledgement of the world of the audience through direct address; explicit references to the dramatic festival; mention of contemporary political figures.

(2) *Poet*: where a poet calls attention to himself, and to the writing of his play, as in the comic parabasis.

(3) *Theatre*: references to the theatre itself and various theatrical techniques.

(4) *Disguise*: where disguise is used to refer self-referentially to theatrical costume and dressing-up.

(5) *Parody*: the deliberate allusion to, and mockery of, other texts.[185]

Taplin argues that all these categories are either relatively or completely absent from tragedy, although he also issues the caveat that the extant comedies and tragedies are not all from the same period.[186] Tragedy and comedy remain distinct, indeed they even define each other by opposition. What examples there are of self-reference in tragedy tend, Taplin argues, to be Euripidean; and it is in Euripides, as well, that comic elements appear more frequently (Taplin terms this 'generic interference'). Much of what Taplin says is acceptable. However, as the appearances of self-reference in tragedy are considered (in categories different to Taplin's), particular points of disagreement will surface. And the generic interference which Taplin takes as especially Euripidean seems to me to be another type of self-reference. For, by introducing conventionally inappropriate comic elements into itself, tragedy calls attention to its own supposedly distinctive generic conventions. It is with comic elements in tragedy that I begin.

It is now generally agreed that there are elements in Euripidean tragedy which mark a change of tone from both Aeschylus and Sophocles. There are the plays of outrageous

---

[184] Taplin (1986).

[185] For the comic parabasis and comic parody of tragedy, see, most recently, Goldhill (1991), 188–222.

[186] Taplin (1986), 163–5.

female sexual behaviour about which the women in Aristophanes' *Thesmophoriazusae* and Aeschylus in the same
author's *Frogs* get so upset. There is the penchant for the
bizarre and grotesque (bestiality in *The Cretan Women*; the
daughters of Pelias boil their own father in *Peliades*).[187] And
there is the consistently anti-heroic tone, whether in the rags
which Electra notoriously wore in *Electra* or in the character
of Orestes in *Orestes* (and see *Frogs* 959ff. for a contemporary
view on the Euripidean incorporation of common themes).
Recently, Michelini has tried to make this obvious difference
the starting point for a detailed study of Euripidean poetics:
'Euripidean theatre is ... a theatre of the unsuitable; and principles of taste or appropriateness are not effective touchstones
when applied to this sort of work.'[188] But it is not just the
incorporation of apparently inappropriate elements which is
important when talking of self-reference; it is also the presence of elements which are inappropriate to tragedy but
appropriate to another genre. Elements from comedy will be
easier to identify when they are generic, e.g. play-structure,
plots, style of staging, cross-dressing.[189] Not all areas of
comic drama, however, can be plundered by tragedy: notably
absent, for instance, is scatology.[190] And identifying what is
simply comic – whether in a line or a scene – is always going
to be difficult. In order to judge the appearance and significance of the comic in Euripides, comparison will have to be
made with both Aeschylus and Sophocles.

Neither Aeschylus nor Sophocles furnishes us with much
that could be called comic. And those examples which have
been cited are unified by the fact that the comedy is supposed
to be produced by a separate and unheroic character of lower
social status, such as a watchman (Aesch. *Ag.* 1ff.), a nurse

---

[187] Michelini (1987), 75–94.

[188] Michelini (1987), 71; see also ibid., 66–7, 86; W. Arnott (1973); Knox,
'Euripidean Comedy' in (1979); Decharme (1893), 359–76. Biffi (1961) notes
how Euripides uses elements of realism to interrupt what he calls the proper
mood of tragedy.

[189] Seidensticker (1978), 305–6 calls these 'comedy elements' as against 'comic
elements'.

[190] Taplin (1986), 172.

(Aesch. *Cho.* 731ff.), a guard (Soph. *Ant.* 223ff.) or a messenger (Soph. *OT* 924ff.).[191] It is even arguable whether any of these characters are, in fact, comic: they could instead be regarded as purveyors of what one critic refers to as a certain lively, albeit untragic, realism.[192] Euripides was not averse to a particular sort of figure for comic purposes, as the Phrygian slave in *Orestes* testifies.[193] A different sort of Sophoclean example altogether is *Philoctetes*, which, with its hero in rags and its plot full of intrigue and its stress on Philoctetes' malodorous foot (*Phil.* 473, 483, 783–4, 876, 890–1, 1032, 1378), seems more typical of Euripides. But this seems more a question of bad taste, of low tone, of the inappropriate than of the comic. It should also be remembered that *Philoctetes* was a late play and was no doubt influenced by some of Euripides' innovations.[194] Throughout the career of Euripides comedy appears not only confined to a single character of a certain type but also throughout whole plays, whole scenes and in single-line jokes said by otherwise serious characters: the comedy seems of a different sort.

The plays of Euripides which seem most difficult to pin down as to their genre come from both early and late in his career. In this category Seidensticker discusses *Alcestis, Helen, Iphigeneia at Tauris* and *Ion*.[195] Here the earliest, *Alcestis*, will be briefly considered, since the difficulties of its generic status cannot be explained away by historical developments or by Euripides' alleged retirement into the writing of romantic comedy.[196] No ancient source describes the play as pro-satyric, but the hypothesis does state that the drama is of a satyric nature.[197] Furthermore, the appearance of Heracles

191 Seidensticker (1982), 242; see ibid., 65–75 for Aeschylus, 76–88 for Sophocles.
192 Ibid., 74–5.
193 Seidensticker (1982), 101–14; on *Orestes* more generally as a play suffused with comic elements, see Dunn (1989). I find taking the Nurse in *Hippolytus* as comic, as Smith (1960), 175 and Michelini (1987), 310–12 do, less plausible.
194 Craik (1979); Greengard (1987), 51–66.
195 (1982), 129–241; see also Knox, 'Euripidean Comedy' in (1979).
196 On *Alcestis*, apart from Seidensticker (1982), see Wilson (1968b), 1ff.; Seaford (1984), 1–2; Conacher (1988), 35–7.
197 Dale (1954), xviii–xxii: the argument that the play is not tragedy depends on the length of the play, the fact that it needs only two actors (but so does *Medea*), and,

heralds the entrance of the comic (*Alc.* 747ff.). For Heracles, the great panhellenic hero, makes rare appearances in tragedy; he is more usually to be found in comedy.[198] Burnett says: 'Heracles comes geographically from afar, and he also comes from another genre.'[199] In this connection we could mention his eating off-stage, his rowdy and hedonistic creed, and his drunkenness. There is also the strange scene where Admetus describes how he will go to bed with a statue of his wife (*Alc.* 348ff.). (By contrast, at Aesch. *Ag.* 416–17 the chorus describe how Menelaus, in his wife's absence, finds statues of Helen no substitute.) How do we approach this? Beye calls it 'ludicrous in the extreme, or disgusting',[200] and, even though its value is hard to determine precisely, perhaps there is something comically grotesque about this simulated woman.

Euripides also makes use of elements which we would expect to find more usually in comedy and inserts them into plays which are otherwise very far from comic. One instance of this is the *Bacchae*. The conventional tragic tone is already challenged perhaps because the action is orchestrated by the god of theatre – of tragedy *and* comedy – himself, and because Dionysus' mask probably remained fixed in a smile.[201] But there are, in particular, two scenes which seem more reminiscent of comedy. The first is the sight of the two old men, Teiresias and Cadmus, gaily garbed in Dionysiac costume (*Bacch.* 170ff.); the second has Dionysus succeed in urging the king of Thebes to don the clothes of a woman (*Bacch.*

---

most especially, the appearance of Heracles. Dale argues that a satyric theme (the triumph of life over death) has been adapted to tragedy; Knox, 'Euripidean comedy' in (1979) says that *Alcestis* should be viewed as a satyr play transformed by a tragic situation, character, chorus and style.

[198] Silk (1985) argues that Heracles is such a dangerously disturbing hero that tragic structure can accommodate him only with difficulty. Heracles' appearance in *Alcestis* may have been his first in tragedy, although that depends on how one dates Sophocles' *Trachiniae*, which may well have been earlier; see Easterling (1982), 19–23.

[199] (1971), 38; see also Dale (1954), xx–xxi. For a different view, see Gregory (1991), 19–49.

[200] (1959), 114; see also Rosenmeyer (1963), 228; Burnett (1971), 36.

[201] On the mask, see Foley (1980); C. Segal (1982), 223ff.; Vernant and Vidal-Naquet (1986), 238–62; Frontisi-Ducroux (1989).

912ff.).[202] Both scenes use the obvious self-referentiality of dressing-up in order to honour Dionysus, which is what the actors have done anyway. They also bring to mind (would parody be the wrong word?) the frequency with which comedy exploits dressing-up in the form of disguise for comic effect. A second example is *Electra*, which has a celebrated parody – another frequent feature of comedy – of the recognition scene in the *Choephori* (*El.* 508ff./Aesch. *Cho.* 164ff.). While the scene has some serious features and functions, there is no doubt that part of the effect is comic.[203] Electra's debunking of the Aeschylean signs of Orestes' presence reported to her is itself undermined by the fact that they are, in fact, genuine.[204]

The final comic element in Euripides is the shocking one-liner. There are two celebrated examples. The first, in *Hercules Furens*, has Lyssa (Madness) pleading with Iris, Hera's representative, that she be allowed not to derange Heracles, as he is such a great hero (*HF* 843–56). Iris' reply puns etymologically on *sōphronein* (saving one's mind; sanity), telling Lyssa that it is not her job to be sensible (*HF* 857). The second example is in *Troades*. The joke here, if it is a joke, comes after the debate between Helen and Hecuba, which itself has a certain comic feel: for all the flashiness of the rhetoric on display, it may not be Helen's words which are persuasive but her very physical presence. Once Menelaus has adjudged Hecuba the winner of the debate, Hecuba implores Menelaus to make sure he executes Helen (1044–5). Menelaus replies that he will be taking Helen home to Argos, and it is at this point we hear this strange couplet (1049–50):

---

[202] Seidensticker (1978), (1982), 116–28; Muecke (1982); C. Segal (1982), 255–7. Sansone (1978) examines satyric elements in the *Bacchae*.

[203] Pucci (1967); Winnington-Ingram (1969), 129; Bond (1974); Knox, 'Euripidean Comedy' in (1979); Goldhill (1986), 247–9; Taplin (1986), 171; Michelini (1987), 181–206. On *Electra* generally Michelini (1987), 182 well states: 'This play challenges the basic split between the laughable (*geloion*) and the serious (*spoudaion*).' Note C. Segal (1986), 222–68 on the mixed genres in Euripides' *Helen*. Gorgias himself (DK 82B12) advises that one should undermine the serious with laughter and vice versa.

[204] In the Sophoclean version Electra also does not believe that the offerings at her father's tomb are signs of Orestes' presence. But her disbelief is not a product of a rationalistic scepticism concerning the signs themselves, but of faith in the story told her of Orestes' death by Orestes' Paedagogus (Soph. *El.* 680ff., 892ff.).

Εκ.   μή νυν νεὼς σοὶ ταὐτὸν ἐσβήτω σκάφος.
Με.   τί δ' ἔστι; μεῖζον βρῖθος ἢ πάροιθ' ἔχει;

Hec.   Do not let her [Helen] on the same ship as yourself.
Men.   Why? Has she put on weight?

What could be the point of this, which Barlow thinks too
feeble even for the banal Menelaus? And in a play which has
provoked critics to describe it as representing total disaster,
cultural crisis, nothingness, total nihilism, etc. Let us consider
the possibilities. It could be a momentary release from the
awful, despondent tale which the audience has so far been
watching. Seidensticker, in accordance with his general views
about comic elements in tragedy, argues that the couplet not
only acts as much-needed contrast to the otherwise desperate
events; it also emphasizes the calamity the play represents,
and, furthermore, it points out the stupidity and insensitivity
of Menelaus.[205] But it should also be stressed that the reply of
Menelaus is singularly inappropriate, because it seems both to
be a joke and, if a joke, a bad one at that. As such the couplet
certainly disrupts the tone of the play. That it is comic also
makes it a disruption of genre. The effects on the audience can
only be guessed: it is probable that the genre of the play was
ironically affirmed.[206] It is even more likely that, once the
self-reference was acknowledged, the response of the audience
would have been divided: even now the couplet remains
strangely disturbing.

In Euripides, then, it is not merely the presence of inappropriate elements (bad taste, the grotesque) which makes
Euripidean tragedy self-referential, but the appearance of elements not only inappropriate to tragedy but strictly appropriate to another genre, namely comedy. By using comedy, and
in the manner of comedy, Euripidean tragedy calls attention
to its own fictional status. As Charles Segal says: 'Euripides

---

[205] (1978), 310; (1982), 89–90; see also Grube (1941), 295; Gellie (1986), 118; Biehl
(1989), 379.
[206] In the language of frames, one would say that the breaking of the theatrical
frame can have the function of reasserting the frame so long as the frame is
acknowledged as frame: see Goffman (1974), 382; Eco (1976), 272; Elam (1980),
90; Waugh (1984), 28–34.

situates his play both within and beyond the conventional form of both genres, a place where his text can explore the power and limitations of its own mimetic mode.'[207]

One of the ways in which comedy is most openly self-referential is through the use of audience address, both in the parabasis and in asides made by individual characters. It is true that this mode of self-acknowledgement is not explicit in tragedy, but the denials of its possibility have perhaps been excessively strenuous.[208] The possibility of audience address in tragedy is not uniquely Euripidean, as Aesch. *Eum.* 681ff. makes clear;[209] but, given what we have seen already of the intrusion of contemporary and comic discourses into Euripidean tragedy, and a certain wilful anachronism, the exclusion of the possibility of audience address in Euripides, not with arguments but with mere preferences to support the exclusion, looks simplistic. For instance, Bain discusses *Or.* 128–9, where Electra, alone on stage, says of Helen, who has just exited:

> εἴδετε παρ' ἄκρας ὡς ἀπέθρισεν τρίχας,
> σῴζουσα κάλλος; ἔστι δ' ἡ πάλαι γυνή.

> Did you see how she snipped her hair at the tips,
> looking after her beauty? It's the same old Helen.

Bain runs through the two common interpretations of these lines. There are silent slaves on stage; it is audience address. He simply denies the possibility of both and plumps instead for 'imaginary listeners'.[210] But why can Electra not address all three of the groups which Bain mentions? Why is it Bain, rather than the audience, who decides whether they are being addressed? Can the audience not be 'imaginary listeners'? And so on. In *Troades* there is a similar possible instance of audience address (or so the scholiast thought) at 36–8, where

---

[207] (1982), 256.
[208] E.g. Taplin (1978), 166: 'The world of the play never acknowledges the world of the audience: the distancing always remains intact.'
[209] Taplin (1977), 131.
[210] (1975), 19. Bain also considers Aesch. *Ag.* 36–9 and Soph. *Aj.* 1028ff. In both cases he again just asserts that there is no need to see audience address. Bain (1987) has reconsidered his position on audience address, but has not changed it.

Poseidon invites anyone ('τις') to look at Hecuba lying on the ground.[211] It should be added that it is only in tragedy, with the exception in comedy of Ar. *Ach.* 27), that one comes across an address to the city (*ō polis*) without any functional, spatial or temporal qualifications (see *Hipp.* 884; *Heracl.* 763, 901).[212] One is tempted to ask whether the audience of tragedy might not be able to take these addresses as to themselves.

There is one final, and less well-defined, area of self-reference. This includes references to poets and poetry and references to, and appearances of, Dionysus. Criticism of Euripides has become increasingly interested in such metafictional aspects, especially in relation to the *Bacchae*.[213] In that play the central character is Dionysus himself: 'the god of theatre appears on his own stage, in costume and disguise, and he will be honoured in the play by the chorus of Dionysus' worshippers – actors trained for the festival in order to honour Dionysus'.[214] Dionysus, in fact, uses 'theatrical weapons'[215] to undermine the opposition of Pentheus, most notably in the scene where Pentheus is costumed as a bacchant (827ff., 925ff.). But, as the bulk of the bibliography testifies, *Bacchae* requires separate and detailed treatment. In *Troades*, however, the appearance of Dionysus is confined to descriptions of the behaviour and state of mind of Cassandra (341, 366–7, 500; see chapter three). That Euripides chooses to confront Dionysus, the god of illusion and fiction, with Cassandra, who always speaks the truth but who in this play contradicts traditional truths, leads to questions about the truth-value of

---

[211] The scholiast's words are: 'frigidly to the theatre' ('ψυχρῶς τῷ θεάτρῳ'); see Lee (1976), 70–1; Biehl (1989), 108.

[212] In the orators the normal address is *ō andres dikastai* (e.g. Lys. 21.22), and in political speeches one usually finds *ō Athenaioi* or *andres Athenaioi* (e.g. Lys. 28.10; Thuc. 1.140).

[213] C. Segal (1982), (1985); Foley (1985); Goldhill (1986), 244–86. On *Hercules Furens*, see Pucci (1980), 175–87. On tragedy as self-referential because it is ritual, see Foley (1985), 64. Taplin (1978), 161 denies this as well, which is excessively zealous given the basic fact of tragedy's performance at a festival. Zeitlin (1980) superbly analyses *Orestes* in terms of its metafictional aspects and shows (p. 69) how the 'repertory of tragedy and epic provides, as it were, a closet of masks for the actors to raid at will, characters in search of an identity, of a part to play'.

[214] Goldhill (1986), 260; see also Foley (1985), 219.   [215] Foley (1985), 223.

the representation which the audience see before them. By using one figure in the representation to question inherited representations, by using Dionysus (the principle of representation) to complicate further the truth of Cassandra's utterances in this representation, Euripides keeps the matter of representation before the audience: *Troades* is self-consciously an artefact.

Amid these engaging problems of metafiction associated with Dionysus, there is also a more general self-reference.[216] This manifests itself in a pervasive anxiety about whether the Trojan War is a proper subject for poetry. Early on Hecuba laments her situation and wishes for the consolation of tearful song (119: 'δακρύων ἐλέγους'). She then says (120–1):

> μοῦσα δὲ χαὔτη τοῖς δυστήνοις
> ἄτας κελαδεῖν ἀχορεύτους.

> But even this is music to the wretched,
> to cry out unhappy [lit.: undanceable] troubles.

That Hecuba should describe the troubles of Troy as undanceable seems both self-referential and inappropriate in a medium which was dominated formally by the presence and songs of the chorus. Yet – and this is again typically Euripidean – the self-reference is not simple ('we know we are performing a play'); instead it declares its self-consciousness by questioning its ability to represent what it is in fact representing.

The chorus agree with Hecuba that the only song that can be sung about Troy is a depressing one (511–15):

> ὢ
> Μοῦσα, καινῶν ὕμνων
> ἄισον σὺν δακρύοις ὠιδὰν ἐπικήδειον.

> O Muse, in new hymns
> sing with tears a funeral lament.

---

[216] Bain (1987) is more flexible than in (1975) or (1977). While still correctly denying – along with Taplin (1977), 133 and Easterling (1985) – that there is anything so explicit as theatrical imagery in tragedy (because the tragedies are recreations of the Homeric world), he does admit that Euripides is a self-conscious dramatist (see esp. pp. 8–13).

The appeal to the Muse is unique in tragedy, although it is characteristic of epic and Homeric hymns.[217] Of more interest, in terms of self-reference, is the word *kainōn*. Describing the dirge which the chorus want to sing, we would normally translate this word as 'strange', 'new', or possibly 'sinister'. McDermott has recently demonstrated that Euripides often signposts his innovations of mythic material by use of the word *kainos* (examples from *Supplices*, *Heracleidae*, *Hecuba*, *Phoenissae* and *Orestes* are examined).[218] The newness of what the chorus say consists in two points. First, their song now compares unfavourably with the happy songs which were being sung in Troy before its destruction (529–30, 544ff.); second, this treatment of war is quite different from epic treatments because it is seen almost entirely through the eyes of women.[219] Once again, the play alludes to itself as a literary artefact, this time in its difference from another genre (epic).

It is also not the view of all the Trojan women that lamentation is the only appropriate response. The chorus' address to the Muse, and their appeal to the Muse to sing laments, is preceded by the very different pronouncements of Cassandra. The prophetess, having completed her paradoxical criticism of the Greeks, summarizes as follows (383–5):[220]

> [ἢ τοῦδ' ἐπαίνου τὸ στράτευμ' ἐπάξιον.
> σιγᾶν ἄμεινον τἀισχρά, μηδὲ μοῦσά μοι
> γένοιτ' ἀοιδὸς ἥτις ὑμνήσει κακά.]

> This is the praise of which the army is worthy.
> It is better to keep quiet about shameful things. Let my muse
> not be a singer who sings of evils.

The muse here is not divine but Cassandra herself; and she will not sing ('ὑμνήσει') in new hymns ('καινῶν ὕμνων'), as the chorus call on their muse to do. The verbal echo of 'ὑμνήσει'/ 'ὕμνων' alerts us to the irony that it is Cassandra who lays

---

[217] Lee (1976), 164.   [218] McDermott (1991).

[219] Lee (1976), 164; Barlow (1986), 184.

[220] All three lines have been suspected and are bracketed by Diggle and Barlow. For arguments against the lines, see Barlow (1986), 177; cf. Lee (1976), 139. One good reason for keeping the lines is precisely that they betray, self-referentially, an anxiety about the tragic discourse of Troy.

more claim to being new, for, in an Aeschylean dismissal of improper subjects (see Ar. *Frogs* 1009ff.), she denies that anything should be said or recited from the point of view of the Greeks about the events which led to the sack of Troy. That is, by concentrating on the effects of the absence of the Greeks from their homes, by describing those effects as shameful and evil ('τἀισχρά', 'κακά'), and by ignoring the conventional advantages and glory issuing from military victory, Cassandra disallows the possibility of singing about conventional epic themes. Through Cassandra, the play self-consciously distinguishes between tragic discourse, of which Cassandra is a part here, and epic, from which she is inherited.

Hecuba, later in the play, continues this new approach to representing the end of Troy, again in sarcastic criticism (note 'αἰσχρόν'; see 'τἀισχρά' at line 384) of the Greeks and their treatment of Astyanax (1188–91):

> τί καί ποτε
> γράψειεν ἄν σοι μουσοποιὸς ἐν τάφῳ;
> Τὸν παῖδα τόνδ' ἔκτειναν Ἀργεῖοί ποτε
> δείσαντες; αἰσχρὸν τοὐπίγραμμά γ' Ἑλλάδι.

> What could
> a poet write on your tomb?
> *This child the Argives killed because*
> *they feared him?* That would be a shameful epitaph for Greece.

The muse on this occasion is neither divine nor divinely inspired. In fact, Hecuba herself, speculating on the appropriate epigram for Greek behaviour, becomes the poet ('μουσοποιὸς'). Again, all that is allowed for is a poetry of criticism, one that represents the victims' point of view. Again, the play distances itself from epic.

Finally, as she laments the failure of ritual to provide divine support, Hecuba finds her consolation in the inevitability of Troy's celebration in song (1242–5):

> εἰ δὲ μὴ θεὸς
> ἔστρεψε τἄνω περιβαλὼν κάτω χθονός,
> ἀφανεῖς ἂν ὄντες οὐκ ἂν ὑμνηθεῖμεν ἂν
> μούσαις ἀοιδὰς δόντες ὑστέρων βροτῶν.

And if god had not
overturned [us], throwing what was above below the earth,
we would have disappeared and would not be celebrated
in song, providing themes for the songs of posterity.[221]

Hecuba here confirms what had been said before ('ὑμνηθεῖμεν', 'μούσαις' and 'ἀοιδάς' all pick up earlier uses; see above): Troy – in the fact rather than the manner of its destruction – can be a subject for poetry. The self-reference is again obvious, for *Troades* is itself evidence of Hecuba's hope. But Euripides is not one to let us comfortably imbibe the more sophisticated aspects of his Dionysiac art, for soon after this great statement of poetic consolation, with an inescapable contradiction, we find that Troy will lose its name, and thus will cease to be the subject of great poetry (1277–8, 1319, 1322–4).[222]

Euripides, then, produces a distinctive dramatic world. It is typified by peculiar scenic arrangements and movements and by a pervasive anachronism, whether that be through the

[221] Line 1242 contains a problem. My quotation follows Diggle's and Barlow's acceptance of Stephanus' emendation of the MSS 'εἰ δ'ἡμᾶς θεὸς'. It seems to me that there are good arguments in favour of both readings, for both make it clear that in accordance with tradition the consolation of poetry is important to Hecuba and neither reading affects the fact of self-reference. The main accusation against the MSS is that the lines do not make sense, but Lee (1976), 272 makes a fairly convincing stab at translation: 'But if the deity had rolled us over, throwing what was on top of the earth beneath it, [in] disappearing we would not be celebrated in song.' The benefit of the MSS reading is that the final and complete destruction of Troy (identifying 'us' with 'Troy'), which occurs a few lines later, is something which Hecuba thinks will not happen. This would fit into a pattern in the play, which Ebener (1954) has discussed extensively, where a character says that something is the case and then, almost immediately after, finds that it is not. The problem with the MSS reading is in thinking that Hecuba should believe that Troy has not already been destroyed. The benefit of Stephanus' emendation is that it is the songs sung about the destruction of Troy which themselves become the cause of consolation.

[222] See n.89. Rutherford (1982), 160 n.69; Halleran (1985), 101. Bain (1987), 10 denies that these lines refer to the theatre specifically, but accepts that they are self-referential about poetry. However, in (1977), 4 the same author had asserted that there was a world of difference between lines uttered by a rhapsode and by an actor: surely that applies here as well. Di Benedetto (1971), e.g. 190–2, 223–8 sees a different significance in these lines, namely, that the experience of war profoundly changed Euripides, who, after *Troades*, retreated into writing beautiful poetry for the relief of grief. For criticism, see Burian (1976). Gellie (1986), 118 takes another view: 'It sounds as though poetry makes war alright and so it does if we stay inside epic and myth.'

presence of small anachronistic detail or of contemporary ideas. In *Troades* the unique *mise-en-scène* – destroyed Troy, the temporary tents – allows for a special consideration of space. Euripides represents the terrible effects of war on the ordered space of the city, heightening the effect by having the women speak nostalgically of Troy in the past, and by giving details of their imminent dispersal throughout the Greek world. The end of Troy – an inherited mythical fact – is reflected on, and argued about, in paradoxical and contemporary terms. And, in the final section of this chapter, we have seen that Euripides lays claim to being the most self-referential of the three tragedians. Oliver Taplin has insisted that tragedy is loth to make use of self-reference, since, by its appearance, the spell which tragedy needs to maintain can be broken. He also notes that, in distinction to comedy, tragedy does not invite interruption.[223] However, even if we accept Taplin's argument in principle, we are left with the fact that Euripides' penchant for self-reference would surely break the spell. Of course, self-reference in itself does not preclude the possibility of drama (as comedy testifies), but it does seem to be the case that, in the final years of the fifth century, the conventions of tragedy were increasingly being adapted, challenged and changed, especially in relation to comedy.[224] And these changes are more often than not associated with Euripides. *Troades* is perhaps not the play we could choose to illustrate Euripidean self-referentiality most forcefully, but it still has some remarkable moments of self-consciousness, produced by the intrusion of humour and by regular mention, both in polemic and in consolation, of Troy as a subject for poetry. It is through these spatial and temporal characteristics that the mythical city *par excellence*, the city represented from the beginning of poetry, is recast as a very distinctive other-place.

---

[223] (1986), 164 and 171–2. Tragedies were, however, interrupted: Euripides is said to have told the angry audience of *Danae* to wait to see what happened to the character who had so offended them (Sen. *Ep.* 115.15). There is also the case of audience reaction to the first *Hippolytus* and to Phrynichus' *Capture of Miletus* (Hdt. 6.21.1–2); see Pickard-Cambridge (1968²), 272ff.

[224] Greengard (1987), 13.

AS IF WAR HAD GIVEN A LECTURE

(Von Clausewitz)

Scholars have not found it difficult to distinguish Euripides from his illustrious predecessors. The difference has often been seen as a genre-threatening decadence, or as an assault on both Aeschylean majesty and Sophoclean classicism. Perhaps the most extreme position to have arisen out of such observations is that Euripides was responsible for the end of tragedy. Nietzsche is the most famous proponent of this view, arguing that Euripides opposed traditional tragedy by bringing the ordinary man in the auditorium onto the stage, thereby vulgarizing tragedy and making possible the degenerate genre of New Comedy.[1] And the opinion persists: to take just one recent critic, Euripides is said to bring tragedy to the brink of its own antithesis.[2] The idea of the end of tragedy – and Euripides' responsibility for it – has been nourished by our lack of fourth-century tragedies and by an idealization of the fifth century. Dependence on the former risks arguing from silence; criticism issuing from the latter can produce distortions. But to talk of the end of tragedy is to raise two separable though possibly interdependent issues. The first is the historical question: did tragedy continue as an institution in the fourth century? The second, still historical but also literary, is: did tragedy continue in the same way in the fourth century, namely, performing the same function and producing the same effects? And we must remember that, even if we answer these questions satisfactorily, we shall not have shown that Euripides brought about the end of tragedy: its demise

[1] Nietzsche (1967), 76–81. For discussions of the origins of Nietzsche's views, see W. Arnott (1984); Henrichs (1986).
[2] Michelini (1987), 66.

could have been coincidental with but otherwise unconnected to the death of Euripides (Sophocles anyway died later).

The answer to the first question must be an unequivocal 'yes'. It is certain that the theatrical festivals continued. And it is erroneous to suggest, as some critics have done,[3] that Aristotle in the *Poetics* refers almost exclusively to fifth-century models and to take that as evidence that he was analysing a genre which by his time was dead. Aristotle, in fact, mentions three fourth-century tragedians (Carcinus: *Poet.* 1454b23, 1455a26; Astydamas the younger: *Poet.* 1453b33; Theodectes: *Poet.* 1455a9, 1455b29), each of whom produced a not inconsiderable number of tragedies (160, 240 and 50 respectively), evidence itself of continuing interest.[4] Also, both Plato and Aristotle take tragedy as a serious contemporary force (see chapter one); indeed the latter, according to some, excludes from his discussion much of what we would identify as important in fifth-century tragedy.[5]

To answer the second question is more difficult. It has been argued that tragedy – as a glamorous and provocative self-examination – was an effect of Athenian self-confidence issuing from successful imperialism. Once Athens had ceased to be a great imperial power in the Greek world,[6] the tragic experiment also ceased.[7] However, if we accept that tragedy was an examination of ideology in the fifth century, there is no reason in principle to think that it was incapable of such a task in the fourth century (and we have no evidence).[8] Possession of empire, and the ensuing self-confidence, are not the only conditions in which public self-examination exists. It has further been asserted that, after the upheavals of the end of the Peloponnesian War, Athenians felt a need to forget the realities of war: 'disturbed by social, political and economic changes at home and threatened by dangers abroad, they

---

[3] Else (1957), 636; Salkever (1986), 302.
[4] Easterling (1993).   [5] Webster (1954), 294–5.
[6] Mossé (1973); Hornblower (1983), 166ff.
[7] Reckford (1987),18: 'The decline in drama after the Peloponnesian War shows how much the spirit of tragedy and comedy depended on Athens' power and prosperity.'
[8] Easterling (1993).

faced a life so full of anxieties that they could hardly face true tragedies'.[9] New Comedy answered demands for a lighter entertainment. But we would surely find it difficult to demonstrate that the fourth century as a whole was more unstable and more threatening than the last quarter of the fifth century, when Athens was engaged in its violent and near-fatal struggle with Sparta.[10] Proof of the failure of the fourth century to match its more idealized predecessor has also been seen in the fact that, from early in the century, revivals of fifth-century plays, especially of the canonized triumvirate of Aeschylus, Sophocles and Euripides, became annual events.[11] But revivals were not a fourth-century invention, and we should not forget that, throughout the fifth century, plays were re-performed at various festivals.[12]

It seems, then, that we cannot state with any conviction that tragedy came to an end at the end of the fifth century: the theatrical festivals continued; many plays were produced; much money and energy was expended on their production. However, there also seems little doubt that the nature of tragedy had changed. Certainly, the production and performance of tragedy became an increasingly cosmopolitan affair in the fourth century, with non-Athenians contributing in all areas, and with perhaps half the audience (by Menander's time) made up of non-Athenians.[13] If this is true, then it seems unlikely that fourth-century tragedy could address Athenian ideology so specifically, and in that case the nature of tragedy had changed.[14] The panhellenization of tragedy and the fact that it could increasingly be seen as having a repertoire (a corpus containing classics) surely contributed to the transfor-

---

[9] Xanthakis-Karamanos (1980), 41.   [10] Easterling (1993).

[11] The performance of an old tragedy first became established as an annual event at the Great Dionysia in 386 BC: IG II.2318. It is possible that the plays of Aeschylus were revived in the fifth century (*Life of Aeschylus* 12; Philostratus *Life of Apollonius* 6.11; Ar. *Ach.* 9–12; *Frogs* 866ff.); see Pickard-Cambridge (1968²), 99–100.

[12] Easterling (1993).

[13] Xanthakis-Karamanos (1980), 4–5; Wiles (1991), 15.

[14] Wiles (1991), 15 argues that fifth-century tragedy asked of its audience whether their loyalties were to *oikos* and *polis*, but that the alternatives offered by fourth-century New Comedy were *polis* or humanity.

mation of tragedy from a political discourse to a more purely literary one.

If Euripides was not responsible for the end of tragedy, was he at least responsible for some of the changes which occurred in the discourse after his death, and which led eventually to New Comedy? Certainly it has been claimed that, with Euripides, we see tragedy unable to cope with the pervasive effects of the Peloponnesian War and with the intrusive and troubling discourses of the sophists. What followed was a literature of resignation, dealing with the less grandiose matters of private life.[15] What was produced by the later fifth century was a tragedy too self-conscious, too overtly cognizant of the problems engendered by its status as representation (most notably, in Euripides' last play, the *Bacchae*), rendering the continuing production of significantly educative tragedy improbable. This amounts to saying that the experiment had run its course, and that Athenian tragedy certainly continued to be produced in the fourth century but, like Athens itself, without the same power or significance.[16] This position has its problems as well – self-conscious fiction does not necessarily prohibit the possibility of unselfconscious fiction, or of fiction *per se*, or of the questioning of ideology, as the example of Old Comedy testifies – but it does have the benefit of relating any changes which may have taken place in tragedy to tragedy's didactic function.

It has been argued in these pages that tragedy had a didactic function, which it achieved by exploring ideology, and which Euripides has been shown to have performed. However, it has also been seen that Euripides presented his audience with a distinctive dramatic world, which posed distinctive questions and which, therefore, amounted to a distinctive didacticism. On the one hand, this was dependent on a more extreme exploration, or questioning, of ideology. In *Troades*, Euripides exploits the context of war, and of the consequent

---

[15] Di Benedetto (1971); Kolb (1979), 516–17.
[16] Foley (1985), 9: 'Although tragedy survived in the fourth century, Athens' enjoyment of self-criticism and iconoclasm in its theatrical festivals did not.'

crisis, to show the problems of polarities constitutive of Athenian ideology in a manner similar to, but still more radical than, the other tragedians. On the other hand, Euripides' distinctiveness lay most importantly in the spatial and temporal constitution of his dramatic world and in the increasing use of self-reference, both of which produced a new relationship between the dramatic world and the audience. The Euripidean scene is characterized by inventive tampering with the conventions of the dramatic site, of which the backdrop of a totally destroyed city in *Troades* is only the most extreme example. But we are still left with two important and interdependent questions. First, what does *Troades* teach and, second, what is the effect of Euripidean polemic, in *Troades* and the other plays I have discussed, on tragedy's didactic function?

In answer to the first question, we start with a contention already made, namely, that *Troades* should be viewed as produced in the context of, and pervaded by, war and sophistic rhetoric. The play, in its extremity, manifests what one critic has called the 'massive dislocation' which Euripidean tragedy effected in Athenian culture.[17] In this light, the various attempts to describe what *Troades* means or teaches all appear rather tame. Of course, the play is about 'the dreadful effects of war',[18] war, the great tragedy of society;[19] it may even be a condemnation of purposeless and excessive bellicosity;[20] more arguably, it could be interpreted as a drama of 'total nihilism',[21] an anti-war, anti-expansionist harangue with Euripides using the voice of Cassandra to preach his message.[22] The willingness of critics to reduce the play to these slogans is evidence of the power of some of its voices. Yet one can and should say more. *Troades* is not merely concerned with the

---

[17] Jones (1962), 268. Yet Meier (1988), 237 is right to point to the fact that, as members of a bellicose society, Athenians did enjoy watching unpleasant representations of war: 'Da wollte die Bürgerschaft, die so viele Kriege begann, auch die so sehr zu Herzen gehende Klage über die Schrecklichkeit des Krieges hören.'

[18] Waterfield (1982), 142; see also Walton (1984), 141.

[19] Luschnig (1971), xx; Sienkiewicz (1978), 84: 'The collective tragedy of a nation'; Whitman (1974), 128: 'one of the most telling anti-war plays ever written'.

[20] Lee (1976), xx; Keuls (1985), 381.

[21] Sartre (1968); see also Scarcella (1959); Orban (1974); Villemonteix (1985).

[22] Delebecque (1951), 261–2; Goossens (1962), 520–34.

material effects of war on the *polis*, the *oikos*, the body and so on; nor with its spiritual effects on the characters. It represents, in addition, the consequences of war for the structures of thought, the beliefs, values – the ideology – in which Athenians lived, and in which tragedy and its function were conceived (and challenged).

But this too is only to assert that Euripides was performing the didactic function of tragedy in the same way as the other tragedians; that is to say, he questioned ideology. What distinguishes Euripides is that through irony and self-reference he examines the didactic function itself.[23] That such an examination should take place is perhaps not surprising, as the didactic function was itself part of Athenian ideology. The focus of the Euripidean criticism of the tragic function lies in the extreme and varied complication of the other. In chapter one it was shown that tragedy performed its didactic function by examining Athenian ideology in a dramatic other-world, distant in time and space and peopled by figures (e.g. heroes, kings, barbarians, slaves and women) very different from the fifth-century Athenian citizen. However, we saw in chapter two that in *Troades* there is no convincing attribution of otherness within the terms of the polarities of Athenian ideology: who is truly more free – Hecuba or Talthybius? Who acts more like a barbarian – Odysseus or Andromache? Euripides, like the Peloponnesian War, which saw the introduction of Persians – the original barbarian other – into Greek armies, makes the identification of Greek as against barbarian problematic. Who can be counted as a *philos*? The play is dominated by the voices of women, women who, at the level of ideology, are excluded as other to men. But the Trojan women do not offer a consistent or coherent criticism of Athenian ideology. Instead, from character to character and from individual characters at different points of the play, conflicting opinions are offered and different sorts of questions are asked. So, even when the words of the play are nearly all uttered by

---

[23] Zeitlin (1980), 51 on *Orestes*: 'Ironic, decadent, "modern", even "post-modern".'

figures as other to men as women are, the other is difficult to define and has many voices. In chapter three, for instance, we saw that Cassandra questioned the fact of Greek victory in the Trojan war, something which all the other women accept. Such difficulties with the attribution and definition of otherness render the self-examination through the other which tragedy enacts more complicated. Furthermore, Euripides presents those difficulties as effects of war, as if war itself, central to the life of the *polis* but defined by Vernant as the 'city facing outwards',[24] has taken centre stage and become the other, the agent of self-examination.

However, it is not only a matter of who, but when and where is the other. For in the preceding chapter I demonstrated that in *Troades* Euripides also complicated the scene of the other, both in its internal construction (the representation of spatial order destroyed, fragmentation and dispersal, groundlessness and homelessness) and in its relationship with the audience (through the use of anachronism, of contemporary argumentation to question inherited myth, and of self-reference). Euripides, then, brought both war and the ungrounded discourses of the sophists into the sacred space of Dionysus at the centre of Athens. From these spatial and temporal characteristics, a distinctive mode of questioning, of self-questioning, emerges. The play interrogates not only the ideology which has produced the carnage represented on stage, and the various reactions to it;[25] it also allows the audience to have an ironic attitude to the authority of this particular tragic representation and of representation in general. Euripides does not destroy the didactic function of tragedy, but he does question it, shifting tragedy into different areas, so that it can deal with different concerns.

In portraying Euripidean tragedy and *Troades* as I have, I have been stressing the questioning as against the affirming

---

[24] Vernant (1980), 25.
[25] E. Segal (1983), 244 says that in *Troades* Euripides presented 'the most unmitigated misery ever witnessed on a stage'.

force of tragedy. However, while some critics adopt one position or the other,[26] the more circumspect allow tragedy the performance of both functions, since the question of affirmation or criticism resides with the audience.[27] Tragedy involves, therefore, both order and disorder;[28] and this certainly seems to be the case with Euripides, where one is confronted by both celebration and inversion, a culture struggling against itself in a war of languages. Such ambiguity issues, in part, from the fact that, although Greek tragedy is a civic discourse which examines the ideology of the *polis*, it is produced and authorized to do so by that same *polis*. As such, it should be expected to have the potential for propaganda, to affirm as well as to question. And we should not be surprised if it betrays elements of prohibition, of the sort of authority that pretends to command and forbid. Yet of course this could only ever be a partial account of tragedy's operation. When Michelini claims that the function of Euripidean art is to say 'no', I take it that she means it not in the sense of repressive power but rather of a hopeless nihilism.[29] But whatever its potential to affirm ideological prescription, tragedy does not just say 'no' (whether nihilistic or prohibitive).[30] Rather, tragedy, like the power it represents (in both senses of the word) and like the god in whose honour it is performed, is polyvalent: a discourse at the centre of Athens, it has affirmative, prohibitive, critical and self-critical potential.[31]

[26] Affirmers: G. Thomson (1941), 360; C. Segal (1981), 48; Heath (1987a), 55, 64–5; des Bouvrie (1988), 65. Questioners: Goldhill (1986), *passim*; Vernant and Vidal-Naquet (1988), 23–48.

[27] Vernant (1970), 282; Chalkia (1986), 285; Euben (1986), 29; C. Segal (1986), 25; Goldhill (1987), 74.

[28] Vernant and Vidal-Naquet (1988), 264.

[29] (1987), 126.

[30] Foucault (1980), 119: 'If power were never anything but repressive, if it never did anything but say "no", do you really think one would be brought to obey it?'

[31] Foucault (1987), 22: 'to negate one's own discourse ... is to cast it ceaselessly outside of itself, to deprive it at every moment not only of what it has just said, but of the very ability to speak'. Zeitlin (1980), 51 quotes Borges (*Labyrinths*, xviii) and well applies it to Euripides: a style which 'deliberately exhausts (or tries to exhaust) its possibilities and borders on its own caricature'. Lynn-George (1988), 122 says something similar of Homer, though, obviously, for different reasons: 'In the space of its own silence the epic produces a statement which profoundly questions the conditions of its possibility as well as its worth.'

The lessons of *Troades* are not always easy to describe; nor always comfortable. I have made much of the similarity between Euripides and Thucydides, arguing that they occupy the same critical space in the disorder of discourse which characterizes the late fifth century. The conjunction of the two authors is at its most powerful when Thucydides in the Corcyra chapter – a central text for my thesis – remarkably and insightfully calls war 'βίαιος διδάσκαλος' ('a violent teacher': 3.82.2).[32] *Troades* in two words: Euripidean polemic, the violent teacher. Yet, even as we seem to be making a conclusive point, the ground is once again pulled from under us. For Euripidean tragedy, like the Thucydidean Cleon (Thuc. 3.36.6), refuses to be bound by the traditional exclusivity of violence and persuasion. Euripides' tragedies therefore become that which the plays depict: a collapse of self-definition through polarity. However, while Thucydides offers his observations about Cleon and about war as the masterful narrator of the true story of the Peloponnesian War, the violent teaching of Euripides – Euripidean polemic – is a product of often vehemently conflicting voices, rhetorics and ideologies.

In his questioning of the mimetic mode of self-examination, Euripides may be said to have something in common with Plato, who wanted to exclude poets from his ideal city and who desired to replace poetry, in so far as it possessed an ethical function, with philosophy.[33] Plato also, like tragedy, invented fictional worlds (utopias) in order to pursue his investigations. But Euripides' questioning (including the questioning of tragic teaching) takes place in a wider variety of dramatic worlds: there are scenes in which figures, though absent, nevertheless seem to be prominent (e.g. *Andromache*); there are scenes characterized by the inability of their human

---

[32] Occasionally, the plays themselves say something explicit about teaching, but normally in the context of opposing what can be taught with what is inherent or natural: *Hipp.* 79–81; *Hec.* 592ff.; *Supp.* 913ff.; see Lesky (1968). See also Menelaus at *Andr.* 682ff. on the experience of war as a teacher.

[33] For an interesting view of the relationship between Euripides and Plato, see Arrowsmith (1963), 51.

inhabitants to function effectively (e.g. *Hippolytus*), and by a recurrent need to look elsewhere for causes and solutions (e.g. *Hippolytus* again). Whether we look at an earlier play like the *Medea*, where the heroine tries to be a man, or a late one like the *Bacchae*, with its inescapable and endlessly multiplying complications of representation, we must surely recognize that in the diversity and complexity of the dramatic worlds he created, Euripides' teaching was problematic. But when we remember the grim and dramatically unique scene of devastated Troy in *Troades*, we must also recognize that, in his polemic identification of impasse, of fragmentation and disruption, Euripides offered to the members of the audience the liberating possibility of acknowledging the complexity of the world which they inhabited and their own fallibility. Nowhere does Euripides produce a dramatic world so conducive to such an acknowledgement as in *Troades*, in which the use of the aftermath of war as the setting of the play allows an especially thorough and extreme questioning of Athenian ideology. It is in this sense that with *Troades* we can say that it is almost as if war had given a lecture.

Appendix

IDEOLOGY AND WAR

Ideology

Modern studies of ideology are both many and complex. For to ask 'what is ideology?' inevitably has implications for theories of culture, of the evolution of society, of the mechanisms and possibilities of change and so on. Also, I am aware that it is impossible to say anything about ideology without being ideological myself. [As Loraux (1986), 330 points out: ideology is often the key word of ideology.] Space does not allow full treatment, but for a working definition of ideology I have used various elements from modern discussions of ideology. Briefly, then, there are three senses of ideology.

The first, termed 'descriptive', has ideology constituted by the beliefs, values, desires, interests etc. held by a society as a whole, as well as by particular groups within society, or as the production of meanings and ideas within a social system. [For a general discussion, see Williams (1977); Larrain (1979); J. Thompson (1984). For the three senses of ideology I am indebted to Geuss (1981): the descriptive sense is discussed on pp. 4–12; on which, also see Williams (1977), 55.] Ober (1989), 38–42 has given a similar definition of ideology. Following M. Finley (1982), esp. p. 17, he defines ideology as the set of ideas, beliefs and attitudes which can facilitate action. [Henderson (1990), 177–8 says much the same.] It is valuable that Ober stresses that ideology is not a philosophy or a theory; that it is not necessarily clearly articulated or logically consistent; and that it is still more organized than a set of prejudices. However, the problem with the descriptive view is that ideology becomes ubiquitous, which may be convenient but robs the term of any explanatory rigour; it runs the risk of making ideology and society synonymous. 'Man cannot live

259

by ideology alone', as M. Finley (1983), 31 says. Finley, of course, has also stated that there was no ideology in ancient Greece [(1973), 50–4, 66], which is controversial but unhelpful; for an answer to this criticism, but also a balanced argument against using ideology too easily, see Loraux (1986), 330–7; also Lanza and Vegetti (1975).

The second sense – the 'positive' – makes ideology necessary for society to function. It acts as an agent of social cohesion and unity; see Geuss (1981), 22–3. However, the diversity of values and beliefs in society can be demonstrated as a cause of stability; see J. Thompson (1984), 5. Also, this view of ideology overlooks possible conflicts of interest both within and between different groups.

The third sense is the 'pejorative'. Ever since the word 'ideology' and its cognates were first used, it has had some negative connotation, employed, on the one hand, to refer to an unjust system of repression and, on the other, to undermine an opponent's claim to truth. In this sense, ideology is always the 'thought of the other' [J. Thompson (1984), 1]. To elaborate, ideology is seen as a system of illusory beliefs, and as a manifestation of false consciousness whereby the domination of one group is maintained. [See Williams (1977); Larrain (1979), 210–11.] Geuss (1981), 12–22 lists three processes leading to false consciousness. First, the distortion of the epistemic qualities of the beliefs which constitute ideology, as when, in classical Athens, the *polis* turns the political and legal realities of servile status into a state of nature, or when one group arrogates to itself the right to speak on behalf of other groups, e.g. men speaking for women in classical Athens. The second process is a false legitimation of the institutions of power and repression, through which the functional properties of ideology are not perceived. The third process is the distortion of the genetic properties of a belief, what Geuss calls a 'tainted origin'. This is a belief held for unacknowledged or unacknowledgeable reasons. For instance, what is the significance of a (hypothetical) statement such as: 'Slaves are not fit to hold political office in Athens' (an Afrikaner might say the same of Blacks)? Given that governing is a difficult business requiring some education and expertise, we would have to accept the truth of the statement, slaves, of course, being denied access to the appropriate education. It might be argued that false consciousness, as I have described it above, amounts to what Bourdieu calls a society's tendency to misrecognize its arbitrary structures; Bourdieu (1977), 164: 'Every established order tends to produce the naturalization of its own arbitrariness'; ibid., 167: 'what is essential goes without saying because it comes without saying'. [On Bourdieu and classical archaeology, see Hodder (1986), 70–6. On slavery in the classical world, see de Ste Croix (1957); M. Finley (1960); Garlan (1988). Slavery as natural: Arist. *Pol.* 1254a18.] However, in the late fifth century Euripides was not alone in questioning the slave/free distinction; see Antiphon DK 87B44b; on which see Kerferd (1981), 156ff. The pejorative sense of ideology has some problems as well, though. For example, not all repression and exclusion is self-evidently unjustified, e.g. repression of those designated criminals (the existence of such a category is not questionable in the same way as the criteria by which people are included within it); see J. Thompson (1984), 4 and 12. And, while the pejorative view describes ideology as everywhere and somehow inexorable, it also claims to see in the future the possibility of a world without ideology, i.e. a world purged by critical theory (the project of the Frankfurt School). Also, the pejorative view fails to take account of the relation between ideology and what in fact may be legitimate. As Geuss (1981), 23 says, ideology has created 'situations in which the agents can satisfy legitimate existential needs only on condition of accepting the repression the ideological world-view imposes'. Here we confront the problem of ideology's relation to science, or to truth; see Larrain (1979), 172–211. [For a survey and criticism of Marxist uses of ideology in archaeology, see Hodder (1986), 61–70. Foucault (1979), 159 restricts ideology to the pejorative sense, and replaces ideology in all the senses I have described with the concepts of power and truth; (1978); (1980), esp. 118, 133. On the relation between truth, myth and history in classical Greece, see Veyne (1988).]

All the views of ideology outlined above have their problems; they also have their roots in analyses of modern capitalist society. As such, they are not necessarily germane to the study of fifth-century Athens. To see how we might apply some of what I have described to classical Athens, it is best to start with something we can identify: the civic discourse of the fifth-century *polis* of Athens. Civic discourse was the collection of utterances, texts and representations produced in and/or by the *polis*, which spoke for and/or about the *polis*. This includes (for us, extant) dramatic texts, reported political speeches (e.g. in Herodotus and Thucydides), oratory, inscriptions from the Athenian Assembly, public art and architecture, vase paintings and so on. Civic discourse (re)presents to the *polis* subjects, questions, values, beliefs, conflicts, self-images – all the diverse and manifold aspects of the *polis* which it sees and hears, as it were, in reflection. It is because of this that I suggest that ideology is produced in civic discourse. Of course, certain discourses may carry more ideological weight than others – the Funeral Oration, for example [see Loraux (1986)]; and certain elements within discourses that are not overtly ideological may be more fruitful in providing evidence of ideology, e.g. marginal utterances, things apparently self-evident placed in parenthesis, jokes. [Jokes about sexual activity in Aristophanes can tell us about attitudes towards sexuality; see especially *Lysistrata* and *Thesmophoriazusae*. Much about male attitudes to the family and marriage can be gleaned from casual remarks in Demosthenes, on which see Vernant, 'Marriage' in (1980). Another place where we might find ideological material is in statements of a proverbial or gnomic flavour; de Grouchy (1984).] Still, what is Athenian ideology? I want to retain aspects of all three senses described above. Athens was a direct but exclusive democracy. The Athenian citizen was a freeborn adult male. Women, slaves, foreigners and children had few or no political and legal rights. In such a structure, based on exclusion and inclusion, it follows that definitions will be required in order to decide who is to be included, who excluded. [Vernant and Vidal-Naquet (1988), 264; and see Whitehead (1984) on immigrants in Antiquity.] For reasons which will become clear (and should anyway be obvious) the most important definition will be that of the citizens, the dominant group. But it was the citizens who provided their own definition: it was a self-definition, produced and sustained in civic discourse. My working understanding of Athenian ideology, then, is that it was *the authoritative self-definition of the Athenian citizen*. This is descriptive in that it obviously describes the ideas, values etc. which inform the self-definition; it is positive in that it assists group cohesion; and it is pejorative inasmuch as the interests of the dominant group caused the self-definition to fall foul of some of the processes which produce false consciousness (attitudes to slavery being a good example). Ideology as self-definition also has the benefit of fulfilling Ober's requirements: ideology can facilitate action; it is not a philosophy or a theory; it need not be logically consistent or clearly articulated; it is more organized than a set of prejudices. Let me lay out my definition of ideology in more detail.

(1) Ideology in fifth-century Athens is produced in civic discourse, access to which is controlled by the citizens. Strictly speaking, this is not to say that all discourse is ideological (though we would be hard pressed to find an example of non-ideological discourse), but that all ideology is in discourse. Non-discursive elements may reflect or provide the material from which ideology is produced, but they are not themselves ideological. In distinguishing between discourse and ideology I differ from Goldhill (1986), 74. Yet, once one accepts that Goldhill uses the terms interchangeably, one cannot help but agree with his observations. He says that discourse/ideology must not be taken as a strictly physical description of the *polis*, nor as the political structure and the history of political institutions, nor as daily life, religious life and so on. Goldhill indicates his agreement with Foucault's 'discursive practice' and Vernant's 'structure of social thought'. His own articulation goes like this: 'the way one's place in the order of things is thought about and organized conceptually' (p. 74). Of course, my interest is not quite in 'one' but in a well-defined group: Athenian citizens.

(2) Ideology refers to those elements of a civic discourse which allow or actively promote the authoritative self-definition of the dominant group. Ideology is therefore a form of legitimation since it seeks to justify the authority of the self.

(3) Athenian self-definition, as is argued in more detail in chapters one and two, was to a large extent based on comparison with a (usually inferior) *other*, e.g. women, slaves, foreigners. Nevertheless, the self-definition of the dominant group can be provided by those others. For example, women may reinforce male self-definition (this is indeed a problem in Greek tragedy).

(4) The self – the citizens – had a number of aspects, since there were a range of others to define itself against. In fifth-century Athens, we have the citizens defining themselves against barbarians, men against women, the free against the enslaved. When there were conflicts between those who satisfied the requirements of being Athenian, free and male, these can be called conflicts *within* ideology (that which united Athenian citizens), as well as conflicts of ideology (that which was shared by oligarchs as against democrats the Greek world over). An example of such internal conflict was the perennial tension in Athens between oligarchs (the propertied?) and democrats (the non-propertied?), which on two occasions led to *stasis* (411 BC and 404 BC). [De Ste Croix (1955): caution is necessary when interpreting ancient sources who say a *polis* did or decided something, for *polis* can describe the state as a whole and all in it, or its empowered groups. Ober (1989) is a fine demonstration of the persistent tensions between the mass and the elite in democratic Athens, as well as a credible summary of how, for most of the fifth century, Athens coped with those tensions. On *stasis*, see de Ste Croix (1981); Lintott (1982); M. Finley (1983); Gehrke (1985); Loraux (1986).] Statements of Athenian self-definition cannot be expected to be transparent, unambiguous or mutually consistent. Anyway, the self-definition was not fixed; it was often being rejected, adapted, challenged and improved. [Geuss (1981), 23: ideology can change interests and vice versa, e.g. the case of Christianity.]

(5) There were various degrees of Athenian citizenship. As Vidal-Naquet says, citizenship could be 'potential or very real'. It was very real in the case of the Plataeans, who, as they say in Thucydides, were allowed to share the rights and privileges of Athenian citizenship; or in the case of individuals who had similarly benefited Athens. On the other hand, there were those who were granted a sort of honorary citizenship, becoming, so to speak, privileged foreigners. In practice, then, inclusion in the dominant group was flexible, even if the arguments about the boundaries of inclusion were fierce. There were also those with a more marginal status, most importantly the metics, who were granted a certain freedom in financial transactions (unlike Athenian women), but who were nevertheless granted no political rights. Therefore, those who constitute the self, the dominant group, are not constantly the same. And they are surrounded not only by *others* but by groups who belong neither to the self nor to the other. [On the degrees of citizenship in Athens, see Vernant and Vidal-Naquet (1988), esp. 351ff. On metics, see Whitehead (1977); (1986); Baslez (1984); Lonis (1988); on their numbers in Periclean Athens, see Duncan-Jones (1980). One group or type I have not mentioned is the *proxenos*, who as a beneficiary may have been given potential or real citizenship; on which, see Baslez (1984), 74–80, 120–2. For the Plataeans, see Thuc. 3.55.3 ('πολιτείας μετέλαβεν'); and Baslez (1984), 104. After 451 BC one could only be an Athenian citizen if born from two Athenians; see Davies (1977); Patterson (1981); Baslez (1984), 94–7; Walters (1983); Ober (1989), 80–1.]

(6) A significant consequence of my definition of ideology is that it implies that ideology only applies to the dominant group. This means that there was no ideology of Athenian women, or of slaves. The self-definition given by a woman or a slave is only ideological inasmuch as it sustains the self-definition of the free adult male. Anyway, we have few self-definitions of slaves or women for the simple but important reason that they were denied access to civic discourse. [It may be stated that property and political power were intimately connected, especially in classical Athens; see Garlan (1975);

Davies (1981); de Ste Croix (1981). Yet there was one property which all Athenian citizens had in common, namely access to the Assembly.] Barthes (1976), 32–3 sums up the position nicely: 'ideology can only be dominant. Correct as it is to speak of an "ideology of the dominant class", because there is certainly a dominated class, it is quite inconsistent to speak of a "dominant ideology", because there is no dominated ideology: where the dominated are concerned, there is nothing, no ideology, unless it is precisely – and this is the last degree of alienation – the ideology they are forced to borrow from the class that dominates them'. [See Whitehead (1977), 3: 'certainly the ideology of the metic is largely the creation of non-metics – the ideology, so to speak, *about* the metic'.]

(7) To serve self-definition, Athenian ideology made prescriptive and normative statements. However, the relation between such statements as still remain, and what Athenian society was actually like, is problematic. For instance, when Pericles (or, more precisely, the Thucydidean Pericles) offers his famous advice to women [not to speak or be spoken of – Thuc. 2.45.2. Loraux (1986), 45: 'As an indissolubly military and political speech, the Funeral Oration recognized only male values'], we could interpret the prescription as a reaffirmation of an already existing condition or, alternatively, as an exhortation to women to change. In both interpretations, the statement is ideological, yet it can either affirm or contradict what was actually the case.

War

Most historians agree that the transformation in battle tactics, sometimes called the Hoplite Reforms, was more or less concurrent with new, less aristocratic forms of political organization. To put it briefly, political structures were established sometime in the seventh century BC whereby some of those previously excluded from full citizenship were included in the dominant group. Salmon (1977) is probably the most balanced and cautious statement on the political significance of the hoplite revolution. Andrewes (1956) tried to attach the hoplite reforms to the seventh-century Argive king, Pheidon; see also Kelly (1970). Snodgrass (1965) saw the reforms as a more gradual development, without special political significance. Detienne (1968), 139 argues that the reforms were a seventh-century invention. Some aspects of the hoplite ethos are already in evidence in the writings of the seventh-century Spartan, Tyrtaeus (fr. 12.1–10, 13–18); see also Pausanias 4.8–12 on the First Messenian War as a hoplite war; on Tyrtaeus, see Pritchett (1971–91) IV.37ff.; Shey (1976); Svenbro (1976), 77–107; Lonis (1979), 15; Tarkow (1983); Ducrey (1985), 66. Of course, armies and revolutions continued to go together, as at Samos and Athens in 411 BC; see Thuc. 8.76 and 93; Mossé (1968), 221–3. It is also controversial whether hoplite tactics continued to predominate after the fifth century, but Lonis (1979), 17–21 demonstrates that they did, at least until the emergence of the Macedonian army under Philip. Certainly, traces of Homeric combat linger on into the fifth century. It is probable that more often than not engagements between phalanxes broke down into a series of discrete individual combats; see Pl. *Laches* 181e–182d. Detienne (1968), 125 incautiously denies any possibility of individual combat in hoplite battle. For more balanced discussions, see Garlan (1975), 123; Lonis (1979), 35; Krentz (1985); Hanson (1989); Lazenby (1991). And the concept of *aristeia* – those accounts of exemplary individual feats which so dominate the *Iliad* – was retained in the classical era, though in a different form; see Pritchett (1971–91) II.276–90. A third Homeric trace lies in the existence of elite groups within the hoplite army. This is not surprising perhaps for the armies of oligarchic states such as Thebes, Sparta and Syracuse; yet there were 300 specially chosen Athenians at the battle of Plataea (Hdt. 9.21), and Cimon had 100 at Tanagra (Plut. *Cim.* 17 and *Per.* 10); see Detienne (1968), 134–9; Pritchett (1971–91) II.221. On the hoplite question, see also Holladay (1982), who argues, against Cartledge (1977), that it was military experience rather than political self-interest which perpetuated what Cartledge calls the impractical style of hoplite warfare; Garlan (1975), 26–31 tries to explain the odd phenomenon of the ritual wars in terms of initiation without any firm evidence; see also Brelich (1961); Cartledge (1977). The best-known example of a ritual war is between the Argives and the Spartans (Hdt. 1.82). For a general discussion, see White (1955) and Ducrey (1985), 49ff., but, most especially, the most recent discussion in Pritchett (1971–91) IV. 22ff., who considers the meaning and occurrence of 'φάλαγξ' in Homer; p. 27 notes effectively the 'hoplite' characteristics of Homeric warfare (see *Il*. 3.15; 4.299; 13.136; 15.306, 395; 16.210–11, 276, 601; 17.262); he sums up on p. 30: 'The essential and final decisions of the *Iliad* hinge on battles of masses.' And on p. 90: 'The idea of the creation of the hoplite phalanx at Sparta in the seventh century BC is an archaeological myth.' That may indeed be true, but in his enthusiasm to debunk that myth, Pritchett neglects to consider what may be the more interesting question, namely, what role hoplites played (whenever they were created) in the creation of new post-aristocratic forms of political organization. For a more cautious approach than Pritchett's, see Kirk (1968).

Anyway, the new citizens are usually thought to have been hoplites. Military and civic organization also merge in that the making of a *politēs* was also in part preparation and training for war; see Vernant (1980), 23. Certainly, by Aristotle's time, the *ephēbeia* had become a military training as well as a sort of national service; Arist. *Ath. Pol.* 42; see Pélékidis (1962); Vidal-Naquet (1986). [One of the pre-play ceremonies at the Great Dionysia was a procession of orphans who had been educated by the *polis*; they processed as newly fledged hoplites; Pickard-Cambridge (1968²), 59; Winkler (1985); Goldhill (1987). On tragic heroes portrayed in ephebic terms, see Vernant and Vidal-Naquet (1988), 175–99 on Sophocles' *Philoctetes*; Bowie (1983) on Sophocles' *Ajax*; C. Segal (1982) on *Bacchae*. A case could certainly be made for Heracles in *Hercules Furens* as ephebic.] But, more precisely, what are these hoplite values? And how do they relate to Athenian military practice in the fifth century?

The values of the hoplite are inseparable from the equipment and tactics developed in hoplite warfare. [Lonis (1979),

15–16; on hoplite armour see Detienne (1968), 133; Ducrey (1985), 49ff.; Anderson (1991).] The hoplite is a heavy-armed infantry soldier who fights in a phalanx, which was designed to maximize the effect of soldiers so armed. (Hoplites are unsuitable for pursuit, siege and mountain warfare.) For the phalanx to be effective it had to be a disciplined unit. Discipline was maintained by a) necessity: a phalanx was only as strong as its weakest member; b) training; c) flute and drums to give marching time. Aristotle asserts that *eutaxia* is necessary to the hoplite art (*Pol.* 1297bff.); and see Pritchett (1971–91) II.236. For the importance of *taxis*, see Hdt. 6.111–12; 7.104; 9.31; Thuc. 2.89.9; 5.66ff.; 6.72.4; 7.77.5; 8.104; see also Detienne (1968), 122. Both Herodotus and Aeschylus dwell on the order in the Greek army as against the Persian; see Benardete (1969); Hartog (1980), (1988); Laurot (1981); Goldhill (1988a). But the hoplite ideal and manner of fighting is most easily understood when contrasted with the sort of warfare depicted in the *Iliad*. The Homeric warrior interests himself in *kleos*, and in the perpetuation of his individual and family name. He fights separately from the massed ranks (the *laos*). The hoplite, by contrast, is one of the *laos* and he depends to a large extent on other members of the phalanx. [Pritchett (1971–91) IV. 7–33; Goldhill (1987); Hanson (1989)]. The importance of individual achievements is diminished: no longer does Homeric warrior frenzy win battles and praise; instead *sōphrosunē* is asserted as the principal military virtue. The overly manic hoplite does not seem to have been encouraged, e.g. Aristodemus at Plataea (Hdt. 9.71); see Lonis (1979), 36. For *sōphrosunē* replacing *menos* as the military virtue, see Detienne (1968), 122; Vernant (1980), 40.

BIBLIOGRAPHY

Adkins, A. (1966) 'Basic Greek values in Euripides' *Hecuba* and *Hercules Furens*', *CQ* 16: 193–219

Adrados, F. (1975) *Festival, Comedy and Tragedy*. Leiden (trans. C. Holme)

Aélion, R. (1983) *Euripide: héritier d'Eschyle*. 2 vols. Paris

Aldrich, K. (1961) *The Andromache of Euripides*. Lincoln, Nebr.

Alexiou, M. (1974) *The Ritual Lament in Greek Tradition*. Cambridge

Allison, R. (1984) 'This is the place: why is Oidipous at Kolonos?', *Prudentia* 16: 67–91

Amerasinghe, C. (1973) 'The Helen episode in the *Troiades*', *Ramus* 2: 99–106

Anderson, J. (1991) 'Hoplite weapons and offensive arms', in V. Hanson (1991)

Andrewes, A. (1953) 'The generals in the Hellespont', *JHS* 73: 2–9

(1956) *The Greek Tyrants*. London

Arnott, P. (1959) *An Introduction to the Greek Theatre*. London

(1989) *Public and Performance in the Greek Theatre*. London

Arnott, W. (1973) 'Euripides and the unexpected', *G&R* 20: 49–64

(1984) 'Nietzsche's view of Greek tragedy', *Arethusa* 17: 135–50

Arrowsmith, W. (1958) 'Introduction to *Orestes*', in D. Grene and R. Lattimore (eds.) *Euripides vol. 4*. Chicago

(1963) 'A Greek theater of ideas', *Arion* 2: 32–56

(1968) 'Euripides' theater of ideas', in E. Segal (1968)

Arthur, M. (1981) 'The divided world of *Iliad 6*', in Foley (1981)

Austin, C. ed. (1968) *Nova Fragmenta Euripidea in Papyris Reperta*. Berlin

Bachelard, G. (1969) *The Poetics of Space*. Boston (trans. M. Jolas)

Bacon, H. (1961) *Barbarians in Greek Tragedy*. Yale

Bain, D. (1975) 'Audience address in Greek tragedy', *CQ* 25: 13–25

(1977) *Actors and Audience: a Study of Asides and Related Conventions*. Oxford

(1987) 'Some reflections on the illusion in Greek Tragedy', *BICS* 34: 1–14

Bakhtin, M. (1981) *The Dialogic Imagination*. Austin (trans. M. Holquist and C. Emerson)

Baldry, H. (1965) *The Unity of Mankind in Greek Thought*. Cambridge

(1971) *The Greek Tragic Theatre*. London

Barlow, S. (1971) *The Imagery of Euripides*. London

(1986) *Euripides: Trojan Women*. Warminster

Barnes, H. (1968) 'Greek tragicomedy', in Wilson (1968b)

Barrett, W. (1964) *Euripides: Hippolytos*. Oxford

Barthes, R. (1973) *Mythologies*. London (trans. A. Lavers)
(1976) *The Pleasure of the Text*. London (trans. R. Miller)
(1986) *The Rustle of Language*. Oxford (trans. R. Howard)

Baslez, M. (1984) *L' étranger dans la Grèce Antique*. Paris

Baumann, R. (1990) *Political Trials in Ancient Greece*. London

Benardete, S. (1969) *Herodotean Inquiries*. The Hague

Benedetto, V. di (1971) *Euripide: Teatro e Società*. Turin

Benveniste, E. (1973) *Indo-European Language and Society*. London (trans. E. Palmer)

Bérard, C. (1989) 'The order of women', in Bérard *et al*. (1989)

Bérard, C. and Bron, C. (1986) 'Bacchos au coeur de la cité', *L'Association Dionysiaque dans les Sociétés Anciennes*. Paris

Bérard, C. *et al*. eds. (1989) *The City of Images*. Princeton (trans. D. Lyons)

Bergren, A. (1983) 'Language and the female in early Greek thought', *Arethusa* 16: 69–95

Bernand, A. (1985) *La carte du tragique*. Paris

Berns, G. (1973) '*Nomos* and *Physis* (an interpretation of Euripides' *Hippolytus*)', *Hermes* 101: 165–87

Betts, J., Hooker, J. and Green, J. eds. (1986) *Studies in T. B. L. Webster's Honour vol. 1*. Bristol

Beye, C. (1959) 'Alcestis and her critics', *GRBS* 2: 109–27

Biehl, W. (1989) *Euripides: Troades*. Heidelberg

Bierl, A. (1989) 'Was hat die Tragödie mit Dionysos zu tun?', *WJ* 15: 43–58

Biffi, L. (1961) 'Elementi comici nella tragedia greca', *Dioniso* 35: 89–102

Blundell, M. Whitlock (1989) *Helping Friends and Harming Enemies: a Study in Sophocles and Greek Ethics*. Cambridge

Bond, G. (1974) 'Euripides' parody of Aeschylus', *Hermathena* 118: 1–14
(1981) *Euripides: Heracles*. Oxford

Bongie, E. (1977) 'Heroic elements in the *Medea* of Euripides', *TAPA* 107: 27–56

Boulter, P. (1966) '*Sophia* and *Sōphrosunē* in *Andromache*', *Phoenix* 20: 51–8

Bourdieu, P. (1977) *Outline of a Theory of Practice*. Cambridge (trans. R. Nice)

Bouvrie, S. des (1988) 'Aristotle's *Poetics* and the subject of tragic drama', *Arethusa* 21: 47–73

Bowie, A. (1983) 'The end of Sophocles' *Ajax*', *Liverpool Classical Monthly* 8.8: 114–15

Bradeen, D. (1969) 'The Athenian casualty lists', *CQ* 19: 145–59

Brandt, H. (1973) *Die Sklaven in den Rollen von Dienern und Vertrauten bei Euripides*. Hildesheim

Brecht, B. (1975) 'Theatre for pleasure, theatre for instruction', in D. Craig (ed.) *Marxists on Literature*. Harmondsworth

Brelich, A. (1961) *Guerre, agoni e culti nella Grecia arcaica*. Bonn

Bruit Zaidman, L. and Schmitt Pantel, P. (1992) *Religion in the Ancient Greek City*. Cambridge (trans. P. Cartledge)

Burian, P. (1974) 'Suppliant and saviour in the *OC*', *Phoenix* 28: 408–29

(1976) 'Euripides the contortionist', *Arion* 3: 96–113

ed. (1985a) *Directions in Euripidean Criticism*. Durham

(1985b) '*Logos* and *pathos*: the politics of *The Suppliant Women*', in Burian (1985a)

Burkert, W. (1966) 'Greek tragedy and sacrificial ritual', *GRBS* 7: 87–121

(1985) *Greek Religion*. Oxford (trans. J. Raffan)

Burn, A. (1962) *Persia and the Greeks*. London

Burnett, A. (1971) *Catastrophe Survived: Euripides' Plays of Mixed Reversal*. Oxford

(1977) '*Trojan Women* and the Ganymede Ode', *YCS* 25: 291–316

Butts, H. (1947) *The Glorification of Athens in Greek Drama*. Iowa Studies in Classical Philology 11. Iowa City

Buxton, R. (1982) *Persuasion in Greek Tragedy*. Cambridge

(1985) 'Euripides' *Alcestis*: five aspects of an interpretation', *Dodoni Philologia Tomos* 1: 75–89

(1987) Review of Foley (1985), *JHS* 107: 199–200

(1988) 'Bafflement in Greek tragedy', *Metis* 3: 41–51

Caillois, R. (1962) *Man, Play and Games*. New York (trans. M. Barash)

Calame, C. (1977) *Les choeurs de jeunes filles en Grèce archaïque*. 2 vols. Rome

(1986) 'Facing otherness: the tragic mask in ancient Greece', *History of Religions* 26: 125–42

Calder, W. (1971) 'Sophoclean apologia: *Philoctetes*', *GRBS* 12: 153–74

Cameron, A. and Kuhrt, A. eds. (1983) *Images of Women in Antiquity*. London

Cantarella, R. (1965) 'Atene: la polis e il teatro', *Dioniso* 39: 39–55

Carrière, J. (1979) *Le carnaval et la politique*. Paris

Cartledge, P. (1977) 'Hoplites and heroes', *JHS* 97: 11–27

(1985) 'The Greek religious festivals', in Easterling and Muir (1985)

Cassio, A. (1985) *Commedia e partecipazione. La Pace di Aristofane*. Naples

Chalkia, I. (1986) *Lieux et espace dans la tragédie d'Euripide*. Thessalonike

Chantraine, P. (1968) *Dictionnaire étymologique de la langue grecque*. Paris

Christ, M. (1990) 'Liturgy avoidance and *antidosis* in classical Athens', *TAPA* 120: 147–69

Cixous, H. (1974) 'The character of "character"', *NLH* 5.2: 383–402

Clairmont, C. (1983) *Patrios Nomos*. Oxford

Cogan, M. (1981) *The Human Thing*. Chicago

Cohen, D. (1989) 'Seclusion, separation, and the status of women in classical Athens', *G&R* 36: 3–15

Coles, R. (1974) *A New Oxyrhynchus Papyrus. The Hypothesis of Euripides' Alexandros*. BICS supp. 32. London

Collard, C. (1970) 'On the tragedian Chaeremon', *JHS* 90: 22–34

(1972) 'The funeral oration in Euripides' *Supplices*', *BICS* 19: 39–53

(1975a) *Euripides: Supplices*. Groningen

(1975b) 'Formal debates in Euripides' drama', *G&R* 22: 58–71

Collinge, N. (1962) 'Medea *ex machina*', *CP* 57: 170–2

Conacher, D. (1967) *Euripidean Drama: Myth, Theme and Structure*. Toronto

(1981) 'Rhetoric and relevance in Euripidean drama', *AJP* 102: 3–25

(1988) *Euripides: Alcestis*. Warminster

Connor, W. (1970) 'Theseus in classical Athens', in A. Ward (ed.) *The Quest for Theseus*. London

(1971) *The New Politicians of Fifth-Century Athens*. Princeton

(1984) *Thucydides*. Princeton

(1990) 'City Dionysia and Athenian democracy', in Fears (1990)

Conradie, P. (1981) 'Contemporary politics in Greek tragedy', *Acta Classica* 24: 23–35

Craik, E. (1979) '*Philoktetes*: Sophoklean melodrama', *AC* 48: 15–29

(1980) 'Sophokles and the sophists', *AC* 49: 247–54

(1990) 'Sexual imagery and innuendo in *Troades*', in Powell (1990)

Cropp, M., Fantham, E. and Scully, S. eds. (1986) *Greek Tragedy and its Legacy. Essays presented to D. J. Conacher*. Calgary

Crotty, K. (1982) *Song and Action: the Victory Odes of Pindar*. Baltimore

Cunningham, M. (1954) 'Medea ἀπὸ μηχανῆς', *CP* 49: 151–60

Daitz, S. (1971) 'Concepts of freedom and slavery in Euripides' *Hecuba*', *Hermes* 99: 217–26

Dale, A. (1954) *Euripides: Alcestis*. Oxford

(1969) *Collected Papers*. Cambridge

Daraki, M. (1985) *Dionysos*. Paris

Davies, J. (1977) 'Athenian citizenship: the descent group and the alternatives', *CJ* 73: 105–21

(1981) *Wealth and the Power of Wealth in Classical Athens*. New York

Davison, J. (1991) 'Myth and the periphery', in D. Pozzi and J. Wickersham (eds.) *Myth and the Polis*. Ithaca

Decharme, P. (1893) *Euripide et l'esprit de son théâtre*. Paris

Delebecque, E. (1951) *Euripide et la guerre du Péloponnèse*. Paris

Deleuze, G. and Guattari, F. (1987) *A Thousand Plateaus*. Minneapolis (trans. B. Massumi)

Denniston, J. (1939) *Euripides: Electra*. Oxford

Derenne, E. (1930) *Les procès d'impiété intentés aux philosophes au Vme et au IVme siècles avant J.-C.* Liège

Derrida, J. (1976) 'Signature, event, context', *Glyph* 1: 172–99

(1981) *Dissemination*. Chicago (trans. B. Johnson)

Desch, W. (1985–6) 'Die Hauptgestalten in Euripides' Troerinnen', *Grazer Beiträge* 12–13: 65–100

Detienne, M. (1965) 'Géométrie, politique et société', *Annales* 20: 425–41

(1967) *Les maîtres de vérité dans la Grèce archaïque*. Paris

273

(1968) 'La phalange. Problèmes et controverses', in Vernant (1968)

(1981) 'Between beasts and gods', in Gordon (1981)

(1986) 'Dionysos en ses parousies: un dieu épidémique', in *L'Association Dionysiaque dans les Sociétés Anciennes*. Paris

Deubner, L. (1959) *Attische Feste*. Hildesheim

Diano, C. (1969) 'Sfondo sociale e politico della tragedia greca antica', *Dioniso* 43: 119–38

Diels, H. and Kranz, W. eds. (1952) *Die Fragmente der Vorsokratiker*. 3 vols. Berlin

Diggle, J. ed. (1981 and 1984) *Euripidis Fabulae*. 2 vols. Oxford

(1981) *Studies on the Text of Euripides*. Oxford

Dihle, A. (1977) 'Das Satyrspiel *Sisyphos*', *Hermes* 105: 28–42

Dilke, O. (1985) *Greek and Roman Maps*. London

Dodds, E. (1960) *Euripides: Bacchae*. Oxford

Donzelli, G. Basta (1985) 'La colpa di Elena: Gorgia ed Euripide a confronto', *SicGym* 38: 389–409

Dover, K. (1972) *Aristophanic Comedy*. London

(1975) 'The freedom of the intellectual in Greek society', *Talanta* 7: 24–54

Dubois, P. (1984) *Centaurs and Amazons*. Ann Arbor

Duchemin, J. (1968²) *L'agon dans la tragédie grecque*. Paris

Ducrey, P. (1968) 'Aspects juridiques de la victoire et du traitement des vaincus', in Vernant (1968)

(1985) *Guerre et guerriers dans la Grèce antique*. Fribourg

Duncan-Jones, R. (1980) 'Metic numbers in Periclean Athens', *Chiron* 10: 101–9

Dunn, F. (1989) 'Comic and Tragic License in Euripides' *Orestes*', *CA* 8: 238–51

Dupréel, E. (1948) *Les Sophistes*. Neuchâtel

Eagleton, T. (1986) *Against the Grain*. London

Easterling, P. (1977) 'The infanticide in Euripides' *Medea*', *YCS* 25: 177–91

(1982) *Sophocles: Trachiniae*. Cambridge

(1984) 'Kings in Greek tragedy', in J. Coy and J. de Hoz (eds.) *Estudios sobre los géneros literarios II*. Salamanca

(1985) 'Anachronism in Greek tragedy', *JHS* 105: 1–10

(1987) 'Women in tragic space', *BICS* 34: 15–26

(1989) 'City settings in Greek poetry', *PCA* 86: 5–17

(1993) 'The end of an era? Tragedy in the early fourth century', in A. Sommerstein *et al.* (eds.) *Tragedy, Comedy and the Polis*. Bari

Easterling, P. and Knox, B. eds. (1985) *The Cambridge History of Classical Literature vol. 1*. Cambridge

Easterling, P. and Muir, J. eds. (1985) *Greek Religion and Society*. Cambridge

Ebener, D. (1954) 'Die Helenaszene der Troerinnen', *WZ Halle* 3: 691–722

Eco, U. (1976) *A Theory of Semiotics*. Bloomington

(1977) 'The semiotics of theatre', *Tulane Drama Review* 21: 107–17

Edmunds, L. (1975a) *Chance and Intelligence in Thucydides*. Cambridge, Mass.

   (1975b) 'Thucydides' ethics as reflected in the description of stasis (3.82–83)', *HSCP* 79: 73–92

Ehrenberg, V. (1947) 'Polypragmosyne: a study in Greek politics', *JHS* 67: 46–67

   (1960) *The Greek State*. Oxford

Eisner, R. (1979) 'Euripides' use of myth', *Arethusa* 12: 153–74

Elam, K. (1980) *The Semiotics of Theatre and Drama*. London

Else, G. (1957) *Aristotle's Poetics: the Argument*. Cambridge, Mass.

Erbse, H. (1984) *Studien zum Prolog der euripideischen Tragödie*. Berlin

Erp Taalman Kip, A. van (1987) 'Euripides and Melos', *Mnemosyne* 40: 414–19

Euben, J. ed. (1986) *Greek Tragedy and Political Theory*. Berkeley

Farnell, L. (1909) *The Cults of the Greek States vol. 5*. Oxford

Fears, J. ed. (1990) *Aspects of Athenian Democracy*. Classica et Mediaevalia Dissertationes 40. Copenhagen

Finley, J. (1938) 'Euripides and Thucydides', *HSCP* 49: 23–68

Finley, M. ed. (1960) *Slavery in Classical Antiquity*. Cambridge

   (1973) *Democracy Ancient and Modern*. New Brunswick

   (1982) *Authority and Legitimacy in the Classical City-State*. J. C. Jacobsen Memorial Lecture. Copenhagen

   (1983) *Politics in the Ancient World*. Cambridge

Finley, M. and Pleket, H. (1976) *The Olympic Games*. London

Fisher, E. (1963) *The Necessity of Art*. Harmondsworth (trans. A. Bostock)

Fitton, J. (1961) '*The Suppliant Women* and the *Herakleidae* of Euripides', *Hermes* 89: 430–61

Fitzgerald, G. (1989) 'Euripides and Hecuba. Confounding the "Model"', *Maia* 41: 217–22

Foley, H. (1980) 'The masque of Dionysus', *TAPA* 110: 107–33

   ed. (1981) *Reflections of Women in Antiquity*. London

   (1982a) 'The "female intruder" reconsidered: women in Aristophanes' *Lysistrata* and *Ecclesiazusae*', *CP* 77: 1–21

   (1982b) 'Marriage and sacrifice in Euripides' *Iphigeneia in Aulis*', *Arethusa* 15: 159–80

   (1985) *Ritual Irony: Poetry and Sacrifice in Euripides*. Ithaca

   (1988) 'Tragedy and Politics in Aristophanes' *Acharnians*', *JHS* 108: 33–47

Fontenrose, J. (1967) 'Poseidon in the *Troades*', *Agon* 1: 135–41

   (1968) 'A response to Wilson's reply on *Troades*', *Agon* 2: 69–71

Fornara, C. (1977) *From Archaic Times to the End of the Peloponnesian War*. London

Foucault, M. (1978) *The History of Sexuality vol. 1*. London (trans. R. Hurley)

   (1979) 'What is an author?', in J. Harari (ed.) *Textual Strategies*. Ithaca

(1980) *Power/Knowledge*. Brighton (ed. C. Gordon)

(1987) *Foucault/Blanchot*. New York (trans. B. Massumi)

Foxhall, L. (1989) 'Household, gender and property in classical Athens', *CQ* 39: 22–44

Fraenkel, E. (1950) *Aeschylus' Agamemnon*. Oxford

Fraisse, J.-C. (1974) *Philia. La notion d'amitié dans la philosophie antique*. Paris

Frontisi-Ducroux, F. (1989) 'In the mirror of the mask', in Bérard *et al.* (1989)

(1991) *Le dieu-masque: une figure du Dionysos d'Athènes*. Rome

Fuks, A. (1971) 'Thucydides and the *stasis* in Corcyra', *AJP* 92: 48–54

Garlan, Y. (1968) 'Fortifications et histoire grecque', in Vernant (1968)

(1975) *War in the Ancient World*. London (trans. J. Lloyd)

(1988) *Slavery in Ancient Greece*. Ithaca (trans. J .Lloyd)

Gehrke, H.-J. (1985) *Stasis: Untersuchungen zu den inneren Kriegen in den griechischen Staaten des 5. und 4. Jh. v. Chr.* Munich

Gellie, G. (1986) 'Helen in *The Trojan Women*', in Betts, Hooker and Green (1986)

Gernet, L. (1981) *The Anthropology of Ancient Greece*. Baltimore (trans. J. Hamilton and B. Nagy)

Geuss, R. (1981) *The Idea of a Critical Theory*. Cambridge

Giles, P. (1890) 'Political allusions in the *Supplices* of Euripides', *CR* 4: 95–8

Gill, C. (1990) 'The articulation of the self in Euripides' *Hippolytus*', in Powell (1990)

Gilmartin, K. (1970) 'Talthybius in the Trojan Women', *AJP* 91: 213–22

Girard, R. (1977) *Violence and the Sacred*. Baltimore (trans. P. Gregory)

Goff, B. (1990) *The Noose of Words: Readings of Desire, Violence, and Language in Euripides' Hippolytos*. Cambridge

Goffman, E. (1969) *The Presentation of Self in Everyday Life*. London

(1974) *Frame Analysis*. Cambridge, Mass.

Goldhill, S. (1984) *Language, Sexuality, Narrative: the Oresteia*. Cambridge

(1986) *Reading Greek Tragedy*. Cambridge

(1987) 'The Great Dionysia and civic ideology', *JHS* 107: 58–76

(1988a) 'Battle narrative and politics in Aeschylus' *Persae*', *JHS* 108: 189–93

(1988b) 'Doubling and recognition in the *Bacchae*', *Metis* 3: 137–55

(1989) 'Reading performance criticism', *G&R* 36: 172–82

(1991) *The Poet's Voice*. Cambridge

Gomme, A. (1959–62) *Thucydides I–V.85*. 3 vols. Oxford

Gomme, A., Andrewes, A. and Dover, K. (1970–81) *Thucydides V.85–VIII*. 2 vols. Oxford

Gomperz, H. (1965) *Sophistik und Rhetorik*. Stuttgart (originally published: Leipzig and Berlin, 1912)

Goossens, R. (1962) *Euripide et Athènes*. Brussels

Gordon, R. ed. (1981) *Myth, Religion and Society*. Cambridge

Gould, J. (1973) 'Hiketeia', *JHS* 93: 74–103

(1980) 'Law, custom and myth: aspects of the social position of women in classical Athens', *JHS* 100: 38–59

(1985) 'On making sense of Greek religion', in Easterling and Muir (1985)

Gouldner, A. (1965) *Enter Plato: Classical Greece and the Origins of Social Theory*. New York

Gow, A. (1950) *Theocritus*. Cambridge

Grande, C. del (1962) 'Euripide, *nomos* e *physis*', *Dioniso* 36: 46–9

Gredley, B. (1987) 'The place and time of victory: Euripides' *Medea*', *BICS* 34: 27–39

Green, A. (1979) *The Tragic Effect*. Cambridge (trans. A. Sheridan)

Greengard, C. (1987) *Theatre in Crisis: Sophocles' Reconstruction of Genre and Politics in Philoctetes*. Amsterdam

Gregory, J. (1991) *Euripides and the Instruction of the Athenians*. Ann Arbor

Grouchy, G. de (1984) *Proverbial and Gnomic Material in Greek Tragedy*. Cambridge (Ph.D. dissertation)

Grube, G. (1941) *The Drama of Euripides*. London

Guépin, J.-P. (1968) *The Tragic Paradox*. Amsterdam

Guthrie, W. (1962) *The History of Greek Philosophy vol. 1*. Cambridge

(1971) *The Sophists*. Cambridge

Hall, E. (1988) 'When did the Trojans turn into Phrygians? Alcaeus 42.15', *ZPE* 73: 15–18

(1989) *Inventing the Barbarian*. Oxford

Hall, F. and Geldart, W. eds. (1907) *Aristophanis Comoediae*. 2 vols. Oxford

Halleran M. (1985) *Stagecraft in Euripides*. London

Halliwell, S. (1984) 'Plato and Aristotle on the denial of tragedy', *PCPS* 30: 49–71

(1986a) *Aristotle's Poetics*. Chapel Hill

(1986b) 'Where three roads meet: a neglected detail of the *Oedipus Tyrannus*', *JHS* 106: 187–90

(1987) *The Poetics of Aristotle*. Chapel Hill

Handley, E. and Rea, J. (1957) *The Telephus of Euripides*. BICS supp. 5. London

Hansen, M. (1976) 'How many Athenians attended the Ekklesia?', *GRBS* 17: 115–34

(1987) *The Athenian Assembly in the Age of Demosthenes*. Oxford

Hanson, J. (1964) 'Reconstruction of Euripides' *Alexandros*', *Hermes* 92: 171–81

Hanson, V. (1989) *The Western Way of War*. London

ed. (1991) *Hoplites: the Classical Greek Battle Experience*. London

Harriott, R. (1969) *Poetry and Criticism before Plato*. London

Harrison, F. (1960) 'Homer and the poetry of war', *G&R* 7: 9–19

Hartog, F. (1980) *Le miroir d'Hérodote: essai sur la représentation de l'autre*. Paris

(1982) 'L'oeil de Thucydide et l'histoire véritable', *Poétique* 49: 22–30

(1988) *The Mirror of Herodotus*. Berkeley (trans. of [1980] by J. Lloyd)

Harvey, F. (1966) 'Literacy in the Athenian democracy', *REG* 79: 585–635

Havelock, E. (1963) *Preface to Plato*. Cambridge

(1968) 'Watching the Trojan Women', in Segal (1968)

(1972) 'War as a way of life in classical culture', in E. Gareau (ed.) *Classical Values and the Modern World*. Ottawa

(1982) *The Literate Revolution in Greece and its Cultural Consequences*. Princeton

Haverfield, F. (1913) *Ancient Town Planning*. Oxford

Heath, M. (1987a) *The Poetics of Greek Tragedy*. Stanford

(1987b) 'Euripides' *Telephus*', *CQ* 37: 272–80

(1989) *Unity in Greek Poetics*. Oxford

Heidel, W. (1937) *The Frame of the Ancient Greek Maps*. New York

Heiden, B. (1991) 'Tragedy and comedy in *The Frogs* of Aristophanes', *Ramus* 20: 95–111

Helgerson, R. (1988) 'The land speaks: cartography, chorography and subversion in renaissance England', in S. Greenblatt (ed.) *Representing the English Renaissance*. Berkeley

Henderson, J. (1990) 'The *Dēmos* and the comic competition', in Winkler and Zeitlin (1990)

(1991) 'Women and the Athenian dramatic festivals', *TAPA* 121: 133–47

Henrichs, A. (1978) 'Greek Maenadism from Olympias to Messina', *HSCP* 82: 121–60

(1981) 'Human sacrifice in Greek religion: three case studies', in Rudhardt and Reverdin (1981)

(1982) 'Changing Dionysiac identities', in B. Meyer and E. Sanders (eds.) *Jewish and Christian Self-Definition vol. 3*. Philadelphia

(1984) 'Loss of self, suffering and violence; the modern view of Dionysus from Nietzsche to Girard', *HSCP* 88: 205–40

(1986) 'The last of the detractors: Friedrich Nietzsche's condemnation of Euripides', *GRBS* 27: 369–97

Herington, J. (1985) *Poetry into Drama: Early Tragedy and the Greek Poetic Tradition*. Berkeley

Herman, G. (1987) *Ritualized Friendship and the Greek City*. Cambridge

Hignett. C. (1963) *Xerxes' Invasion of Greece*. Oxford

Hodder, I. (1986) *Reading the Past*. Cambridge

Hogan, J. (1972) 'Thuc. 3.52–68 and Euripides' *Hecuba*', *Phoenix* 26: 241–57

(1980) 'The ἀξίωσις of words at Thuc. 3.82.4', *GRBS* 21: 139–49

Holladay, A. (1982) 'Hoplites and heresies', *JHS* 102: 94–103

Hornblower, S. (1983) *The Greek World*. London

Hourmouziades, N. (1965) *Production and Imagination in Euripides*. Athens

How, W. and Wells, J. (1912) *Herodotus*. 2 vols. Oxford

Hude, C. ed. (1926) *Herodoti Historiae*. 2 vols. Oxford

Hughes, D. (1991) *Human Sacrifice in Ancient Greece*. London

Huizinga, J. (1955) *Homo Ludens*. Boston

Humphreys, S. (1978) *Anthropology and the Greeks*. London

   (1983) *The Family, Women and Death: Comparative Studies*. London

Immerwahr, H. (1966) *Form and Thought in Herodotus*. Cleveland

Irwin, T. (1983) 'Euripides and Socrates', *CP* 78: 183–97

Jacob, C. (1988) 'Inscrire la terre habitée sur une tablette', in M. Detienne (ed.) *Les savoirs de l'écriture*. Lille

Jaeger, W. (1939) *Paideia vol. 1*. Oxford (trans. G. Highet)

Jameson, F. (1984) 'Postmodernism, or the cultural logic of Late Capital', *New Left Review* 146: 53–92

   (1988) *The Ideologies of Theory vol. 2*. Minneapolis

Jameson, M. (1990) 'Private space and the Greek city', in Murray and Price (1990)

Jones, J. (1962) *On Aristotle and Greek Tragedy*. London

Jones, S. and Powell, J. eds. (1942) *Thucydidis Historiae*. 2 vols. Oxford

Jouan, F. (1966) *Euripide et les légendes des chants cypriens*. Paris

Jouanna, J. (1981) 'Les causes de la défaite des barbares chez Aeschyle, Hérodote et Hippocrate', *Ktema* 6: 3–15

Just, R. (1989) *Women in Athenian Law and Life*. London

Kahn, C. (1979) *The Art and Thought of Heraclitus*. Cambridge

Kaimio, M. (1970) *The Chorus of Greek Drama within the Light of the Person and Number Used*. Helsinki

Kamerbeek, J. (1960) 'Mythe et réalité dans l'œuvre d'Euripide', in Reverdin and Rivier (1960)

Keesey, D. (1979) 'On some recent interpretations of catharsis', *CW* 72: 193–205

Kelly, T. (1970) 'Did the Argives defeat the Spartans at Hysiae in 669 BC?', *AJP* 91: 31–42

Kennedy, G. (1963) *The Art of Persuasion in Greece*. London

Kerferd, G. (1981) *The Sophistic Movement*. Cambridge

Kern, S. (1983) *The Culture of Time and Space 1880–1919*. Cambridge, Mass.

Keuls, E. (1985) *The Reign of the Phallus*. New York

King, H. (1983) 'Bound to bleed: Artemis and Greek women', in Cameron and Kuhrt (1983)

King, K. (1985) 'The politics of imitation: Euripides' *Hecuba* and the Homeric Achilles', *Arethusa* 18: 47–66

Kirk, G. (1968) 'War and the warrior in the Homeric poems', in Vernant (1968)

   (1981) 'Some methodological pitfalls in the study of ancient Greek sacrifice', in Rudhardt and Reverdin (1981)

Kitto, H. (1961³) *Greek Tragedy: a Literary Study*. London

Knox, B. (1952) 'The *Hippolytus* of Euripides', *YCS* 13: 3–31

   (1961) 'The *Ajax* of Sophocles', *HSCP* 65: 1–39

(1964) *The Heroic Temper: Studies in Sophoclean Tragedy*. Berkeley

(1977) 'The *Medea* of Euripides', *YCS* 25: 198–225

(1979) *Word and Action: Essays on the Ancient Theater*. Baltimore

(1985) 'Books and readers in the Greek world', in Easterling and Konx (1985)

Kolb, F. (1979) 'Polis und Theater', in G. Seeck (ed.) *Das griechische Drama*. Darmstadt

Koniaris, G. (1973) '*Alexander, Palamedes, Troades, Sisyphus*. A connected tetralogy? A connected trilogy?', *HSCP* 77: 85–124

Kovacs, D. (1983) 'Euripides *Troades* 95–7: is sacking cities really foolish?', *CQ* 33: 334–8

(1987) *The Heroic Muse*. Baltimore

Kraemer, R. (1979) 'Ecstasy and possession: the attraction of women to the cult of Dionysus', *HTR* 72: 55–80

Krentz, P. (1985) 'The nature of hoplite battle', *CA* 4: 50–61

Kristeva, J. (1981) *Desire in Language*. Oxford (trans. T. Gora, A. Jardine and L. Roudiez)

Kuch, H. (1978) *Kriegsgefangenschaft und Sklaverei bei Euripides*. Berlin (1984) *Euripides*. Leipzig

Kyle, D. (1987) *Athletics in Ancient Athens*. Leiden

Labellarte, R. (1982) *Passato, Presente nelle Troiane di Euripide*. Bari-Adriatica

Lacey, W. (1968) *The Family in Classical Greece*. London

Laín Entralgo, P. (1970) *The Therapy of the Word in Classical Antiquity*. Yale (trans. L. Rather and J. Sharp)

Lanza, D. and Vegetti, M. (1975) 'L'ideologia della città', *QS* 2: 1–37

Larrain, J. (1979) *The Concept of Ideology*. London

Laurot, B. (1981) 'Idéaux grecs et barbarie chez Hérodote', *Ktema* 6: 39–48

Lawler, L. (1964) *The Dance in Ancient Greece*. London

Lawrence, A. (1979) *Greek Aims in Fortification*. Oxford

Lazenby, J. (1991) 'The killing zone', in V. Hanson (1991)

Lear, J. (1988) '"Katharsis"', *Phronesis* 33: 297–326

Lebeck, A. (1971) *The Oresteia*. Washington

Lee, K. (1976) *Euripides: Troades*. London

Lefkowitz, M. (1976) *The Victory Ode*. Park Ridge

(1989) '"Impiety" and "Atheism" in Euripides' dramas', *CQ* 39: 70–82

Lesky, A. (1968) 'Euripides und die Pädogogik', *WHB* 11: 16–19

Lévêque, P. and Vidal-Naquet, P. (1973) *Clisthène l'Athénien*. Paris

Levine, D. (1985) 'Symposium and the *polis*', in T. Figueira and G. Nagy (eds.) *Theognis of Megara: Poetry and the Polis*. Baltimore

Lévi-Strauss, C. (1963) *Structural Anthropology vol. 1*. New York (trans. C. Jacobsen and B. Schoepf)

(1967) 'The story of Asdiwal', in E. Leach (ed.) *The Structural Study of Myth and Totemism*. London

(1969) *The Elementary Structures of Kinship*. New York (trans. J. Bell and J. Sturmer)

Lintott, A. (1982) *Violence, Civil Strife and Revolution in the Classical City*. London

Lissarrague, F. (1989) 'The world of the warrior', in Bérard *et al.* (1989)
(1990a) 'Around the *krater*: an aspect of banquet imagery', in Murray (1990)
(1990b) *The Aesthetics of the Greek Banquet*. Princeton (trans. A. Szegedy-Maszak)

Lloyd, G. (1966) *Polarity and Analogy*. Cambridge
(1979) *Magic, Reason and Experience*. Cambridge
(1988) *The Revolutions of Wisdom*. Berkeley

Lloyd, M. (1984) 'The Helen scene in Euripides' *Troades*', *CQ* 34: 303–13
(1992) *The Agon in Euripides*. Oxford

Lloyd-Jones, H. and Wilson, N. eds. (1990) *Sophoclis Fabulae*. Oxford

Longo, O. (1990) 'The theatre and the polis', in Winkler and Zeitlin (1990)

Lonis, R. (1979) *Guerre et religion en Grèce à l'époque classique*. Paris
ed. (1988) *L'étranger dans le monde grec*. Nancy

Lonnoy, M.-G. (1985) 'Arès et Dionysos dans la tragédie grecque: le rapprochement des contraires', *REG* 98: 65–71

Loraux, N. (1978a) 'La gloire et la mort d'une femme', *Sorcières* 18: 51–7
(1978b) 'Sur la race des femmes et quelques-unes de ses tribus', *Arethusa* 11: 43–87
(1981a) 'Le lit, la guerre', *L'Homme* 21: 37–67
(1981b) *Les enfants d'Athéna*. Paris
(1982) 'Mourir devant Troie, tomber pour Athénes', in J.-P. Vernant and G. Gnoli, G. (eds.) *La mort, les morts dans les sociétés anciennes*. Paris
(1986) *The Invention of Athens*. Chicago (trans. A. Sheridan)
(1987) *Tragic Ways of Killing a Woman*. Cambridge, Mass. (trans. A. Forster)
(1990) 'Kreousa the Autochthon', in Winkler and Zeitlin (1990)

Luschnig, C. (1971) 'Euripides' *Trojan Women:* all is vanity', *CW* 65: 8–12
(1976) 'Euripides' *Hecabe*: the time is out of joint', *CJ* 71: 227–34
(1988) *Time Holds the Mirror: a Study of Knowledge in Euripides' Hippolytus*. Leiden
(1992) 'Interiors: imaginary spaces in *Alcestis* and *Medea*', *Mnemosyne* 45: 19–44

Lynn-George, M. (1988) *Epos: Word, Narrative and the Iliad*. London

McDermott, E. (1989) *Euripides' Medea: the Incarnation of Disorder*. Pennsylvania and London

Macherey, P. (1978) *A Theory of Literary Production*. London (trans. G. Wall)

Macherey, P. and Balibar, E. (1981) 'Literature as an ideological form', in R. Young (ed.) *Untying the Text*. Brighton

Macleod, C. (1983) *Collected Essays*. Oxford

BIBLIOGRAPHY

(1991) 'Double meaning and mythic novelty in Euripides' plays', *TAPA* 121: 123–32

Marrou, H. (1956) *A History of Education in Antiquity*. London (trans. G. Lamb)

Martin, R. (1989) *The Language of Heroes: Speech and Performance in the Iliad*. Ithaca

Mason, P. (1959) 'Kassandra', *JHS* 79: 80–93

Maxwell-Stuart, P. (1973) 'The dramatic poets and the expedition to Sicily', *Historia* 22: 397–404

Mead, L. (1938–9) 'The *Troades* of Euripides', *G&R* 8: 102–9

Meier, C. (1988) *Die politische Kunst der griechischen Tragödie*. Munich

Meiggs, R. (1972) *The Athenian Empire*. Oxford

Meiggs, R. and Lewis, D. eds. (1969) *A Selection of Greek Historical Inscriptions to the End of the Fifth Century*. Oxford

Merck, M. (1978) 'The city's achievement: the patriotic Amazonomachy and ancient Athens', in S. Lipshitz (ed.) *Tearing the Veil. Essays on Feminism*. London

Meridor, R. (1984) 'Plot and myth in Euripides' *Heracles* and *Troades*', *Phoenix* 38: 205–15

Michelini, A. (1987) *Euripides and the Tragic Tradition*. Madison, Wis.

Moline, J. (1975) 'Euripides, Socrates and virtue', *Hermes* 103: 45–67

Mossé, C. (1968) 'Le rôle politique des armées dans le monde grec à l'époque classique', in Vernant (1968)

(1973) *Athens in Decline*. London

Muecke, F. (1977) 'Playing with the play: theatrical self-consciousness in Aristophanes', *Antichthon* 11: 52–67

(1982) '"I know you – by your rags". Costume and disguise in fifth-century drama', *Antichthon* 16: 17–34

Mullen, W. (1982) *Choreia*. Princeton

Murray, G. ed. (1913) *Euripidis Fabulae*. 3 vols. Oxford

(1946) 'Euripides' tragedies of 415 BC: the deceitfulness of life', in *Greek Studies*. Oxford

Murray, O. ed. (1990) *Sympotica: a Symposium on the Symposium*. Oxford

Murray, O. and Price, S. eds. (1990) *The Greek City From Homer to Alexander*. Oxford

Myres, J. (1953) *Herodotus. Father of History*. Oxford

Nagy, G. (1990) *Greek Mythology and Poetics*. Ithaca

Nauck, A. ed. (1964²) *Tragicorum Graecorum Fragmenta*. Hildesheim

Nestle, W. (1901) *Euripides: der Dichter der griechischen Aufklärung*. Stuttgart

Neuberger-Donath, R. (1970) 'Die Rolle des Sklaven in der griechischen Tragödie', *C&M* 31: 72–83

Newiger, H. (1973) *Untersuchungen zu Gorgias' Schrift über das Nichtseiende*. Berlin

Nielsen, R. (1976) 'Alcestis: a paradox in dying', *Ramus* 5: 92–102

Nietzsche, F. (1967) *The Birth of Tragedy*. London (trans. by W. Kaufman of *Die Geburt der Tragödie*. Leipzig, 1872)

Nisetich, F. (1989) *Pindar and Homer*. Baltimore

North, H. (1966) *Sophrosyne: Self-knowledge and Self-restraint in Greek Literature*. New York

Nussbaum, M. (1986) *The Fragility of Goodness*. Cambridge

Ober, J. (1989) *Mass and Elite in Democratic Athens*. Princeton
  (1991) 'Hoplites and obstacles', in V. Hanson (1991)

Ober, J. and Strauss, B. (1990) 'Drama, political rhetoric and the discourse of Athenian democracy', in Winkler and Zeitlin (1990)

O'Connor-Visser, E. (1987) *Aspects of Human Sacrifice in the Tragedies of Euripides*. Amsterdam

Oldenziel, R. (1987) 'The historiography of infanticide in Antiquity', in J. Blok and P. Mason (eds.) *Sexual Asymmetry*. Amsterdam

O'Neill, E. (1941) 'The prologue of the *Troades* of Euripides', *TAPA* 72: 288–320

Orban, M. (1974) '"Les Troyennes": Euripide à un tournant', *LEC* 42: 13–28

Osborne, C. (1987) *Rethinking Early Greek Philosophy*. London

Osborne, R. (1985) *Demos: the Discovery of Classical Attika*. Cambridge

Owens, E. (1991) *The City in the Greek and Roman World*. London

Padel, R. (1974) '"Imagery of the elsewhere": two choral odes of Euripides', *CQ* 24: 227–41
  (1983) 'Women: model for possession by Greek daemons', in Cameron and Kuhrt (1983)
  (1990) 'Making space speak', in Winkler and Zeitlin (1990)

Page, D. ed. (1972) *Aeschyli Tragoediae*. Oxford

Parker, R. (1983) *Miasma: Pollution and Purification in Early Greek Religion*. Oxford

Patterson, C. (1981) *Pericles' Citizenship Law of 451–450 BC*. New York

Pavel, T. (1986) *Fictional Worlds*. Cambridge, Mass.

Pearson, L. (1962) *Popular Ethics in Ancient Greece*. Stanford

Pélékidis, C. (1962) *Histoire de l'éphébie attique*. Paris

Pelling, C. ed. (1990) *Characterization and Individuality in Greek Literature*. Oxford

Pellizer, E. (1990) 'Outlines of a morphology of sympotic entertainment', in O. Murray (1990)

Petersmann, G. (1977) 'Die Rolle der Polyxena in den Troerinnen des Euripides', *RhM* 120: 146–58

Pickard-Cambridge, A. (1968²) *The Dramatic Festivals of Athens*. Oxford (rev. J. Gould and D. Lewis)

Pleket, H. (1976) 'Games, prizes, athletes and ideology', *Stadion* 1: 49–89

Podlecki, A. (1971) 'Theseus' bones on Skyros', *JHS* 91: 141–3
  (1975–6) 'A Pericles prosopon in Attic tragedy', *Euphrosyne* 7: 7–27
  (1986) '*Polis* and monarch in early Attic tragedy', in Euben (1986)

Pohlenz, M. (1954²) *Die griechische Tragödie*. Göttingen

Poliakoff, M. (1987) *Combat Sports in the Ancient World*. Yale

Polignac, F. de (1984) *La naissance de la cité grecque*. Paris

Pomeroy, S. (1975) *Goddesses, Whores, Wives and Slaves: Women in Classical Antiquity*. New York

Poole, A. (1976) 'Total disaster: Euripides' *The Trojan Women*', *Arion* n.s. 3: 257–87

Powell, A. ed. (1990) *Euripides, Women and Sexuality*. London

Prendergast, C. (1986) *The Order of Mimesis*. Cambridge

Pritchett, W. (1971–91) *The Greek State at War*. 5 vols. Berkeley

Pucci, P. (1967) 'Euripides *Heautontimoroumenos*', *TAPA* 98: 365–71

(1977) 'Euripides: the monument and the sacrifice', *Arethusa* 10: 165–95

(1980) *The Violence of Pity in Euripides' Medea*. Ithaca

Purcell, N. (1990) 'Mobility and the *polis*', in Murray and Price (1990)

Rankin, H. (1983) *Sophists, Socratics and Cynics*. London

Reckford, K. (1968) 'Medea's first exit', *TAPA* 99: 329–59

(1972) 'Phaethon, Hippolytus and Aphrodite', *TAPA* 103: 405–32

(1974) 'Phaedra and Pasiphae: the pull backward', *TAPA* 104: 307–28

(1985) 'Concepts of demoralization in the *Hecuba*', in Burian (1985a)

(1987) *Aristophanes' Old and New Comedy*. Chapel Hill

Redfield, J. (1975) *Nature and Culture in the Iliad: the Tragedy of Hector*. Chicago

(1990) 'Drama and community', in Winkler and Zeitlin (1990)

Reinhardt, K. (1960) 'Die Sinneskrise bei Euripides', in *Tradition und Geist*. Göttingen

Reverdin, O. and Rivier, A. eds. (1960) *Euripide*. Entretiens sur l'antiquité classique 6. Fondation Hardt, Geneva

Ricoeur, P. (1984) *Time and Narrative*. Chicago (trans. K. McLaughlin and D. Pellauer)

Ridley, R. (1979) 'The hoplite as citizen: Athenian military institutions in their social context', *AC* 48: 508–48

Robinson, J. (1973) 'On Gorgias', in E. Lee, A. Mourelatos and R. Rorty (eds.) *Exegesis and Argument*. Assen

Rohdich, H. (1968) *Die euripideische Tragödie*. Heidelberg

Romilly, J. de (1965) 'Les Phéniciennes d'Euripide ou l'actualité dans la tragédie grecque', *RPh* 39: 28–47

(1968a) *Time in Greek Tragedy*. Ithaca

(1968b) 'Guerre et paix entre cités', in Vernant (1968)

(1973) 'Gorgias et le pouvoir de la poésie', *JHS* 93: 155–63

(1975) *Magic and Rhetoric in Ancient Greece*. Cambridge, Mass.

(1986) *La modernité d'Euripide*. Paris

Romilly, J. de ed. (1982) *Sophocles*. Entretiens sur l'antiquité classique 29. Fondation Hardt, Geneva

Rose, P. (1976) 'Sophocles' *Philoctetes* and the teachings of the sophists', *HSCP* 80: 49–106

Rose, V. ed. (1886) *Aristotelis Fragmenta*. Leipzig

Rosenmeyer, T. (1955) 'Gorgias, Aeschylus and ἀπάτη', *AJP* 76: 225–60.
   (1963) *The Masks of Tragedy*. Austin

Rousselle, A. (1988) *Porneia*. Oxford (trans. F. Pheasant)

Rudhardt, J. and Reverdin, O. eds. (1981) *Le sacrifice dans l'antiquité classique*. Entretiens sur l'antiquité classique 27. Fondation Hardt, Geneva

Russell, D. (1981) *Criticism in Antiquity*. Berkeley

Rutherford, R. (1982) 'Tragic form and feeling in the *Iliad*', *JHS* 102: 145–60

Ryle, G. (1967) 'Review of K. Popper, *The Open Society and its Enemies*. London, 1962²', in R. Bamborough (ed.) *Plato, Popper, and Politics*. Cambridge

Saïd, S. (1978) *La faute tragique*. Paris
   (1989) 'L'espace d'Euripide', *Dioniso* 59: 107–36

Ste Croix, G. de (1955) 'The character of the Athenian empire', *Historia* 3: 1–41
   (1957) 'Review of Westermann, W. (1955) *The Slave Systems of Greek and Roman Antiquity*. Philadelphia', *CR* n.s. 7: 54–9
   (1972) *The Origins of the Peloponnesian War*. London
   (1981) *The Class Struggle in the Ancient Greek World*. London

Salkever, S. (1986) 'Tragedy and the education of the *demos*', in Euben (1986)

Salmon, J. (1977) 'Political hoplites?', *JHS* 97: 84–101

Sansone, D. (1978) 'The *Bacchae* as a satyr play', *ICS* 3: 40–6

Sartre, J. (1968) 'Why the Trojan Women?', in E. Segal (1968)

Scarcella, A. (1959) 'Letture Euripidee. Le *Troadi*', *Dioniso* 22: 60–70

Schaps, D. (1977) 'The woman least mentioned: etiquette and women's names', *CQ* 27: 323–30
   (1978) *The Economic Rights of Women in Ancient Greece*. Edinburgh
   (1982) 'The women of Greece in wartime', *CP* 77: 193–213

Schein, S. (1984) *The Mortal Hero*. Berkeley
   (1988) 'Φιλία in Euripides' *Alcestis*', *Metis* 3: 179–206

Schlesinger, A. (1963) *The Boundaries of Dionysus*. Cambridge, Mass.

Scodel, R. (1980) *The Trojan Trilogy of Euripides*. Göttingen

Scully, S. (1990) *Homer and the Sacred City*. Ithaca

Seaford, R. (1981) 'Dionysiac drama and the Dionysiac Mysteries', *CQ* 31: 252–75
   (1984) *Euripides: Cyclops*. Oxford
   (1987) 'The tragic wedding', *JHS* 107: 106–30

Seale, D. (1982) *Vision and Stagecraft in Sophocles*. London

Searle, J. (1975) 'The logical status of fictional discourse', *NLH* 6: 319–32
   (1976) 'Reiterating the differences', *Glyph* 1: 198–208

Segal, C. (1962) 'Gorgias and the psychology of the *logos*', *HSCP* 66: 99–155

(1971) *The Theme of the Mutilation of the Corpse in the Iliad*. Leiden

(1981) *Tragedy and Civilization: an Interpretation of Sophocles*. Cambridge, Mass.

(1982) *Dionysiac Poetics and Euripides' Bacchae*. Princeton

(1985) 'The *Bacchae* as metatragedy', in Burian (1985a)

(1986) *Interpreting Greek Tragedy*. Ithaca

(1990) 'Violence and the other: Greek, female, and barbarian in Euripides' *Hecuba*', *TAPA* 120: 109–31

(1991) 'Violence and dramatic structure in Euripides' *Hecuba*', in J. Redmond (ed.) *Violence in Drama*. Cambridge

Segal, E. ed. (1968) *Euripides: a Collection of Critical Essays*. Englewood Cliffs

(1983) 'Euripides: poet of paradox', in E. Segal (ed.) *Oxford Readings in Greek Tragedy*. Oxford

Seidensticker, B. (1978) 'Comic elements in Euripides' *Bacchae*', *AJP* 99: 303–20

(1982) *Palintonos Harmonia*. Göttingen

Shapiro, H. (1983) 'Amazons, Thracians and Scythians', *GRBS* 24: 105–14

Shaw, M. (1975) 'The female intruder: women in fifth-century drama', *CP* 70: 255–66

Shey, H. (1976) 'Tyrtaeus and the art of propaganda', *Arethusa* 9: 5–28

Sienkiewicz, T. (1978) 'Euripides' *Trojan Women*: an interpretation', *Helios* 6: 81–95

(1980) 'Helen: scapegoat or siren?', *CB* 56: 39–41

Sifakis, G. (1986) 'Learning from art and pleasure in learning', in Betts, Hooker and Green (1986)

Silk, M. (1985) 'Heracles and Greek tragedy', *G&R* 32: 1–22

Simon, B. (1978) *Mind and Madness in Ancient Greece*. Ithaca

Slater, P. (1968) *The Glory of Hera*. Boston

Smith, W. (1960) 'Staging in the central scene of *Hippolytus*', *TAPA* 91: 162–77

Snell, B. (1937) *Euripides' Alexandros und andere Strassburger Papyri*. Hermes Einzelschriften V. Berlin

(1964) *Scenes from Greek Drama*. Berkeley

Snodgrass, A. (1965) 'The hoplite reform and history', *JHS* 85: 110–22

Steidle, W. (1968) *Studien zum antiken Drama*. Munich

Stevens, P. (1956) 'Euripides and the Athenians', *JHS* 76: 87–94

Stinton, T. (1965) *Euripides and the Judgement of Paris*. London

(1986) 'The scope and limits of allusion in Greek tragedy', in Cropp, Fantham and Scully (1986)

Strauss, B. (1986) *Athens after the Peloponnesian War: Class, Faction and Policy 403–386 BC*. London

Strohm, H. (1957) *Euripides: Interpretationen zur dramatischen Form*. Munich

Suzuki, M. (1989) *Metamorphoses of Helen*. Ithaca

Svenbro, J. (1976) *La parole et le marbre: aux origines de la poétique grecque*. Lund

Synodinou, K. (1977) *On the Concept of Slavery in Euripides*. Ioannina

Taplin, O. (1977) *The Stagecraft of Aeschylus*. Oxford

(1978) *Greek Tragedy in Action*. London

(1982) 'Sophocles in his theatre', in de Romilly (1982)

(1983) 'Tragedy and Trugedy', *CQ* 33: 331–4

(1986) 'Fifth-century tragedy and comedy: a *synkrisis*', *JHS* 106: 163–74

(1987) 'The mapping of Sophocles' *Philoctetes*', *BICS* 34: 69–77

Tarkow, T. (1977) 'The glorification of Athens in Euripides' *Heracles*', *Helios* 5: 27–35

(1983) 'Tyrtaeus 9D: the role of poetry in the new Sparta', *AC* 52: 48–69

Tedeschi, G. (1978) 'Euripide nemico del popolo?', *QFC* 1: 27–48

Thompson, H. (1952) 'The Altar of Pity in the Athenian Agora', *Hesperia* 21: 47–82

Thompson, J. (1984) *Studies in the Theory of Ideology*. Cambridge

Thomson, A. (1898) *Euripides and the Attic Orators*. London

Thomson, G. (1941) *Aeschylus and Athens*. London

Turner, V. (1982) *From Ritual to Theatre*. New York

(1986) *The Anthropology of Performance*. New York

Tyrell, W. (1984) *Amazons: a Study in Athenian Myth-Making*. Baltimore

Untersteiner, M. (1954) *The Sophists*. Oxford (trans. K. Freeman)

Vellacott, P. (1975) *Ironic Drama: a Study of Euripides' Method and Meaning*. Cambridge

Verdenius, W. (1981) 'Gorgias' doctrine of deception', in G. Kerferd (ed.) *The Sophists and their Legacy*. Wiesbaden

Vernant, J.-P. ed. (1968) *Problèmes de la guerre en Grèce ancienne*. Paris

Vernant, J.-P. (1970) 'Greek tragedy: problems in interpretation', in E. Donato and R. Macksey (eds.) *The Structuralist Controversy*. Baltimore

(1980) *Myth and Society in Ancient Greece*. Brighton (trans. J. Lloyd)

(1981) 'Théorie générale du sacrifice et mise à mort dans la θυσία grecque', in Rudhardt and Reverdin (1981)

(1982) *The Origins of Greek Thought*. London

(1983) *Myth and Thought among the Greeks*. London

(1989) *L'individu, la mort, l'amour*. Paris

(1991) *Mortals and Immortals: Collected Essays*. Princeton (ed. F. Zeitlin)

Vernant, J.-P. and Vidal-Naquet, P. (1981) *Tragedy and Myth in Ancient Greece*. Brighton (trans. J. Lloyd)

(1986) *Mythe et tragédie en Grèce ancienne vol. 2*. Paris

(1988) *Myth and Tragedy in Ancient Greece*. New York (trans. J. Lloyd of (1981) and (1986))

Veyne, P. (1988) *Did the Greeks Believe in their Myths?* Chicago (trans. P. Wissing)

Vickers, B. (1973) *Towards Greek Tragedy*. London

Vickers, M. (1987) 'Alcibiades on stage: *Philoctetes* and *Cyclops*', *Historia* 36: 171–97

Vidal-Naquet, P. (1981) 'Land and sacrifice in the *Odyssey*: a study of religious and mythical meanings', in Gordon (1981)

(1986) *The Black Hunter*. London (trans. A. Szegedy-Maszak)

Villemonteix, J. (1985) 'Le sens du tragique dans les Troyennes d'Euripide', *Hommages à Henry Bardon*. Brussels

Voegelin, E. (1957) *Order and History vol 2: the World of the Polis*. New Orleans

Walbank, F. (1951) 'The problem of Greek nationality', *Phoenix* 5: 41–60

Walcot, P. (1976) *Greek Drama in its Theatrical and Social Context*. Cardiff

(1977) 'The Judgement of Paris', *G&R* 24: 31–9

Walker, S. (1983) 'Women and housing in classical Greece: the archaeological evidence', in Cameron and Kuhrt (1983)

Walsh, G. (1984) *The Varieties of Enchantment*. Chapel Hill

Walters, K. (1983) 'Perikles' Citizenship Law', *CA* 2: 314–36

Walton, J. (1984) *The Greek Sense of Theatre*. London

Waterfield, R. (1982) 'Double standards in Euripides' *Troades*', *Maia* 34: 139–42

Waugh, P. (1984) *Metafiction*. London

Webster, T. (1954) 'Fourth-century tragedy and the *Poetics*', *Hermes* 82: 294–308

(1967) *The Tragedies of Euripides*. London

(1970²) *Greek Theatre Production*. London

Westlake, H. (1953) 'Euripides *Troades*: 205–29', *Mnemosyne* 6: 181–91

White, A. and Stallybrass, P. (1986) *The Politics and Poetics of Transgression*. London

White, M. (1955) 'Greek tyranny', *Phoenix* 9: 1–18

Whitehead, D. (1977) *The Ideology of the Athenian Metic*. Cambridge

(1984) 'Immigrant communities in the classical *polis*', *AC* 53: 47–59

(1986) 'The ideology of the Athenian metic: some pendants and a reappraisal', *PCPS* 32: 145–58

Whitman, C. (1974) *Euripides and the Full Circle of Myth*. Cambridge, Mass.

Wiles, D. (1987) 'Reading Greek performance', *G&R* 34: 136–51

(1991) *The Masks of Menander: Sign and Meaning in Greek and Roman Performance*. Cambridge

Wilkins, J. (1990) 'The state and the individual: Euripides' plays of voluntary self-sacrifice', in Powell (1990)

Williams, R. (1977) *Marxism and Literature*. Oxford

Williamson, M. (1990) 'A woman's place in Euripides' *Medea*', in Powell (1990)

Wilson, J. (1967) 'An interpolation in the prologue of Euripides' *Troades*', *GRBS* 8: 205–23

(1968a) 'Poseidon in the *Troades*: a reply', *Agon* 2: 66–8

ed. (1968b) *Twentieth-Century Interpretations of Euripides' Alcestis*. Englewood Cliffs

Winkler, J. (1985) 'The ephebes' song', *Representations* 11: 26–62 (reprinted in Winkler and Zeitlin (1990))

Winkler, J. and Zeitlin, F. eds. (1990) *Nothing to do with Dionysos? Athenian Drama in its Social Context*. Princeton

Winnington-Ingram, R. (1948) *Euripides and Dionysus*. Cambridge

(1960) '*Hippolytus*: a study in causation', in Reverdin and Rivier (1960)

(1969) 'Euripides: *poiētēs sophos*', *Arethusa* 2: 127–42

(1980) *Sophocles: an Interpretation*. Cambridge

Woodbury, L. (1986) 'The Judgment of Dionysus: books, taste and teaching in the *Frogs*', in Cropp, Fantham and Scully (1986)

Woodhead, A. (1970) *Thucydides on the Nature of Power*. Cambridge, Mass.

Wycherley, R. (1949) *How the Greeks Built Cities*. London

Xanthakis-Karamanos, G. (1980) *Studies in fourth-century Tragedy*. Athens

Zeitlin, F. (1965) 'The motif of corrupted sacrifice in the *Oresteia*', *TAPA* 96: 463–508

(1970) 'The Argive festival of Hera and Euripides' *Electra*', *TAPA* 101: 645–69

(1978) 'The dynamics of misogyny: myth and myth-making in the *Oresteia*', *Arethusa* 11: 149–84

(1980) 'The closet of masks: role-playing and myth-making in the *Orestes* of Euripides', *Ramus* 9: 51–77

(1982a) *Under the Sign of the Shield: Semiotics and Aeschylus' Seven Against Thebes*. Rome

(1982b) 'Cultic models of the female: rites of Dionysus and Demeter', *Arethusa* 15: 129–57

(1985a) 'The power of Aphrodite: Eros and the boundaries of the self in the *Hippolytus*', in Burian (1985a)

(1985b) 'Playing the other: theater, theatricality and the feminine in Greek drama', *Representations* 11: 63–88

(1986) 'Thebes: theatre of self and society in Athenian drama', in Euben (1986)

(1991) 'Euripides' *Hekabe* and the somatics of Dionysiac drama', *Ramus* 20: 53–94

Zuntz, G. (1955) *The Political Plays of Euripides*. Manchester

(1972) 'Contemporary politics in Euripides', in *Opuscula Selecta*. Manchester

GENERAL INDEX

INDEX OF PASSAGES CITED

Page references which are italicized signify that the lines indexed are quoted in Greek.

Troades (*cont.*)

252	*88*
253–5	88
267	105, 107, 111, 116
277	105
278ff.	106
288	107, 116
289	105
294	106, 200
296–7	202
298–302	73, 89
299ff.	200
300–1	202
301	105
302–3	100, 111
304	200
305	105
306–7	73
307	133
308	88, 198, 200
308ff.	86, 229
308–40	73, 88
313	105
315ff.	73
318	117
322–30	73
331–7	229
332–4	73
336–8	73
341	133, 243
341–2	230
342	105, 198
347	88
349–50	88
353	131
353ff.	229
353–405	215
356–60	74
357	*88–9*, 132
357–8	141
357–60	215
359–60	*128*
360	130
361ff.	229
361–4	215
363	132
365–7	216
365–405	229–30
366–7	*133–4*, 229, 243
367ff.	216
368ff.	93, 107, 221–2
368–9	123
368–85	123–6

369	124
370	116
370–1	*123*
370–2	124
371	106
371–2	89, 127
372	123
373	123
374–9	127
375	194
376	126
376ff.	116
376–9	74
377	127
377–8	124
378	127
380	124
381–2	74, 124, 124 n11
383–5	*245–6*, 245 n220
386	126
386ff.	127 n20, 195, 216
386–402	126–7
387	126
387–90	74, 127
389–93	127
395–7	127
397	91
398	80, 95
398–9	95 n53, 141
400	107, 127, 127 n20
401–2	*131*
403–4	87
404–5	128, 132
405	88, 131
406–7	230
408	133
408–9	133 n32
413	105
420	89
423	105
424–6	100
427–30	203
428ff.	230
432	105
432ff.	128
432–3	*128*
433ff.	202
444	230
445	76, 89
446–7	74
447	105
448–50	74, 202

304

WIDENER UNIVERSITY WOLFGRAM LIBRARY CHESTER, PA.